In Experts We Trust

In Experts We Trust

Knowledge, Politics and Bureaucracy
in Nordic Welfare States

Åsa Lundqvist
Klaus Petersen (eds.)

University Press of Southern Denmark 2010

© The authors and University Press of Southern Denmark 2010
Printed by Special-Trykkeriet Viborg a-s
Cover Design by Donald Jensen
Cover Photos: Scanpix. From left to right: Gunnar Myrdal (1898-1987),
Nic Waal (1905-1960), Alva Myrdal (1902-1986), Signe Höjer (1896-1988),
Axel Höjer (1890-1974), Gustav Cassel (1866-1945).
University of Southern Denmark Studies in History and Social Sciences vol. 397

ISBN 978 87 7674 497 7
ISSN 1602-5962

University Press of Southern Denmark
Campusvej 55
DK-5230 Odense M
Phone: +45 6615 7999
Fax: +45 6615 8126
www.universitypress.dk

Distribution in the United States and Canada:
International Specialized Book Services
5804 NE Hassalo Street
Portland, OR 97213-3644 USA
www.isbs.com

Distribution in the United Kingdom:
Gazelle
White Cross Mills
Hightown
Lancaster
LA1 4 XS
U.K.
www.gazellebooks.co.uk

Table of Contents

Preface   7

Experts, knowledge and the Nordic
welfare states. An introduction   9
Åsa Lundqvist & Klaus Petersen

Part I
On the Role of the Experts in the Welfare State

Politics out of time – Historical expertise
and temporal claims in Swedish governmental reports   *35*
Sara Edenheim

Communication as control: Infra-politics,
social diplomacy, and social engineering   *59*
Carl Marklund

Part II
Knowledge and Bureaucracy in Nordic Reform Policy

Between social radicalism and Christian socialism:
Intellectuals, social knowledge and the building
of the early Danish welfare state   *89*
Lars Schädler Andersen

The making of Nordic unemployment. Experts
and public policy in Denmark and Sweden, 1890–1910   *119*
Nils Edling

The 'psy-experts' and the minds of children:
Transfer of knowledge in inter-war Norway and Sweden   *149*
Kari Ludvigsen

Power, knowledge and acknowledgement of expertise:
Signe and Axel Höjer's strategies to launch
public health ideas, 1919–1970   *181*
Annika Berg

Experts at work. A micro-study of architects
and school buildings in Denmark, 1940–1970   *223*
Ning de Coninck-Smith

Part III
Experts, Research and the Nordic Welfare State

Gendered understandings of agrarian
population in early Finnish social studies   *249*
Ann-Catrin Östman

From the common good to the efficiency of policy means
– Research on alcohol and drugs in Nordic social science   *269*
Svanaug Fjær

Notes on contributors   *289*

Preface

In the early summer of 2008 the Nordic Centre of Excellence Nordwel organised a seminar on the role of experts and knowledge in the making and development of the Nordic welfare state. Over two sunny days in beautiful Kivik on the east coast of Skåne a group of historians and social scientist engaged in a cross-disciplinary discussion of who the experts of the Nordic welfare state were, what role they had played and their strategies. We would like to thank all the participants at the seminar and especially the commentators: Professor Bente Rosenbeck (University of Copenhagen), professor Sven Hort (Södertörn University) and professor Pauli Kettunen (University of Helsinki). After the seminar in Kivik the authors elaborated their arguments into the book chapters you'll find here.

We would like to thank NCoE Nordwel for supporting the seminar and the publication. Three anonymous referees have combined critical comments and constructive suggestions for the individual contributions. John Irons has helped through the mysteries of the English language. Mai Hostrup Brunse assisted in the last rounds of editing.

NCoE Nordwel is part of the Nordforsk initiated centre of excellence program for welfare state studies.

Experts, knowledge and the Nordic welfare states. An introduction

Åsa Lundqvist & Klaus Petersen

The Nordic welfare state model is a particularly well-established category in international welfare research. Since the 1970s, many articles and books have been written about the model's distinctive characteristics, challenges and historical preconditions – so many that it is almost impossible to gain an overview and knowledge of all the details. The nature, function and history of the welfare states has become a field for experts. In this book some of these 'historical experts' will study and discuss the role of the experts in developing the Nordic welfare model.

It is often claimed that we now live in a knowledge society – as a marker for our age and a distinguishing mark from other historical periods, which are then assumed to be characterised by other relations. The development towards a knowledge society is not least assumed to have to do with an increased spread of knowledge and its easy access. The most powerful expression of this development is of course the Internet.

Alongside other technologies, the Internet has enabled an increasing number of citizens to act as experts, even if the role of expert has thus become conditionalised. Here, there is a clear distinction between now and earlier periods in history – the role of expert is negotiated, embedded in an additional societal context; the citizen occasionally tries to outdo the expert. This is a process that has also been supported by political parties, who have encouraged people to reject the concept of experts governing society. The former Danish prime minister, Conservative Anders Fogh Rasmussen, used his first TV-broadcast New Year Speech in 2002 to make a head-on attack on 'the experts' (especially those that disagreed with the right-wing government):

> 'We spent the twentieth century building up the Danish welfare state. We now have to develop it into a modern welfare society that is adapted to peo-

ple living in the 21st century ... We want to put people before the system. The individual must have a greater freedom to shape his or her life. We want to do away with rigid systems that claim people are incapable and with uniformity. We believe that people can best choose for themselves. We do not need experts and arbiters of taste to decide things for us. In recent years, a veritable wilderness of governmental councils and committees and institutions has shot up everywhere. Many of them have developed into state-authorised arbiters of taste who lay down the law as to what is right and wrong in various areas. There is a tendency towards a 'tyranny of experts' which runs the risk of suppressing free popular debate. The Danish population must not accept admonishing fingers from so-called experts who think they know best. Experts are fine when it comes to conveying actual knowledge. But when it comes to making personal choices, all of us are experts.'

This conditionalised democratisation is, however, only one facet of the importance of knowledge in present-day society. Running parallel with this, the dependence of citizens and politicians on the knowledge of experts has probably never been so comprehensive as it is today. The complexity of the regulation of the financial market, the organisation of the pensions system, the effects of the taxation system or climatic risks also mean that these areas are mainly the domains of experts – with citizens or politicians hardly able to question the necessary claims on knowledge required. Citizens and politicians are thus involved in expert knowledge: they have to handle it and relate to not infrequently contradictory or partial claims on knowledge. They are also expected to act on the basis of it – but not always with the possibility of predicting effects and consequences of various alternatives for action.

A not unusual assumption is then that our age is characterised by a historically unique interlacing of expert knowledge, politics and bureaucracy (which is then called a 'knowledge society'). Our intention with this publication is to point to historical continuities rather than sharp breaks in this interlacing. For it is by no means a new phenomenon. The importance of expert knowledge in the formulation of various societal issues, just as the handling of them, is an important part of the modernisation of the Nordic societies and the creation of modern welfare societies. There are changes and shifts – among other things in the form of a more relativised expert role and partially new relations between experts, citizens and politicians – but in the main the interaction between expertise, politics and citizens has been in existence and in operation for more than a century.

Research in the development of the welfare states: The usual suspects

How has this interaction been assessed in welfare state research? Any overview of international welfare state research paints a picture of a large number of diverse empirical and theoretical studies. They reflect various analytical strategies and levels, schools of research, scientific traditions and perspectives, political points of view and definitions of the welfare state.[1]

To provide an easier overview, research can broadly speaking be divided into a number of main types: structural explanations, studies of political and social agents and a wide range of institutional analyses. Research discussions, however, do not only take place between the various types of investigation but also within each one of them, where researchers with, for example, an actor-oriented perspective can have many and long disagreements about which players in a given context are the key ones. Most of the more comprehensive analyses of welfare-political developments will, though – in the name of truth – argue in favour of an interaction between several factors, and there is also to a considerable extent an acknowledgment of the fact that an explanation that makes good sense in one welfare-political field is not necessarily also a main explanation within a different area.

The researchers who tend towards structural explanations have mainly been interested in the early socio-political development, and not least the emergence of the first modern social legislation of the 1880s and 1890s. Here, connections have been pointed out between industrialisation, modernisation and social reforms. The argument is that industrialisation and the processes linked to it, such as urbanisation and technological innovations, break down the existing social relationships, creating new social problems that the state has to resolve via social reforms.[2] There can be no doubt that there is a close connection between industrialisation and the need for social reforms. But it is obvious that the industrialisation argument finds it more than difficult to explain why reforms come at particular points in time, and why they contain what they do. This also applies to the second predominant structural explanation, even though it has widened the horizon by apart from industrialisation including democratisation and the political mobilisation that is linked to it.[3] This also creates a more dynamic explanation of the national differences, although it still fails to provide any convincing explanation of the choice of various socio-political solutions.

In analyses of the development of the welfare state in the Nordic countries it is most often the Social Democratic Party that is the main player. The qualitative and quantitative nature of the welfare state is seen as an expression of the ability of the organised working class to shift the struggle for power from the market over into a political sphere.[4] In this connection, a number of distinctive characteristics of the Scandinavian welfare states are emphasised – a high level of organisation, strong Social Democratic parties, strong links between Social Democrats and the trade union movement, and a political tradition for political compromises. According to Gøsta Esping-Andersen, the welfare state is both a product of the efforts of the Social Democratic party and an expression of social democratic power strategy:

> 'The welfare state strategy is a natural consequence of social democratic mobilization ... The institutionalization of universalistic public and collective programs can be a mean of supplanting narrow group identities or individualism with broad social solidarity, for such programs help create a large, if not universal, electoral constituency whose welfare and happiness is wedded to a social democratic state.'[5]

There are a large number of Nordic researchers who have pursued this approach further and discussed the significance of the social democratic labour movement and the Social Democratic Party for the development of the welfare state at both the local and the national level. Some researchers have more directly questioned the narrative of the crucial importance of the Social Democratic party and, to a greater or lesser extent, stressed the vital role of other players. In this connection, a great many actors have been emphasised, from the right-wing political parties via particular individuals to social movements.[6] This applies not least to the Women's Rights Movement. It is above all feminist-inspired research that has analysed the importance of the Women's Rights Movement for the growing policy of reform. Here, analyses of the role of female players in the history of the welfare stage have contributed to a greater understanding of the development of the social reform programmes – not least the roles of various experts.[7]

The tendency has, however, been towards a softening-up of positions, so that the social democratic influence is discussed to a great extent in interaction with other political players: parties, social movements, institutions and experts.

Experts matter

Other researchers have pointed to the role of single individuals in the development of the welfare state. This more biographical approach is not utilised as a distinct alternative explanation, but rather has the nature of a shading of the player perspective, with clear links as well to the historical-institutional perspective. In the unofficial list of welfare state 'monarchs', practically all the royals have a background in, or clear link to, the central authorities as officials, civil servants and/or experts.

Thereby, clear links are also made to the more heterogeneous group of research contributions that can be gathered under the title historical-institutional studies of the history of the welfare state. Key elements here are state capacity, social learning, ideas and institutions. Internationally, such a perspective has been advocated by a whole series of researchers, including the American sociologist Theda Skocpol, who has tried to explain the special nature of the American welfare state precisely by referring to a lack of state capacity.[8] A prerequisite for the establishment and development of a modern welfare state is that one can plan, finance, administer, etc.

If one further pursues this approach, one can investigate what happens within the institutions. How do institutions think and act? The American political scientist Hugh Heclo, in a classic study, has pointed out how this learning 'accumulates' through time (becomes institutionalised), so that a solution that works within one area is re-used for others.[9] The Swedish historian Carl-Axel Gemzell, in a study of British welfare policy from the 1930s and 1940s, has analysed how a new type of rationality arises that subsumes a strong trust in science and its use in politics.[10] There is all in all a comprehensive amount of research that includes studies of professions, ideas and paradigms, etc.

In the history of Nordic research from this perspective, much interest has been shown in so-called 'social engineers'. This group of academically trained experts (e.g. architects, physicians – and in particular political economists) came to play a crucial role for societal development from the 1930s onwards. A main player – both then and in Nordic research of the following decades – was the Swedish intellectual couple Gunnar and Alva Myrdal. What did they want? To quote economist Gunnar Myrdal's own words from an article in the Swedish journal *Spektrum* from 1931:

'This new socio-political ideology has within it strongly radical and to a certain extent revolutionary possibilities. It is intellectualistic and coldly rationalistic, while the old ideology, which still reigns, was sentimental to a considerable degree. It has a lot less respect for the rationality of what at present exists. To a great extent it has been liberated from liberalist curbs on ideas. On the other hand, it is far too technically oriented to be able to lose itself in purely general and unworldly ideal constructions. For it is matter-of-fact. Its romanticism is that of the engineer.'[11]

Also Alva Myrdal argued for a similar development in her book *Folk och familj* [People and Family] from 1944:

'A scientific treatment of social policy has not yet been set on trial. But since social politics must transform into social planning, and since social planning must be carried out under rational control, and not just by fumbling policies, the time has come for social science scholars to step out of their isolation. In order to create social change, they must go beyond registration of facts and consistent analysing to raise rational plans for special purposes.'[12]

In these modernistic visions it was possible to unite a number of the socio-political watchwords of the time – prevention, planning, comprehensive thinking, rationality – and create the (social) scientific basis for a more offensive and effective welfare policy. A consequence of this was that welfare policy was developed through an interplay between scientific production and political regulation and became increasingly a matter for the state (or the public sector). At the same time, this interplay between science and welfare state policy meant that the discussion could be lifted out of political-ideological harassments. It was – so to speak – a strategy to depoliticise welfare policy and make it a matter for the rational experts. That, at any rate, was what Myrdal felt, along with many of the then important officials, experts and politicians, who belonged to a kind of epistemic community that believed in rationality, science and planning.[13]

This is an important part of the history of the Nordic welfare state model. At the same time, however, it is important to keep things in proportion. The experts of the inter-war and early post-war period were prepared to take the lead, but they far from always had the opportunity to do so. They were held back by politicians who had the power of decision by a population that voted with its feet when, for example, it came to communal dwellings with communal kitchens, too functionalist furniture, etc. The experts gained power both when it came to setting the agenda and formulating concrete solutions, but they also met with resistance, scepticism and specific defeats. Even though it is possible to talk about an interplay between science and welfare policy, it must be remembered that it can be politicised all the time both from above and from below.

One of the questions that arise in connection with this discussion is whether there exists a specifically Nordic relation between experts and the development of the welfare state. One sometimes gets that impression – not least within the more critical (and partly normatively oriented) research into the role of the experts. One of the most striking examples is the study by the Swedish historian Yvonne Hirdman of Swedish Welfare State Policy in the book 'Att lägga livet tillrätta' [Organising life] (1989), where, with keen, critical edge, she analyses the Myrdal-inspired plans for a far-reaching rationalisation of Swedish society. The villains in this narrative are precisely the social engineers, who want to regulate all aspects of life, from macro-economy to everyday family life. The idea of a specifically Nordic alliance between experts and political power is also found in the debate on inter-war eugenic legislation and sterilisation policy, which was initially considered in connection with social politics.[14]

This type of study is reminiscent of the critical perspectives on society that can be found in the international debate in such social analysts as Michel Foucault and Zygmunt Baumann, where societal rationality, taken to its furthest extreme and with precisely scientific expertise as its point of departure, ends up abolishing large areas of individual freedom. It is a critical perspective that is important and a great deal to be said for it, but one that is hardly specifically Nordic. It can, for example, be pointed out that both Foucault and Baumann see this as being precisely a general phenomenon and base their analyses on non-Nordic conditions. If one is to speak of something specifically Nordic, it must be linked to the ambitious development of the welfare states (particularly on the service side) that took place from the 1950s onwards. Considerable freedom to act was created for the experts and their ideas, although one must also note that these ideas were often fetched from outside. Social engineers were not a specifically Nordic invention but a transnational phenomenon.

All the above perspectives are analyses with the nation state as the possessor of the natural and given role. This even applies to the structurally oriented analyses. The nation state and the welfare state are historically speaking so closely knit that they provide a natural starting point for the analysis. On the other hand, the national arena must not become a closed container for examinations of the history of the welfare state. Since the first socio-political seeds were sown in the last part of the 19th century, cross-border comparison and learning have been a key part of the history of the welfare state. This has been pointed out both by political scientists with an interest in cross-border diffusion and learning and by more historically oriented studies of socio-political cooperation, transnational networks, etc.[15] In a Nordic context, inspiration from in particular Germany – even though it often served as a negative model – was crucial for the first wave of reforms up to 1900, while from the inter-war period onwards it was not least Sweden toward which the other Nordic countries oriented themself.[16] The Nordic model thereby tended to close in on itself. This was the argument put forward at the Nordic Social Political meeting in 1947, when the Icelandic Minister of Social Affairs Stefán Jóhann Stefánsson argued in favour of:

> '... a comprehensive account for the social political development in the Nordic countries, which could be comparative, and other countries might benefit from. I, for my part, think the Nordic countries are the highest ranking when it comes to social political legislation.'[17]

A few years later, in 1953, the Nordic Ministers of Social Affairs jointly published a volume entitled Freedom and Welfare, in which was stated that

> 'That the people are realists, and in their 'social engineering' they have never followed any one general formula. Planning has been carried out on a strictly pragmatic basis, drawing upon past experiences but freely adapting it to changed circumstances. This approach may be lacking in drama, but it has proved well suited to the psychology of these nations and has yielded practical results.'[18]

The Nordic model became an international brand in the post-war period and attracted international attention as a model for comprehensive social security systems. However, more recent research has pointed out that this Nordic model not only was based on comparisons with the outside world and other welfare state models – it was also in certain respects directly influenced from the outside.[19]

About the book

In Experts We Trust deals with how the interaction between experts and politicians has influenced the organisation of the Nordic welfare states. The contributions to the book mainly draw attention to the early period in the history of the welfare state, i.e. the years between 1880 and the post-war culmination around 1970, although contemporary sequences of development are also analysed.

The all-embracing theme is how the interaction between various groups of experts and politicians has influenced the Nordic countries.[20] The question that all the chapters of the book deal with is the nature of the relationship between science and policy in the Nordic welfare states, and what role expertise has played in this development. In attempts to narrow down this theme a number of questions are asked in the chapters of the book. How were social politics and social science interwoven in attempts to create national identities? What new perspectives and problem formulations emerged in the wake of the interplay between policy and, for example, social, economic and medical knowledge? Who were the experts? Within which areas did the emerging expertise regarding the welfare state operate? How were social problems – and which problems – constructed by this scientific expertise, and how were these analyses received in political contexts? Furthermore, how have the experts influenced the planning of social life in the Nordic welfare states?

As is often the case, historical investigations do not provide any clear, unequivocal answer. Naturally, there are a number of common features when it comes to the experts' strategies and ways of arguing. Not least when it comes to the use of scientific and professional legitimacy. Nor is it surprising that the experts often belong to the professional groups that are strong and trend-setting in society: economists, doctors, architects and a wide range of university people. The expansion of the welfare state from the first reforms at the end of the 19th century up to the 1960s is a period with a strong belief in scholarship and experts. At the same time, however, it is also clear that – when taking a cross-section of the contributions into consideration – that the historical context is important. The status and role of the experts changes through time, and from sector to sector. The political context also plays a role. It is vital for the experts' strategies who they can enter into an alliance with. The close alliance between Social Democratic parties and experts after the Second World War has often been emphasised, but several of the contributions to the book show how the experts also played a key role before the power breakthrough of the labour movement in the inter-war years. Without taking the sting out of the book's chapters, it is important to make clear that the experts are unable on their own to explain the development of the welfare state – they acted in a political, cultural and socio-economic context that must be included in the analysis. It is also important to remember that the same groups of experts that are paraded as the 'engineers of the welfare state' often represented the environments from which the most trenchant critics of the welfare state were recruited.

The book is divided into three parts. In the first part the theoretical perspectives that have been adopted in political contexts in the Nordic countries – and under what conditions – are discussed. In the second part of the book, the concrete results of the interaction between the knowledge production and politics is examined. In this part, space is provided for rich, empirical illustrations – with examples from various areas of policy, e.g. population policy, labour market policy, psychiatry and housing policy. In the third part of the book the relationship between the internal dynamics of research disciplines and research environments are highlighted, underlying the researcher's (normative) role in knowledge-producing processes.

The chapter analyses, then, the development within different areas in three different countries. The Nordic countries are obviously distinctive because of their specific historical contexts, but there are also similarities.[21]

Part I. On the Role of the Expert in the Welfare State

In studies of political systems the importance of national variations has been emphasised, and in connection with this that the specific forms of the nation state laid the foundation for the emergence of specific welfare state models. In these – normally comparative – studies, policy outcomes are related to institutional structure. The organisation of the welfare state is thus seen both as an effect of political mobilisation and as a driving force behind this self-same mobilisation.

There is, then, an interaction between institutional organisation, policy outcome and social mobilisation. This understanding of the dynamics of policy development is dealt with thoroughly by the so-called historical institutionalism.[22] The explanatory ambition in this perspective is elucidated in the dynamic understanding of the relations between institutions, preferences and players. There are various different approaches within this perspective. One studies economic development and the importance of the institutions for this, a second deals mainly with how institutions form structures and patterns of behaviour within organisations. A third – and in this context central – perspective studies the importance of the institutions (and its embedded experts) for political paths of action and strategic choices of policies. One example is the relation between policies, academic discourses and the role of experts. In her chapter, Sara Edenheim, analyses precisely the relation between the role of politics, science and expertise with the ambition to further understand how the choice of scientific – and other kinds of expertise – takes place.

Sara Edenheim dwells on a similar complex of issues, where precisely the relation between the role of politics, science and expertise is paid attention to, not least by demonstrating the importance of understanding and fully perceiving how the choice of scientific – and other – expertise takes place. Certain theoretical perspectives are chosen, others are not. She argues that Swedish historical research has not dealt with how *history as a concept and an institution* is used and negotiated in liberal democracy. Edenheim bases her analysis on both governmental commission reports and historical research concerning social movements (mainly the feminist and gay movements) – movements in which the 'experts' and the 'activists' are not infrequently one and the same person. As her point of departure, she uses already established research to do with social movements, but at the same time she approaches – in her terminology – the liberal paradox from a feminist perspective, where for example Wendy Brown's problematisation of the American civil rights movements (mainly *women's* and *gay liberation*) constitutes a key theoretical influence, just as the works of Walter Benjamin and Jacques Derrida concerning the problematisation of the past in present-day politics.

One of her conclusions is that the requirement of a common history was essential if the governmental commission reports were to be able to absorb and define the agenda of the social movement, no matter which expert groups dominated the investigations (physicians and psychiatrists during the first half of the twentieth century; sociologists and other social scientists during the latter half).

Carl Marklund dwells on similar complex issues. By using the concept *social engineering*, Carl Marklund tries to bridge the gap between the institutionalist and Foucaultian perspectives in welfare state research. The concept 'social engineering' has come to be used very frequently in the Nordic historiographical debate concerning the rise of the welfare state and the interaction between politics, science and expertise – especially when talking about the formative inter-war years. Marklund carries out a comparative study of some of the people who made use of the concept during the 1930s in the USA and Sweden and demonstrates that the entry of science onto the political arena was by no means as self-evident and natural as it has often seemed in retrospect. Marklund also shows that it was by no means self-evident exactly which theoretical position was going to influence policy. Social Darwinism – and to an even greater extent *laissez-faire* liberalism – placed a strong curb in many places on the policy direction that was advocated by the self-appointed social engineers. That such a policy also means that knowledge becomes politicised was not something that completely escaped the notice of the 'experts' of that era, either. Instead, it was precisely here that the dividing line went, according to Marklund: between activists that became 'experts' and those groups that continued to believe in an objective world picture and who remained 'scholars'. One of the insights that seem to have been shared by most of those who used the concept social engineering in positive terms was precisely that science is ultimately political to the same extent as it is the result of human and social action. The idea of objective, neutral science is therefore often described by the social engineers as a 19th century liberalist fiction without any basis in reality.

It seems as if the actual concept social engineering played quite an important role in the attempts to de-dramatise what was radically new – and therefore threatening – in what many of the inter-war social scientists represented. So the concept became important for making the vision of a – in Marklund's terminology – new 'social diplomacy' credible.

Part II Knowledge and Bureaucracy in Nordic Reform Policy

An important part of the creation of modern welfare state policy has been the alliance between *science and policy*. Throughout the twentieth century, scientific studies have underpinned or paved the way for political reforms. With the aid of social science in particular, the form and content of politics has been able to be tested and further developed. Politics has sought and gained support in academic analysis when it has wanted to expand its understanding of how society works. Academic scholars, for their part, met with a powerful ally when their chartings and theoretical investigations could be incorporated into reform efforts that were large, broad and politically anchored.[23]

In the second part of the book a number of various political areas – as well as their organisation and objectives – are problematised against a background of a reform policy based on interplay between science and policy. Here, in other words, we meet the experts in a more concrete fashion. The experts of the welfare state – officials, academics, doctors, architects, etc. – early on became part of a legal arrangement in the European national states which, to begin with at least, was thought to be above other social and economic interests in civil society. Their role in the state is found in Max Weber's analysis of modern bureaucracies.[24] In his ideal-typical bureaucracy the official is seen as an unusually powerful player (but also as the auxiliary arm of politics, neutral, etc.). Politicians are electable and therefore interchangeable: officials, however, who have arisen out of a 'demystification' of society, retain their posts for a fairly long period, amass a great amount of knowledge and expertise within their particular fields and gradually come to enjoy an important – even predominant – position within the political system, which gives them considerable influence on the policies that are actually adopted. Bureaucracy, as Weber sees it, was an inevitable consequence of modern society. And here bureaucracy played a decisive role in how society was organised.

Other early state bureaucracy theorists have aired the danger of the so-called 'bureaucratisation of the world', where government officials are seen as belonging to the *administrative despotic culture* that in the final instance threatens the entire democratic system, principally because of the politicians' dependence on them.[25] In Marxist theory, the emergence of the 'state of officialdom' is viewed as a product of the class struggle. For example, the Marxist political philosopher James Burnham claimed that once the means of production had been handed over by the capitalists, it was not the working class that was to take them over but rather the officials and business executives that assumed the role of the powers that be – of the economy as well as politics.[26]

Even in more contemporary analytical programmes, the question of the importance of democracy in the state has been an important basis for an understanding of which players and institutions influence political change. In a well-known book by Theda Skocpol i.a., a state-centred perspective of political change is presented.[27] A key role in the organisation and implementation of important political reforms is ascribed to high-ranking civil servants, who therefore also acquire a strategic role beyond the mere implementation of already completed ideological programmes. Implicit in the analysis is an understanding of high-ranking civil servants as a group that has awareness and self-understanding that is distinct from that of the political elite – with a reasoning intelligence concerning the direction of society, and not merely reflections of social relations in society as a whole. Skocpol's analytical programme can be criticised for overestimating the actual autonomy of governmental officials.[28] At the same time, it emphasises an important and formerly neglected aspect of societal change – the leading stratum of civil servants, their convictions and evaluations as well as their role in the transformation of society.

So Skocpol offers an important point of departure for an understanding of the administrative elite as an agent of change. The administration is interpreted as a relatively independent force that has to be mobilised for the shaping and implementation of reformist policies. As a number of the following chapters will show, even the Nordic countries seem to show similar patterns regarding government-appointed experts.

Precisely this complex of issues is analysed in Lars Schädler Andersen's chapter, where he deals with how a number of doctors, statisticians and national economists gained increasing influence over Danish social policies towards the end of the nineteenth century. Via an analysis of 'social experts', such as Harald Westergaard, Th. Sørensen and Marcus Rubin, Andersen attempts to understand the importance of this intellectual expertise in Danish society at the turn of the twentieth century. Andersen assumes that this expertise comprises a knowledge-generating network.

Andersen's point of departure is that social science was (and is) an active player in societal change. In that way, he wants to complement a traditional politico-historical analysis with a sociological one, where interest is on the relation between social expertise and the political reform process. It is first and foremost the relation between political decisions and expert basic data from social statisticians and economists that is analysed in Andersen's chapter.

Another distinctive feature of the Nordic countries would seem to be the variable role of officials within administration. Whereas the classic civil servant carried out his work assignments in a strict relation to pre-defined political aims and ambitions, government officials in the post-war period seem to an increasing extent also to have been involved in the formulation of the political aims and ideological programmes, characterised by Social Democratic governments. A clear example of this is the ever more trendsetting role played by labour market policy in the Nordic welfare states: a whole cadre of government officials is appointed on the basis of their experience in and commitment to the labour movement rather than on the basis of a more formal education.[29] In that way, the role of the civil servant became linked to a Social Democratic programme.

In his contribution, Nils Edling analyses the early development of the construction of the unemployment problem at the turn of the twentieth century in Denmark and Sweden. The emergence of expert knowledge concerning statistics, municipal job provision and publicly supported voluntary insurance is at the centre of his presentation. Voluntary unemployment insurance and public job provision are seen by Edling as regulatory tools that are also intended to reduce the damaging effects of unemployment and separate 'real' job-seekers from all those who are more or less 'work-shy'. These regulations were drawn up and introduced by the new experts within the social sphere: the statisticians and social economists.

The lively transnational exchange in this matter was an important element in the formulation of local and national solutions, but these naturally differed, depending on the particular political, economic and social contexts. This was the case in the Scandinavian countries. The experts entered into various networks, both intra-Nordic and European, and in Edling's chapter the role of the experts in the creation of national unemployment 'measures packages' and the importance of the various networks in this process are examined. The contribution deals partly with the period prior to the depression of the 1930s, when the problem of unemployment was nationalised, and partly with Nordic meetings on issues linked to unemployment insurance (from 1949).

In Kari Ludvigsen's chapter, attention is paid to the role of psychological and psychiatric expertise during the inter-war and early post-war periods. She takes as her starting point the discourse concerning a good childhood. In her chapter she describes how psychiatric and psychological expertise helped to define the view of children and childhood as well as mental health and illness in children and young people in the inter-war and early post-war years in Norway and Sweden. The point of departure is historically and sociologically inspired research work concerning the establishment of Norwegian child psychiatry, where Norwegian politics and expertise in the field are contrasted with their Swedish equivalents.

In both Sweden and Norway, the psycho-dynamically oriented form of therapy became predominant in the building up and institutionalising of child psychiatry during the 1950s and 1960s. Both Swedish and Norwegian experts found inspiration in the international mental hygiene movement and 'The Child Guidance Movement', where societal prevention of mental suffering and social problems were key problem areas. A number of studies have shown, however, that the practical counselling work with children and parents assumed various forms in the countries, which indicates that influences from international movements were ascribed various meanings in different national contexts. Ludvigsen is of the opinion that thoughts concerning child psychiatric treatment and its practice were established in an interaction between an institutional and a political context and between professional relations in the two countries.

The relation between the production of knowledge, expertise and policies is complex. In this contribution, the social experts are seen as independent players that are also in many respects linked to the political field. It is therefore difficult to find examples of a more 'neutral' production of knowledge in the expertise where information is made use of in political contexts. Normative – and at times even moral – considerations are emphasised and embedded in basic data and utterances.[30]

Such an example is provided in Annika Berg's chapter, which deals with the Swedish couple Signe Höjer and Axel Höjer and their ideas on public health. Signe Höjer (1896–1988) was a nurse and a social worker, but gradually became increasingly recognised as a politican and peace activist and later on as a writer. Axel Höjer (1890–1974), a qualified doctor, became known as the radical director-general of the Swedish National Board of Health (then called Medicinalstyrelsen) between 1935 and 1952. Both of them were influential in building up the Swedish welfare state and later also became active in issues to do with international health.

In Berg's chapter, the changes in the Höjer's ideas about the aims and methods of health care between 1919 and 1960 are analysed. Furthermore, an analysis is provided of how the couple came to establish themselves as part of an expertise for the emerging welfare state. Berg does so by using a Foucault-inspired analysis of experts in modern societies. She combines this point of departure with a gender-sensitive analysis of experts as mediators of knowledge between various national arenas, partly as independent players but also as parts of international organisations, scientific communities and social movements.

In her chapter, Ning de Coninck-Smith analyses how pedagogical ideas influenced architects and planners in post-war Denmark. Her point of departure is taken from the rising number of pupils in the education system who to an increasing extent took the lower secondary school leaving examination. In connection with this explosive development in education a number of so-called central schools were built throughout Denmark, and education changed from having been a private matter to becoming a task of the welfare state. In terms of architecture, this work was inspired by developments in Sweden. Even the pedagogical ideas were based on Swedish ideals – more precisely in the form of Alva Myrdal's writings – as well as the ideas in the Swedish population commission which was set up in 1935.

The ambition of the chapter is to study analytically the dialogue that took place between the architects and educationalists that aimed at transforming modern childhood – not only as a result of new ways of treating children but also as changed spatial practices. If one views developments from such a perspective, the education system is an excellent example of how ideas about modernity and a growing public welfare are made concrete in the form of new spaces for children. The role of the experts was central here, since prominent architects, educationalists and artists were involved in the work of modernising childhood.

Part III. Experts, Research and the Nordic welfare State

The individual research traditions have their own well-established traditions for the writing of the history of their disciplines development, the major figures and the classic internal conflicts. There are also a number of attempts to view these issues from a more theoretical point of view – best known is probably the paradigm theory of the science historian Thomas S. Kuhn, which attempts to explain how the discipline-internal power-knowledge relation is enacted around particular conceptions (paradigms) and the defence and challenging of these.[31] In general, however, researchers are surprisingly reluctant to engage in analysing themselves as 'political' players. The requirements concerning contextualisation, analyses of motives, etc. that appear banal for the ordinary analysis of society do not seem to apply to the same degree when researchers analyse themselves.[32] Even the most critical analyses stick to analysing the scholarly statements (articles, books) and shy away from discussing the scholar's personal (or the group's) ideological, normative, religious, economic, etc. motives.

One of the most obvious exceptions is the relatively comprehensive research on the role of the economists in the development of the welfare state. Here, there is the above-mentioned research into the role of the state-bearing national economists in the heyday of the welfare state from the 1930s to the 1960s as well as the predominantly critical research connected with the paradigm shift of the economists towards a more neoliberal and critical discourse of the welfare state in the 1980s.[33]

In the final two chapters of the book, the authors attempt to widen the perspective to include other disciplines. Ann-Catrin Östman's chapter analyses the studies of social problems in the Finnish rural areas that were carried out at the end of the 19th century and during the early twentieth century by researchers with a background in History. Östman shows that historians in Finland were influenced by lectern socialism, historical statistics and a historically oriented national economy. Societal interest in scientific knowledge was channelled via *Kansantaloudellinen Yhdistys* – The Finnish Economic Association – which initiated research that was felt to be socially relevant. In the mid-1880s, a proclamation was made concerning the need to study economic conditions in rural areas. Among those who signed the proclamation were the professors of history J.R. Danielsson-Kalmari and Yrjö Koskinen. In their opinion, statistical and economic research could promote and underpin social reforms. Those groups that were considered to be neglected could gain improved conditions and thereby a more unified nation would be created. In that development history research was not considered to be an end in itself but was explicitly connected to societal needs. In Östman's analysis, this history is emphasised – focusing in particular on conceptions of femininity, masculinity and family.

As initially mentioned, the history of the welfare state is also a history of the establishing of a number of new professions and the research areas and academic disciplines which belong to them. Some of these came into being because of the welfare state and are only found in strongly institutionalised welfare states such as the Nordic varieties, while others are areas of research which, in various ways, come to interact closely with the welfare state. This applies not least to research that is connected with social problems and their resolution. A whole number of such research areas can be named, such as: social work, child psychiatry, pedagogic and research into forms of abuse. Svanaug Fjær's analysis of the organisation and prioritisation of Nordic alcohol and drug research reveals a similar development to that in Östman's chapter, but within a completely different policy area – that of intoxicants. Traditionally speaking, the Nordic authorities have placed considerable emphasis on knowledge-based alcohol and drugs policies. Research has thus had a strong position, while at the same time it has been framed by clear, normative assumptions about seeking to contribute to what is best for the population in such issues.

Nordic alcohol and drug researchers have experienced a whole series of interesting changes over the past decade. Fjær analyses how these changes can be understood on the basis of the transformation of public administration and the shifts of perspective that have taken place in research into alcohol and drug abuse. In this connection, Fjær discusses how the role of research has been linked to the emergence of New Public Management, which she feels has been of importance for both the relation of research to administration and politics – and the knowledge that authorities ask for. The question is to what extent the development of the past ten years has changed the focus of research – away from the social scientific issues that have traditionally been linked to social, cultural and historical conditions in relation to the consumption of alcohol and drugs towards research that is more interested in medicinal factors. She therefore questions whether the changes of recent years have changed the balance between social scientific and medical research on drugs and alcohol.

Concluding remarks

Where does all this point to? That is – as one often says when under pressure – a really good question. Taking away the nuances and complexity of the empirical cases we find:

Firstly, that research into the interaction between experts, power and welfare state policy has come to stay. It is a complex of themes that has established itself and matured, so that experts are no longer analysed as the heroes of history or reduced to the role of clear villains of the piece. Instead, they are seen as a highly central ingredient in the explanation of the development and organisation of the welfare state.

Secondly, that the theme cannot be examined within one single theoretical framework. A whole range of theoreticians and frameworks of analysis must be drawn on – in the same way as in the introduction to this book, and welfare state research in general. In the long term, the objective must be to 'merge' welfare state research and expert research to a greater extent than is at present the case. Not least recent trends within research into the historical development of the welfare states inspired by institutional analysis and transnational studies[34] make this patently obvious. This book is an attempt to take a single step in that direction.

Thirdly, that research so far has concentrated on the classic disciplines as physicians and economists. This also applies to the contributions in this book, although it also includes 'new' areas such as architects, alcohol and drug researchers and social historians. The task in the future will be to involve more groups – also including a wide range of semi-professional experts that are a direct result of the development of the welfare state: family counsellors, activation inspectors, etc. Furthermore, one ought to a greater extent to be aware of cooperation and conflicts between various groups of experts and professions.

Many more and other possible conclusions can certainly be arrived at. Our hope is that this book, taken as a whole, will be included in a discussion of the role of experts in the history of welfare states, and that the individual chapters can be seen as possible empirical contributions to this history. That, at any rate, is its intention.

Notes

1 See for example Søren Kolstrup, 1994; Klaus Petersen, 1997; Asbjørn Sonne Nørgaard, 1999.
2 Harold L. Wilensky, 1975. See also Gaston V. Rimlinger, 1971.
3 Jens Alber & Peter Flora, 1981.
4 See i.a. Walter Korpi, 1981; Gøsta Esping-Andersen & Walter Korpi, 1984; Gøsta Esping-Andersen, 1985. See also Julia O'Connor & Greg M. Olsen (eds.), 1998.
5 Gøsta Esping-Andersen, 1985, p. 33f.
6 See for example Peter Baldwin, 1990; Peter A. Swenson, 2002.
7 Janet Fink & Åsa Lundqvist (eds.), 2010; Roger Klinth, 2002; Åsa Lundqvist,

2007; Kari Melby, Anna-Birte Ravn & Christina Carlsson Wetterberg (eds.), 2008; Kari Melby, Anu Pylkkänen, Bente Rosenbeck & Christina Carlsson Wetterberg, 2006; Hilda Rømer Christensen, 2003, pp. 125-135.
8   Theda Skocpol, Margaret Weir & Ann Shola Orloff (eds.), 1988.
9   Hugh Heclo, 1974.
10 Carl-Axel Gemzell, 1989, 1993 & 1989.
11 Quoted from Jan Olof Nilsson, 1994, p. 164.
12 Alva Myrdal, 1944, p. 20.
13 Ron Eyermann, 1985, pp. 777–807; Klaus Petersen, 1998.
14 For a discussion based on the Swedish case see Mattias Tydén, 2000, pp. 73-143.
15 For historically oriented research see in particular Christoph Conrad, Haupt & Kocka (eds.), 1996; Daniel T. Rodgers, 1998.; Pauli Kettunen & Klaus Petersen, 2010 (Forthcoming). There is also a great deal of political-scientific research on diffusion, transfer, etc. One historically oriented example of this is Stein Kuhnle, 1996.
16 For the Nordic perspective, see Klaus Petersen, 2006, pp. 67–98.
17 Klaus Petersen, 2006, p. 90.
18 George R. Nelson (ed.), 1953, pp. 38-39.
19 Cf. Henriette Buus, 2008; Frederik W. Thue, 2006.
20 The articles in the book deal with Sweden, Norway, Finland and Denmark – but not Iceland. On the other hand, in several of the articles there is a fairly broad international frame of reference with links in particular to British and American research.
21 See the discussions in Niels Finn Christiansen, Klaus Petersen, Nils Edling & Per Haave (eds.), 2006.
22 See for instance Sven Steinmo, Kathleen Ann Thelen & Frank Longstreth (eds.) 2001; Ellen Immergut, 1994; Bo Rothstein & Sven Steinmo (eds.) 2001.
23 Klaus Petersen, 1998; Lundqvist, 2007.
24 Max Weber, 1977.
25 Henry Jacoby, 1973.
26 B. Guy Peters, 2001.
27 Theda Skocpol, 1988.
28 Bob Jessop, 1990; Bob Jessop, 2002.
29 Bo Rothstein, 1992; Bo Rothstein, 1996.
30 Dietrich Rueschemeyer & Theda Skocpol (eds.), 1996.
31 Thomas S. Kuhn, 1962.
32 Michéle Lamont, 2009.
33 See for example Agneta Hugemark, 1994. See also Kristina Boréus, 1994; Klaus Petersen, 1998.
34 For an introduction to transnational history see Sissel Bjerrum Fossat, Anne Magnussen, Klaus Petersen & Nils Arne Sørensen (eds.), 2009.

References

Alber, Jens & Peter Flora 1981: 'Modernization, Democratization and the Development of Welfare States', P. Flora & A.J. Heidenheimer (eds.), *The Development of Welfare States in Europe and America*, New Brunswick.

Baldwin, Peter 1990: *The Politics of Solidarity. Class Bases of the European Welfare State 1875-1975*, Cambridge.
Boréus, Kristina 1994: *Högervåg. Nyliberalismen och kampen om språket i svensk debatt 1969-1989*, Stockholm.
Buus, Henriette 2008: *Indretning og efterretning. Rockefeller Foundations indflydelse på den danske velfærdsstat 1920–1970*, Copenhagen.
Christensen, Hilda Rømer 2003: 'Kvindeorganisationer, magt og velfærdsstat', K. Petersen (ed.), *13 historier om den danske velfærdsstat*, Odense.
Christiansen, Niels Finn, Klaus Petersen, Nils Edling & Per Haave (eds.) 2006: *The Nordic Model of Welfare – A historical Re-appraisal*, Copenhagen.
Conrad, Christoph 1996: 'Wohlfarhrtsstaaten im Vergleich', Haupt & Kocka (eds.), *Geschichte und Vergleich. Ansätze und Ergebnisse international vergleichender Geschichtsschreibung*, Frankfurt aM.
Esping-Andersen, Gøsta & Walter Korpi 1984: 'From Poor Relief to Welfare State', *Tidsskrift for politisk økonomi*, no. 1, pp. 7-49.
Esping-Andersen, Gøsta 1985: *Politics Against Markets. The Social Democratic Road to Power*, Princeton.
Eyermann, Ron 1985: 'Rationalizing Intellectuals. Sweden in the 1930s and 1940s', *Theory and Society*, vol. 14, pp. 777-807.
Fink, Janet & Åsa Lundqvist (eds.) 2010: *Changing Relations of Welfare. Family, Gender and Migration in Britian and Scandinavia*, Aldershot, Ashgate.
Fossat, Sissel Bjerrum, Anne Magnussen, Klaus Petersen & Nils Arne Sørensen (eds.) 2009: *Transnationale historier*, Odense.
Gemzell, Carl-Axel 1989, 1993 & 1989: *Om politikens förvetenskapligande och vetenskapens politisering. Kring välfärdsstatens uppkomst i England*, Del I: Teoretisk inledning, Del II: Ställföreträdarna, Del III: Föreningen av motsatser, Copenhagen.
Heclo, Hugh 1974: *Modern Social Politics in Britain and Sweden*, London.
Hugemark, Agneta 1994: *Den fängslande marknaden. Ekonomiska experter om välfärdsstaten*, Lund.
Immergut, Ellen 1994: *Health Politics. Interests and Institutions in Western Europe*, Cambridge.
Jacoby, Henry 1973: *The Bureaucratisation of the World*, University of California, Berkeley.
Jessop, Bob 1990: *State Theory. Putting the capitalist state in its place*, Cambridge.
Jessop, Bob 2002: *The future of the capitalist state*, Cambridge.
Kettunen, Pauli 2000: 'Internationalla jämförelser som nationell och övernationell praktik – Ett historiskt perspektiv på globalisering och nationella arbetslivsinstitutioner', Nordic Council of Ministers, *Norden i verden og verden i Norden*, TemaNord.
Klinth, Roger 2002: *Att göra pappa med barn. Den svenska pappapolitiken, 1960-95*, Umeå.
Kolstrup, Søren 1994, 'Forskning i velfærdsstatens rødder. Strategier, resultater, huller'. *Historisk Tidsskrift*, 2, pp. 314-336.
Korpi, Walter 1981: *Den demokratiska klasskampen*, Stockholm.
Kuhle, Stein 1996: 'International Modelling, State and Statistics – Scandinavian Social Security Solutions in the 1890s', Rueschemeyer, Dieter & Theda Skocpol (eds.), *States, Social Knowledge and the Origins of Modern Social Policies*, Princeton.
Kuhn, Thomas S. 1962: *The Structure of Scientific Revolutions*, Chicago.
Lamont, Michéle 2009: *How professors think. Inside the curious world of academic judgement*, Cambridge Mass.

Lundqvist, Åsa 2007: *Familjen i den svenska modellen*, Umeå.
Melby, Kari, Anna-Birte Ravn & Christina Carlsson Wetterberg (eds.) 2008: *Gender Equality and Welfare Politics in Scandianvia*, Bristol.
Melby, Kari, Anu Pylkkänen, Bente Rosenbeck & Christina Carlsson Wetterberg 2006: *Inte ett ord om kärlek. Äktenskap och politik i Norden ca 1850-1930*, Lund.
Myrdal, Alva 1944: *Folk och familj*, Stockholm.
Nelson, George R. (ed.) 1953: *Freedom and Welfare. Social patterns in the Northern countries of Europe*, Copenhagen.
Nilsson, Jan Olof 1994: *Alva Myrdal. En virvel i den moderne strömmen*, Stockholm.
Nørgaard, Asbjørn Sonne 1999, 'Viden og videnskab om velfærdsstaten: Findes der en dansk velfærdsstat', *Grus*, 1999, No. 56/57, pp. 6-39.
O'Connor, Julia & Greg M. Olsen (eds.) 1998: *Power Resource Theory and the Welfare State: A Critical Reader*, Toronto.
Peters, B. Guy 2001: *The Politics of Bureaucracy*, London.
Petersen, Klaus 1997: 'Fra ekspansion til krise. Forskning, velfærdsstatens udvikling efter 1945', *Historisk Tidsskrift*, 1997, No. 2, pp. 356-375.
Petersen, Klaus 1998: *Legitimität und Krise. Die politische Geschichte des dänischen Wohlfahrtsstaats 1945-1973*, Copenhagen.
Petersen, Klaus 2006: 'Constructing Nordic Welfare? Nordic Social Political Cooperation 1919-1955', N.F. Christiansen et al. (eds.), *The Nordic Model of Welfare. A historical re-appraisal*, Copenhagen.
Rimlinger, Gaston V. 1971: *Welfare Policy and Industrialization in Europe, America and Russia*, New York.
Rodgers, Daniel T. 1998: *Atlantic Crossings. Social Politics in a Progressive Age, 1890–1945*, Princeton.
Rothstein, Bo 1992: *Den korporativa staten. Intresseorganisationer och statsförvaltning i svensk politik*, Stockholm.
Rothstein, Bo 1996: *The Social Democratic State. The Swedish Model and the Bureaucratic Problem of Social Reforms*, Pittsburgh and London.
Rothstein, Bo & Sven Steinmo (eds.) 2001: *Restructuring the welfare state. Political institutions and policy change*, New York.
Rueschemeyer, Dietrich & Theda Skocpol (eds.) 1996: *States, Social Knowledge and the Origins of Modern Social Policies*, Princeton.
Skocpol, Theda 1988: 'Bringing the State back in', M. Weir, A.S. Orloff & T. Skocpol (eds.), *The Politics of Social Policy in the United States*, Princeton.
Steinmo, Sven, Kathleen Ann Thelen & Frank Longstreth (eds.) 2001: *Structuring politics. Historical institutionalism in comparative analysis*, Cambridge.
Swenson, Peter A. 2002: *Capitalist against Markets. The Making of Labor Markets and Welfare States in United States and Sweden*, Oxford.
Thue, Frederik W. 2006: *In Quest of a Social Order. The Americanization of Norwegian Social Scholarship 1918-1970*, Oslo.
Tydén, Mattias 2000: *Från politik till praktik. De svenska steriliseringslagarna 1935-1975*, Stockholm.
Weber, Max 1977: *Vetenskap och politik*, Göteborg.
Wilensky, Harold L. 1975: *The Welfare State and Equality. Structural and Ideological Roots of Public Expenditure*, Berkeley.

Part I
On the Role of the Experts in the Welfare State

Politics out of time - Historical expertise and temporal claims in Swedish governmental reports

Sara Edenheim

'We inherit the traces of the dead even when we were not the intended recipients, but in the moment that we give away our own words, we participate in a certain wild future of inheritance, one for which no framework for kinship exists. We are not sure 'who' survives, but there is a surviving that takes place, spectral, haunted, in and through the trace.' [1]

'But what will we say, if it must be averred that faults were committed in the name of the same principles as our own, […]?'[2]

'[…] until at last it came to me that time was suspect.'[3]

The official governmental report (SOU) is a relatively unique Swedish welfare state version of the White Paper, not perhaps because of its final effect on the legal system, but because of its formation and positioning in the public community. This implies that the result of the reports, i.e. actual laws, may not necessarily differ from laws in other liberal democracies, but the specific structuring of the preceding debate in the form of public reports themselves provides a homogenous material for analysis that may have been more difficult to carry out under other circumstances. The governmental report is usually seen as having two, mutually interacting, purposes: to provide a long-term policy for social and legal change (preparatory function) and to negotiate between different organisations and parties by supplying arguments based on the work of a committee consisting of both politicians and appointed experts (deliberative function).

When described by political scientists, one can sometimes discern a certain (national) pride concerning the report: 'the system of deliberation is at once the principal expression and the best symbol of the traditional political culture in Sweden. Internationally compared, it is a unique apparatus for long-term political decision making.'[4]

This specific deliberative tradition can probably be seen as a normative ideal, based on a national self-image consisting of superior democratic values, scientific rationality and equality. These ideals, of course, coincide with the welfare state project, but also with modernity and the liberal subject in a more generally Western context. Hence, the governmental reports can be analysed both as specifically Swedish (as to their structure) and as a product and reproducer of certain universalised ideals (as to their claims). In a study of these reports, the specific structure can consequently be used as a means to grasp a multitude of claims through a single, but still significant, framework.

This study will concentrate on temporal claims. Such claims are usually already naturalised and can therefore be introduced in a governmental discourse without any prior discussion. This creates an opening for a hegemonic discourse to use these claims in strategic manners without risking an exposure or conflict. The aim of this study is to map out how these claims are used and what consequences they have for our definition of democracy. The analysis is part of a wider methodological project mainly concerned with how a philosophy of history denotes a possibility for history as a field of research to study itself.[5] This will concern historiography in relation to some social movements that have played vital roles in the 'autobiographical' version of Swedish (and Western) democratic discourse; mainly those women's and gay movements that have had a major influence on the legal system and our understanding of citizenship.

Hence, it is the emancipatory aspect of the social movements that is of interest, and the implied paradoxes that have already been studied and theorised in various ways by feminists like Denise Riley[6], Joan Scott[7] and Wendy Brown.[8] Their concern is the stabilisation and essentialisation of an identity (e.g. woman) through the appeal to history and civic rights. One of the questions brought up by these researchers concerns the role of historiography within liberal democracy. There are divergent opinions on this issue, where, e.g., political scientist Wendy Brown states that a significant feature of both liberalism and neo-liberalism is a 'postmodern' disrespect for history. Brown does not ascribe a specific value to this statement; she is simply ascribing liberalism a constructivist ideology and hence presumes, as compared to the conservative or (neo)marxist fixations on the past, a liberal disinterest in ontology in general.[9] I do not wich to contradict the observation that liberalism is (or can be) constructivist and postmodern; the widespread use of social constructivism within identity politics is quite enough evidence of that.[10] I would, however, like to scrutinise the suggestion that such a constructivist or postmodern theory automatically eliminates any historical and narrative claims. That histories are multiplied or 'made more complex', does not necessarily mean that narratives or ontologies are being disrupted. They are rather imposed even further and in additional layers.

Hence, when I wish to analyse shifts, deliberations, and foreclosures concerning temporal claims in governmental discourse, I do not want to insist on a historical connection where texts (i.e., governmental reports) have to 'know' each other by means of references and authors (even though often enough there are such connections to be found in these specific texts). I would rather assert an important differentiation between *historicising* and *contextualising*, where the latter could conceivably be characterised as a revised form of genealogy where a non-hermeneutical reading takes the text 'seriously' in the sense that the text is given a legitimacy (and interest) on its own – and only in relation to other texts – no matter their specific time of production. This does not imply a traditional philosophical methodology, since a contextualisation of this kind does take into account the impossibility of understanding and is therefore not concerned with finding universal principles in any text. The 'colonisation' of a text is hence taken for granted instead of foreclosed. Historicising, though used by some poststructuralist genealogists in a somewhat inconsistent manner (including Foucault), implies a quite different methodology, where a text is seen as a passage to another time, as a source which has to be 'grounded' in a specific historical network to be able to inform us about this other time-period. Historicising, in this sense, can only be either a positivist search for 'what really happened' or a hermeneutic search for 'understanding'. As a result, neither of them can be of productive use in this project.[11]

This paper consists of a short introduction to a critical philosophy of history and then continues with an analysis concerning some governmental reports that will be studied in order to analyse the legal claims on the political subject in relation to the past. A discussion follows, concerning the role that temporal claims play for the understanding of our relationship to the past, the writing of history and present political strategy. The paper investigates the relationship between history and liberal democracy, between history and postmodernism, and perhaps most importantly, between history and the past, through which I believe it is possible to discern foreclosed political and social relations.

The politics of double time

There are many ways to write history, but all are based on an assumption about a past, a present and a future, each of which is supposed to be able to say something about the other two 'entities' of time. The historian has turned this into her full-time job: trying to say something about the present through investigations into the past, trying to say something about the future by comparing the past with the present, or, as in the case of the specifically Foucauldian genealogy, trying to say something about the past through the present, or even, as in some strange – and inversely consistent – cases, trying to say something about the past for the sake of the past.

One effect of the assumption of what Elizabeth Deeds Ermarth calls *representational time* is the idea of time as something that can be 'out of joint'.[12] This Shakespearean figure of speech, found in many different Western discourses and elaborated on by philosophers such as Benjamin, Derrida, Laclau, Žižek, or Brown, plays a central part in the governmental reports concerning law proposals against discrimination. To assume that time can be out of joint is to assume two parallel dimensions of time: one dimension that is either utopic or dystopic and one that is 'backwards' and dangerous.[13] Hence, there seemingly exists a true path of time that an entire legal system or even a whole society can digress from. It is therefore the duty of any progressive legal system or society to make sure that they are 'in sync with time' by turning 'everything all right'. This almost Hollywoodian cliché is most apparent in governmental reports concerning the function of the very report itself in relation to legal history as a whole: e.g., statements such as 'homosexuality was not decriminalised *until* 1944', or 'unfortunately there *still* exists prejudices', or 'the legal system is at risk of *falling behind*'. From this it is possible to discern a historiography based on determinism and teleology – a subtle European version of 'Manifest destiny!' – where legal righteousness always has to be prepared to step in against the dark forces of 'untimeliness' that wishes to delay the determined path towards (the now already accomplished) perfection. In other words, the restoration of time has already taken place in and through the reports' claim – in and through the passed law – and hence the 'pure' present time is, in a quite intriguing way, always already reproduced as perfect while the past is not only rendered incomplete but also contagious. Those untimely forces that aspire to destroy the true path of time are consequently also defined as coming from the past in the form of 'remains' (*kvarlevor*, *rester*). Hence, nothing that is 'on time' is bad, while everything that is 'out of joint' is not only bad but can never, according to this logic, inhabit anything but the past.[14]

In some senses this may seem to be an unnecessary part of the law proposals; one might define it as rhetorical jargon to make the report look good in comparison to the older, unmodern, totalitarian legal system that we (since 1944, or 1993, or, take your pick) have left 'behind us'. It is furthermore a historiography that seemingly uses modernist metaphors (the progressive state, the struggle for enlightenment, the determined path to utopia) rather than neoliberal or postmodern ditto. This last observation, of course, just makes it more interesting, since the laws that are proposed (and passed) constitute the pillow-stones of present day identity politics (gay marriage, adoption, anti-discrimination clause). Brown assigns such 'modernist' historiography a mere fetishist function in late modernity, where its emergence is more about not having found any other alternative to this rhetoric, even though we 'very well know' that this kind of historiography represents a myth.[15]

However, Brown does not completely dismiss the place of history in late modernity; she rather ascribes it an ambivalence: 'As the past becomes less easily reduced to a single set of meanings and effects, as the present is forced to orient itself amid so much history and so many histories, history itself emerges as both weightier and less deterministic than ever before.'[16] Hence, when she describes the present as 'disoriented by the literal loss of trajectory following the collapse of historical metanarratives […],'[17] this might seem contradictory to the reports produced in the model state of liberal democracy of Sweden. Brown is, however, referring to the 'dark times' called the global state, which is indeed 'fraught with injustice and misery and not only apocalyptic danger.'[18] In this global state of affairs, there is most probably a sense of loss of direction, a lack of 'a forward movement', a sort of stale time. What the reports are trying to do is to provide us with an answer to this loss, an answer that perpetuates the very same world order by foreclosing the loss altogether and, as I am trying to show here, making all evils (including its responsibility) a thing of the past. In other words, the present may be at a loss and without direction, but liberalism is all too eager to take advantage of the situation and put us all 'back' on track towards an everlasting present.

It is this eagerness that I would like to investigate further by claiming that the use of what Robyn Wiegman calls 'double time' and its very much intended by-product – that which I am tempted to call 'the hero of time restoration' – are vital parts of the formation of liberal democracy.[19] Or, to put it in other (and psychoanalytical) terms, such statements are more than a figure of speech, more than 'just' a fetish; rather, they are, *like all fetishes*, very noteworthy symptoms of a constituting lack.

This becomes apparent if one introduces the question of responsibility; to claim the existence of 'remaining prejudices' (*kvardröjande fördomar*) is after all to claim that the responsibility for this existence lies in the past – they are not the fault of the present society or legal system. When prejudices are defined as anachronistic remains, rhetorical figures like 'hidden prejudices' (*dolda fördomar*) that can be 'lanced' (*slå hål på*), 'tossed out' (*slänga ut*) or 'thrown onto the garbage heap' (*kastas på sophögen*), produce prejudices as almost physical entities that take up an autonomous space in relation to present day society. Prejudices are hence defined as misapprehensions (*vanföreställningar*) about specific groups of people that have no productive meaning or function in the present. Once again, we are dealing with an imagery almost taken from science fiction, where a black hole – with its origin in the past – reaches into the present at the risk of creating an anarchy of time by 'sucking up' anyone that gets in its path.

Enlightenment is seen as the solution here; only (true) knowledge can fill up this hole and prevent it from spreading. Knowledge about specific groups of people is consequently defined as a product of the present – as a fundamental part of a democracy – and it is here that the legal preparations for the official reports and their assigned research put forward by the reports, play a fundamental part. Research reports from such government authorities as the National Institute of Public Health (*Statens folkhälsoinstitut*) or The Living History Forum (*Forum för Levande Historia*) often consist of extensive survey studies, aiming at providing the basis for revealing 'the conceptions and attitudes of the Swedish population' towards any given group of people.[20] From these surveys one can discern that the difference between misapprehension (prejudices) and comprehension (knowledge) is based on two mutually dependant assertions: 1) that the past existence of a present group is beyond doubt (ontological claim), 2) that a positive attitude towards this existence derives from knowledge of the temporal stability and homogeneity of the group (epistemological claim). It is at this point that historiography fulfils its most important duty within the (con)text of the legal report.

History and the political choice

As a rule, one can locate examples of this when both surveys and reports find the correlation between homophobia and the 'misconception' that homosexuality is not a stable trait very significant. Actually, the most central concern of *all* reports concerning homosexuality in late modernity is, by far, the importance of a guarantee that homosexuals cannot 'recruit' heterosexuals.

> 'To sum up, no certain evidence would seem to exist according to research as to what causes homosexuality. Different reasons have been advanced for various factors – even combinations of these. However, there would seem to be broad agreement that, no matter which factors may be significant, *they must make an impact at a very early stage*, either genetically at the moment of conception, hormonally during the embryonic phase, or psychologically during the earliest childhood years.'[21]

> '[homosexuality] cannot be 'treated' and is not contagious. It is rather characterised as a personality trait. According to current research it is not possible to tell why some people become heterosexuals and others homosexuals. Those who have conducted research on the matter do, however, agree on that sexual disposition is founded, *at its latest*, during the early years of childhood.'[22]

The concluding argument against the 'prejudice' that homosexuality is contagious is the declaration that the number of homosexuals in any given population and time is constant. Here, however, we find two different ways of how a temporal ontological claim can be used:

1) When it comes to the matter of decriminalisation (1944), e.g., the entire argumentation is based on history as the sole and direct proof of homosexuality's constituting character. The current law (Penal Code, ch. 18 §10) is in this case argued against (mainly for being insufficiently effective when it comes to implementing against 'homo-

sexuality's destructive effects on society') by an active and visible dispute over homosexuality in history. The writer of the proposal, the well-known legal reformer Wilhelm Lundstedt, refers to an appendix by an anonymous writer who, by means of a vast system of scientific references, wants to impose the inherited (biological) constitution of homosexuality, the main argument being that homosexuals have existed in all periods and places. Hence, he states that it is 'less likely that the occurrence of homosexuals should change between different periods of time and different cultural epochs' and 'that homosexuality to us in the present appears to have been so generally widespread in the old Greek and Roman cultures, is surely due to the Greeks' and Romans' view of homosexuality, and other manifestations of the sexual drive, as nothing remarkable and that the ethics brought in by Christianity were unknown to them, which, due to a greater tolerance and understanding, made it possible for homosexuals to more openly display their sentiments, instead of, as in our case, being condemned to conceal them. Indeed, homosexuality must be viewed as a valid constant for all of humanity, as a necessity included in the order of nature.'[23]

However, the author of the bill following the first commission, who was also the Minister of Justice at the time, answered by claiming that homosexuality is not a completely constitutive trait and *therefore* cannot be decriminalised. This is argued for through the following use of history: '[t]he circumstance that homosexuality during certain periods of time and among some populations has reached an especially high extent seems to amount to significant evidence that even social factors can play an important part in this context.'[24] The Minister's aim is to deny homosexuality a common and linear history. In other words, it is by ascribing homosexuals a *contingent* and *fractional* part of the past that he wishes to be able to discredit the entire legal proposal. The final legal report that implements the decriminalisation ends by rejecting every single claim made by the minister in the bill, conspicuously and scrupulously, by borrowing generously from both Lundstedt's proposal and the above-mentioned appendix.

What we can discern from this is that a contingent past (and hence a contingent present and future) is sorted out as an illegitimate foundation, not primarily for a conservative agenda, but for a democratically defined legal system. The decriminalisation was all about the constitutive character of homosexuality (and hence, also, heterosexuality), where legal ethics considered the possibility of choice as defining a criminal. Hence, where indecent acts but no free choice were involved, no one ought to be punished. In this respect, the governmental bill against decriminalisation was part of the same liberal ethics as Lundstedt; it is only the conclusion concerning the ontology of homosexuality that does not fit the liberal way of dealing with indecent acts. The author of the bill rather implies that people can be homosexuals *without* a constituting past and hence he also runs the risk of revealing that the question of decriminalisation, ultimately, is (or ought to be seen as) a *moral* choice between a) No matter its ontology, (homo)sexuality is a legal concern, or b) No matter its ontology, (homo)sexuality is *not* a legal concern. Where Lundstedt covered up this standpoint by introducing the parameter of history to use as a guide towards his (likewise) heteronormative definition of deviant desire, the Minister of Justice's refusal opens up the past and makes it contingent, even though he finally finds such contingency immoral. In other words, this line of argumentation could be seen as making a truly *political* choice possible; a possibility that is 'dribbled away' *by means of history* in the final legal report.

2) In the other example of how history is implemented, we find few, if any, references to (historic) scientific research in the selfsame legal reports when they concern themselves with the ontology of homosexuality. The scientific claim is either bantered around in very general terms ('most researchers believe…', 'it has been shown that…', etc.), or, in a more common and characteristic manner, it is *construed as true by making clear that it is undemocratic to believe otherwise*. In the case of a study from the National Institute of Public Health, this argumentation is part of an on-going field of (sociological) research, where one finds references to key-researchers that have constructed a 'scale of homophobia' where answering in the affirmative to statements like 'homosexuality is unnatural' categorises a respondent as homophobic.[25] A reference to these researchers occurs in the context of the governmental study and backs up statements like the following:

> 'The question whether homosexuality is genetically conditioned or an acquired disposition is important in relation to how the attitudes of the Swedes are constructed. If you believe in a genetic disposition, i.e. a biological inheritance, homosexuality is perceived as something incontrovertible that one cannot be blamed for, as opposed to a disposition that is established in the course of life.'[26]

This, of course, is the same legal ethics as that used by Lundstedt, but with an interesting twist somewhat reminiscent of Slavoj Žižek's well-known 'postmodern parent'. The passage is seemingly without any ontological claim, but instead of giving us a *political* choice between two dissimilar moralities, the only alternative given is already more than implied – it is all over the place – making it in effect politically impossible to claim a different ontology of homosexuality than the one(s) supported by the law.[27] Hence, there may be no need for a naturalisation of homosexuality through scientific and/or historical referential systems; within this postmodernist form of Nietzsche's moralism, the claim on ontology is not declared directly as in the above-mentioned case, but rather a cemented and determined history appears as a sort of melting pot for both the 'biologist' and 'culturalist' standpoint; as most of the reports themselves repeatedly point out, it does not matter if you believe in genes *or* social constructions – as long as the deviant constitution has already taken place 'in the past' (*'at a very early stage'*; *'at the latest'*). After all, it is *history* that assists at the liberal inclusion of any chosen ontology necessary so that nothing but linear and complete time can cement categories and make them legitimate. Everyone who wants to be part of the democratic project requires a history, a narrative, a story to be told so that the law will listen and, eventually, help. The liberal law is in that sense a very narcissistic law, seeking to be told stories in a way that reflects the law as the hero, where certain temporal claims are necessary elements to enable a retrospectively and apolitically dependant legal and social system.

The historical subject and liberalism – a discussion

The philosophers of history that I assume as my platform in this text all describe the writing of history as a high-risk, if not even a downright vain, occupation. They enquire why a linear narrative or an ontological claim is seen as desirable even though (or, rather, because) we can never achieve and complete such desires. To desire a history is to be in need of a sense of meaning and wholeness through the idea of events as part of valuable and comprehensible causes and effects in time. Hence, to 'know your history' can never be an innocent decree, but on the other hand, at the moment it cannot be a *political* decree either.

This becomes clear when the claim of history is brought forward as obvious and non-objectionable, where its intention is not to create a discussion or a political standpoint concerning history per se. In those cases, the claim rather refers to a dogmatic 'common sense' supposedly shared by all sides involved and history is always and already legitimate and legitimising. Any actual protest against the claim would most likely disqualify the protester from the democratic agenda and hence from the definition of legitimate forms of politics. Consequently, the demand for history is probably more properly categorised as an *apolitical* demand as defined by Chantal Mouffe, where *the political* is the opposite of consensus and common sense, and therefore more likely to be based on the recognition of conflicts (not necessarily leading to an *antagonistic* conflict). The 'right to our own history' does not eliminate canonical history (national or universal), it merely acknowledges it as its *only* antagonist partner and thereby forecloses an opinion concerning history per se, which hence is rendered impossible to even utter and therefore cannot be defined as a political claim since 'properly political questions always involve decisions which require us to make a choice between conflicting alternatives.'[28]

Can the desire for history become political within present-day society dominated by liberal democratic discourse? If not, are there perhaps other ways of 'being' political in late modernity? Mouffe would answer with a distinct 'no': the mechanism of liberalism is to hide and exterminate that which is political and hence nothing political, historical or not, can come out of liberalism.[29] The remaining question, then, would be whether *the claim on history is exclusively used as a liberal project or not*? In other words, can history be liberated from its 'liberal chains' or is the idea of history per se invariably interconnected with a liberal subject? To be able to answer such questions we are in need of some criteria as to what constitutes historiography and, respectively, what constitutes the liberal subject. To start with both at the same time, it is telling that the left-right scale of the Swedish welfare state is usually associated with two different kinds of historiography: the right-wing's devotion to a canonical and universalist historiography connected to the nation, its leading men and great wars (or, as in the modern Swedish case, its great peace); and, in contrast, the left-wing's commitment to the historiography of the underdog and the marginalised, where the everyday, the oppositional and the excluded are given a narrative. We are used to interpret this as the constituting difference between a conservative and a radical historiography, especially since most of the left-wing historians are explicit Marxists of one sort or another.³⁰ Where then, is the liberal to be found?

According to Brown, liberalism in late modernity cannot be defined as one explicit branch of the parliamentary scale. Another, more delicate tool of classification is therefore needed; preferably a classification based on the conceptualisation of the subject. Hence, the differentiation made by Brown between a *liberalism of individual freedom* and *a liberalism of equal rights* can be quite helpful to acknowledge a variation between the Swedish left and right without having to exclude a quite possible shared liberal base.³¹ Those are similarities that Mouffe would point out as characteristic of a liberal democracy and hence in themselves an example of the hegemonic position of the apolitical politics of liberalism where constituting antagonisms are not only rendered invisible but all together foreclosed by the ideal of consensus.³² Therefore, parliamentary politics in late modernity only make it even clearer that we have to turn to the very maxim of liberalism – the possibility of a free individual with equal rights, living in a community of equally free individuals – to continue the investigation into the criteria of liberal historiography.

Usually these criteria are criticised for producing a kind of historiography that, somewhat derogatory, does not take power in consideration, i.e., there is no taking into account the subjectivating effects of power in any given context. This definition would place a range of historiographies outside the compromising range of liberalism: historical materialism, religious history, gender history, postmodernist history, etc., since they all, in different ways, concern themselves with a constituting power (economy, God, patriarchy, language). According to this definition though, quite ironically, even the 'invisible hand' of Adam Smith would be excluded from liberalism, since it, too, implies a power that constitutes societies and hierarchies by means of correcting, adjusting or (mis)leading pre-social agents in(to) a pre-programmed world, either filled with abundance (Smith) or filled with a slightly hidden abundance, quite easily found behind the veils of capitalism, patriarchy or secularism. What these historiographies all share, then, is a certain kind of revolutionary paradigm where revolution is an emancipatory fight for a utopia with free individuals having equal rights?

What most standard ideas of revolution may be said to have in common is a belief in the possibility of *abundance* in a near future.

This is at least why certain aspects of Marxism, feminism, or messianism, are defined as revolutionary. It is, however, a revolution that shares both the definition of subject and freedom with liberalism and in that sense, liberalism encompasses this revolutionary paradigm. In practice, however, liberalism has made its own use of the paradigm in a slightly different manner: by somewhat shifting the revolutionary narrative, liberalism promises abundance here and now, not in a post-revolutionary after-life. It is a quite efficient inversion: by claiming abundance in the present, the need for change is minimised by means of blame: 'if you do not have, you are free to take. If you do not take, you do not deserve to have.'[33] Not surprisingly (since they share the same revolutionary paradigm), this same method can be found in neo-marxism (e.g., Hardt/Negri), deradicalised feminist/queer-activism and constructivist historiographies in general as they, somewhat paradoxically, turn to identitarian claims. In those cases, it is foremost the assumed abundance of *identities* that functions as the principle for blame: It is subversive to be whoever you want to be and the choice is unlimited, so just do it! This constant navigation in abundance – between 'mountains of things' – can hence be said to be assumed in quite the same manner no matter if power is defined as productive (as in Smith or religion) or repressive (as in neo-marxism or identitarian feminism) or both (as in Foucault or constructivist feminism). That which foremost lies at the base of an assumed free and equal individual can thus not accurately be defined as a lack of power but rather a *lack of lack*.[34]

To clarify this point, liberalism is a modernist ideology, just like (neo-)marxism, but where both modernism and Marxism are defined as ongoing social processes with a not-yet-realised future, liberalism presents itself as a finished project, at the end of history, with no limits concerning what it will (always already) encompass. Since liberalism assumes that it encompasses everything, it can define itself as a non-ideology. This is why liberalism is willing to absorb both modernism and postmodernism at the same time. As well as universalism, relativism, positivism, constructivism, realism, rationalism, idealism, and even (neo-)marxism... and, it might be added, this is also how all these different -isms become legible within the liberal democratic context. Instead of allowing a theory of lack, (neo-)marxism and other more traditionally messianic ideologies are given an opportunity to 'use' the liberal subject as a medium to communicate a (deradicalised) revolutionary agenda.[35] One may be tempted to call it a 'liberal matrix', where the deviant (e.g., Marxism; globalisation movements; et al.) confirms the norm (liberalism) by being subjectificated through the same matrix. The process is in that sense similar to Judith Butler's heterosexual matrix, where heterosexuality is not only a norm confirmed by speech-acts, but also a normative institution that simultaneously and necessarily makes possible the opposite category (homosexuality). [36] And just as in the case of the heterosexual matrix, other possibilities, categories, materialisations, and ethics are being repeatedly foreclosed.

This 'double positioning' of liberalism is, I believe, important to bear in mind, since it turns liberalism into exactly that which it also claims to be, i.e. a non-ism; in this sense, liberalism is a unique medium for turning paradoxes into an invisible perpetuation of differences without simultaneously producing the means for neither identifying nor criticising them. As opposed to some parts of modernism then, liberalism is by necessity an anti-intellectual movement where critique is only of value if it can be assimilated within the liberal project.[37] This is why the acknowledgement of the complex matter of lack, i.e. human impotency, is an abject impossibility within liberalism, no matter if we choose to define lack in the Freudo-Lacanian sense or not.

If academic liberalism can include almost any scientific premise, this version of scientific 'tolerance' is somewhat mirrored in a legal context by legal policies concerning everything from the protection of private property to anti-discrimination and human rights. If this may already seem to be a narrowing down of possibilities, that impression is further enforced when it comes to the economic trademarks of liberalism: the free market, homo economicus, individual entrepreneurships, and privatisation of the state. This is where the 'neo-' finds it place in front of liberalism, or to put in other (and quite Marxist) terms: wherever the 'real' action takes place, the less tolerant liberalism becomes.[38]

As Brown has pointed out, and thoroughly analysed, tolerance plays an important part in liberal discourse[39] and in combination with the above-mentioned 'lack of lack' we can now perhaps formulate a version of the liberal creed: the absolute mark of liberalism is *its claim on completeness*. As will be argued for below, it is the *claim* that is of importance here, not the actual outcome, because it is the claim that creates an absorbing effect on anything standing in liberalism's way. It is of minor concern to liberalism whether an actual inclusion is possible or not (or, rather, it is of importance that it is *not* possible, since that perpetuates the claim).

The claim on complete inclusion needs to be taken into careful account, since it also implies a specific *temporal* claim not unlike the inverted revolutionary discourse of abundance in the present mentioned above. The ideal of a holistic (cosmopolitarian) society driven by reason and incorporated citizens, that, no matter their inborn or constructed differences, sensibly adhere to universal human rights as their common denominator, is not only a utopian ideal in the futurist stance. It is foremost used in a double stance of closing off the future-to-come by means of a (meticulously) prescribed future, filled with the historically legitimised (a)politics of the present.[40] In other words, when an official governmental report states that its proposal *is* democratic, we have an ad hoc where the existence of a certain law, and indeed the very talk about the inclusion of a defined group in the law, is treated as an assertion that the true intention of the law always already includes the named group and it is only due to anti-democratic forces that this inclusion now needs to be stressed explicitly. The performativity of the law hence not only manages to hide its production of a discriminated group, it also turns the legal speech concerning democracy into verification of a democratic society. The same goes for concepts such as freedom and justice, where the faith in their performative power far surpasses any claim of action.[41] When the speech on democracy, freedom and justice passes *as* democracy, freedom and justice per se, it ought to be clear that something is amiss, that the speech taking place is rather trying to avoid interruptions, protests and claims on other definitions of democracy, freedom and justice.

The Politics of Untimeliness – a concluding suggestion

If all things bad come from the past, it is quite ironic that the liberal reports, wanting to give equal rights to homosexuals, repeatedly refer the constitution of deviance to the past. In that respect, it is no wonder that the governmental report on homosexuals' right to adopt[42] mainly concerns itself with establishing as a fact that the children of homosexuals do not, under any circumstances, become either homosexuals or suffer from 'other' gender identity disorders to any higher degree than other children. Children are, as we are persistently reminded, 'the future', and the report's immense concern with rendering a possible 'gay future' impossible is in this case telling. It is, however, not telling enough. Any human trait that wants to legitimate itself as an identity – deviant or not – is given an ontology in quite the same manner within liberal democracies. Therefore it is the 'giving of ontologies' that is interesting, rather than exactly who or what is given one. In this case, the specific double time of liberalism is therefore of more interest and foremost the radical potentiality in its by-product of 'untimeliness'.

Because it seems that it is not only the conservative or the religious fundamentalist that are rendered enemy to the true time inherited in liberalism, even though that is the official version. Perhaps being declared 'untimely' can also be a sign of radicalism, a signal that you are on to something that the current hegemonic discourse wishes to foreclose by deeming it impossible in relation to 'true time'.[43]

Even if Brown at one point declared history to be a 'mere' rhetorical figure in late modernity, she has also observed the radicalism of untimeliness and applies it to philosophers as diverse, but equally critical, as Benjamin, Connolly, Derrida, Jameson, Nietzsche and Wolin.[44] Jameson's definition of postmodernity as a time of an eternal present – '[a] present experienced as eternal is a present experienced as Total, with no imagined elsewhere.'[45]– leads Brown to Nietzsche's warning that an endless present, as '[u]nbroken time is the time of eternity, death's time.'[46] In this context, the untimely – in Brown's version equal to critical theory (not least since that is how critical theory is usually argued against: 'this is not the right time to be critical, wait until the time is right') – is rendered powerful because 'to insist on the value of untimely political critique is [...] to contest settled accounts of what time it is, what the times are, and what political tempo and temporality we should hew to in political life.[...] Intellectual and political strategies of successful untimeliness therefore depend on a close engagement with time in every sense of the word. They are concerned with timing and tempo. They involve efforts to grasp times by thinking against the times. They attempt, as Nietzsche put it, to 'overcome the present' by puncturing the present's 'overvaluation of itself', an overcoming whose aim is to breathe new possibility into the age.'[47]

This quest, however, is neither an innocent one for utopia nor an attempt to dismiss the past, and when dissecting Benjamin's sixteenth thesis of 'Thesis on the Philosophy of History', Brown calls attention to the difference between 'historicism' (here equal to conventional history) and 'historical materialism' (here equal to critical theory), where the former strives toward an 'empty time' of universal history and the latter strives towards a 'still(ed) time' where 'this notion [of stillness] *defines the present in which [the historical materialist] himself is writing history.*'[48] This is genealogy with a twist, where we will have a present that is 'not automatically overcome by time, a present that is out of time in both senses, is a present that calls to us, calls to us to respond to it.'[49] It is only by accounting for the experience of a past (e.g. in the form of spectres à la Derrida), while at the same time not naming this experience *history*, that the philosopher of history can start scrutinising the present's historiography. In other words, being untimely involves knowing that your untimeliness is a product of the present, of historiography, and not an autonomous thought outside all time and space. Hence, as Brown concludes, by referring to Benjamin's call to blast open the continuum of history, '[critical theory] becomes a non-violent mode of exploding the present.'[50]

Maybe it is possible to rephrase this in order to make clear that the untimely does not seek to become 'timely', i.e., there is no desire to be included by the rights of liberalism on 'new', or any other, terms. Rather, the proposal to refuse (to use) history *as* history is probably defined as preposterous by the legal and scientific discourses alike, and therein lies the possibility of forcing liberalism to unveil itself and start arguing *for* its cause (instead of against everyone else's). This would mean that liberalism would no longer be able to pass as the only moral alternative. To point out temporal claims on the past within governmental discourse, then, does not aim (over and over again) to expand this discourse; the untimely does not want to be liberalism's psychoanalyst and point out its foreclosures to help it avoid making the same mistake again (which of course would be impossible anyway since liberalism is 'unmistakable'). The aim is rather to create an opposition that is not unaware or independent of liberalism, but still strives towards making another *moral* visible. This can only be done by forcing liberalism to listen to 'stupid' questions (where a questioning of time and history may be one such example): if refusing to answer, liberalism will expose its limits of tolerance, and if trying to answer, it will have to argue for its sake in a manner where history can no longer serve as an unquestioned legitimiser for a certain ideological system. Hence, we would have one (identified) ideology trying to argue against another (equally identified) ideology, where the contingent possibilities of the future-to-come have to be taken seriously. In other words, the effect might be such a rare thing as a *political* democracy.

Notes

1   Judith Butler, 2005, p. 32.
2   Jean-Luc Nancy, 1990, p. 107.
3   Einstein, cited in Ronald Clark, 1971, p. 84.
4   Andersson, Mellbourn, Skogö, 1983, p. 54. The status of the governmental report is not, however, without changes itself. The numbers of reports and committees appointed have, for example, sky-rocketed during the last decades, creating an impression of inflation rather than increased importance. This trend, however, has diminished since the right-wing parties assumed government. Instead the one-man report is currently in fashion, where the main purpose rather seems to be to go through the mandatory procedure as smoothly and fast as possible without consulting more than one expert.
5   It is no easy matter to name this field: 'philosophy of history' has certain Hegelian connotations, while 'intellectual history', the term commonly used within the field of history, has nothing but strange connotations (e.g., 'intellectual' as opposed to what?). 'Historiography', as used in the Scandinavian context, is limited to quite traditional over-views regarding specific historians and their influences on historical research. 'Theoretical history' (*historieteori*) may be an alternative choice, but runs the risk of differentiating 'theory' from 'empiric studies' in a way more comfortable for the non-theoretical historian than for the other.
6   Denise Riley, 1988.
7   Joan Scott, 1996; 1999; 2002.
8   Wendy Brown, 2001; 2005; 2006.
9   Wendy Brown, 2005.
10 Cases of liberal use of constructivism can be found in many Governmental Official Reports concerning equity. The most explicit constructivist report, however, concerns intersexuals (SOU, *Om intersexuellas könstillhörighet*, 1968, p. 23) and the need for surgical intervention (see also Erika Alm, 2006; Sara Edenheim, 2005). Liberal feminism and its argument for equality based on the fact that what is considered feminine or masculine (not female/male) varies depending on time and place, is another well-known example.
11 I have elaborated on this issue elsewhere, see Sara Edenheim (forthcoming), 'The Haunted Hermeneutics of History'. A shorter version can be found in Sara Edenheim, 2009.
12 Elisabeth Ermarth, 1992.
13 See Robyn Wiegman, 2000, for a very interesting discussion on this 'Double Time' in relation to feminism and some of its apocalyptic effects.
14 When one commonly speaks of a person as being 'ahead of his time' it is usually used in retrospective, implying that this person was better than everyone else in *his* time, but equal to us since we share his standpoint and like to think of him as part of our own, more progressive, time. Hence, it is a temporal claim that serves the same reinstating of a hierarchical relation between the past and the

present as the claim that 'time is out of joint'. Another version on this theme can be found when a governmental report argues for *not* changing a law, by claiming that *society* is not yet ready for such a change (simultaneously implying that the *legal* system might be ready, but only because the legal system is always 'ahead of its time').

15 Wendy Brown, 2001, p. 3ff.
16 Wendy Brown, 2001, p. 5.
17 Wendy Brown, 2005, p. 10.
18 Wendy Brown, 2005, p. 10.
19 Robyn Wiegman, 2000.
20 For a selection of quotes, see also Sara Edenheim, 2005:155ff.
21 SOU, 1984:63, p. 4.
22 SOU, 1993, p. 98, 1; my italics. 'Sammanfattningsvis syns enligt forskningen några säkra kunskaper om orsakerna till homosexuell inte finnas. Argument har framförts för olika faktorer och även för sammanträffande av sådana. Man syns dock vara enig om att, oavsett faktorerna som kan vara av betydelse, så måste dessa inverka mycket tidigt, de genetiska i befruktningsögonblicket, de hormonella under fosterstadiet och de psykologiska under de första barnaåren.' (SOU, 1984:63, p. 34f) 'Den [homosexualiteten] går inte att 'bota' och är inte heller smittsam. Den kan snarast karaktäriseras som en personlighetsinriktning. På forskningens nuvarande ståndpunkt går det inte att säga varför en del blir heterosexuella och andra [sic] homosexuella. De som har forskat i dessa frågor är dock överrens om att sexuell läggning grundläggs senast under de tidiga barnaåren.' (SOU, 1993:98, p. 51).
23 '[…] föga troligt, att homosexualitetens förekomst skulle växla med olika tidsskeden och olika kulturepoker.' Han fortsätter med en förklaring till att det förvisso kan verka som om så ändå vore fallet: 'Att homosexualiteten för oss nutidsmänniskor förefaller hava varit så allmänt utbredd inom den gamla grekiska och romerska kulturvärlden, beror säkert på att greker och romare ej ansågo homosexualitet och andra yttringar av könsdriften vara något märkvärdigt, att den med kristendomen införda etiken var dem främmande, och att därför till följd av den större toleransen och förståelsen de homosexuella mera öppet kunde visa sina känslor och ej som hos oss voro förvisade till det fördolda. Nej, homosexualiteten måste anses som en för hela mänskligheten giltig konstant, som en i naturens ordning ingående nödvändighet.' (bilaga till Vilhelm Lundstedt, 1933, p. 49)
24 '[d]en omständigheten att homosexualiteten under vissa tider och bland vissa folk nått en särskilt stor spridning synes utgöra ett talande vittnesbörd om att även sociala faktorer kunna spela en betydande roll i detta sammanhang.' (Prop. 1937:187, p. 91; also quoted in SOU, 1941:32, p. 11.)
25 Sune Innala, 1995; Mikael Landén, 2000. For anyone who has read the excellent study of Celia Kitzinger (1987) this field of research is quite familiar.
26 'Frågan om huruvida homosexualitet är en genetiskt betingad eller en förvärvad läggning spelar stor roll för hur svenskarnas attityder byggs upp. Om man tror på genetisk läggning, således ett biologiskt arv, upplevs homosexualiteten som något ovedersägligt man inte kan rå för, jämfört med en läggning som etableras under livet.' (FHI, 2002, p. 32).
27 Žižek retells the story of the totalitarian parent who tells the child that he has to come and visit grandmother 'no matter what', while the postmodern parent

tells the child that his grandmother loves him a lot, but it is 'really up to the child' if he wants to come or not. The effect of the latter is that not only does the child have to go to grandmother 'no matter what', he has to *like* it too. In the above context we have a postmodern research study that tells us that not only is homosexuality a stable category through time and space, but that the final proof for this is that it is also only by believing so that you can become a true democrat. Hence, homophobes are rendered undemocratic, but at the same time, so am I and so are other feminists who argue for the denaturalisation of sexual desire.

28 Mouffe divides the political from politics by ascribing to the latter an ontic level consisting of 'the set of practices and institutions through which an order is created, organizing human coexistence in the context of conflictuality provided by the political.' She then continues, 'it is the lack of understanding of 'the political' in its ontological dimension which is at the origin of our current incapacity to think in a political way.' (Chantal Mouffe, 2005, p. 9).

29 Perhaps a discussion on Lukes' three-dimensional power can provide an idea on how power is not only attributed a function of mystification, not unlike the fetish of Marx (see, e.g., Wendy Brown, 2000) or the internalisation of Foucault, but also an additional third dimension consisting of the conservative effect of the consensus. Power that causes conflicts and change can no longer be hidden and hence power is more efficient where there are no (visible) conflicts. In Mouffe this would be a description of liberalism, rather than power in general, but the idea of power as ontologically conservative can also be found in Freud's death drive. In any case, it is necessary to ask in what ways conservatism and liberalism adhere to and differ from each other (see Wendy Brown, 2006b), but also to problematicise the ontological claims on power as *either* inherently logical *or* contingent: does power follow a mechanic? Is mechanics *equal* to logic? Is the contingent the *opposite* of logic? Is power *equal* to logic? Is power a *claim* on logic? Can the contingent coexist with a logical power?

30 The term 'radical' seems to have a quite interesting genealogy within liberalism. The Swedish media discourse has more or less abandoned the terms 'left-wing radicals' (*vänsterradikala*) and 'right-wing extremists' (*högerextremister*) in favour of 'left-wing extremists' (*vänsterextremister*) and 'right-wing radicals' (*högerradikala*) in those cases when the former consists of members of certain unions and anti-racist organisations and the latter consists of neo-Nazis. A simple search on the web-based sites of the leading national newspapers confirms this beyond doubt. In other words, a kind of derogation of 'radical' is taking place, where the term becomes more and more impossible to use in a positive manner, while at the same time any form of politics 'left of the left' is delegitimised by the term 'extremist'. For an academic and European example of this same process, ponder this quote from an invitation to the international conference *The State and 'the Others': Reacting to Xenophobia* in Leipzig 2008: '[…] Right-wing radicalism has been drawing a great deal of attention from media, civil society protagonists, and social scientists. […] We want to compare and discuss ways of dealing with radicalism in EU countries, different premises under which this problem can be seen and the sort of subjects formation that is connected with the different approaches.' (*Call for papers*, 2007).

31 Wendy Brown, 1995, p. 67. A later Brown (2006b) differentiates between (neo) liberalism and (neo)conservatism within domestic politics of the U.S., where

(neo)conservatism openly rejects a free subject with equal rights. The Swedish left-right scale of parliamentary politics does not officially cover this version of (neo)conservatism, even though I would not be prepared to claim its complete absence in certain instances, mainly concerning religious claims.
32   Chantal Mouffe, 2005.
33   For an elaborate discussion on responsibility within (neo)liberalism, see Emilie Hache, 2007.
34   It ought to be clear that I do not consider feminists like, e.g., aforementioned Butler to be constructivist. Her project is rather a reaction against constructivist feminism, and one could say that her critique is based on a revision of both constructivism and psychoanalysis with the intention to simultaneously introduce the concept of lack within feminism and the concept of power within psychoanalysis.
35   One might want to ask why this subject is not simply defined as Western or Judeo-Christian here, instead of the seemingly narrower liberal. However, these other terms need a historicising and/or geographical narrative to be rendered 'meaningful' in the present, while liberalism defines an ideology that is very much present and active today, both globally and nationally – no matter its (glorious or grimy) 'history'.
36   Judith Butler, 1991; 1993.
37   It may be interesting to study what parts of modernism liberalism forecloses. One suggestion is the foreclosing of 'grand ideologies', i.e., oppositional politics where different economic systems can be played out against each other, where ideas about different social systems and relations can be part of a legitimate political discussion.
38   This is probably why I prefer talking about liberalism rather than (just) capitalism; capitalism comes in plural (state capitalism, Keynesian capitalism, monopoly capitalism, laissez-faire capitalism, merchant capitalism) and could work under certain forms of socialism (e.g. Kibbutzim) and conservatism (e.g. Protestantism) as well as liberalism. Capitalism is certainly dependent on alienation, a monetary market and fetishist surplus value, but it is *not* dependent on free individuals with universal rights. Hence, because liberalism can only work together with capitalism while capitalism can work without liberalism, liberalism can be seen as a way of 'colonising' capitalism for liberalism's own sake by rendering the idea of capitalism as 'just' an economic system (among other possible systems) obsolete. However, this is not necessarily done by 'veiling the truth' by naturalising capitalism, *but rather by making naturalisation itself irrelevant*. Liberalism, then, could be said to be that ideology which Marx could not foresee; the very ideology that implodes the base and the superstructure and goes beyond the claim on nature used by the bourgeoisie in Marx' take on capitalism; hence *any* ontology – even constructivist historicising – can do the trick for liberalism simply because it relies on narration and closure.
39   Wendy Brown, 2006.
40   See e.g., the Habermasian description of the future and its extreme attention to details.
41   See Wendy Brown, 1995, pp. 105ff or Zlavoj Žižek, 2001, pp. 170ff for more on this matter. For those who are not persuaded by their arguments on the liberal (over)use of performatives (as defined by J.L. Austin), a field trip to the main university library in Malmö (*Orkanen*, which also holds the teacher training)

might help. One of the inscriptions on its postmodern façade consists of the word *frihet* (freedom), repeatedly duplicated in long lines and in several languages, supposedly promoting a feeling in those who enter that the repetition of the inscriptions generates some mystical spell, guaranteeing that this is indeed a 'house of freedom', where the words automatically constitute anything and anyone – no matter their (linguistic) differences - in accordance to this all-embracing freedom. Even though it is truly nothing but an inscription on a façade.

42 SOU, 2001, p. 10.
43 An interesting twist on this issue is found in the debate concerning The Living History Forum (*Forum för Levande Historia*), where research on genocide is directed by the government through a special authority outside the circuit of other kinds of research. Recently, this authority received a vast amount of funding to produce research on communist genocides, especially directed towards public information in high schools and libraries. Critical academics were met with the argument that if you are publicly against state-sponsored research on Communist genocide, you should have been equally publicly critical of the same research on Nazi genocides that was a topic more than a decade ago (not even taking in account the low age of some of the critics). They are hence accused of 'being too late' and their critique could be dismissed as being nothing but a pro-communist agenda *because* of its focus on a present issue. The fact that there *was* and still exists an academic criticism towards the state sponsored Holocaust project as well, could (and was) used as an answer to this. That should, however, not be relevant. Rather it is by asking 'why did you not say anything publicly *then?*' that is of interest since it derives from a use of double time (and ditto standard) that manages to render critique of a neoliberal state project towards communist genocides even *more* impossible to criticise than a (ditto liberal) social democratic state project towards the Nazi genocides (if you criticised the present project, you are by definition using *both* the former critique of the research on the Nazi genocides, *and* the research itself, in an immoral way to *defend* the communist genocide...). Ironically, this mind- (and time-) boggling moralism renders possible a very *timely* opportunity on behalf of liberal historians and public columnists to bash the present intellectual critique as nothing but desperate communist propaganda from the past. Not surprisingly then, the project was carried out according to plan, and now every high-school student in Sweden is taught that any ideology left of the Social democrats is based on the promotion of mass genocide. (see, e.g. Häfte från Forum för Levande historia: *Brott mot mänskligheten under kommunismens regimer*, 2008. www.levandehistoria.se; www.omkommunismen.se).
44 Wendy Brown, 2005.
45 Wendy Brown, 2005, p. 9.
46 Wendy Brown, 2005, p. 11.
47 Wendy Brown, 2005, pp. 4f.
48 Benjamin in Wendy Brown, 2005, p. 12, my italics.
49 Wendy Brown, 2005, p. 12.
50 Wendy Brown, 2001, p. 14.

References

Alm, Erika 2006: *'Ett emballage för inälvor och emotioner' – föreställningar om kroppen i statliga utredningar från 1960- och 1970-talen*, Göteborg.
Andersson, Simon & Anders Mellbourn & Ingemar Skogö 1983: *Myndigheten i samhället: Problem och utvecklingslinjer i Statsförvaltningen*, Stockholm.
Badiou, Alain 1988: *L'Être et l'événement*, Seuil.
Barker, Jason 2002: *Alain Badiou – a critical introduction*, London.
Barthes, Roland 1981: 'The discourse of history', *Comparative criticism*, no. 3.
Brown, Wendy 2001: *Politics out of history*, Princeton.
Brown, Wendy 2005: *Edgework – critical essays on knowledge and politics*, Princeton.
Brown, Wendy 2006: *Regulating aversion – tolerance in the age of identity and empire*, Princeton.
Brown, Wendy 2006b: 'American Nightmare – Neoliberalism, Neoconservatism, and De-democratization', *Political Theory*, no. 6, vol. 34.
Butler, Judith (2005): 'On Never Having Learned How to Live', *Differences: A Journal of Feminist Cultural Studies*, no. 3, vol. 16, pp. 690-714.
Clark, Ronald 1971: *Einstein – the Life and Times*, New York.
Derrida, Jacques (1992): *The Gift of Death*, Chicago 1996.
Derrida, Jacques (1993): 'Marx spöken – skuldstaten, sorgearbetet och Den nya internationalen', *Daidalos* 2001.
Edenheim, Sara 2005: *Begärets lagar – moderna statliga utredningar och heteronormativitetens genealogi*, Stockholm.
Edenheim, Sara 2007: 'Döden och historikern: hauntologiska parafraseringar av Marx riktade mot liberalismens begär till evigheten', *Forum för teoretiska interventioner*, no. 2/3.
Edenheim, Sara 2007a: 'History Out of History – A Critique of Common Concepts Within (and Outside) the Field of History', *Forum för teoretiska interventioner*, no. 1.
Edenheim, Sara 2009: 'Den kulturella förevändningen – om historieämnet, poststrukturalismen och konflikten som inte får finnas', *Scandia*, 75:1.
Ermath, Elizabeth Deeds 1992: *Sequel to History – Postmodernism and the Crisis of Representational Time*, Princeton.
Folkhälsoinstitutet (FHI) 2002: *Föreställningar/Vanföreställningar – allmänhetens attityder till homosexualitet*, Statens folkhälsoinstitut (also published as *Svenska befolkningens attityd till homosexuella och homosexualitet*, 2000).
Hache, Émilie 2007: 'La responsabilité, une technique de gouvernementalité néolibérale?', *Raison politique – études de pensée politique*, no. 28.
Hardt, Michael and Antonio Nigri 2000: *Empire*, Harvard University Press.
Innala, Sune 1995: 'Structure and development of homophobia', Gothenburg *psychological reports* 25:2.
Kitzinger, Celia 1987: *The Social Construction of Lesbianism*, Sage.
Landén, Mikael 1999: *Transsexualism : epidemiology, phenomenology, regret after surgery, aetiology, and public attitudes*, Göteborg.
Lukes, Steven 1974: *Power – A Radical View*, London.
Lundstedt, Vilhelm 1932: Om upphävandet av 18 kap. 10 § strafflagen m.m. med bilaga, motion i andra kammaren.
Mouffe, Chantal 2005: *On the Political*, New York.
Nancy, Jean-Luc (1990): 'Our History', *Diacritics* 20.3.
Proposition 1937:187. Kungliga majestäts proposition till riksdagen med förslag till

lag om ändringar i vissa delar av strafflagen, m.m.

Riley, Denise 1988: *'Am I that Name?': Feminism and the Category of 'Women' in History*, Basingstoke.

Scott, Joan W. 1996: *Only paradoxes to offer – French feminists and the rights of man*, Boston.

Scott, Joan W. 1999: *Gender and the politics of history*, New York.

Scott, Joan W. 2002: 'Feminist reverberations', *Differences* 13:3.

SOU, 1935:68, *Promemoria angående ändringar i strafflagen beträffande straffsatserna för särskilda brott*.

SOU, 1941:32, *Homosexualitetens samhällsfarliga yttringar*.

SOU, 1984:63, *Homosexuella och samhället*.

SOU, 1993:68, *Om partnerskap*, del A och B.

SOU, 1997:175, *Förbud mot diskriminering i arbetslivet på grund av sexuell läggning*, (SEDA).

SOU, 2001:10, *Barn till homosexuella*.

SOU, 2001:39, *Ett effektivt diskrimineringsförbud – om olaga diskriminering och begreppen ras och sexuell läggning*.

Wiegman, Robyn 2000: 'Feminism's Apocalyptic Futures', *New Literary History*, no. 4, vol. 31, pp. 805-825.

Žižek, Slavoj 2001: *Did Somebody Say Totalitarianism? – five interventions in the (mis) use of a notion*, London.

Communication as control: Infra-politics, social diplomacy, and social engineering[1]

Carl Marklund

Introduction

The relationship between 'expertise' and 'welfare' is a close yet complex one: On the one hand, social policy-makers have drawn heavily upon the research of social scientists not only for the formulation of policy goals but also for the practical implementation of these goals.[2] To some extent, social science itself has evolved in response to the need of the modern state to meet the challenges brought about by 'modernity.' On the other hand, the modern state has also been criticised for exactly this dependency upon expertise and science.[3]

Not only totalitarian regimes but also welfare states have been the target of this criticism, as both have indeed relied upon scientific expertise in their attempts at promoting the happiness, the welfare, and the (self-)control of the wider population. Both welfare states and totalitarian regimes have been accused of 'social engineering' in controlling and guiding the behaviour of their populations as well as promoting a kind of 'technocracy' in which the logic of cost-benefit analysis are given primacy in public policy-making, where the means overtake the ends and politics succumbs to science.[4]

This chapter will seek to examine this tension between expertise and welfare by exploring the origins and many different meanings of the vocabulary of social engineering. By looking at this rhetoric, the chapter aims to problematise the relationship between 'politics' and 'science' and between 'technology' and 'ideology' in the modern state. While social engineering is most often used to denote a relationship between politics and science where the latter dominates the former, the present chapter seeks to map alternative usages, primarily focusing upon the rhetorical function of this supposedly scientific language of social knowledge in the USA from the Progressive Era to the early Post-War years.

The USA is often considered a liberal 'welfare regime.' As such, it has often been compared and contrasted with the social democratic welfare regimes of Scandinavia, representing the so-called 'Nordic model.'[5] While it is a question for debate to what extent the USA can be understood in terms of 'welfare state' – despite many early starts – recent research has revealed the important impact of American social science upon the management of business, communication, and governance in the Scandinavian welfare states as well as globally during the Post-War Era. Also, more general American interpretations of the promise and peril of modernity have exercised a considerable influence upon the formulation of the Nordic model, both as contrast and as example. Interestingly, while the vocabulary of social engineering only rarely found any use in the emergent social democratic welfare regimes in interwar Scandinavia (before it became a central accusation of this very same welfare regime in the neo-liberal 1990s, that is) it has been commonplace in the advocacy for a scientific, purposivist, and activist social science from the 1920s to the 1950s in the USA.[6]

The present chapter will therefore take a closer look at this concept as it developed in concert within three different academic disciplines,[7] namely institutionalism, legal realism, and cybernetics.[8] First, however a brief account of the more general relationship between languages of social knowledge and that which they seek to not only diagnose but also remedy, namely 'society', may be relevant.

Expertise and welfare, politics or science?

Modern welfare policies have rested upon the assumption that society somehow is capable of acting upon itself for its own improvement – much like the legendary Baron Münchhausen pulling himself up by his bootstraps – either through more or less representative action 'from above' or through more or less popular mobilisation 'from below'. Thereby, society is made into an intentional acting 'subject' as well as reacting object, 'subjected' to these very same actions.[9] As society emerges as both an object of study and control as well as a subject of action and desire of change, the competition about the character of 'the social' becomes a central aspect of 'the political.'[10] To articulate what society is (or a significant part of it, such as its economy, its culture, or its politics), what it needs, and what may threaten it, thus becomes a fundamentally political enterprise, whether it is presented as such or not.[11] As a result, various academic disciplines, political ideologies, and administrative institutions compete with one another in their descriptions and prescriptions about society.[12]

While this competition about the meaning and direction of society may at times be caustic and even violent, the eventual victory also requires some degree of successful communication. The communication of the successful perspective is often phrased in terms of the 'public interest' of the society which is under debate. In the era of mass politics, different actors may attempt to make themselves the champions of society, identifying themselves as its 'friends' and their opponents as its 'foes'. The friends of society must not only persuasively demonstrate their own commitment to the public interest, such as the 'security' or the 'welfare' of society, but must also show how the self-interest of the foes threaten to tear it apart.[13]

This dual concern with the social as both object and subject has generated a merging or even hybridisation between politics and science as science is increasingly used to provide advice as well as criticism of politics, while politics more and more determines the task and scope of science in a mutual process which Carl-Axel Gemzell has aptly described as the 'scientization of politics' and the 'politicization of science'.[14] This symbiosis between science and politics plays an important role in what Gemzell has seen as a wider attempt at *föreningen av motsatser*, 'the unification of opposites', a basic characteristic of the modern welfare state.[15]

Social engineering as anti-politics

This symbiosis between science and politics has for the most part been considered a rather happy marriage. Importantly, science has contributed to open up and expand the horizon of political expectations, for better and for worse. For better, as it has contributed to raising the quality and efficiency in the production of public goods (within public health, educational systems, and legal regulation, as well as public administration), as well as the predictability and possibly also the fairness by which these goods are being redistributed. For worse, as science, if allowed to influence politics *too* much, runs the risk of 'colonising' it, either by determining the outcome of political contests irrespective of public opinion or by simply doing away with political decision-making altogether through massive bureaucratisation and widespread dependency upon expertise.

However, it is not just *any* combination of science and politics but the symbiosis between *some* particular science and some particular politics which is met with suspicion today: On the one hand, citizens, civil society, and media often use science in their criticism of current administration and politics, which is required to become more accountable, more efficient, more just, and more rational, making use of relevant and reliable 'evidence' if available. Here, then, science is in high political demand. If, on the other hand, a political initiative or a proposed reform is considered either unimaginative or lacking in political vision or – quite the contrary – overly ambitious in its aspiration to change society to the better, it is not seldom criticised for attempting to substitute politics with science, and as such an example of social engineering and/or technocracy.[16] Especially this is so if a reform is presented as 'rational' or 'apolitical', based upon 'the one best way' as outlined by expertise rather than as based in popular consent.

This apolitical, or perhaps even 'anti-political', stance is in its turn often connected with the 'society as machine' metaphor which became very widespread in the late nineteenth century and early twentieth century, after having been initially formulated during 18th century Enlightenment. Indeed, this mechanistic metaphor did not only correspond to the widespread awe caused by the expansion of industry and impressive engineering feats of modern Western civilization at the time. It also quite accurately visualised the increased influence of the organised, the rational, the systemic, the technical, and the scientific – in short, the mechanical – in modern society.[17]

Institutionalism and social peace in the Progressive Era

For all the popularity of engineers, machines, and 'hard' physical matter at the turn of the nineteenth century, this mechanicism found itself competing with the 'society as body' metaphor. The bodily metaphor dominated much of the worldview of Western political elites for half a century. Indeed, if the nineteenth century was an era of strong belief in the supremacy of rational coordination and civilized cooperation, it was also the age of imperialism, *laissez-faire* liberalism, and Social Darwinism. These dogmas all emphasised the role of 'natural selection' through uncompromising and merciless competition between species, races, and civilisations, as well as between empires, nations, and individuals. Interestingly, it seems as if it is in the meeting between these opposite characterisations of humans living together – whether society is best understood in terms of competition or in terms of cooperation – that we apparently for the first time begin to see the explicit usage of the concept of social engineering, at least in English.[18]

By the end of the nineteenth century, the political establishment in most Western societies accepted conflict as not only natural and normal but in fact also necessary for the 'progress' of society. Yet, these elites also perceived a need for maintaining the social order, and thus some measure of what would become known as 'social peace'. However, the conflict between labour and capital – especially the scientific diagnosis of society presented under the banner of socialism – brought out the tension within these dogmas of competition: Socialism showed how competition in economy could transform into conflict in the rest of society, into *guerre sociale*, 'social war', as the leader of the French Socialist Party, Jean Jaurès, had warned in an influential speech before the French Chamber in 1906.[19]

This tension between competition (in the interest of progress and liberty) and cooperation (in the interest of peace and discipline) presented a critical dilemma to the theory of liberalism, social biologism, and Social Darwinism. British comparative jurist and historian Henry James Sumner Maine interpreted this dilemma as a tension between cooperation brought about voluntarily through agreement between more or less consenting agents ('the system of contract') and compulsory cooperation created by the exercise of power over more or less voluntary subjects ('the system of status').[20] British philosopher Herbert Spencer found Maine's phrasing congenial, as it convincingly showed that any alternative to cooperation through competition must immediately lead to cooperation through compulsion. It thus served as a powerful argument in favour of liberalism and social biologism against the challenge of socialism.[21]

However, in 1891, American economist Thorstein Veblen contested Maine's and Spencer's position, arguing that status and contract in fact presented no absolute opposition: Firstly, corporations (operating according to the system of contract) were increasingly making use of bureaucracy (operating according to the system of status) in the late nineteenth century, through the increased tendency towards economic concentration into 'trusts' as well as industrial management by 'engineers', thus mixing the two categories which Maine and Spencer viewed as mutually exclusive. Secondly, the system of modern constitutional government, impersonal law, and the 'free institutions' of the English, did not fall under either of these categories, but presented a mixture as well, Veblen argued. Since both industry and society – as systems of social organization – could be seen as buildings, made by humans over time out of cultural 'materials', a 'constructive social engineering' could bridge the uncompromising dilemma posed by Maine and Spencer and pave an alternative route between either cut-throat capitalism and *laissez-faire* liberalism on the one hand or socialist bureaucracy on the other. Veblen held out the promise that – without specifying how – it should be possible to construct social organisation without falling into either the control of status or the competition of contract.[22]

There was another important message in Veblen's answer to Maine's and Spencer's dilemma. In his emphasis of the role of human intention and ingenuity in constructing institutions for the organisation of social life, Veblen made a seminal contribution to the emerging Progressivism which questioned the conformism, individualism, traditionalism, and religiosity of American culture and politics as being outmoded and out of pace with modern America. Most importantly, Veblen contributed to institutionalism in bourgeoning American social science, especially in economics and sociology. His institutionalism contrasted with both *laissez-faire* liberal and Social Darwinist ideas (both supporting themselves upon 'scientific' dogmas first established within biology and economics, respectively) that society should best be left alone so that the 'natural' competition may have its way, harmonious 'balance' ensue, and society evolve by itself, with as little 'artificial' human intervention as possible.[23] Often espousing liberal beliefs, these institutionalists doubted that the aims of liberalism, a well-balanced society characterised by liberty of self-determination, could be brought about solely by liberal means.[24]

Mostly based in Chicago, from where they could have a first-hand experience of the promise and peril of life in the proverbially modern metropolis, these institutionalists argued that society in fact was the result of constant and continuous redesigning and reconstruction of social affairs. Consequently, social science should assist in these processes, through what one of their leading names, sociologist Albion W. Small, called 'social telesis'.[25]

Especially, at a time acutely aware of how easily the 'economic machinery' of capitalism could self-combust (or possibly set ablaze by various radicals), these American institutionalist social scientists prized social peace greatly.[26] [27] In 1900, Small for example argued that the know-how on how the 'distance [...] between the elements that make up society [...] may be bridged, how channels of intercommunication may be opened and kept open' should be the concern of what he called 'social technology'.[28]

To cooperate was thus apparently something which could be learnt as well as taught. As such, it could also be approached as a technique. The problem was that cooperation demands some kind of community in order to carry some hope of success (for example, one must hold largely similar views about what one is cooperating for, or what one is cooperating in order to avoid). Community was, however, exactly what American public intellectuals found wanting in modern USA: It was widely assumed that modern society's need for such intercommunication had increased, at the same time as its capacity for such intercommunication had dramatically decreased, due to the dissolution of a traditional sense of community, a loss which was most evident in the rapid secularisation of American society. A considerable number of institutionalist sociologists and economists joined the so-called Social Gospel movement, which sought to combine religious ends with scientific means, arguing that the modern clergy will have to integrate knowledge of modern social science into their work and learn how to engage in what institutionalist economist Henry Carter Adams, Professor of Political Economy at University of Michigan, in 1902 explicitly called 'social engineering', in order for religion to become of relevance to contemporary and modern Americans.[29]

Some of the earliest usages of social engineering rhetoric – and related concepts of social technology – thus seem to have been very closely associated with an interest in bypassing various liberal and social biological dogmas of conflict, emphasising the need for conscious and calculated cooperation among humans in constructing the institutional framework for ensuring social peace at a time of great upheavals, growing radicalisation, and more frequent social protest.[30]

Legal realism and social reconstruction in the Inter-war Era

Despite the apparent desirable aspects of such a social peace, many American social scientists concluded together with sociologist Edward A. Ross that such a peace would be improbable on purely moral grounds. Especially given the 'folkways' of the American people, stressing the importance of individualism and praising the 'self-made man', it would be unrealistic to strive directly towards social peace. Yet, every society had more or less appropriate forms of 'social control' for that society to continue to exist, Ross argued.[31] If one could identify the sources of this social control in a certain society, it would also be possible to establish some measure of social peace upon this basis.[32] Given the increasing specialisation in labour and the resulting interdependence between different groups in modern society, social science would possibly be able to show exactly how much a certain group could win and how much it could risk losing if adopting a policy of confrontation in an upcoming conflict. It would thereby be possible to forestall unnecessary, counter-productive, or outright dangerous social conflict to a greater extent than before. Through increased social organisation of corporations, interest groups, and social movements it would also be possible to see which social values were on the rise and which were becoming less prevalent. In order for cooperation instead of competition to take place it would be necessary to rebuild community. Community, however, presupposed some form of social control and social control must be upheld by law, Ross found.[33]

American law at the time, however, was firmly in the grip of *laissez-faire* liberal and Social Darwinist dogma. Yet, there was also a powerful criticism rising against these deterministic beliefs. Already in 1916, Harvard law professor Roscoe Pound turned against what he saw as nineteenth century liberal or 'necessitarian' determinism, which had held 'that the most that legal science could do for us was to teach us to observe nature's machine in operation, and to warn us to keep our itching fingers out of the cogs and to avoid becoming caught in the belts and shafting.' By contrast, Pound called 'for voluntaristic theories of lawmaking on the part of jurists and judges.'[34] Law should not be understood as a neutral machine producing just and predictable results as prescribed by natural law jurisprudence and cherished by liberals. Instead, Pound suggested, law should be studied as 'action' (much in line with what American pragmatists proposed) and as a process determined by the competition between various interests, the outcome of which could hardly be said to be neutral by definition.[35]

Rather than pretending to provide objective justice, uphold 'formal rights' and to defend liberties, law should aspire to be 'realistic' in protecting those private interests and 'real rights' which could be legally entitled from the perspective of 'public interest' against those private interests which could not.[36] Legal exegesis should similarly aspire to be functionalistic, studying the consequences of law as action. Naturally, Pound's view of law had considerable consequences for his view of the source of the authority of the law, namely the state:

> 'Let us for the moment think of the state, not legally as a relation created by a social compact, nor metaphysically as the personified general will, nor biologically as a huge super-organism, but functionally as the chiefest [sic!] of human agencies by which human society achieves its tasks of social engineering—its tasks of conserving the goods of existence and the values of civilization, of eliminating waste and friction in human enjoyment of them, and in adjusting conflicting human claims so as to bring about the widest possible satisfaction with the least friction and the least waste. The state is by no means the sole of these agencies. Religious organizations, fraternal organizations, professional and vocational organizations, social and benevolent organizations and even business organizations do a large part. The state is only the chiefest [sic!] and most enduring and most efficacious of these agencies of social engineering.'[37]

By connecting law to the developing disciplines of psychology and sociology, Pound pioneered what he himself had in 1908 called a 'sociological jurisprudence' as an alternative to what he called the 'mechanical jurisprudence' of the past.[38] Pound's advocacy for a stronger link between state and law and a more activist interpretation of law would have immense influence upon generations of American lawyers, who would consider him, alongside with Justice Oliver Wendell Holmes and Justice Benjamin Cardozo, as the main inspiration for American Legal Realism.[39]

The advent of the Great Depression in 1929 intensified the demands for 'social reconstruction' which had been heard since the beginning of the Progressive Era.[40] Indeed, from 1932 and onwards, President Franklin D. Roosevelt openly sought support in the emerging social sciences not only for the legitimacy of his ambitious New Deal policies, but also for their implementation.[41]

While the New Deal first relied upon rather explicit 'planning'[42] ideals as developed since the 1890s in the nexus between welfare capitalists and scientific managers on the one hand, and institutionalist economists and sociologists on the other (the so-called Brain Trust representing both), the second phase of the New Deal after 1935 represented rather a victory of the lawyers over the social scientists with regard to political influence. To New Deal lawyers, the United States Constitution provided the support for a sociological jurisprudence and a more active role for government, as indeed outlined by Pound, but it prohibited any kind of federal programme for the social and economic planning of the entire Union. Lawyers, in effect, not social scientists, would be the ultimate social engineers in the ongoing social reconstruction of American society as partly represented by the New Deal.

Subsequently, a rather different interpretation of social engineering entered the language of everyday political debate in the USA, yet retaining the original emphasis on the role of government and academia in working towards the reconciliation of opposed social interests and in empowering cooperation for the conscious reconstruction of American society. While reconciliation of opposed social interests remained the focal point of American discussions on planning and social engineering until the outbreak of World War II, the Great Depression also resulted in a widespread disbelief in the capacity of democracy alone to control either a complex capitalist economy in crisis or a rapidly changing modern society. The urgency of the economic crisis did indeed contribute considerably to make the symbiosis of politics and science more feasible, yet it was only the political and military crisis of World War II which finally ensured the entry of science into politics and politics into science in the USA,[43] as well as establishing planning as an acceptable means as well as goal of American politics.[44]

Cybernetics and social truce in the Post-war Era

The question arose: Could the sense of community necessary for social control and social planning somehow be actively created and, if so, how and by whom? New professions and new technologies, such as social psychology, human relations, and propaganda (using new media such as film and radio) suggested that under conditions of rapid social change human behaviour as well as 'public opinion' could indeed be 'adjusted'. However, they might just as well become 'maladjusted', worried social scientists noted. Either way, those 'who understand the mental processes and social patterns of the masses […] pull the wires which control the public mind,' Public Relations guru Edward Bernays concluded in 1928. Indeed, Bernays continued,

> 'The conscious and intelligent manipulation of the organized habits and opinions of the masses is an important element in democratic society. Those who

manipulate this unseen mechanism of society constitute an invisible government which is the true ruling power of our country. [...] This is a logical result of the way in which our democratic society is organized. Vast numbers of human beings must cooperate in this manner if they are to live together as a smoothly functioning society.'[45]

While Bernays saw the new professions and technologies of guiding human behaviour as an indispensable part of any functioning democratic polity in the era of mass communication, sociologist E. W. Burgess feared that these new instruments could just as well be used by totalitarians, as indeed could be witnessed in Germany and Italy. Science, noted sociologist William F. Ogburn, could be seen as a knife, equally good in the hands of a surgeon as it would be bad in the hands of a criminal, and the same went for scientific planning.[46]

Although World War II had shown the necessity as well as power of scientific planning it also prompted a discussion on whether planning – as a mode of governance – was desirable or even feasible under any other conditions than extreme duress. Austrian economist Friedrich von Hayek famously argued against planning, opening that perfect planning requires not only omnipotence on the part of the planner, which is undesirable, but also omniscience, which is impossible. The resulting mismatch between action and knowledge would force society on 'The Road to Serfdom', Hayek concluded.[47]

About the same time, fellow Austrian philosopher Karl Popper suggested that Hayek's characterisation of planning concerned a specific form of planning rather than all types of planning, pleading for a distinction between what he called 'Utopian social engineering' *vis-à-vis* 'piecemeal social engineering'.[48] While the former indeed relied upon ideals about the ultimate good of society, as determined by the laws of history (e.g. Marxism), thus using social engineering as an instrument to bring about 'the end of history' once and for all, the latter rather strove to eliminate the most obvious social evils in society, as apparent in the preferences of the citizenry, using social engineering as one of the many tools available to the citizens of an 'Open Society', and as such always subjected to criticism and possible to reverse if proven either faulty or lacking in popular support.[49] In effect, Popper's piecemeal social engineering pleaded for the application of experimental method to social and political affairs, thus allowing for an expansion of the politically possible.[50]

In Popper's and Hayek's discussions, the question was rather whether planning could deliver on its promise of a perfectly ordered world than whether it could assist in bridging critical oppositions within society. Yet, the latter appeared as one of the main points in the advocacy for 'scientific social engineering' of Swedish economist Gunnar Myrdal as he in 1944 concluded his work on the social situation of African Americans. Myrdal predicted not only wide-scale racial conflict unless deliberate measures were taken to improve the situation of African Americans but also that the USA would suffer moral collapse if fighting against racism abroad, yet tolerating it at home.[51] The structure of racism in American society could only be broken by a coalition of social science and political forces. Indeed, Myrdal argued that 'social science is essentially a 'political' science' as it seeks to be relevant and useful in dealing with matters of social consequence.

Unlike the straw men of planning critics – e.g., Hayek's omniscient planner and Popper's omnipotent Utopian – Myrdal's 'scientific social engineering' did not require that 'all the facts are in' (as urged by positivists), since they never will be unless history comes to an end and society ceases to function. Instead, the social scientist shall analyse the values actually held by people in society as 'social facts' and then seek to identify discrepancies between these values and the actual situation in society as well as the technical ways of how to bridge this gap, much as Popper had proposed. Rather than either hoping that society itself would through conflict arrive at some measure of harmony – a liberal belief derided by Myrdal as mere superstition – or striving to establish such an balance through the detailed regulation of every aspect of society – which he considered as impossible as undesirable – Myrdal proposed that social engineering could be used surgically and strategically to break vicious circles of deprivation and turn them into what he called 'virtuous circles' or 'accumulation'.[52]

The end of World War II provided a unique opportunity for reformist social science and social expertise as the practical experience of war-time planning and control of human behaviour on a massive scale, the analysis of the causes of 'the Authoritarian Personality', and the fear of a new Cold War conspired with the concrete needs of global 'post-war reconstruction' in promoting the creation of the United Nations. Already during the war a series of *Science, Philosophy and Religion* symposia were arranged in New York to discuss the prospects of scientific 'bridge-building', 'cross-fertilisation' and 'group understanding' in order to propose ways in which to avoid future global conflict between cultures, ideologies, races, and religions.[53]

By the end of the war, the concept of planning had become almost synonymous with social engineering. However, while planning had become accepted as normal, '[a] color of derision and disdain has been cast over the words 'social engineering' and 'manipulation',' American journalist Lyman Bryson noted in 1947, when commenting on these symposia: '[S]ometimes [this is done] by those who deliberately want to obfuscate the issue, sometimes by those who innocently think that all forms of eloquence are something else than manipulation,' Bryson found, continuing that

> '...the attempt to change the behavior of other men, or of men in general, is a normal human activity in which anyone who breathes and speaks takes part. It is to be judged not by its motives but by its means and ends. The means must be effective to good ends; in this case 'good' is what leads to freedom.'[54]

In effect, the journalist and the expert communicator argued – much in line with Bernays – that at the heart of democracy rests demagoguery. As half of Europe and Asia lay in ruins as the result of totalitarian and imperialist aggression and as the Cold War had just begun, democracy and 'freedom' did not need much motivation among Westerners. Instead, it was science which needed to be defended, after its nefarious potential had been revealed in the war. Bryson summarised that

> '...science as a method, or predominant social habit, is on trial before mankind. This is true far more than most Westerners, satisfied in their cultural parochialism, can realize. [...] Since they have never shared the habit, the rest of mankind, in fact the most of mankind, may be simply not convinced.'[55]

If all culture was engineering to some extent, partly artificial and partly subject to willed change, it also became important to decide exactly which kind of engineering of culture – or 'engineering of consent' in Bernays' memorable phrase – could be considered legitimate inasmuch as it was rational and promoted 'freedom'.[56]

In addition to making freedom the rallying cry of the American war effort, the war also had a profound impact upon the politics-science nexus. Especially, new theories of control and regulation of 'systems', in particular the control of chaotic situations on the battlefield and the complex meeting between weapons systems and human behaviour emerged, most notably 'cybernetics'.[57] In his pioneering work in this discipline, American mathematician Norbert Wiener suggested that any system – whether a machine, an organism, an organisation, or even a whole society – interacts with its environment through the interpretation of information ('input') from the environment being processed and adjusting its own behaviour accordingly ('output'). [58] In other words, control is simply the sending of messages that modify the behaviour of the person (or animal) or machine which receives them. In Wiener's cybernetics, then, communication effectively equals control.[59]

All system behaviour is determined by the flow of negative or positive feedback between these two poles. If this flow is hampered, the capacity to purposively bridge the gap between desired ends and constantly changing means breaks down and the system ceases to function. In this sense there is no difference between humans and machines (especially means of communication) Wiener argued. However, in its emphasis upon dynamism, openness, and flexibility (which allows for autonomous self-regulation and autopoietic self-creation), Wiener's cybernetic mechanicism differed from the more deterministic and unilinear mechanicism of the past. Certainly, a balance between input and output is necessary for the system to be capable to manage disturbances and to maintain itself, but the system cannot in most cases eliminate such disturbances. Therefore, it is of the utmost importance that the continuous circulation of communication may flow freely for the survival of the system.[60]

This cybernetic view was soon exported as an analogy by which to explain society, the complex system of humans living together, partly by Wiener himself.[61] Society could be seen as a systems of communications, as a vast network of messaging. However, there could be no perfect balance or 'homeostasis' in this gigantic network. Consequently, there could be no social peace either. Instead, the primary objective of cybernetics would be to combat tendencies towards the 'anti-homeostatic' concentration of communication and conformity in information, and to promote pluralism and exchange in the interest of an improved yet not perfect balance, a kind of social truce based on a minimum of consensus: not peace, but not quite war either.[62]

Conclusion

The vocabulary of social engineering emerged in a confrontation between two different ways in viewing the 'genesis' as well as 'telesis' of society:[63] On the one hand, there was the idea that society does work automatically, quite independently of human purpose, and that one has to discover the laws which govern the operation of this gigantic machine and abide by them to make it work the best – e.g., mechanicism, determinism, technocracy, and anti-politics. On the other hand, there was the idea that society does not work very well, unless humans act purposively to make it do so, and that one has to invent the laws by which to govern the operation of this gigantic construction to make it work better – e.g., constructivism, voluntarism, social engineering, and what may be called 'infra-politics' (see below).

The former view has been more closely associated with various biological social metaphors, while the latter has been more often expressed through various technological social metaphors. However, this metaphorical distinction should not be overdrawn, especially not since metaphors exactly allow opposites to unite in everyday rhetoric: The main difference between them lies instead rather in the type of 'quality' society has to live up to in order to qualify as a 'good' society according to these views: Are humans living together due to the relative peace, prosperity, and cooperation of their togetherness, or are humans living together despite the conflict, disparity, and competition in their togetherness?

The ambitions of those who used the social engineering vocabulary went from a slightly idealistic hope in establishing social peace through cooperation between free institutions in the 1890s, *via* a belief in the need to create community to maintain social control for the sake of social reconstruction in the wake of crisis in the 1920s, to the more moderate assumption that communication is the *sine qua non* for the governance or even survival of any system. As such, cybernetics aimed less at homeostasis and social peace than at relative consensus through social truce in the 1950s.

Social engineering as infra-politics

In these accounts, society does not appear as a smoothly operating machine, but rather as a rickety construct, built over time by competing contractors. As such it is elastic and durable, yet unstable, and could do with a scaffolding or social infrastructure to protect the entire structure from breaking up due to the innumerable and inevitable cracks within the social matter. This infrastructure requires a political culture of communication in the interest of national and social integration as well as the controlled communication between opposite interests (which one neither can nor should do away with) in order to avoid potentially disruptive conflict. In other words, what I would like to call a kind of 'social diplomacy' to combine otherwise opposite social ends, such as individual and collective, tradition and modern, private and public, labour and capital.[64]

In very much the same manner as international diplomacy seeks to do, this social diplomacy did not only attempt to manage internal fears and risks, but also to find mutually acceptable solutions to common challenges through the idea of a public interest about which there can be a public opinion.[65] As such, social engineering rhetoric approximates more a special kind of security policy, in rhetorically transforming uninsurable 'uncertainty' into insurable 'risks'.[66] Rather than an anti-political attempt at abolishing politics, social engineering rhetoric was being used to promote the need for a kind of infra-politics by which to ensure productive communication between different social interests.

In conclusion, this study suggests that social engineering did not only serve to expand the imaginary reach of human agency in society and to reduce political conflicts into less contested technical issues. It entered the language of social knowledge to alleviate the tension between these two conflicting perspectives on humans living together, between the 'over-competitive' perspective on the one hand and the 'over-cooperative' perspective on the other.

Communication and control, democracy or efficiency?

This conflict is still very much with us, as is the general preference for a relative pacificity in social relations. High levels of social integration and relative political pacificity are still regarded as probable causes for 'successful modernisation', in Scandinavia as well as in the USA, and continue to be held out as a prime benefit of a sound 'civil society'.[67] 'Postmodern' welfare states, too, must also seek to fulfil the demands of both efficient meritocracy and just democracy at the same time, just as once modern welfare states attempted to do, at least if it is to live up to its promise of accommodating the consensus within the majority with the dissension of the minority. In other words, the democratic welfare state must allow for both 'input legitimacy' through participation and representativity and 'output legitimacy' through anticipation and responsibility.[68]

Given this similarity between the welfare state of the past and the postmodern welfare state, it becomes interesting to take a final look at the rhetorical manoeuvres of contemporary social expertise. While the explicit vocabulary of social engineering is anathema in contemporary languages of administration and politics, several 'new' ethical concepts do show some intriguing functional, if not formal, affinities with the rhetoric of social engineering and its derivates. For example, expert notions of 'human capital' and 'social investment' play a significant role for social scientists, public intellectuals, think tanks, political parties, and social movements attempting to pave a 'Third Way' between neo-liberal non-interventionist 'workfare' policies and social democratic activist welfare policies.[69]

In a sense, these concepts also come with a desire to 'educate' the citizenry about the realities of postmodern society, placing a heavy emphasis upon our individual ability to use new technologies, new communication, and new intelligence as means of self-help in living up to the responsibility of continuously developing, educating, and re-creating the Self.[70]

Also, new technologies of communication are sometimes taken to herald a more inclusive form of democracy, allowing for improved feedback through the blogosphere, through e-democracy, and through media more generally. In assessing the legitimacy of these complementary processes of input and output, contemporary media fulfil an important function by providing negative as well as positive feedback on the integration of politics, science, and society. Indeed, media has taken over much of the communication on and competition about the (de-)construction of society and its needs once nearly monopolised by academic disciplines and scientific professions. The latter primarily gain access to public debate through the filter of the former. Admittedly, then, certain media may serve as a kind of infra-politics in creating and maintaining consensus about the public interest. At the same time, however, media also operates according to a more explicitly conflict-driven logic than did the social engineering of the past.

Obviously, then, dramatisation of conflict fulfils an important role in contemporary democracy, as does reconciliation of conflict.[71] Contemporary social expertise, whether found in media or in academia, provides us with both. When thinking about the role of expertise in the shaping of the past welfare state as well as the present, it might be valuable to keep in mind Wiener's insight: All communication aspires to some measure of control to be meaningful, while all control requires some measure of communication to be successful.

Notes

1 The author wishes to gratefully acknowledge comments and criticism on earlier versions as well as excerpts of this text made by the participants of the conference 'Välfärdsstatens experter', Kivik, 12-13 June 2008 and the workshop 'The Limits of Nordic Universalism', Korpilampi, 25 January 2009, especially by Svanaug Fjær, Pauli Kettunen, Chris Lloyd, Klaus Petersen, and Johanna Rainio-Niemi as well as an anonymous referee.
2 While the concept of expertise may include any kind of knowledge, academic as well as non-scientific, of society and human relations which makes a claim of being particularly reliable, whether presented by politicians, intellectuals, artists, journalists, and, since the rise of consumerism, advertisers, public relations experts, consultants, and 'life-coaches'. Yet, much of the expertise on society will most often aspire to the legitimacy of science, especially if the information provided has to be convincingly 'sold' to a corporation, an institution, an organization, a group, or the electorate in general.
3 These challenges include for example capitalism, democratisation, industrialisation, and urbanisation as well as migration. See Peter Wagner, Björn Wittrock & Richard Whitley, 1991; Johan Heilbron, Lars Magnusson & Björn Wittrock, 1998; Peter Wagner, Carol Hirschon Weiss & Björn Wittrock, 1991.
4 The accusation of social engineering has sometimes been the medium of an even more grave accusation, namely that of seeing the welfare state as a relative of the totalitarian state. For a critical discussion of this tendency in the debate on Swedish social engineering, sterilisations, and welfare policy, see Norbert Götz, 2002.
5 The Nordic countries and Scandinavia will here be used in accordance with international standard, i.e., interchangeably, although strictly speaking only the former includes Finland, while the latter excludes it. For the seminal discussion on welfare regimes, see Gøsta Esping-Andersen, 1990.
6 For activism and purposivism in American social science, see for example Mary O. Furner, 1975; Mark C. Smith, 1994; Martin Bulmer, 1984; Dorothy Ross, 1991.
7 The chapter will thus examine social engineering more in terms of rhetoric than in terms of practice, as expressed in general social diagnosis rather than as found in more specific social reforms. This is not to deny that applied social science has had a very direct and tangible influence upon welfare policies, as is indeed evident in several of the contributions to this volume. Rather, it is to acknowledge that the way in which the relationship between expertise and welfare and between politics and science has been 'spoken' of has had a considerable impact upon the development of the welfare state: Beyond making scientific 'means' available for political 'ends', convincing rhetoric and political

persuasion has been a prerequisite not only for the successful implementation of the welfare state, but also for creating the basic consensus and dissuading critical dissension about the idea of welfare as a 'public interest' and as a viable political goal in itself.

8   This focus will arguably leave aside many relevant themes, such as for example human relations, scientific management, and Taylorism in industry during the progressive era; behaviourism, institutionalism, and symbolic interactionism in social science (primarily economics and psychology) during the inter-war era; as well as sociotechnics, structural functionalism, and systems theory during the post-war era.

9   Welfare has thus not only been closely connected with the discovery or invention of society in itself. It has also become a legitimate goal for society to seek to achieve as well as a measure of its relative 'failure' or 'success'. The notions of welfare, welfare policy, and the welfare state have contributed to this double vision of society as an 'object' which can be dispassionately studied from without as well as a 'subject' which is somehow capable of feeling and expressing its own needs and desires through the formation of public opinion. See Jacques Donzelot, 1984; Pauli Kettunen & Hanna Eskola, 1997; Alain Touraine, 1997.

10 For a discussion of 'the social', see for example Dennis Bryson, 1998.

11 There is of course the risk of using a too wide concept of politics. However, it should be noted that the demarcation between the modern Western understanding of 'the social' and the *ditto* conceptualisation of 'the political' is in fact a political enterprise in itself, and the site of much political debate. Implicitly or explicitly, these contests also negotiate the limits of politics.

12 The late nineteenth century witnessed the rise of academic disciplines and scientific professions which strove to make the administration of corporations, organisations, and institutions more effective, as well as the emergence of scientific paradigms supporting various political ideologies, such as Social Darwinism supporting *laissez-faire* liberalism and historical materialism underpinning communism, for example.

13 This characterization is inspired by the work of the so-called Copenhagen School of International Relations. See for example Barry Buzan, Ole Waever & Jaap de Wilde, 1998; Ole Waever, 2008.

14 In a similar way, the call for evidence-based policy-making (EBP) has recently come under criticism for resulting in what has ironically been termed policy-based evidence-making. For an earlier and parallel line of thought, see Alvin W. Gouldner, 1976. See also Carl-Axel Gemzell, 1993; Anne-Lise Seip, 1989.

15 While any form of democratic politics may have to perform such a unification of opposites in order to survive over time, it has been particularly important for the formulation of durable welfare policies, as these place a very high demand on establishing a relative consensus on the character of welfare.

16 Adam Podgórecki, Jon Alexander & Rob Shields, 1996; James C. Scott, 1998.

17 For accounts that rely heavily upon this connection between mechanicism and social engineering, see Henrik Björck, 1995; Yvonne Hirdman, 1989; John M. Jordan, 1994; Jessica Wang, 1999.

18 The concept may of course very well have been used earlier in other forms and constructions which has not been possible to study in full detail as of yet, such as e.g., social technology, social mechanics, social art, social physics, *etcetera*.

19 'The economic civil war, the social war, will continue—sometimes visibly, some-

times covertly, sometimes violently, sometimes sullenly, but always with the same sufferings, the same exasperation, the same iniquity, so long as the world of production be disputed by two antagonistic forces. There is no means—hear what I say, gentlemen—to reconcile definitely these two forces. You may palliate the strife, you may soften the shocks, but you cannot remove the abiding, fundamental, antagonism resulting from the privilege of property itself. There is but one means to abolish this antagonism, and that is to reabsorb capital in labor—to make but one possessive and controlling force, the creative force of labor.' Incidentally, an extreme leftist journal appeared the same year under the editorship of prominent French pacifist and socialist (and later French fascist) Gustave Hervé, entitled *La Guerre sociale* (1906-1916), as if to prove to Jaurès' audience that his analysis was correct. Jaurès' speech is available in English translation in William Jennings Bryan, 1906.

20 On Maine, see George Feaver, 1969.
21 Herbert Spencer, 1891.
22 Thorstein B. Veblen, 1891.
23 The literature on progressivism is vast, emphasising different aspects of this as heterogeneous as influential trend in public opinion in the USA. The uniting feature of Progressivism that most students of this phenomenon agree upon was the insistence that 'progress' was not the automatic result of just about any human activity, but the result of conscious effort and social cooperation, again in stark contrast to the dogmas of competition. See for example Daniel T. Rodgers, 1982.
24 A typical example may be found in John R. Common, 1908.
25 In 1892, Veblen joined the first Department of Sociology at the University of Chicago under the direction of Albion W. Small. In promoting his new department, Small claimed that social science had a 'telic value' for the increase of 'human happiness': Not only should it explain 'social genesis', i.e. the roots of human interaction, but it should also seek to promote social telesis, i.e. the goals of human interaction.
26 Apparently, the concept of 'social peace' had been used in 1886 by American historian Herbert L. Osgood, but would become more widely used in the USA after German Protestant liberal politician Gerhard von Schulze-Gaevernitz's 1890 book on English nineteenth century social policy with that title, which was frequently reviewed in Great Britain as well as the USA from 1891 and onwards. See Gerhard von Schulze-Gaevernitz, 1890.
27 While some voices within the American business community indeed agreed to this call for social peace and accepted the legitimacy of worker organisation in line with German antecedents, many did not. However, there was a strong interest within American business to increase productivity and at the same time lower the risk for worker unrest. For discussions on usage of the concept of social engineering in doing so, see Benny Carlson, 2003; David Östlund, 2003.
28 The concept of social technology was later taken up by another prominent institutionalist and social gospeller, C. R. Henderson. See C. R. Henderson, 1901; 1912; Albion W. Small, 1900.
29 Adams' paper, entitled 'Higher Education and the People', was presented at a joint meeting between the Michigan Political Science Association and the Michigan Farmers' Institute, see 'Notes and Abstracts', *The American Journal of Sociology*, Sep. 1902.

30 It is perhaps no coincidence that we see the rise of this language at the very same time as the Panic of 1893 showed that frequent economic turmoil would have to be expected in the speculative capitalist economy and set off some of the most massive social protests the USA had yet witnessed, most notably, Coxey's Army and the Pullman Strike, both in 1894.

31 In *Social Control through Law* (New Haven, 1942), Roscoe Pound (see below) would link his legal realism (see below) to the concept of social control as originally outlined by Ross and later developed further within American sociology. See Morris Janowitz, 1978, p. 42.

32 See especially Ross' series on the concept of 'social control', where he also expounds upon his understanding of the origins of and requirements for 'social peace' in Edward A. Ross, 1896a, 1896a, 1898.

33 Ross would formulate this view later in life, when his opinion had already become an established truth among American sociologists. See Edward A. Ross, 1936.

34 It is significant that Pound was speaking at the 25th Anniversary of the University of Chicago – the centre of not only institutionalist social science but also of the Social Gospel movement. See Roscoe Pound, 1917.

35 Roscoe Pound, 1959 [1922]; Jessica Wang, 2005.

36 Niklas Luhmann has in passing showed how Pound's definition of legitimate interests itself will by necessity be based upon one conception of liberty and rights or the other. Niklas Luhmann, 2004.

37 Roscoe Pound, 1921, pp. 103-118.

38 Roscoe Pound, 'Mechanical Jurisprudence', *Columbia Law Review*, (1908), vol. 8, pp. 605-623.

39 The international influence of American Legal Realism falls outside the scope of this brief chapter, but it is interesting to note the many common traits between this school and Scandinavian Legal Realism, which had a certain influence upon the formulation of at least Swedish and Danish art of social engineering, although founded in 'value nihilism' rather than pragmatism. See Ola Sigurdson, 2000.

40 The perception that there was a need for manipulation of the social – a need for 'social reconstruction' – came partly from the Progressive movement which since the 1890s had argued that American civilisation – a 'frontier civilisation', as it were – would need to 'adjust' to the new conditions when there was not much more free land which could work as a vent for social conflict coming to a boil in the great cities on the Eastern Seaboard. The failure of traditional political and scientific elites and their theories in predicting and controlling the crisis also allowed for new and sometimes more radical scientists to step forward. Institutionalism, for example, now became the mainstream in American economics.

41 Roosevelt relied upon sociologist William F. Ogburn's famous notion that there was a 'cultural lag' between technological development and social development, creating not only a mismatch between the two, but also evident in the lack of social control over technical development and its consequences. In 1936, the President called upon engineers to not leave these issues 'wholly in the hands of bankers, Government officials or demagogues,' but pay more attention to the social consequences of engineering, or 'human engineering,' as Roosevelt called it. See Franklin D. Roosevelt, 1938.

42 The concept of 'planning' had long been treated carefully, at least in the USA since the so-called Red Scare of 1919, as it was easily associated with the socialist experiment in the Soviet Union. The initial preference for social engineering over social planning in American debates may very well reflect the possibly more neutral or American sound of 'engineering' over the more socialist and Soviet ring of 'planning'. See Carl Marklund, 2008.
43 For the usages of social science by American government and armed forces during World War II, see, among others, Rebecca M. Lemov, 2000; Bosse Holmqvist, 2004; Jessica Wang, 1999; for the consequences of the war upon American social science, see Stephen P. Turner & Dirk Käsler, 1992.
44 See Otis L. Graham Jr., 1976.
45 See Edward Bernays, 1928, especially Chapter I. Organizing Chaos, and Chapter XI. The Mechanics of Propaganda.
46 Initially, the fascist and Nazi experiments in social planning attracted a great deal of positive attention in the USA, only to become anathema at the outbreak of World War II. See E. W. Burgess, 1935; Wolfgang Schivelbusch, 2006. For the 'science as knife' metaphor, see William F. Ogburn 1949, p. 208.
47 Friedrich A. von Hayek, 1944.
48 Karl Popper, 1974 [1945], 1957 [1944/1945].
49 In effect, Popper's version of piecemeal social engineering is not very different from Charles Lindblom's notion of 'muddling through'. See Charles E. Lindblom, 1959, pp. 79-88.
50 For a discussion on the notion of expanding the limits of politics, see Charles S. Maier, 1987.
51 Despite the Enlightenment values formally expressed in the United States Constitution and informally embraced by Americans in their everyday life as 'the American Creed'.
52 Gunnar Myrdal, 1996 [1944], vols. 1 & 2, especially vol. 1, Appendix 2, pp. 1044-1045.
53 For the proceedings of these symposia, see Lyman Bryson, Louis Finkelstein & R.M. MacIver, 1947.
54 Lyman Bryson, 1947, p. xi. See also Lyman Bryson, 1948.
55 Lyman Bryson, 1947, p. 80.
56 Edward Bernays, 1947, pp. 113-120.
57 From the Greek *kybern't's*, steersman, governor, or pilot, incidentally related to the concepts of 'government' and 'governance'. On the influence of cybernetics on Post-War American governance and social science, see Steve J. Heims, 1991.
58 Norbert Wiener, 1961 [1948], p. 6.
59 Norbert Wiener, 1950. See also Bosse Holmqvist, 2004, pp. 66-68.
60 Norbert Wiener, 1950. See also Bosse Holmqvist, 2004, pp. 73-75.
61 Cybernetic perspectives were soon integrated with the vocabulary of structural functionalism and behaviourism in sociology and psychology, see for example Talcott Parsons, 1951; B. F. Skinner, 1953; Robert K. Merton, 1949.
62 There is a distinct affinity between Wiener's praise of circulation of information and free communication and Popper's insistence upon the Open Society, the enemies of which could be equally well represented in the 1950s by media moguls and McCarthyism in the USA as by censorship and the KGB in the Soviet Union.
63 For these concepts, see note 26 in this chapter.

64 While diplomacy never is neutral but only approximates a language of neutrality, it does fulfil an important function in international relations as it provides the codes by which various security interests and risks can be managed and aligned with one another without having to resort to 'politics by other means' – i.e., war.

65 Naturally, this type of social diplomacy requires that the social and political system is more or less corporatist, with well-organised and representative interest organisations. Incidentally, between the Progressive Era and the Post-War Era, American 'civil society' and organisational life expanded considerably and the First New Deal indeed sought to promote a higher level of public participation through social organisations, notably legalising trade unions for example. As such, it can be subjected to very much the same criticism as corporatism, i.e. of silencing dissent, streamlining opinion, and excluding minorities. See for example Bo Rothstein & Jonas Bergström, 1999.

66 Diplomacy is sometimes viewed as the art of managing fear. See for example Barry Buzan, Ole Waever & Jaap de Wilde, 1998.

67 This integrating, infra-political function, while potentially detrimental to democracy, also appears as a central component of democracy. Pacificity and social peace may perhaps be understood as the *pharmakon* of democracy, as both its poison and its remedy. For the notion of 'successful modernisation', see Håkan Arvidsson, 2001.

68 Fritz W. Scharpf, 1999.

69 There is one important distinction, though: If the logic of social engineering of the past equalled an expansion of the public into the private, the human capital and social investment logic of the largely represent an advance of the private into the public, in many ways reminiscent of the way in which identity politics and resource politics have merged since the 1960s. For the connection between social investment and social engineering, see discussion in Jenny Andersson, 2004.

70 Nikolas Rose, 1989, 1996.

71 See for example Peter Wagner & Nathalie Karagiannis, 2005.

References

Almqvist, Kurt & Kay Glans (eds.) 2001: *Den svenska fremgångssagan?*, Stockholm.

Andersson, Jenny 2004: 'A Productive Social Citizenship? The Metaphor of Productive Social Policies in European Perspective 1850-2000', Bo Stråth & Lars Magnusson (eds.), *A European Social Citizenship? Future Preconditions in Historical Light*, Brussels.

Arvidsson, Håkan 2001: 'Reflektioner kring moderniseringens dilemma', Kurt Almqvist & Kay Glans (eds.), *Den svenska framgångssagan?*, Stockholm.

Bernays, Edward 1947: 'The Engineering of Consent', *The Annals of the American Academy of Political and Social Science*, no. 1, vol. 250, pp. 113-120.

Bernays, Edward 1928: *Propaganda*, New York.

Björck, Henrik 1995: 'Ett perspektiv på social ingenjörskonst', *Teknisk idéhistoria*, Stockholm.

Brauch, Hans Günter et al. (eds.) 2008: *Globalization and Environmental Challenges:*

Reconceptualizing Security in the 21st Century, vol. 3, Berlin & Heidelberg.

Bryan, William Jennings (ed.) 1906: *The World's Famous Orations*, vol. VII., Continental Europe, New York.

Bryson, Dennis 1998: 'Lawrence K. Frank, Knowledge, and the Production of the 'Social'', *Poetics Today*, no. 3, vol. 19, pp. 401-421.

Bryson, Lyman 1947: *Freedom and Science*, New York.

Bryson, Lyman, Louis Finkelstein & R. M. MacIver (eds.) 1947: *Approaches to Group Understanding: Sixth Symposium*. Conference on Science, Philosophy and Religion in Their Relation to the Democratic Way of Life, New York.

Bryson, Lyman (ed.) 1948: *The Communication of Ideas. A Series of Addresses*, New York.

Bulmer, Martin 1984: *The Chicago School of Sociology: Institutionalization, Diversity, and the Rise of Sociological Research*, Chicago.

Burgess, E. W. 1935: 'Social Planning and the Mores', E. W. Burgess & Herbert Blumer (eds.), *Human Problems of Social Planning*, Chicago.

Buzan, Barry, Ole Waever & Jaap de Wilde 1998: *Security: A New Framework for Analysis*, Boulder.

Carlson, Benny 2003: *Amerikansk välfärdskapitalism och social ingenjörskonst*, Stockholm.

Commons, John R. 1908: 'Is Class Conflict in America Growing and Is It Inevitable?', *The American Journal of Sociology*, no. 6, vol. 13, pp. 756-783.

Donzelot, Jacques 1984: *L'invention du social: Essai sur le declin des passions politiques*, Paris.

Esping-Andersen, Gøsta 1990: *The Three Worlds of Welfare Capitalism*, Cambridge.

Feaver, George 1969: *From Status to Contract: A Biography of Sir Henry Maine 1822-1888*, London.

Furner, Mary O. 1975: *Advocacy and Objectivity: A Crisis in the Professionalization of American Social Science 1865-1905*, Lexington.

Gemzell, Carl-Axel 1993: *Om politikens förvetenskapligande och vetenskapens politisering. Kring välfärdsstatens uppkomst i England*, vol. 2: Ställföreträdarna, Copenhagen.

Götz, Norbert 2002: 'Att lägga historien tillrätta. Försöket att göra folkhemmet folkhemskt', *Tvärsnitt*, no. 1.

Gouldner, Alwin W. 1976: *The Dialectic of Ideology and Technology: The Origins, Grammar, and Future of Ideology*, New York & Toronto.

Graham Jr., Otis L. 1976: *Toward a Planned Society: From Roosevelt to Nixon*, New York.

Hayek, Friedrich A. von 1944: *The Road to Serfdom*, London.

Heilbron, Johan, Lars Magnusson & Björn Wittrock (eds.) 1998: *The Rise of the Social Sciences and the Formation of Modernity: Conceptual Change in Context, 1750-1850*, Dordrecht & London.

Heims, Steve J. 1991: *Constructing a Social Science for Post-war America. The Cybernetics Group, 1946-1953*, Cambridge, Mass.

Henderson, C.R. 1912: 'Applied Sociology (Or Social Technology)', *The American Journal of Sociology*, no. 2, vol. 18, (Sep.), pp. 215-221.

Henderson, C.R. 1901: 'The Scope of Social Technology', *The American Journal of Sociology*, no. 4, vol. 6, (Jan.), pp. 465-486.

Hirdman, Yvonne 1989: *Att lägga livet till rätta—studier i svensk folkhemspolitik*, Stockholm.

Holmqvist, Bosse 2004: *Individens tidsålder är förbi. Några nedslag i femtiotalets människosyn*, Stockholm/Stehag.

Janowitz, Morris 1978: *The Last Half-Century. Societal Change and Politics in America*,

Chicago & London.
Jordan, John M. 1994: *Machine-Age Ideology: Social Engineering and American Liberalism, 1911-1939*, Chapel Hill & London.
Kettunen, Pauli & Hanna Eskola (eds.) 1997: *Models, Modernity and the Myrdals*, Helsinki.
Lemov, Rebecca M. 2000: *The Laboratory Imagination: Experiments in Human and Social Engineering* (Unpublished Ph.D.), UC Berkeley.
Lewis, John Brumm (ed.) 1921: Educational Problems in College and University.
Lindblom, Charles E. 1959: 'The Science of 'Muddling Through'', *Public Administration Review*, no. 2, vol. 19, (Spring), pp. 79-88.
Luhmann, Niklas 2004: *Law as a Social System*, Oxford.
Maier, Charles S. 1987: 'Introduction', Charles S. Maier (ed.), *The Changing Boundaries of the Political: Essays on the Evolving Balance Between the State and Society, Public and Private in Europe*, New York.
Maier, Charles S. (ed.) 1987: *The Changing Boundaries of the Political. Essays on the Evolving Balance between the State and Society, Public and Private in Europe*, New York.
Marklund, Carl 2008: *Bridging Politics and Science: The Concept of Social Engineering in Sweden and the USA, Circa 1890-1950* (Unpublished Ph. D.) EUI, Florence.
Merton, Robert K. 1949: *Social Theory and Social Structure*, New York.
Myrdal, Gunnar 1996 [1944]: *An American Dilemma: The Negro Problem and Modern Democracy*, vols. 1 & 2, New Brunswick, N.J.
'Notes and Abstracts', 1902: *The American Journal of Sociology*, no. 2, vol. 8, (Sep.), pp. 281-288.
Ogburn, William F. 1949: 'Science and Society', Robert C. Stauffer (ed.), *Science and Civilization*, Madison.
Östlund, David 2003: *Det sociala kriget och kapitalets ansvar. Social ingenjörskonst mellan affärsintresse och samhällsreform i USA och Sverige 1899-1914*, Stockholm.
Parsons, Talcott 1951: *The Social System*, Glencoe, Ill.
Podgórecki, Adam, Jon Alexander & Rob Shields (eds.) 1996: *Social Engineering*, Ottawa.
Popper, Karl 1974 [1945]: *The Open Society and Its Enemies*, vol. 1, London.
Popper, Karl 1957 [1944/1945]: *The Poverty of Historicism*, London.
Pound, Roscoe 1917: 'Juristic Problems of National Progress', *The American Journal of Sociology*, no. 6, vol. 22, (May), pp. 721-733.
Pound, Roscoe 1908: 'Mechanical Jurisprudence', *Columbia Law Review*, vol. 8, pp. 605-623.
Pound, Roscoe 1921: 'The Place of the University in Training for Citizenship', John Brumm Lewis (ed.), *Educational Problems in College and University*. Addresses delivered at the Educational Conference held at the University of Michigan, October 14-16, 1920, pp. 103-118, Ann Arbor.
Pound, Roscoe 1959 [1922]: *An Introduction to the Philosophy of Law*, New Haven.
Pound, Roscoe 1942: *Social Control through Law*, New Haven.
Rodgers, Daniel T. 1982: 'In Search of Progressivism', *Reviews in American History*, no. 4, vol. 10, The Promise of American History: Progress and Prospects (Dec.), pp. 113-132.
Roosevelt, Franklin D. 1938: 'Are You and I Paying Enough Attention to 'Human Engineering'?'—Address to the Third World Power Conference, Washington, D. C., September 11, 1936, Samuel Irving Rosenman (ed.), *The Public Papers and Ad-*

dresses of Franklin D. Roosevelt, vol. 5, pp. 349-356, New York.
Rose, Nikolas 1989: *Governing the Soul: The Shaping of the Private Self*, London.
Rose, Nikolas 1996: *Inventing Our Selves: Psychology, Power and Personhood*, Cambridge.
Rosenman, Samuel Irving (ed.) 1938: The Public Paters and Adresses of Franklin D. Roosevelt, vol. 5, New York.
Ross, Dorothy 1991: *The Origins of American Social Science*, Cambridge.
Ross, Edward A. 1896: 'Social Control', *The American Journal of Sociology*, no. 5, vol. 1, (Mar.), pp. 513-535.
Ross, Edward A. 1896a: 'Social Control. V. Religion', *The American Journal of Sociology*, no. 3, vol. 2, (Nov.), pp. 433-445.
Ross, Edward A. 1936: 'Some Contributions of Sociology to the Guidance of Society', *American Sociological Review*, no. 1, vol. 1, (Feb.), pp. 29-32.
Ross, Edward A. 1898: 'Social Control. XII. Social Valuations', *The American Journal of Sociology*, no. 5, vol. 3, (Mar.), pp. 649-661.
Rothstein, Bo & Jonas Bergström 1999: *Korporatismens fall och den svenska modellens kris*, Stockholm.
Scharpf, Fritz W. 1999: *Governing in Europe: Effective and Democratic?*, Oxford.
Schivelbusch, Wolfgang 2006: *Three New Deals: Reflections on Roosevelt's America, Mussolini's Italy, and Hitler's Germany 1933-1939*, New York.
Schulze-Gaevernitz, Gerhard von 1890: *Zum socialen Frieden. Eine Darstellung der socialpolitischen Erziehung des englischen Volkes im neunzehnten Jahrhundert*, Leipzig.
Scott, James C. 1998: *Seeing Like A State: How Certain Schemes to Improve the Human Condition Have Failed*, New Haven.
Seip, Anne-Lise 1989: 'Politikkens vitenskapeliggjøring. Debatten om sosialpolitikk i 1930-årene', *Nyt Norsk Tidsskrift*, no. 3, vol. 6, pp. 210-225.
Sigurdson, Ola 2000: *Den lyckliga filosofin: Etik och politik hos Hägerström, Tingsten, makarna Myrdal och Hedenius*, Stockholm.
Skinner, B. F. 1953: *Science and Human Behavior*, New York.
Small, Albion W. 1900: 'The Scope of Sociology. VI. Some Incidents of Association', *The American Journal of Sociology*, no. 3, vol. 6, (Nov.), pp. 324-380.
Smith, Mark C. 1994: *Social Science in the Crucible: The American Debate Over Objectivity and Purpose 1918-1941*, Durham & London.
Spencer, Herbert 1891: 'From Freedom to Bondage', *Essays: Scientific, Political, and Speculative. Library Edition, containing Seven Essays not before republished, and various other Additions*, vol. 3, London.
Stauffner, Robert C. (ed.) 1949: *Science and Civilization*, Madison.
Stråth, Bo & Lars Magnusson (eds.) 2004: *A European Social Citizenship? Future Preconditions in Historical Light*, Brussels.
Touraine, Alain 1997: *Critique of Modernity*, London.
Turner, Stephen P. & Dirk Käsler (eds.) 1992: *Sociology Responds to Fascism*, New York.
Veblen, Thorstein B. 1891: 'Some Neglected Points in the Theory of Socialism', *Annals of the American Academy of Political and Social Science*, vol. 2, (Nov.), pp. 57-74.
Waever, Ole 2008: 'Peace and Security: Two Evolving Concepts and Their Changing Relationship', Hans Günter Brauch et al. (eds.), *Globalization and Environmental Challenges: Reconceptualizing Security in the 21st Century*, vol. 3, Berlin & Heidelberg.
Wagner, Peter, Björn Wittrock & Richard Whitley (eds.) 1991: *Discourses on Society: The Shaping of the Social Science Disciplines*, Dordrecht & London.

Wagner, Peter, Carol Hirschon Weiss & Björn Wittrock (eds.) 1991: *Social Sciences and Modern States: National Experiences and Theoretical Crossroads*, Cambridge.

Wagner, Peter & Nathalie Karagiannis 2005: 'Towards a Theory of Synagonism', *Journal of Political Philosophy*, no. 3, vol. 13, pp. 235-262.

Wang, Jessica 2005: 'Imagining the Administrative State: Legal Pragmatism, Securities Regulation, and New Deal Liberalism', *The Journal of Policy History*, no. 3, vol. 17, pp. 257-293.

Wang, Jessica 1999: *American Science in an Age of Anxiety: Scientists, Anticommunism, and the Cold War*, Chapel Hill.

Wiener, Norbert 1961 [1948]: *Cybernetics: Or the Control and Communication in the Animal and the Machine*, Cambridge, Mass.

Wiener, Norbert 1950: *The Human Use of Human Beings: Cybernetics and Society*, London.

Part II
Knowledge and Bureaucracy in Nordic Reform Policy

Between social radicalism and Christian socialism: Intellectuals, social knowledge and the building of the early Danish welfare state

Lars Schädler Andersen

Researchers on the early Danish social policy of the 1890s tend to emphasise the political, social and economic conflicts preceding legislation such as old age assistance, sickness insurance, accident insurance and unemployment insurance. Social science and the social experts are mentioned but often as a by-product of mainstream research. On the other hand, the complex and dynamic relationship between the modern state, social science and social policy has been at the centre of a still growing international literature. International scholars are now investigating the role of social experts, knowledge-generating institutions, intellectual traditions and the history of social surveys.[1]

A few Danish studies argue that neutral social experts were able to overcome difficulties with antagonistic political ideologies.[2] Once social problems were established as a scientific fact, it became reasonable to find political solutions. This way a statistical representation of society bridged a gap between conservative landowners and industrial employers, liberal farmers and socialist workers on social political issues. This is a sound judgement, but several questions still remain. Were these social experts in fact ever neutral? Although available social knowledge seems to have been a precondition for social policy, there is hardly any automatic or instrumental links between science and politics.[3]

This points to the central research question: What determines the influence of social science and social experts? And why did some social experts succeed in influencing social policy while others failed? To answer this we must carefully study the strategies deployed by these experts. The following study investigates thus the 'utilisation' of social knowledge and social science in social policy formation. In the words of Björn Wittrock, it tries to understand '...the difficult dialogue between producers and users of social research' .[4]

It addresses the question of a policy/science nexus at a time when a new ameliorative social science emerged as well as did new social political institutions. Furthermore, several scholars argue that varying political and cultural national contexts surely were of great importance in explaining the exact profile of social experts.[5] Because of this, different kinds of experts deployed varying strategies to gain influence.

The origin of the early Danish social policy is a case in point. This article will argue that social experts, in a favourable political context, might appear as 'innovating ideologists' – a term coined by historian Quentin Skinner. In his influential works on political history, he defines innovating ideologists as persons who wrest '...an available moral language to their own ends', while 'seeking at the same time to challenge conventional moral beliefs'.[6] That is, in trying to legitimise new ideas, the innovating ideologist tries rhetorically to inscribe new and even controversial ideas in conventional contexts by turning the weapons of their opponents against themselves. Skinner argues that political change is actually determined by the ability to legitimise such changes as truly 'social', 'patriotic', 'democratic', 'moral', etc.[7]

Social experts seem to be in a favourable position to make ideological innovation based on scientific evidence as the new powerful tool. But, on the other hand, it can easily turn out to be a strategic move in order to further an intellectual career or even a political agenda.[8] Intellectuals always run the risk of becoming political actors in the process of legitimising their ideas. The following study reveals the complicated and equivocal relationship between modern social science and the origin of social policy and therefore suggests a more explicit research approach to the role of experts in the utilisation of social scientific evidence.

The origin of the Danish welfare state revisited

According to political scientist Tim Knudsen '...the historian and statistician Marcus Rubin and the economist Harald Westergaard played a decisive role in the social political breakthrough of the 1890s'.[9] In the spring of 1891, the Danish parliament passed an act on old age assistance. It is widely accepted among Danish scholars that these two social experts in the mid-1880s provided policymakers with the social statistical evidence to support a new kind of social policy.[10]

Prior to the old age assistance act, the political elites of the 1870s and 1880s believed that if workers had problems providing for themselves and their families, it was caused by laziness and bad moral behaviour. In a liberal economy, workers had to rely on their own mutual associations for social aid, or otherwise, private charity. If, eventually, poor relief from the state was the only way out, the state in return stripped the citizen of his political and juridical rights. People in need of public aid were clearly regarded as second-class citizens, and poor relief was obviously designed to prevent people from claiming it in the first place.

Rubin and Westergaard (1886) showed that many needy fieldworkers ended up on poor relief though not everyone could be characterised as lazy. What was perceived as the last resort in fact turned out to be a widespread reality for the working population. These investigations paved the way for old age assistance, providing all citizens from the age of 60 with an economic benefit, notably without the stigmatising effects of poor relief. In covering all citizens in 'worthy need' and paid for by public taxation this was a unique model when compared with the rest of Europe. Elsewhere, the question of old age assistance was addressed as a matter of extension of life insurance or, as in Germany, compulsory wageworker insurance. As it was in Denmark in the 1870s and early 1880s, although, as shown in detail by Jørn Henrik Petersen and in general by others, the question was completely reversed in 1890, due to new statistical findings, party political cleavages, and the economic interests of farmers.[11] Petersen points to Marcus Rubin as a central figure. Rubin drew up a bill on public old age assistance to be presented by a faction of radical Liberals in parliament in order to deadlock negotiations between the Conservative government and moderate Liberals.

However, even if the political discussions on the old age assistance act have been well researched, another story has certainly not. Rubin and Westergaard are treated as a social science duo, paving the way for universalist tax-financed social policy. But in this article I intend to argue that they highly disagreed about the proper way to solve the problem of old age assistance. Rubin favoured state-organised public aid whereas Westergaard preferred extension of self-help insurance. Clearly, Marcus Rubin won this battle, and furthermore no one has yet revealed that along with the political discussions between liberal and conservative politicians came a dispute between a 'social radical' and a 'christian socialist'. The explanation is quite simple. The winner writes history and certainly Marcus Rubins interpretation of the making of the old age assistance act prevailed through time. Rubin did not mention any conflict with Westergaard.[12]

But the question still remains: Why did Marcus Rubin succeed while Harald Westergaard failed? A close examination of this question will tell us a great deal about the way in which social experts exercised an influence on social policy in late-nineteenth century. Before analysing in detail the battle between Rubin and Westergaard, I will shortly outline some relevant accounts of Danish political and cultural development in the second half of the nineteenth century. This is necessary in order to understand the context within which social experts operated.

Constitutional struggle, labour questions and two intellectual oppositions

After the decline of absolute monarchy in 1849, a liberal constitutional state was formed. The new state promised freedom of trade, which was realised through legislative measures in the 1850s.[13] The economic development to follow was accompanied by emigration from rural areas to emerging industrial towns, especially from the 1870s, and the abolition of the old guilds created a wage-earning working class with little or no social security. Social problems grew and finally became visible to the authorities. The bloody events following the socialist upheaval in Paris in the spring of 1871 sent shockwaves through bourgeois Europe. Even in less industrialised Denmark, the fear of socialism was present. In 1872, a fierce battle in Copenhagen between workers and police fuelled this anxiety even further. The Danish establishment had now witnessed the appearance of revolutionary socialism in Denmark.

During the 1870s, another struggle emerged, known as the constitutional struggle. Historian Ove Korsgaard has characterised Denmark during the second half of the nineteenth century as a bureaucratic landowner state.[14] The state bureaucrats and the landed aristocracy united in the Conservative Party around 1870, sharing a common interest in keeping the majority of the people from political influence. In the upper chamber of the Danish parliament, the Conservatives held the majority of seats, whereas in the lower chamber the Liberals clearly did. The 1880s was a period of fierce political strife. The Liberals, united in 1870, demanded cabinet responsibility and the abolishment of limited suffrage in the upper chamber. The Conservatives on the other hand argued for upper chamber supremacy and the royal election of government. This constitutional struggle was the context of all social political discussions in the 1880s and the early 1890s.

The conservative rule of the 1870s and 1880s spurred on an intellectual response known as the radical intellectual opposition.[15] A young Jewish scholar, Georg Brandes, disturbed the educated classes and the Conservative establishment in Denmark. In 1871, he held his famous lectures at the University of Copenhagen. He gave a powerful introduction to European literature, stressing science, secularism and internationalism as new guidelines of action rather than tradition, religion and crown. Georg Brandes, his brother and fellow literary man Edvard Brandes, and the philosopher Harald Høffding now became leading figures in the attempt to establish a *radical liberal* intellectual opposition to conservative rule. Around 1880, the radical intellectual group, who believed strongly in a positivist empirical science, formed an alliance with a group of liberal politicians in the lower chamber of parliament, notably Viggo Hørup and Christian Berg.

After graduating in political economics in 1874, the young secular Jewish scholar Marcus Rubin was drawn to this group of left-wing intellectuals, equally opposing established conservatism as well as rising socialism. For the next 20 years he served as a dynamic and extremely successful statistician at the Copenhagen municipal authorities. Especially in the 1880s, he was a fierce opponent of Conservative attempts to carry out provisional finance acts not voted for by the Liberals of the lower chamber.[16]

In the middle of the 1880s, another intellectual opposition emerged. The rapid social and economic changes in Copenhagen in the late nineteenth century gave rise to a fear of a dechristianization of the city among churchgoers.[17] Devoutly religious laymen and women from the Copenhagen bourgeoisie took over the work out of a frustration with the radical intellectual attack on religion as well as the inactivity of the Conservative government and the established church. New, active congregational ideals on the basis of Anglican church ideas were introduced as well as the need for the separation of state and church.[18] One of the leading figures of this movement was the professor of political economy Harald Westergaard. He was deeply influenced by a *Christian socialism* of the kind John Malcolm Ludlow had introduced into Britain around 1850.[19]

This ideology, according to Westergaard, was a practical 'non-partisan' and 'non-statist' socialism, one which argued that proper societal integration of the working population should be carried out through the spread of socially minded Christianity and not foremost by political and democratic reforms. The central institutions of society were the mutual self-help organisations of workers. The state should only interfere to support these institutions as the cornerstones of the education of workers. Westergaard and his fellow Christian socialists believed that neither science nor the state could solve social problems. Christianity alone could create a social consciousness to bridge the cleavages between classes of society.[20] Christian socialists highly disagreed with German 'socialists of the chair' on the role of the state as the primary neutral instrument to resolve social problems from above. Christian socialism envisaged a social Christian revolution from below.[21]

Westergaard and Rubin shared the same interest in statistical scientific work, but with highly different views as regards the state, politics and science. The debate on old age assistance exposed this difference.

State-subsidised life insurance, public assistance or local savings banks?

Until the beginning of the 1880s, the political majority believed that the problem of workers' old age assistance would be solved by life insurance. In 1871, old life insurance companies from the days of the absolute monarchy were reformed under the *State Institution of Life Insurance* (Statsanstalten for Livsforsikring), the idea being that better ways of calculating mortality and a state guarantee would make life insurance, previously a privilege of higher civil servants, cheaper and thus suitable for the working population. The working population was expected to include life insurance as a necessary expense, on a par with rent, clothes and food.[22]

The results were unpromising. In 1881 Westergaard published a great work on international mortality statistics. He concluded that life insurance in Denmark had not spread into the lower classes of society.[23] The reason was obviously that it was difficult to persuade young workers to take out a life insurance as early as the age of 20. He considered the possibility of a limited compulsory state-subsidised life insurance for every worker between the ages of 15 and 22.[24]

He believed that temporary compulsion would convince workers to continue contributing on a voluntary basis. Westergaard was around this time in favour of life insurance.

In the early 1880s, Westergaard was working as a statistician at the *State Institution of Life Insurance*. His knowledge of the death tables of this institution convinced him of another problem besides the working man's lack of foresight. The death tables could be seen as only expressing the mortality of the middle classes. Using these tables to measure working-class mortality would give rise to difficulties in measuring the proper contribution of workers. Westergaard further argued in favour of further investigations of the mortality of the working population. Marcus Rubin also noted in subsequent memoirs the lack of knowledge in the early 1880s concerning any 'socially conditioned mortality'.[25]

In 1883, the Conservative government proposed a voluntary publicly-subsidised life insurance for every Danish citizen.[26] In this way, the government hoped to stimulate an extension of life insurance to the working class, the state financing one third of the costs of purchasing a life insurance from the age of 55 years. This bill was the subject of intense debate at a meeting in early 1884 of the *Association of Political Economy* (Nationaløkonomisk Forening). Both Westergaard and Rubin attended this meeting. A manager of a Danish fire insurance company, G.F. Tvermoes, stated that this bill was epoch-making in its acceptance of a state subsidy without the stigmatising implications of poor relief. However, he argued that the government bill would still benefit the middle classes at the expense of the lower classes. He doubted that young workers could afford to participate at a young age.[27] Tvermoes then proposed an old age assistance for needy old people entirely financed by public taxes. In order to estimate the costs of this proposal, he suggested an investigation be made of mortality in different social classes.

Rubin and Westergaard, both eager to submit social mortality to thorough scientific investigation, took up this task. However, they had different ideas as to the use of such a study in social policy. Rubin endorsed Tvermoes's idea of public assistance without the stigmatising implications of poor relief. Rubin actually mentioned the taxation of distilled spirits to finance this.[28] Westergaard had a quite different agenda. He voiced his reluctance regarding the progressive ideas of Rubin and Tvermoes. And later that same year he published an article with a different proposal.

In 1872, the *Danish Workers' Bank* (Dansk Arbejderbank) was established as a savings bank as well as a loan fund and old age assistance fund. Westergaard championed this institution, partly for succeeding in attracting the working-class population, something that the big life insurance institutions had not been able to do, and partly for its resemblance to British small-scale savings banks in cooperation with mutual workers' associations such as friendly societies and co-operative workshops.[29] The idea behind *Danish Workers' Bank* was that members of the old age fund received, besides market interest from their payments, part of the surplus from the savings bank, which made it fairly cheap for a worker to save up enough money to buy life annuity in the life insurance companies. On the other hand, to attract savers to the savings bank, members of the old age fund as well as the savings bank were able to obtain cheap loans. Rather than feeding stockholders, the purpose was to promote mutuality among savers and loaners among the lower classes of society. Critics argued that a savings bank based on workman capital would jeopardise the solidity of the bank if the workman was unable to repay loans. But since 1872 the history of the *Danish Workers' Bank* had proven the critics wrong, Westergaard argued. The explanation for this was the local connection between self-help associations and the bank. The administrative capacity and personal relations in workers' associations provided a kind of security for the savings bank. These principles could probably not be applied at a national level, but Westergaard strongly called upon other local savings banks to embark along this road. It seemed to be the best way to solve the question of old age assistance.[30]

This was a quite different view of managing old age assistance than the national life insurance for workers proposed by the government, or the tax-financed public assistance proposed by Rubin. It was in accordance with Westergaard's strong belief in the need of building on and strengthening workers' own self-help measures. The English Christian socialists had also promoted this principle of 'cooperative banking' in the mid-nineteenth century.[31]

Social mortality. The 1886 survey

Rubin and Westergaard took on the job of providing social mortality statistics. Major industrial employers and influential people from the finance sector of Copenhagen promised to raise money to pay for this private social-scientific study. Two years later, the result was published in *Landbefolkningens Dødelighed i Fyens Stift. Et Bidrag til en Dødelighedsstatistik* (1886). This book is regarded as a pioneer in the history of mortality statistics, due to Westergaard's application of a certain statistical method: 'The method of expected number of deaths'. This was a method known from the embryonic European insurance statistics of the late 18th century, but almost forgotten in the nineteenth century.[32] It was a way of calculating socially determined mortality from an indirect standardisation of death tables from society in general.

Marcus Rubin wrote the introduction to this scientific study. He stated that the relation between the state and the social questions was in a time of change. Nevertheless, the idea of the present investigation was to argue neither in favour of public assistance nor subsidised self-insurance, but only to shed light on the positive scientific facts. In this way, the conclusions balanced carefully between Rubin's and Westergaard's social views.

The investigation was confined to the *rural* areas of the island of Funen. Ruben, as a practical statistician, carefully worked out schemes to be distributed among clergymen and schoolteachers across the island. On the basis of parish registers and death certificates, these 'statistical assistants' were instructed to report all deaths in the period from 1876 to 1883. Furthermore, these deaths were to be registered according to twenty-two occupational categories. The 'interpolated' number of deaths in 1880 could then be compared to the number of inhabitants of Funen according to the population census of February of 1880: approximately 170,000.

Westergaard then took over and conducted the actual analysis of these data. As stated earlier, Westergaard wanted to investigate the social mortality more accurately than just by relying on death tables for society in general. This was important in the debate on workers' old age assistance. The method of the expected number of deaths was all about calculating '…the number of deaths that would occur in every class, as if mortality was the same as in society in general, and then comparing these results with the actual number of deaths'.[33] A known death table thus served as a standard for every social class. Then, if the real number of deaths in a certain social class turned out to be higher than the calculated and expected number of deaths, this would indicate excessive mortality. On the other hand, if the expected number of deaths was higher than the real number, this would indicate a lower mortality. The main findings can be summed up in table 1:

Table 1: Observed and expected number of deaths. Diocese of Funen, 1876-1883, males and females above 5 years of age.

	Working		Not working		Total	
	obs.	exp.	obs.	exp.	obs.	exp.
Officials	117	102	22	21	139	123
Teachers	98	106	46	32	144	138
Other minor officials	190	223	62	61	252	284
Tradesmen, shopkeepers	206	245	–	–	206	245
Craftsmen	1825	2,146	175	130	2,000	2,276
Seamen and fishermen	224	313	–	–	224	313
Capitalists	0	0	177	203	177	203
Landed aristocracy	70	70	–	–	70	70
Farmers	3,325	3,276	1,656	1,539	4,981	4,815
Smallholders with land	2,865	2,669	1,711	1,627	4,576	4,296
Smallholders without land	2,513	2,140	254	274	2,767	2,414
Servants	981	1,443	–	–	981	1,443
Paupers	0	0	1,550	1,331	1,550	1,331
Others	23	33	–	–	23	33
Total	12,435	12,766	5,653	5,318	18,088	18,084

Source: Rubin & Westergaard 1886: 62.

These data point to an overall excessive agricultural mortality compared to the mortality in trade and craft. it is perhpas hardly surprising that paupers also suffered from excessive mortality. Westergaard now proceeded by dividing the data into mortality according to age, discovering that excessive agricultural mortality was a dominant feature among elderly farmers and smallholders with land.[34]

Smallholders without land and paupers fared worst. The data from both these groups revealed an excessive mortality. His final estimates for the lowest classes thus made him conclude that

> '... a third, maybe even half of the property-less proletariat may die as paupers. Here is a social problem of a great significance, one that will probably

not be solved without measures being undertaken by the state and municipalities as well as great courtesy from the propertied classes.'[35]

Rubin and Westergaard's investigation made it clear that by using new scientific statistical methods it was possible to say something new about the social mortality of the rural population of Funen. Westergaard suggested that any political measures should await further investigations from other parts of the country. But the general surprising conclusion was that a system of poor relief as a last resort for the minority of undeserving poor actually turned out to be the final stage in many fieldworkers' life.

The question now is: How is this social scientific evidence to be used? How did this knowledge of a severe social problem affect policy making? The next section will examine the way in which both Westergaard and Rubin tried to influence social policy around 1890.

The Christian socialist strategy

In 1879, Westergaard wrote an article praising the widespread network of mutual workers' associations in Britain, the so-called friendly societies. Legally protected by the state but economically independent, these societies had accomplished a great deal in solving the social problems in Britain as well as educating the British working class.[36] Westergaard stated that if all countries adopted this British model, it would eliminate the need of state subsidies as well as prevent the growth of radical socialism.

During the 1880s, he believed that old age assistance should be organised around the cornerstone of self-insurance and mutual workers' associations.[37] Any state attempt to de-mutualise workers' own efforts through direct state interference, as in Germany, should be opposed. In several speeches and letters he unfolded his version of Christian socialism.[38] Believing that Christianity was the ultimate remedy for society, he called upon Christian laymen to take up the task of alleviating social problems. Christians were by far the best able to educate and lead the working classes into local mutual associations like savings banks, health insurance societies, trade unions and other associations for the working people. A 'cultural mission' for the broad layers of society he later called this agenda.[39]

Churchmen should not only spread the word of God but also act as the vanguard of social reform in the local community. One could interpret this as a way of establishing networks of 'social communions' in civil society. In the words of Ludlow's biographer, N.C. Masterman, a parish-structured embryonic welfare, organised by churchmen.[40]

Christian socialism should be the social conscience of society. Westergaard believed that '...it is first and foremost among Christians that one can hope to find people who will work intensively for social political reforms, because they are animated by a living conscience regarding the sufferers of society'.[41] Many clergymen actually opposed Westergaard's Christian socialist strategy. They argued that besides a small-scale parish charity and spiritual support to prevent the dechristianisation of society, the church had no business in the struggle for broad social reforms of society. There was a fear of mixing religious community with activities of civil secular society. Westergaard's idea of both religious and social reform found many critics from both sides, while socialists on the other hand considered Christian socialism as typical religious hypocrisy.

In accordance with his Christian socialism, Westergaard breathlessly took part in reform activities in the late 1880s, old age assistance being no exception. The social survey of 1886 made Westergaard ever more convinced that his ideas from 1884 had to be pursued more intensely. Apart from *Danish Workers' Bank* another savings bank called *Bikuben* [The Beehive] also had an old age fund. This institution was established in 1857 under the impression of the simultaneous breaking-down of old guilds. In order to attract workers, the tontine-principle of insurance was chosen. The principle was a sort of group life insurance where all contributors are placed in annual sections. Each investor pays a fixed sum to the insurance company and receives interests from this sum. When investors die, his share of interest is divided among the surviving members of the annuity group. When all members are dead, the next annuity group inherits the remaining capital.[42] The tontine-principle was chosen in order to appeal to workers. Partly because it provided a much cheaper insurance than life insurance, though much less predictable, and because the founders of *Bikuben* believed that supposedly higher working-class mortality in time would enhance the possibility of receiving high payments, if a worker were to live long. On the other hand, many would not live to benefit from this model of insurance.

I 1886, Westergaard was appointed to a seat in the leading three-member committee of *Bikuben*. His first task was a thorough investigation of the old age fund and he proved its failure to attract working-class members. As with life insurance companies, only the middle classes insured themselves through *Bikuben*.⁴³ Furthermore, when there was statistical evidence of relatively high working-class mortality, one could not expect workers to join the same tontine as the middle classes, the latter having a greater chance of benefiting from this scheme. And finally, if people from the middle classes lived longer, as *Bikubens* statistical material seemed to reveal this in turn would postpone the age of receiving the highest interest from the tontine.⁴⁴

He then convinced *Bikuben* to revise the insurance principles in accordance with *Danish Workers' Bank*. He carefully worked out a new scheme of old age insurance in 1889. Instead of annuity groups, each investor was given a separate account, and besides market interest, the investors received an interest surplus from the ordinary banking activities of *Bikuben*. This scheme came into effect in 1890 and Westergaard had really high hopes that this would attract workers. Much later, he bitterly regretted that it actually failed. The augmentation was low in the 1890s and it was soon to be abolished.⁴⁵

His efforts to reform *Bikuben* in order to support a strategy of establishing institutions combining banking and old age assistance as a way of building on workers' own self-help without state interference thus failed. Much likely, the very 'statist' public old age assistance act of 189 got in the way.

Alcohol, public taxes and social policy

During his efforts to reform *Bikuben*, Westergaard was forced into a direct confrontation with Marcus Rubin. Westergaard was aware of Rubin's ideas on the taxation of alcohol to pay for old age assistance. In early 1888, this question became urgent when the liberal *Association of Tariff Reform* (Toldreformforeningen) proposed a reduction of import duty on especially coffee and sugar to be financed by a tax on beer and distilled spirits. Marcus Rubin now launched a campaign in the radical liberal newspaper *Politiken*, arguing that taxation on alcohol should be used to finance not only lower duties on consumer items but also workers' social protection.⁴⁶

In July of 1888, several Nordic political economists gathered for a meeting in Copenhagen. Here Westergaard delivered a powerful speech on drunkenness in Denmark compared to Norway and Sweden. He pointed out that consumption of alcohol in Denmark by far exceeded the Swedish and Norwegian experiences. There were two explanations for this. Firstly, data showed a vast amount of liquor stores in Denmark. In Norway and Sweden there was a liquor store for every 4-5,000 inhabitants. In Denmark there was a liquor store for every 200 inhabitants. The worst 'liquor grotto' was Copenhagen, with a liquor store for every 90 inhabitants, practically on every street corner.[47] Secondly, alcohol taxation in Denmark was among the lowest in Europe.

He outlined two possible solutions. Firstly, a monopolisation of the sale of alcohol, the so-called 'Gothenburg model'. According to this, the sale of alcohol was restricted to certain companies unable to profit from any increase in sales. Any surplus was to be handed over to local municipal authorities. This would reduce the incentive to sell more alcohol and likewise reduce the propensity to open new liquor stores. Regarding the question of taxation, Westergaard believed that a tax on distilled spirits would be highly desirable, but difficult because of the present political circumstances. However, a taxation of beer was a promising solution. He then mentioned the debate on a tariff reform in early 1888 as an indicator of this. But he strongly argued: 'It is not the purpose of such a tax to give a financial surplus. It should only be enforced in order to reduce consumption. If it is profitable, then it is mistaken'.[48]

In other words, no alcohol taxation should be used to finance any social policy. The Nordic economists highly welcomed Westergaard's speech. This encouraged Westergaard to propose a resolution to be adopted by the conference. In this, the Danish government was urged to undertake measures necessary to reduce drunkenness, either through reducing the sale of alcohol or by taxes on alcohol. Then, all of a sudden, Marcus Rubin took the rostrum, arguing that a Nordic conference ought not to adopt any resolution aimed at the government of only one of the nations.[49] This was in fact a clash between Rubin and Westergaard on the issue of alcohol taxation and social policy. Even though Westergaard finally withdrew his proposal, he had made a powerful impact also on the Danish public. His speech was published a couple of months later, and *Politiken* was surprised by the actual amount of alcohol consumed in Denmark: 'Even Russia, the most notorious liquor country, does not consume as much alcohol as Denmark'.[50]

Even though he succeeded in avoiding a resolution, Rubin wrote rather disillusionedly about the costs of publicly financed old age assistance later that same autumn. He calculated that even a modest taxation on distilled spirits, assuming that consumption remained stable, would provide the necessary yield to finance old age assistance for every citizen from the age of 65. But he stated, '...that the social question should not, as rightfully mentioned at the congress of political economists, be closely connected with any public taxation scheme'.[51] Rubin was actually very doubtful about his project, now that Westergaard had effectively turned the Nordic academic establishment of economists against it.

Furthermore, in the wake of Westergaard's truly agenda-setting speech, liberal total abstainers in the Danish parliament presented a bill to tighten up the appropriation act in order to reduce alcohol consumption. During the discussion there were many references to Westergaard's speech, and a parliamentary committee investigated this bill in early 1889. A political majority suggested that any licence to sell alcoholic beverages were to be approved by local authorities as well as the Ministry of the Interior. Opening hours were to be heavily restricted, and licencees had to pay annual duties to the state and the local authority.[52] These ideas were clearly influenced by Westergaard's speech on the Gothenburg model, aimed at reducing the very incentive to sell beer and distilled spirits and reducing the incentive to open liquor trades.

Given the fact that a majority vote in the lower chamber in favour of total abstainers was close at hand, even the Conservative government had to react. In October 1889, the Minister of Finance, J.B.S Estrup, presented a new bill on the taxation of beer and distilled spirits in the upper chamber. Especially taxation of distilled spirits was in fact an old Conservative idea. Urban workers predominantly consumed beer while the rural population mainly consumed distilled spirits. Alcohol taxation would benefit public finances. But in order to comply with the rising political demands on the reduction of alcohol consumption, Estrup argued that the taxation of alcohol was being proposed in order to reduce consumption as well.[53] This seemed to be a strategic move in order to deadlock the discussion in the lower chamber as well as to further the idea of reducing tariffs on other consumer items. The minister of finance may well have known, as Westergaard also pointed out at the meeting of Nordic political economists, that moderate Liberals did not favour a taxation on distilled spirits. The government was surely more interested in the other part of the bill, a tax on beer. Estrup was eager to tax the growing consumption of beer to finance the abolition of a sugar tariff.[54] The main motive of the government was the fiscal part.

Now, the discussion centred on a taxation on beer, but certainly not in the way Westergaard would have preferred. Furthermore, there was no sign of Rubin's connection between alcohol taxation and workers' social protection. Rubin had once more in the summer of 1889 campaigned on public old age assistance as a social right and not as poor relief in any way. It was not justifiable for elderly workers to be treated as paupers, when the only cause of their work inability was age.[55] On the contrary, the government presented in the lower chamber in October 1889 a bill on a revision of the poor law, with specific rules regarding elderly people.[56] Limited relief measures, based on self-help ideology, without the stigmatising effects of ordinary poor relief were proposed. But this bill was still clearly within the framework of poor relief. The bill was indirectly based on the insurance principle. Only needy members of health insurance societies and contributors of private old age insurance associations were entitled to assistance free of the stigmata of poor relief.[57]

The social radical strategy

Furthermore, party political strategies threatened to isolate Rubin's original idea of old age assistance financed by alcohol taxation. In 1890, a faction of the Liberal party, the moderate Liberals, led by Frede Bojsen, embarked on a more compromising strategy towards the Conservatives. An election in early 1890 had favoured another Liberal faction, the radical Liberals, led by Chr. Berg and Viggo Hørup. Bojsen believed that a compromise with the Conservatives would improve the position of the moderate Liberals. And in the summer of 1890 he decided that beer taxation to finance tariff reduction on sugar was such a field for compromise.[58] Then, in the autumn of 1890, Rubin could predict a tariff reform and a poor law reform that would deadlock his ideas.

But on the other hand, a compromise between moderate Liberals and the Conservative government opened a window of opportunity This compromise would isolate radical Liberals – and the radical leaders were strongly opposed to these minor attempts to negotiate with the government while the major political issue of cabinet responsibility still remained unsolved. Furthermore, they believed that the tariff reform was socially wrong if the beer-drinking workers of

Copenhagen were to pay for cheaper sugar for the better-off classes of society.

Radical Liberals wanted to deadlock this compromise and Rubin used his strong connections with radical political leaders in order to realise his social radical scheme. Rubin now drew up a bill on old age assistance.[59] Every citizen above the age of 62 should be entitled to old age assistance financed by an earmarked tax on beer and distilled spirits. A new state insurance office was to measure payments on the basis of fixed rates, and the administration was to be carried out by local authorities. No self-help measures were connected to this scheme. Public old age assistance was the social right of every citizen.

He presented this bill to a reluctant Viggo Hørup in December 1890. Still opposed to beer tax, he hesitated, but then Rubin explained to him, that he himself would publish it for everyone to use as they pleased. Hørup then accepted for political reasons.[60] He feared that other compromising Liberals might gain an advantage from a publication of Rubin's proposal. Either way, the bill could be used to deadlock negotiations between Moderates and government. Hørup and Berg then presented it in the lower chamber on December 17 1890, leaving the Moderates in a tight corner, now that both Liberal groups were suddenly in favour of a beer tax.

Rubin gave a speech in early-January 1891 at a well-attended meeting of the *Association of Political Economy*. He gave a thorough introduction to the social ideas behind his bill. The main principle was that when work inability was caused by age, old age assistance should be separated from the poor law. He pointed out that according to the constitution it was a state responsibility to provide every citizen with a regular social right to old age assistance. Every attempt to demand self-help measures was not only unjust but also unrealistic when scientific studies, as the one he and Westergaard had conducted in 1886, showed that many poor elderly people would not survive to benefit from any self-insurance. Previous social statistical studies, carried out by medical practitioner Th. Sørensen, showed that workers could afford membership of a health insurance society, but they could not afford to insure themselves in old age. In short, the only logic to be derived from the scientific studies of the 1880s was that the state had to grant every citizen an old age benefit of a non-contributory origin.

When the government bill of 1889 stated that recipients of poor relief before the age of 60 were excluded from old age assistance this was also unjust. It was nothing but a punishment for being poor. He also strongly opposed the social aspects of the government's bill on beer tax as a part of a tariff reform. This way the beer-drinking workers would pay for cheaper consumption of products used by the population as a whole, according to the consumer capacity of every social class. This way the only just thing to do was to abolish a reduction of the sugar tariff and earmark the surplus from beer tax entirely to old age assistance.[61]

The following discussion at the *Association of Political Economy*, as well as the public debate more generally, showed that many of Rubin's fellow economists and social experts disagreed with him. Not only Harald Westergaard but also another professor of political economics at the University of Copenhagen, V. Falbe-Hansen, opposed the principle endorsed by Rubin. Furthermore, his comments revealed the dilemma. He stated: 'As far as the technical aspect of the proposal, its formal preparation and the basic calculations, he could highly appreciate it'.[62] But nevertheless he was opposed to the fundamental principles as far as providing public assistance with no contribution from workers themselves. This was morally wrong, threatening to destroy workers' responsibility and thrift.

Around 1890, the majority of social experts actually supported the notion of 'help to self-help' and recommended different kinds of workers' self-insurance as the starting point of any kind of old age assistance, though there was acknowledgement of the statistics behind Rubin's proposal.[63] This really indicates that the issue, even among experts, was highly intertwined with moral views on social policy. This actually highlights Rubin's social radicalism as well as his efforts to let scientific evidence matter directly.[64]

The political implications were also a matter of dispute. In the discussion following his proposal on old age assistance, Conservatives attacked Rubin, arguing that gratuitous assistance without a forfeit of civil rights would produce laziness and provide paupers with political rights in order to produce left-wing voters. Rubin answered that every culturally developed society had to provide citizens with political and social rights in order to make them act as responsible citizens.[65] The traditional Conservative and Liberal view was that political and social rights were a reward granted to worthy citizens. Rubin's social radicalism held another view, namely that extended political and social rights would raise the moral and living standards of the population as a whole. It was not only a matter of social knowledge but a politicised political matter as well. Generally speaking, Rubin was certainly no spokesman for any consensual social scientific segment. But he stood out as the only one willing to draw the most logical conclusions from the social statistical evidence produced by social scientists in the 1880s. A scheme to work immediately in favour of elderly people was needed, and not an insurance scheme.

At the start of his speech in January 1891, he stated very clearly the two main conclusions from the social investigations that had led to his turning down the idea of self insurance: 'This is a foresight that one cannot expect from those who seldom have more than their daily livelihood, often less than that, and who have relatively small chances of reaching the age to enjoy these savings'.[66] The case was more than obvious to Rubin.

Marcus Rubin is accurately described in Quentin Skinner's term as an 'innovative ideologist'. This explains why his proposal was not easily turned down by a political majority, which was close to agreeing on an insurance model inscribed in the poor law. Though arguing for a highly controversial social scheme, wholeheartedly supported by none of his fellow experts, he at the same time succeeded in questioning the very social political foundation of the government and not only the poor law bill of 1889. The government had embarked on a 'social' path in the late 1880s by presenting bills on accident insurance, sickness insurance, and a revised poor law. The ruling politicians wished to present themselves as socially responsible. At the same time, the government seemed to have invested social experts, and thus 'social science', with authority in setting up expert commissions and supporting surveys like the one conducted by Westergaard and Rubin.[67] Rhetorically, Rubin then challenged the government with its own weapons. Passing the poor law bill would in fact undermine this 'social raison d'être' as well as the endavour of letting social science matter, Rubin argued in January 1891.

In this way, Rubin placed the principle of tax-financed old age assistance without self-help measures as the true 'social' principle, based on scientific evidence. For that reason, his scheme could not easily be turned down, and central parts of his bill were passed in the Danish parliament in the spring of 1891.

The final act

Berg and Hørup did not actually succeed. Rather than deadlocking negotiations, this bill catalysed the political process. The Moderates tried to maintain the upper hand in the negotiations and finally in March of 1891 an agreement with the government was reached. According to the Old Age Assistance Act of 1891 every citizen in 'worthy need' was from the age of 60 entitled to payments financed by public taxes. Payments were measured out based on the discretion of local authorities. Finally the moderate Liberals and the government reached an agreement on beer tax in order to reduce sugar tariffs. This way, the old age assistance was financed by public taxes, but not earmarked or equivalent to revenue from beer taxes.[68] Obviously, this resulted in a much more limited old age assistance than Rubin had prescribed. According to his plan, 78,000 people would receive payments from fixed rates, rising to DKK 8.6 mill. In contrast, 44,000 people received old age assistance in 1892, and the total expenses were DKK 2.6 mill.[69]

The development in the discussion of old age assistance from 1889 to 1891 can be described as follows:

Table 2: The old age assistance bills from 1889-1891.

	Government bill (1889)	Marcus Rubin (1890)	Final Act (1891)
Age of recipients	60	62	60
Criterion for assignment	Needy members of health insurance societies and contributors to private old age insurance associations	Every needy Danish citizen	Every citizen in terms of 'worthy need'*
Criterion for measuring	Discretion	Fixed tariffs	Discretion
Financing	State subsidised selfhelp	Taxation of beer and distilled spirits**	Public municipal taxes with state refunding
Administration	Local authorities	State office and local authorities	Local authorities
Social principle	'Help to self-help'	Social right	Indirect 'help to self-help'

*Worthiness was described as good citizenship, whereas unworthiness was conceived as self-inflicted need: Pauperism, wastefulness, disorderliness, vagrancy and begging.
**Hørup and Berg abolished the distilled spirits in order to appeal to Moderate Liberals unwilling to tax the 'liquor-drinking' rural population.

Marcus Rubin thus had to accept several changes. His idea of beer tax to pay for old age assistance was obstructed by moderate Liberals and Conservatives not being in favour of Copenhagen beer-drinking workers. A strong inclination to self-help ideology then precluded fixed tariffs and the idea of an unconditional social right. But on the other hand, Rubin's proposal was indeed a turnover in the political process in two ways; 1) the fact that universal citizenship was chosen as the principle of assignment, and 2) that those payments were to be financed entirely from public taxes with no contribution from either worker or employer. Cornerstones of the Danish welfare 'path' were this way introduced as the result of strategic, and innovative, moves of a social radical economist trying to reconcile the political groups unwilling to impose beer tax with the political groups unwilling to grant public gratuitous old age assistance. The compromise had extremely far-reaching consequences for the development of the Danish welfare state.

The surprisingly strong effect of Rubin's proposal can well be illustrated by quoting a contemporary insurance expert and Conservative politician, Ludvig Bramsen. The development from government proposals of the 1880s, based on positive self-help measurers, until the final act of 1891, he described as a remarkable "...round trip, reaching at first the station 'self-help', then 'help to self-help', only to get off at the station of 'public assistance'.[70] Bramsen himself was a supporter of the insurance principle which had been at the centre of all discussions for two decades, but in the course of a couple of months this was replaced by another principle, due to Rubin's campaign and specific party-political circumstances. In addition, a tax-financed solution would affect society immediately, as opposed to the long-term perspective of an insurance scheme. Liberal farmers, troubled by the economic crisis, could eventually accept this in order to put a damper on rural depopulation.[71]

But it is worth mentioning that the most influential social and economic experts of that time highly disagreed with Rubin – not only Westergaard and Bramsen but also Dr. Th. Sørensen, from 1892 the head of the national health insurance office, as well as the professors of political economics at the University of Copenhagen disagreed.

Social experts and the origins of Danish social policy

What conclusions can be derived from this study of the role of social-political intellectuals in the making of late-nineteenth century social policy? In general, the study confirms the argument of social scientists and social experts as crucial to the way social problems were perceived in public and political discussions. But focusing on the relationship between two very different kinds of experts, Rubin and Westergaard, on the same social policy area, this general view can be further refined. In this concluding chapter I will highlight two aspects of the complex relationship between social experts and social policy in the late nineteenth century.

Firstly, it seems clear that Westergaard and Rubin highly disagreed on the proper way to solve the question of old age assistance. This especially applies to the use of alcohol taxation and the role of the state. Alongside the political discussions on social policy an equally important conflict between two social experts existed – previously unheard of, because Marcus Rubin won the battle and succeeded in orchestrating future interpretations of the birth of old age assistance. Acting as an innovative ideologist, Rubin turned the discussion away from focusing on insurance principles and direct self-help measures. The differences between Rubin and Westergaard stem from different social-political views. Westergaard's Christian socialism stressed the mutual self-help measures and the insurance institutions of civil society, whereas Rubin's social radicalism highlighted the constitutional responsibility of the state to provide citizens with unconditional social rights.

The present study reveals that a scientific study such as the mortality study of 1886 in fact produced highly different expert conclusions. There was no instrumental expert interpretation of the data, even though Westergaard and Rubin co-worked closely on the survey. In Westergaard's eyes, it was ever more urgent to promote a Christian socialist strategy. This actually failed in the case of *Bikuben*, where he tried to reform an old age insurance association in order to attract the lower classes.

On the other hand, the social survey of 1886 proved decisive for Rubin in a quite different way. Until then, as Rerup points out,[72] Rubin had shown little interest in social policy. He was like many of his fellow radical intellectuals predominantly occupied with the overall political conflicts over democracy and cabinet responsibility. But the study of 1886 convinced him of the existence of great social problems. The vast rural pauperism and excessive mortality among fieldworkers made him realise that public assistance was needed.

The score on alcohol taxation was in fact even between Rubin and Westergaard. Rubin did not succeed in earmarking alcohol taxes to be used for old age assistance, and nor did Westergaard prevent the Conservative government's strong fiscal motives behind alcohol taxation.

The *second* feature is the fact that experts deploy different strategies of seeking influence. Jørn Henrik Petersen argues that social experts operate in a field in which new ideas of social policy float between the political and intellectual sphere. The power of new ideas, such as Rubin's, depended on intellectual access to central political policy makers.[73] Rubin used a strategy of permeation through political parties and parliament. In this process his authority as an expert was clearly used to fuel his overall aim of turning down governmental bills on poor law and tariff reform. Faced with the possibility of Rubin publishing his bill as a private one, the radical Liberals were finally convinced? and presented it in the lower chamber. This suggests that social experts could exercise great influence when directly confronting the political parties and members of parliament. And clearly the party political strife opened a window for Rubin. The radical Liberals needed a counterstroke to the compromising strategy of the moderate Liberals in late 1890.

On the other hand, Westergaard's Christian socialism prevented him from forming an alliance with, say, moderate Conservatives. Some conservatives tried to persuade him, but he always refused having his scientific legitimacy associated with any form of party politics. In his view party politics and Christianity were incompatible, a notion he shared with many of his religious fellows. His strategy was indeed non-partisan and extra-parliamentary. He tried to enlighten both workers and the educated classes about the true remedy of Christianity and the power of workers' mutualism. But in pursuing this he was actually cut off from any *direct* influence on the social policy making around 1890. In addition, other Conservatives developed highly sceptical attitudes towards his strong religious feelings and his Christian socialism. Conservative cavalier types in fact despised his religious revivalism.

In this article only a single example of the actions of social experts between social policy and social science is examined. Nevertheless, it has made it clear that experts deploy different strategies in order to influence policy-making. This calls for more research on the difficult dialogue between users and producers of social knowledge, especially when it becomes obvious that social experts might act as both.

Notes

1. Rune Ervik & Stein Kuhnle (eds.), 1993; Dietrich Rueschemeyer & Theda Skocpol (eds.), 1996; Wisselgren, 2000; Lawrence Goldman, 2002.
2. Jørgen Dalberg-Larsen, 1993; Anne Løkke, 2002.
3. Stein Kuhnle, 1996, p. 258.
4. Björn Wittrock, 1991, p. 336.
5. Björn Wittrock & Wagner, 1996, p. 93. A well-known international example is the difference between the authority of conservative university professors of Verein für Sozialpolitik (Association for Social Policy) in authoritarian imperial Germany and the influence of 'amateur science' and 'men of letters' in The Fabian Society in liberal constitutional Britain (Rune Ervik, 1993; Dietrich Rueschemeyer & Ronan van Rossem, 1996; Per Wisselgren, 2000). There was clearly some difference as regarding to the channels of influence. The German 'socialists of the chair' claimed to represent a non-partisan position in society and regarded the state as the only institution to reconcile class conflicts. The idea behind 'Kathedersozialismus' was the notion of the strong state as the only neutral element in the social struggles of the time. They believed science to be morally superior to politics and tried to influence the Imperial state and bureaucracy. Their British intellectual counterparts in the Fabian Society used a permeation strategy, addressing the public opinion, parliamentary political groups and parties more directly in order to exercise influence. Their interpretation of the policy/science nexus was quite different. Fabians regarded social science, though objective and sound, as a tool to promote the political agenda. Policy this way assumed primacy in determining societal values. The political and cultural context explains this variation. In Germany universities were closely connected to the imperial power structure and this German 'Bildungsbürgertum' was a fairly homogeneous conservative social group, connected to universities and excessive state bureaucracy. Development of social science in Germany was a part of and sponsored by the state. This was not the case in Britain, where universities were less bound up with state power and bureaucracy was smaller. Lawrence Goldman states that in pluralist societies, contrary to authoritarian, non-academic experts were in fact crucial in the process of establishing a social science (Lawrence Goldman, 2002, pp. 372-374).
6. Quentin Skinner, 2002, pp. 178-179.
7. Frank Beck Lassen & Mikkel Thorup, 2009, p. 10.
8. Ron Eyerman, 1994, pp. 104-105.
9. Tim Knudsen, 2000, p. 18.
10. Jørn Henrik Petersen, 1985; Jørgen Dalberg-Larsen, 1993; Anne Løkke, 2002.
11. Jørn Henrik Petersen, 1985; 2007; Peter Baldwin, 1990; Asbjørn Sonne Nørgaard, 2000.
12. Marcus Rubin, 1911; 1924. The tendency to view Rubin and Westergaard as taking some of the same stands on social policy (e.g. Knudsen, 2003, p. 40) has ac-

tually led to rather simplified interpretations. Economist Niels Kærgård points to Westergaard in an argument of the relation between Christianity and the social policy around 1890 (Niels Kærgård, 2005, p. 45). There may be good arguments for this relation in general (Uffe Østergaard, 2005) and also regarding Westergaard's contribution to the social political discourse. But the specific Danish model of tax-financed old age assistance of 1891, ever so crucial to the Danish 'Sonderweg', was in no way supported by Westergaard in the late 1880s, though some 25 years later he seemed to acknowledge it (Jørn Henrik Petersen, 2007: 106). Investigating the conflict between Rubin and Westergaard will enable us to separate myth from reality.

13 Asbjørn Sonne Nørregaard, 1943, pp. 61-82.
14 Ove Korsgaard, 2004, p. 310.
15 Kristian Hvidt, 2005, pp. 13-19.
16 Lorenz Rerup (ed.), 1963, pp. 32-40.
17 Lars S. Andersen, 2008, pp. 15-17.
18 Elith Olesen, 1996.
19 N.C. Masterman, 1963; Torben Christensen, 1976.
20 Harald Westergaard, 1886; Harald Westergaard, 1899.
21 Lawrence Goldman, 2005.
22 Anne Løkke, 2007, pp. 200-202.
23 Harald Westergaard, 1881b, p. 547.
24 Harald Westergaard, 1881a.
25 Marcus Rubin, 1924, p. 152.
26 Jørn Henrik Petersen, 1985, pp. 80-81.
27 G.F. Tvermoes, 1884, p. 20.
28 G.F. Tvermoes, 1884, p. 37.
29 Harald Westergaard, 1884.
30 Harald Westergaard, 1884, pp. 326-329.
31 Philip N. Backstrom, 1963, p. 316.
32 Niels Keiding, 1987; Alain Desrosières, 1998, pp. 166-169.
33 Marcus Rubin & Harald Westergaard, 1886, p. 61.
34 Marcus Rubin & Harald Westergaard, 1886, pp. 76-79.
35 Marcus Rubin & Harald Westergaard, 1886, p. 102.
36 Harald Westergaard, 1879.
37 Harald Westergaard, 1888b.
38 Harald Westergaard, 1886, Harald Westergaard, 1889.
39 Harald Westergaard, 1903, p. 311.
40 N.C. Masterman, 1963, pp. 93-94.
41 P. Helweg-Larsen (ed.), 1955, pp. 50-51.
42 Harald Westergaard, 1936, pp. 26-27; Jørn Henrik Petersen, 1985, pp 164-165.
43 Harald Westergaard, 1907, p. 72.
44 Harald Westergaard, 1887, pp. 2-4.
45 Harald Westergaard, 1936, pp. 42-43.
46 *Politiken*, 28/2 1888; 1/3 1888.
47 Harald Westergaard, 1888, pp. 13-14.
48 *Politiken*, 8/7 1888.
49 Aleksis Petersen-Studnitz (ed.), 1888, pp. 250-251.
50 *Politiken*, 28/9 1888.
51 Marcus Rubin, 1888, p. 358.

52 Rigsdagstidende 1888-1889, Tillæg B, pp. 2281-2282.
53 Rigsdagstidende 1889-1890; Landstingets Forhandlinger, pp. 80-81.
54 Kristian Hvidt, 1963, p. 44.
55 Marcus Rubin, 1889.
56 Jørn Henrik Petersen, 1985, pp. 91-94.
57 Jørn Henrik Petersen, 1985, p. 92.
58 Kristian Hvidt, 1963, pp. 188-192.
59 Marcus Rubin, 1891.
60 Lorenz Rerup, 1963, pp. 318-321.
61 Marcus Rubin, 1891.
62 Marcus Rubin, 1891, p. 61.
63 Other active social reformers like Doctor Th. Sørensen and insurance expert Ludvig Bramsen as well had published articles in favour of self-insurance (Ludvig Bramsen, 1890; Th. Sørensen, 1890).
64 Rubin's biographer, the historian Lorenz Rerup, finds clear evidence of his view on science in the historical writings of Rubin. Rubin wrote highly acknowledged books on Danish political, economics and social history of the first half of the nineteenth century. Rerup highlights the difference between the radical historian Rubin and the national historian A.D. Jørgensen, both writing on the same period. Whereas a national romantic framework and its use for popular education determined the scientific method deployed by Jørgensen, Rerup states that the scientific method used by Rubin was to let scientific evidence speak for itself. He was more dedicated to enlightenment thoughts and not constrained by the national, political and moral discourses of Danish society in the late-nineteenth century (Lorenz Rerup, 1963, pp. 51-53). Maybe this relative scientific independence made it easier for him to present a completely new bill on old age assistance in 1890, when other scholars were constrained by the dominant social discourse, and Harald Westergaard in particular by his Christian socialism.
65 *Politiken*, 9/1 1891.
66 Marcus Rubin, 1891, p. 47.
67 Marcus Rubin, 1924, pp. 151-152.
68 Marcus Rubin, 1911, p. 239.
69 Lorenz Rerup, 1963, p. 47.
70 Ludvig Bramsen, 1892, p. 490.
71 Jørn Henrik Petersen, 2007, chapter 3.
72 Lorenz Rerup, 1963, p. 37.
73 Jørn Henrik Petersen, 2007, p. 48.

References

Andersen, Lars Schädler 2008: 'Folkekirkens entreprenører. Striden om Det københavnske Kirkefond 1896-1907', *Historie*, no. 1, pp. 35-87.
Andersen, Lars Schädler 2009: 'The discovery of professional risk: Social science and the industrial accident in Denmark, 1880–1900', *Ideas in History*, no, 1, pp. 37-70.
Backstrom, Philip N. 1963: 'The Practical Side of Christian Socialism in Victorian England', *Victorian Studies*, no. 4, vol. 6, pp. 305-324.
Baldwin, Peter 1990: *The Politics of Social Solidarity. Class Bases of the European Welfare*

State 1875-1975, Cambridge.
Bluhme, C. A. & Marcus Rubin 1889: *Om bajersk Øl og Brændevin*, Copenhagen.
Bramsen, Ludvig 1890: *Ubemidledes Forsørgelse under Sygdom, Arbejdsudygtighed og Alderdom samt Arbejdsforsørgelse efter Ulykkestilfælde*, Copenhagen.
Bramsen, Ludvig 1892: 'Cordt Trap, Statens Stilling til Ubemidledes Alderdomsforsørgelse' (review), *Nationaløkonomisk Tidsskrift*, pp. 473-494.
Christensen, Torben 1976: 'Harald Westergaard og John Malcolm Ludlow. Optakten til den kristelig-sociale bevægelse i Danmark', *Kirkehistoriske Samlinger*, pp. 292-326.
Clausen, Johan (ed.) 1886: *Det kirkelige Møde i Kjøbenhavn, den 25de-27de Maj 1886*, Copenhagen.
Dalberg-Larsen, Jørgen 1993: 'The Role of Professions and the Administrative Personnel in Danish Social Policy 1850-1918', *Jahrbuch für europäische Verwaltungsgeschichte*, pp. 293-312.
Desrosières, Alain 1998: *The Politics of Large Numbers. A History of Statistical Reasoning*.
Ervik, Rune & Stein Kuhnle (eds.) 1993: *Kunnskap, risiko og sosialpolitikk: Institusjonelle perspektiver på skandinavisk utvikling*, Bergen.
Ervik, Rune 1993: 'Tysk 'katetersosialisme' og sosialpolitisk intellektuelle: Noreg og Sverige i komparativt perspektiv', Ervik, Rune & Stein Kuhnle (eds.), *Kunnskap, risiko og sosialpolitikk: Institusjonelle perspektiver på skandinavisk utvikling*, Bergen.
Eyerman, Ron 1994: *Between Culture and Politics. Intellectuals in Modern Society*, Cambridge.
Goldman, Lawrence 2002: *Science, Reform, and Politics in Victorian Britain. The Social Science Association 1857-1866*, Cambridge.
Goldman, Lawrence 2005: 'Civil Society in Nineteenth-century Britain and Germany: J. M. Ludlow, Lujo Brentano and the Labour Question', Harris, José (ed.), *Civil Society in British History. Ideas, Identities, Institutions*, Oxford.
Helweg-Larsen, P. (ed.) 1955: *Kirkens Venners Korrespondance. Af Kirkefondets Forhistorie*, Copenhagen.
Hvidt, Kristian (ed.) 1963: *Frede Bojsens politiske Erindringer*, Copenhagen.
Hvidt, Kristian 2005: 'Det Radikale Venstre og brudfladerne i dansk politik', Pedersen, Sune & Bo Lidegaard (eds.), *B. Radikalt 1905-2005*, Copenhagen.
Keiding, Niels 1987: 'The Method of Expected Number of Deaths, 1786-1886-1986, Correspondent Paper', *International Statistical Review*, no.1, pp. 1-20.
Knudsen, Tim 2000: 'Tilblivelsen af den universalistiske velfærdsstat', Knudsen, Tim (ed.), *Den nordiske protestantisme og velfærdsstaten*, Århus.
Knudsen, Tim 2003: 'De nordiske statskirker og velfærdsstaterne', Petersen, Klaus (ed.), *13 historier om den danske velfærdsstat*, Odense.
Kuhnle, Stein: 'International Modeling, States, and Statistics: Scandinavian Social Security Solutions in the 1890s', Rueschemeyer, Dietrich & Theda Skocpol (eds.): *States, Social Knowledge, adn the Origin of Modern Social Policies*, Princeton, New Jersey.
Kærgård, Niels 1997: 'Tre økonomiske professorers teologi', *Kirkehistoriske samlinger*, pp. 129-198.
Kærgård, Niels 2005: 'Den lille kristne velfærdsstat. Historie og dilemmaer', Schjørring, Jens H. & Jens T. Bak (eds), *Velfærdsstat og kirke*, Copenhagen.
Kærgård, Niels & Th. Davidsen 1998: 'Harald Westergaard: From Young Pioneer to established Authority', Samuels, Warren J. (ed.), *European Economists of the Early*

20th Century, vol. 1, Northhampton.
Lassen, Frank Beck & Mikkel Thorup 2009: 'Introduktion til Quentin Skinner og intellektuel historie', Lassen, Frank Beck & Mikkel Thorup (eds.), *Quentin Skinner. Politik og historie*, pp. 7-45, Copenhagen.
Løkke, Anne 2002: 'Creating the Social Question: Imagining Society in Statistics and Political Economy in Late Nineteenth-Century Denmark', *Histoire sociale/Social History*, pp. 393-422.
Løkke, Anne 2007: 'Tryghed og risiko – forsikring i Danmark 1850–1950', Feldbæk, Ole et al., *Drømmen om tryghed. Tusind års dansk forsikring*, Copenhagen.
Masterman, N. C. 1963: *John Malcolm Ludlow. The Builder of Christian Socialism*, Cambridge University Press.
Nørgaard, Asbjørn Sonne 2000: 'Party Politics and the Organization of the Danish Welfare State, 1890-1920: The Bourgeois Roots of the Modern Welfare State', *Scandinavian Political Studies*, no. 3, pp. 183-215.
Olesen, Elith 1996: *De frigjorte og trællefolket. Amerikansk indflydelse på dansk kirkeliv omkring år 1900*, Copenhagen.
Petersen, Jørn Henrik 1985: *Den danske alderdomsforsørgelseslovgivnings udvikling I. Oprindelsen*, Odense.
Petersen, Jørn Henrik 2007: *Den danske alderdomsforsørgelseslovgivnings udvikling II 1891–1933 - fra Skøn til ret*, Odense.
Petersen-Studnitz, Aleksis (ed.) 1888: *Forhandlingerne paa Det nordiske Nationaløkonomiske Møde i Kjøbenhavn 1888*, Copenhagen.
Rerup, Lorenz 1963: 'Indledning', Rerup, Lorenz (ed.), *Marcus Rubins Brevveksling I, 1870-1892*, Copenhagen.
Rigsdagstidende, Folketingets Forhandlinger.
Rigsdagstidende, Landstingets Forhandlinger.
Rubin, Marcus & Harald Westergaard 1886: *Landbefolkningens Dødelighed i Fyens Stift. Et Bidrag til en Dødelighedsstatistik*, Copenhagen.
Rubin, Marcus 1888: 'Hvad koster en Alderdomsforsørgelse for de danske Arbejdere?', *Nationaløkonomisk Tidsskrift 1888*, pp. 351-358.
Rubin, Marcus 1889: 'Om Arbejderforsikringen med særligt Hensyn til Alderdomsforsørgelsen', *Beretning om Forhandlingerne i den danske Kjøbstadsforenings 8. Samling i Randers den 10de og 11te Juli*, pp. 88-111, Copenhagen.
Rubin, Marcus 1891: 'Alderdomsforsørgelsesforslaget. Foredrag i Nationaløkonomisk Forening d. 6. Januar 1891', *Nationaløkonomisk Tidsskrift*, pp. 43-53 and pp. 54-72.
Rubin, Marcus 1911: 'Alderdomsunderstøttelsesloven af 1891. Erindringer og Betragtninger', *Nationaløkonomisk Tidsskrift*, pp. 230-259.
Rubin, Marcus 1924: *Nogle Erindringer*, Copenhagen.
Rueschemeyer, Dietrich & Theda Skocpol (eds.) 1996: *States, Social Knowledge, and the Origins of Modern Social Policies*, Princeton, New Jersey.
Rueschemeyer, Dietrich & Ronan van Rossem 1996: 'The Verein für Sozialpolitik and the Fabian Society. A Study in the Sociology of Policy-relevant Knowledge', Rueschemeyer, Dietrich & Theda Skocpol (eds.):*States, Social Knowledge, adn the Origin of Modern Social Policies*, Princeton, New Jersey.
Schørring, Jens H. & Jens T. Bak (eds.) 2005: *Velfærdsstat og kirke*, Copenhagen.
Sørensen, Th. 1890: 'Antydninger til en eventuel Alderdomsforsørgelse', *Nationaløkonomisk Tidsskrift*, pp. 257-274.
Skinner, Quentin 2002: *Visions of Politics. Vol. I: Regarding Method*, Cambridge, U.K. & New York.

Tvermoes, G. F. 1884: 'Lovforslaget om billig Alderdomsforsørgelse. Foredrag i Nationaløkonomisk Forening', *Nationaløkonomisk Tidsskrift*, pp. 1-37.
Wagner, Peter et al. (eds.) 1991: *Social Sciences and Modern States. National Experiences and Theoretical Crossroads*, Cambridge.
Westergaard, Harald 1879: 'Foreningsliv i England', *Nordisk tidskrift för vetenskap, konst och industri*, pp. 617-632.
Westergaard, Harald 1881a: 'Spørgsmaalet om Alderdomsforsørgelse', *Nationaløkonomisk Tidsskrift*, pp. 1-31.
Westergaard, Harald 1881b: 'Hovedresultaterne af den nyere Dødelighedsstatistik', *Nordisk tidskrift för vetenskap, konst och industri*, pp. 521-557 and pp. 587-617.
Westergaard, Harald 1884: 'Dansk Arbejderbank', *Nationaløkonomisk Tidsskrift*, pp. 319-329.
Westergaard, Harald 1885: *Fra Forargelse til Tro. Et Lægmandsvidnesbyrd*, Copenhagen.
Westergaard, Harald 1886: 'Kristendommen og det sociale Spørgsmaal', Clausen, Johan (ed.), *Det kirkelige Møde i Kjøbenhavn, den 25de-27de Maj 1886*, Copenhagen.
Westergaard, Harald 1887: *Direktør, Prof. Harald Westergaards Meddelelser i Bikubens Bestyrelsesmøde den 25de Mai 1887*, Copenhagen.
Westergaard, Harald 1888a: *Drikfældigheden i Danmark og Midlerne derimod, med Henblik paa Forholdene i Norge og Sverige, især Gøteborgsystemet*, Copenhagen.
Westergaard, Harald 1888b: 'P. Knudsen: Sygeforsikring og Alderdomsforsørgelse (review)', *Nationaløkonomisk Tidsskrift*, pp. 293-299.
Westergaard, Harald 1889: 'Kirkelig Fattigpleje', Schrøder, Johannes (ed.), *Det tredje kirkelige Møde, den 21de-23de Maj 1889 i Aarhus*, Copenhagen.
Westergaard, Harald 1899: 'Praktisk Socialisme', *Dansk Tidsskrift*, pp. 12-31.
Westergaard, Harald 1903: 'Kreaturforsikringen i Danmark', *Tidsskrift for Landøkonomi*, pp. 310-364.
Westergaard 1907: *Bikuben. Dansk Spare-, samt Børne- og Alderdomsforsørgelsesforening 1857-1907*, Copenhagen.
Westergaard, Harald 1936: *Bikubens Bidrag til Løsning af Samfundsopgaverne*, Copenhagen.
Wisselgren, Per 2000: *Samhällets kartläggare. Lorénska stiftelsen, den sociala frågan och samhällsvetenskapens formering 1830-1920*, Stockholm.
Wittrock, Björn 1991: 'Social knowledge and public policy: Eight models of interaction', Wagner, Peter et al. (eds.), *Social Sciences and Modern States. National Experiences and Theoretical Crossroads*, Cambridge.
Wittrock, Björn & Peter Wagner 1996: 'Social Science and the Building of the Early Welfare State: Toward a Comparison of Statist and Non-Statist Western Societies', Rueschemeyer, Dietrich & Theda Skocpol (eds.): *States, Social Knowledge and the Origins of Modern Social Policies*, Princeton.
Østergaard, Uffe 2005: 'Lutheranismen og den universelle velfærdsstat', Schjørring, Jens H. & Jens T. Bak (eds.), *Velfærdsstat og kirke*, pp. 147-184, Copenhagen.

The making of Nordic unemployment. Experts and public policy in Denmark and Sweden, 1890–1910

Nils Edling

Introduction

The Danish census on 1 February 1901 introduced a new category to Nordic official statistics: the unemployed. Each and everyone in paid work must in the form name the person or company where he or she was employed and state the nature of that work. Those who lacked work must write 'A' for 'arbejdsløs', i.e. 'unemployed'.[1] According to the census, Denmark had 25,243 men and 2,099 women out of work in industry, commerce and transport, and the figures indicated that shortage of work was an urban problem – about half of all those registered as being out of work lived in Copenhagen, which at that time housed twenty % of the entire population.[2] Modest claims were made in the published report, where the census was described as a first attempt to survey the entire national labour market at a given date. Despite its known weaknesses, the census – said the report – provided a reasonably accurate picture of the situation in different branches and age groups, and the data would also be useful for comparisons with the statistics collected by the unions among their members.[3] The lack of information in the census about the causes and duration of the measured unemployment posed an obvious shortcoming, stated the statisticians and listed three possible causes: sickness, strikes and shortage of work. Unfortunately, no further information was given about the listed causes and it's not known why lockouts were omitted and what the wide and vague 'shortage of work' (*mangel paa arbejde*) could mean. Inadvertently, the census in this way illustrates the difficulties involved in distinguishing the individuals who were out of work from the economically inactive persons – and it clearly shows that the nebulous new concept of unemployment lacked a precise definition.

This problem concerning proper and practical definitions was not in any sense unique to Denmark. Unemployment was a new concept, a product of new categorisations of the dependent population and a new language of social classifications centred upon the relationship between the individual and the labour market.[4] This generalisation holds for both the major economies of Europe and North America and the smaller states of northern Europe, and the intensive international exchange of information helps explain certain similarities in the timing of conceptual changes, debates and reform proposals in different countries.[5]

During the first years of the new century, Norwegian and Danish Commissions, requested by their respective parliaments, prescribed national unemployment policies which were enacted with the laws on public support to union-linked funds in 1906 and 1907, two of the first national insurance programmes in any country. In Norway, the insurance was linked to a national labour exchange act, introduced that same year, and this combination constituted the first comprehensive labour market programme, predating the well-known British reforms from 1909–1911.[6] Neighbouring Sweden, on the other hand, was a latecomer, not introducing unemployment insurance until 1934, seventeen years after the Finnish programme with public labour exchanges, substantial public works and unemployment insurance dating from the decisive autumn of 1917. All four insurance programmes were based on the Ghent system, i.e. a voluntary, publicly supported insurance administered by union-linked funds.[7]

Of course, no single factor can explain the differences between the Nordic countries, and the diverging reform timetables, which complicate any argument about a common Nordic model of social policy, will be left aside here.[8] This paper, limited both topically and chronologically, addresses differences between Denmark and Sweden by studying the crucial role played by statisticians and economists in the making of labour market policies prior to 1914. Denmark and Sweden have been selected as contrasting cases. They adopted different policies, and the proposed argument is that the experts influenced public policies in important and different ways, and that they did so by framing social problems, evaluating reforms introduced abroad and recommending certain solutions. A substantial literature now exists on the role of the knowledge producing experts, and they belong to 'the usual suspects' in explaining the making of modern social policies at the turn of the last century.[9] In Denmark, however, such studies – which shift the focus from social forces and economic interests to knowledge production and experts – are relatively rare, which lends a certain Danish bias to this contribution.[10]

The interplay of the emerging social sciences and modern social policies, which were both institutionalised in the late nineteenth and early twentieth centuries, constitutes an important theme in the literature.[11] The rise of the 'social question', fuelled by the political concerns created by rapid industrial and urban growth – or the fear of such changes in the future – and the demands from growing working-class movements, expanded the market for new social knowledge. Social scientists benefited from this demand for detailed surveys and inquiries into wages, working and living conditions that shaped the content of the 'social question/labour question' and made the need for remedying answers to sustain the social order evident and urgent.[12] In a corresponding way, the interlinked professionalisation of social inquiry worked to their benefit reinforcing the privileged position of the knowledge-bearing groups. The statisticians and economists were certainly not neutral in the sense that they shied away from the political scene all the time, lacked sympathies for one party or the other or were uninterested in strengthening their own positions; however, their influence was not based on party membership but on their recognised expert knowledge.

Stressing the importance of the experts in making of unemployment policies and the novelty of the concept does not mean that all other societal actors necessarily made negligible contributions or that economic conditions can be disregarded. The growth of wage-labour in a capitalist economy provided a structural precondition, and this gradual and uneven process can be summed up in the catch-phrases 'from household to factory' regarding people's livelihood and 'from famine to depression' concerning the causes of economic crisis. In Denmark, the total population in agriculture dropped from about 55 % in 1870 to 36 % forty years later, the Swedish agricultural population decreasing from 72 to 49 %, with industry increasing its share from a meagre 15 to 32 % between 1870 and 1910.[13] During those decades, Stockholm grew from 136,000 to 340,000 inhabitants and Copenhagen almost trebled its population to over 500,000. As noted, contemporaries viewed the shortage of work as an urban problem, one which became a concern when the usual seasonal fluctuations in the labour market were aggravated in bad years. The sharp downturns in the building industry – an expanding business in the rapidly growing capitals – in the 1880s (and then again during the first years of the following decade) had repercussions throughout the entire urban economy. In some cases, local officials introduced temporary relief measures during the winter months – partially a response to demands from workers wanting bread and work, not poor relief.[14] Sometimes protests led to open conflict, as in Stockholm on 1 February 1892, when the short-lived unemployed union, which claimed to have 2,500 members, staged a series of rallies demanding work and clashed with the police on several occasions before the showdown at *Stortorget*, the main square in the old city centre. About 40 persons were arrested, most of them were fined for disturbing the public order and two were sentenced to jail for disobedience and incitement to riot. In the aftermath of this event, the city officials instigated the first public inquiry into the new social problem.[15] Events of this kind took place in Helsinki the following winter, and in a related way, the severe crash in Kristiania in 1899, which ended a decade of an unprecedented boom, provided the social background for the intensified agitation from organised labour for national public works programmes and support for union-run provision schemes.[16]

Labour and unemployment insurance

The established interpretation of the making of the Danish unemployment insurance in 1907 can be labelled 'social democratic' since it focuses on the labour movement. In 2007, sociologist Per Jensen forwarded the claim that all experiences from Denmark and abroad confirm 'that it is the demands and struggles of the labour movement which have initiated the making of the insurance'.[17] That starting point can be easily questioned – a comparison with Nordic neighbours Norway and Finland instead of Jensen's choice of Italy, Great Britain and Sweden would definitely complicate his argument – and it is unclear what 'initiate' actually means. According to historian Søren Kolstrup, the labour movement was the dynamic force behind the reform and it exerted vital indirect pressures which led to the class compromise in 1907.[18] 'Dynamic force' and 'indirect pressures' are also vague terms, but both Jensen and Kolstrup are undoubtedly correct when they point to the efforts of the labour organisations, both unions and party, to shift the responsibility for being out of work from the individual to society and convince the authorities about the gravity of the situation. Clearly, they did so with growing success.

The young Trade Union Confederations (*Landsorganisationen*) in

Denmark, Norway and Sweden tried to piece together information gathered from the unions about their members' employment and these figures, it was said, would once and for all reveal the harsh conditions under which the workers lived at the same time as they 'gave a terrifying impression'.[19] The Swedish Confederation declared that statistics produced by the unions would be 'an effective instrument to pressure state and local authorities to take action' but it failed completely in attracting any interest from the unions, since shortage of work was not a major issue according to them. In Denmark, the large and well-organised Confederation managed to involve the unions in the collecting and reporting of unemployment data and it used the gradually more comprehensive statistics in the political campaigns for public support. These were intensified in the winter 1901–02, and clearly contributed to making both the public and the decision-makers aware of the issue.[20] Many unions set up benefit funds: in 1904 there were 80 funds with a total of 50,000 members, or about half of all unionised workers, and these union-linked funds would provide the institutional foundation for the reasonably successful Danish unemployment insurance programme. As Jensen notes, the support from the unions was a key factor behind this success.

Both Jensen and Kolstrup rightly underline the significance of the extended suffrage; Denmark had general male suffrage, which opened for partisan competition for the workers' vote and politicisation of issues relating to the working population's living conditions.[21] The substantially more elitist Swedish *Riksdag* of the early 20th century – 'one of the most reactionary of European parliaments, surpassed only by the Prussian Landtag' – still had influential conservative groups who successfully opposed expensive social policy experiments in general and reforms that might be disadvantageous to the rural population in particular.[22] Great importance had the pivotal changes in Denmark in 1899, when the general agreement between employers and unions established a system for centralised collective bargaining together with guarantees for the employers' managerial control and both parties' right to organise, and in 1901 when parliamentary democracy finally triumphed and the Liberals (*Venstre*) came to power. This reshuffled the political scene in a fundamental way; the old liberal opposition, supported by the Social Democrats, was finally in government.[23] These are non-controversial positions, but the two studies are one-sided in their focus on the labour movement. Jensen tends to interpret all demands made by the Social Democrats, who from the start favoured direct financial support to the organised workers and their benefit funds and public works programmes, as support for the insurance, which was finally introduced in 1907. Such an argument overemphasises the direct continuity in the labour movement's activities from the 1880s to the reform of 1907. Kolstrup notes that the early bills forwarded by the labour MPs – still very few in number –were rejected by the other parties until in 1901 they gave up their resistance when confronted by labour's successful campaign for the insurance. In this way, he clearly reduces the contributions made by other actors besides the Social Democrats and wrongly claims that no one outside the labour movement took an interest in unemployment before 1901.[24] We have to remember that the Social Democrats, although growing rapidly, were still very much junior partners in national politics. In 1901, they had an impressive fourteen representatives in the Danish *Folketinget* (out of 114) – a high share compared to Norway's *Stortinget* with a single MP in 1901 (out of 114, four more from 1903) and a meagre four MPs in the Swedish *Riksdag's* lower house (out of 230 after the elections in 1901 – nine more were elected in 1905).

By focusing on the labour movement, both Jensen and Kolstrup completely exclude the statisticians and economists, the intellectuals who for several years had been interested in that new problem of unemployment and more generally in charting and interpreting societal conditions. The unemployment insurance was imported, introduced and promoted by them and in this way the social scientists took a very active part in setting the agenda for reform.

Paving the way for the Danish unemployment insurance

Danish social economists – to use the apt Danish word for scholars who combined political economy and statistics with an interest in social policy – had a forum of their own, the Economics Association (*Nationaløkonomisk Forening*), founded in 1872, devoted to all kinds of domestic and foreign economic and social topics. It was in the association's journal *Nationaløkonomisk Tidsskrift* that professor Harald Westergaard (1853–1936) in 1894 published his 'On Measures against Unemployment' ('Om Forholdsregler mod Arbejdsløshed'), a survey of the newest policies introduced at the local level in Swiss and English towns and a discussion of the many difficulties involved in defining this novel concept.[25] Westergaard, an internationally renowned scholar, held the chair in economics and statistics at the university in Copenhagen and was Denmark's leading social scientist.[26] His expertise in social policy matters received wide recognition, especially after the introduction of the old age insurance in 1891, where Westergaard's surveys provided the theoretical foundation for the reform. A dedicated and active Christian throughout his life, he had an avid interest in self-help and took active part in different initiatives such as the philanthropic savings association The Beehive (*Bikuben*) which he led for several decades. Self-help as principle and practice and a Christian social conscience constituted central features in the ideological make-up of this influential social conservative university professor (cf. Lars Andersen's contribution).

Westergaard's article from 1894 was his first – but not his last – on unemployment, and other economists shared this interest in the growing discussion abroad.[27] The problems in defining unemployment proper and separating those fit for work from the work-shy and unemployable was Westergaard's starting point, and he devoted his article from 1894 to the many weaknesses he found in the new foreign reform experiments. Highly critical of all compulsory insurance schemes, he simultaneously openly recognised the potential gravity of the problem. Unemployment was, he declared, without a doubt a dangerous social evil: 'Shortage of work has become the plague of society in our age, insidiously sneaking around and threatening to burst out in Sudden Violence. Workers and employers live in constant fear of it.'[28] He repeated this dictum several times: unemployment was 'an Achilles' heel of modern industrial society', 'an ominous cloud hanging over society' and 'a pestilence of contemporary economic life'. Reforms were absolutely necessary to heal the deep wounds and protect the worker who was willing and able to work from the great perils of unemployment. Westergaard held on to this position from 1890s onwards.

Professor Westergaard was cautious and he paid great attention to the many deficiencies in the new policies introduced in Berne, St Gall, Basle, Cologne and elsewhere, whilst also lauding their efforts to find a working solution. During the 1890s, he continuously surveyed foreign developments with the aim of finding an effective and ideologically acceptable solution. The new policy tried out in Ghent in the first years of the new century relied on self-help and limited public contributions, resembling the voluntary Danish sickness insurance with its state-supported self-help funds. According to Westergaard, the union benefit funds were in a position to fulfil a task similar to the sickness funds in the fight against unemployment: they could keep a close eye on work-shy members and it was in their own best interest to help the unemployed find a new job as soon as possible. As they were firmly based on self-help, such funds could count on public sympathy and hopefully recognition of the fact that the unions stood for more than struggles with the employer – in between the conflicts, both parties were actually able to loyally cooperate, Westergaard stressed, in order to show how the unions might be suited to carrying out an insurance reform and handle the daily administrative chores.[29]

Not all economists shared Westergaard's conviction about the urgent need to find remedies to the problem of unemployment. In his review in *Nationaløkonomisk Tidsskrift*, the editor Aleksis Studnitz-Petersen (1846–1935), who opposed far-reaching public regulation of social matters, denied the gravity of the problem and criticised Westergaard for inadvertently accepting some of the tenets forwarded by socialist theorists.[30] For him, unemployment was a relatively simple problem of imbalance between supply and demand which was best solved by the self-regulatory powers of the economy itself. All the same, Studnitz-Petersen showed interest in the problem and contributed to the ongoing review of the different reform proposals forwarded in the international literature, such as the scheme for compulsory individual saving accounts for workers instead of insurance – a German idea which received some attention in Denmark.[31] The establishment of publicly organised, free labour exchanges – labour registries – was another novel idea in the discourse on unemployment, an import from Germany in the mid-1890s. But municipal placement activities never gained the status of being the most important reform required to alleviate shortage of work. Westergaard, for one, was happy with the expanding placement activities, but they did not in any way make the insurance unnecessary.[32] This separates Denmark from its Nordic neighbours, where labour exchanges received a lot of public attention.

Despite the abundance of practical problems – such as the inclusion of seasonal workers into the insurance – and for want of a better solution, Westergaard gave his open support to the voluntary insurance. He did this at a meeting of the Economics Association in January 1903, his proposal gaining support from fellow statisticians Theodor Sørensen (1839–1914), national inspector of the sickness insurance, and Marcus Rubin (1854–1923), former head of the National Bureau of Statistics and newly appointed chief of the national tax administration.[33] Westergaard, Sørensen and Rubin, without a doubt the leading experts in social statistics and social policy in Denmark, all came out in favour of the voluntary insurance at a time when the problem of shortage of work was receiving quite a lot of public attention. As noted above, the Social Democrats had intensified their winter campaigns for unemployment provision from 1900–01 onwards and they had introduced private bills in *Folketinget* requesting direct financial support for the union-run benefit funds and large investments in counter-cyclical public work programmes. These proposals, which dealt more with financial support to the unions than insurance, were turned down each year but they nevertheless helped push the issue forward, and the question of how to provide for those out of work gained political momentum year by year. In 1902–03, both Conservatives and Social Democrats in *Folketinget* spoke out for a reform and the parliamentary Unemployment Commission was appointed in March 1903, a direct result of a private bill presented by a Conservative MP.[34] This proposal followed the formula laid out by Westergaard: a voluntary insurance based on the principles of self-help, mutual control and limited public support to neutral, i.e. union-independent, benefit funds with full financial responsibility and controlled by a new state inspectorate. With relatively few and minor modifications, this proposal four years later became the national unemployment insurance, a law which was passed by a unanimous parliament in April 1907.

The close resemblance between Westergaard's insurance design, worked out in his different essays and reviews 1894–1903, and the final reform of 1907 is by no means a coincidence. As leading experts, Professor Westergaard and Doctor Sørensen were members of the Commission 1903–06 and in a position to set their mark upon the report and its proposals – and they had in fact already been involved in designing the private bill which set the political process in motion in 1903.[35] On 1 April 1903, Westergaard, who rarely made public political statements, gave full support to the bill's proposal in the leading newspaper *Berlingske Tidende*, openly stating that it had been drawn up in cooperation and close connection with the principles laid out and discussed at the Economics Association's meeting in January that same year.[36] The parliamentary commission had already been established, but Westergaard even so went ahead and made his statement because of the vital importance of the reform. The link between expertise and party politics is here directly visible: a leading social policy intellectual and proponent of unemployment insurance took an active part in designing a reform proposal which closely followed the principles he himself had laid out during the preceding decade. In this very concrete way, Westergaard and the other social economists paved the way for the unemployment insurance. Their different contributions regarding unemployment, its character and remedies established *arbejdsløshed* as a legitimate, yet nebulous, concept in political discourse and as category for public policy. They designed the unemployment insurance and their endorsement made the reform acceptable to the established parties and politicians.

The experts were connected to the transnational networks of social reform via their journals, associations and congresses, and the insurance – the Ghent-model – was imported and adjusted to fit the national political and institutional setting.[37] They were instrumental in this process of learning from foreign examples and the shaping of policy innovations for domestic use. As Hugh Heclo puts it: 'The unemployment insurance being talked about by internationally aware reformers reverberated in political discussions and gradually appeared to be a 'natural' alternative for any reform-minded party.'[38] Heclo's description of the situation in Sweden in the early 1910s, where the idea of a voluntary insurance was starting to gain acceptance, applies even better to Denmark ten years earlier.

The experts' important contribution to the making of social policies had another facet: the growing production of statistical enquiries and investigations. All economists shared this interest in statistics. Westergaard, Sørensen and Rubin were all statisticians and produced scholarly important and politically influential social surveys, and even Studnitz-Petersen, generally and inadequately labelled a diehard 'liberal of the Manchester school', was a fervent advocate of developed, publicly organised labour statistics. At the Nordic political economy meeting in Copenhagen in 1888, he stated that labour statistics gained special value in the age of social policy simply because decisions about policies and reforms had to be based on substantial empirical knowledge. Reliable statistics of that kind were lacking.[39] A few years later, a colleague, like so many Danes working in the field highly critical of the inadequate leadership in the current organisation, declared that official statistics constituted a still underrated administrative instrument; they should be used by administrative and legislative organs, 'like the probe in the doctor's hand, to make the shortcomings in societal functions evident, and then later, to observe the effects of the introduced rectifying measures.'[40] In short, states needed statistics and trained experts to collect and interpret the data and this gave them a key role: the experts discovered and quantified social evils and evaluated the public policies. When the bureau was reorganised in 1895–96 under the leadership of Marcus Rubin, the collection of social statistics became a primary task, including surveys of living conditions for different classes, their incomes and consumption, and above all data on the workers' conditions including wages, savings and insurance.[41]

The new tasks, clearly in line with the recent recommendations for the advancement of labour statistics forwarded by the International Statistical Institute in The Hague, supplemented the existing moral and occupational statistics, and the question of unemployment included in the census 1901 should be seen in the light of this quest to combine occupational data with social classifications in order to make the proper detailed grouping of the entire population.[42] Albeit there are its preliminary results, it is obvious that the census established a new category in social statistics at a national level. This made the census important: unemployment was a national problem. Of course, the scholarly discussion among the economists on unemployment, supplemented by the Social Democrats' agitation and the new proposals in the parliament, provided the background for this interest in statistical data. The official statistics reinforced these interests in the manner described by Rueschemeyer & Skocpol: 'Official statistical capacities afforded technical support for certain kinds of legislation and administration, and they also helped to make extra-state actors comfortable with the idea that government should actively address social problems.'[43]

The social economists also supplied the educated public – and their students – with general surveys, and this growing body of work is important since it interpreted social changes and made accurate, i.e. conforming to the academic standards of the times, descriptions of Denmark, its geography, population, industries, public arrangements, and so on. The monumental *Danmarks Statistik* in five volumes 1878–91 was followed by the abridged statistical description in 1898 by Westergaard and Michael Koefoed (1867–1940), number two at the National Bureau of Statistics, the *Statistiske Departments*, and the last major description in the 650-page-long *Haandbog i Danmarks statistik* (1909–1913), the first one to include a chapter on unemployment, by social economist Jens Warming (1873–1939) at the Bureau of Statistics.[44] These general descriptions were supplemented by a number of studies on the performance of the Danish economy since the 1860s and the effects of the recurring downturns published in 1903–04. These studies did not deal directly with unemployment but they tried to describe and analyse the ups and downs of the economy and in that way indirectly shifted the focus from individual actions to overall economic performance. The Social Democrats already argued along these lines, but their argument was political and interest-based whereas the studies provided a scholarly analysis of production, trade and finances. The general point is that they provided new knowledge about the workings of the national economy and opened up for a better understanding of structural changes and problems at a time when shortage of work and its remedies were subjects of intensified public concern.[45]

The primacy of labour exchanges in Sweden

As Hugh Heclo made clear in the 1970s, the experts' policy preferences affect the design of reforms and policies; state administrators 'provided the most constant analysis and review underlying most courses of government action'.[46] The Swedish case illustrates this well. Sweden and Denmark were of course different in a great many respects: Sweden was less democratised and more rural – important aspects of Swedish industrialisation had a distinctively rural character and Stockholm's position in the national economy was not as dominant as that of Copenhagen in the Danish economy. These structural preconditions, which included high levels of emigration and economic growth, made shortage of work a relatively minor macro-economic problem and it was regarded as a local issue best handled at that level. The first investigation into unemployment was undertaken by the officials in Stockholm 1894–95 in order to evaluate the relief work programmes of the preceding years, introduced as a response to the demands from local unions. Although the commission recognised shortage of work as a social problem, it turned down all proposals for new policies – poor relief, self-help and private placement agencies were best suited to solve the problem.[47] A similar lack of interest surfaced a few years later in the unions' replies to the Trade Union Confederation's efforts to organise a concerted campaign for the introduction of public unemployment relief at the national level.⁴⁸

Furthermore, Denmark was far more advanced in the field of social policy following the introduction of a new old age insurance and a revised poor law (1891), a successful sickness insurance (1892) and legislation on industrial accidents (1898). The *Riksdag* had passed laws on sickness insurance in 1891 and on industrial accidents ten years later, but both reforms were limited and regarded as inadequate by contemporaries. As Norwegian political scientist Rune Ervik noted in a comparative study on nascent unemployment policies, the context of poor relief and poor law reform played a central part in the Swedish discussions on unemployment whereas the Norwegian discussion – and the Danish – centred on the insurance.⁴⁹ Sweden was more 'backward' and poor law reform remained a central concern for the social reformers who gathered in the new Central Association for Social Work, founded in 1903 (*Centralförbundet för Socialt Arbete*). Undoubtedly, the priorities and preferences of these knowledge-bearing specialists and activists, many of them with close ties to the Liberal party, had lasting effects and the same holds for the ways in which the economists framed the problems of the labour market.

Prominent and later world-famous Swedish economists Knut Wicksell (1851–1926) – in political matters regarded as a dangerous radical – and Gustav Cassel (1861–1945) – for decades a prolific contributor on economic issues to the leading newspaper *Svenska Dagbladet* – took an interest in unemployment and the challenging problem of definitions. They were certainly Westergaard's juniors with regard to academic position and political clout; both became full professors in 1904 at *Lunds universitet* and *Stockholms högskola* respectively and they lacked experience in designing successful social reforms. And their interest in unemployment was of a cursory nature compared to Westergaard's lifelong commitment to social reform. Wicksell's lecture on unemployment from 1901 was never published during his lifetime, whereas Cassel's lectures of the following year were published in his *Socialpolitik*, a book which saw three editions 1902–22, and this of course makes him far more important.⁵⁰ The book was above all a critique of classical liberalism and an effort to distinguish social policy from socialism – the two were still often confounded in Swedish public discourse. Like Westergaard, Cassel had a fundamentally positive view of unions and their self-help activities, at the same time as he devoted quite a lot of energy to a critical evaluation of socialist economic doctrines and policies. '[F]ashioning a purposeful and consistent social policy in place of a fumbling philanthropy guided by sentimentality or a cold and blind faith in the dead phrase known as free competition', he in 1903 summarised his general view on the task of social policy.⁵¹ Such a policy was above all an instrument for progress, i.e. economic growth and efficient deployment of resources.

Cassel was no proponent of unemployment insurance, at least not of any publicly organised and subsidised system. According to him, insurance could meaningfully be applied only to a certain type of unemployment, the shortage of work due to unforeseen changes in the economy, and never to seasonal or cyclical unemployment:

> It seems that an insurance against normal or regularly occurring unemployment is rather unnecessary, if not useless. People *insure* against events that are *uncertain* to happen, whereas they *prepare* themselves for events that they *know* to happen. Normal unemployment in seasonal professions is not a *risk* that needs to be spread across many people to compensate for the damage that a few of them suffer... The right kind of insurance against regularly occurring unemployment is a [mutual] savings and loan association.⁵²

Seasonal shortages, the dominating form of joblessness in Sweden, were not involuntary unemployment proper and therefore non-insurable. Westergaard and Cassel reached completely different conclusions; the former focused on the social problem and its injurious effects on the individual and the social fabric, whereas the latter concentrated on the performance of the labour market and the conditions for economic growth. Interested mainly in questions concerning wage structures, union policies and the effects of different regulatory measures, Cassel gave few and vague policy recommendations, leaving the insurance to the unions and forwarding counter-cyclical public work programmes supplemented by better vocational training of apprentices as the best public policies against unemployment. Ten years later, he came out hard against such artificial job-creation by the state in order to combat economic downturns, a position he would defend for the rest of his life.⁵³

Cassel's short book on social policy, dating from the same year as the new journal *Social Tidskrift* devoted to all social topics, was 'extremely influential' and as Heclo also notes, his work on trade cycles broadened the general understanding of the workings of the economy.⁵⁴ Of course, Cassel was not alone and other Swedish economists and statisticians produced textbooks and surveys, and similarly a number of detailed empirical studies on social issues, many of them founded by the Lorén foundation, were also published.⁵⁵ These publications, with their many differences in style and content, help to make the social question more known to the general public in ways similar to the above-mentioned Danish studies, but they did not change dominant conceptions concerning the labour market. Other leading economists shared Cassel's macro-economic perspective, which was also generally accepted among the political parties and which laid the theoretical foundations for Swedish labour market policy up to the 1930s.⁵⁶ It provided the underpinnings for the relief work programme, where the wages were set far below union rates to test the willingness to work among the unemployed applying for assistance, which constituted the salient characteristic of Swedish unemployment policies from the 1910s to the 1930s. During the first decade of the century, another new feature was at the centre of attention: the optimised organisation of labour markets through public placement. Cassel had not touched directly upon the importance of labour exchanges as an instrument to handle shortages of work, but he was one of the academic fathers of the new men in charge of designing and coordinating these policies at a national level. The new experts at the Department of Labour Statistics at the Board of Trade (*Kommerskollegii Afdelning för Arbetsstatistik*), established in 1902–03, would remain at the centre of Swedish social policy for many years. Head of department was Henning Elmquist (1871–1933), who completed his doctoral dissertation in statistics on the workers in the tobacco industry in 1899, and next to him worked his friend from the years at Uppsala University, Gunnar Huss (1871–1939), with a Ph D in economic statistics from 1902. Both of them would have long and distinguished careers right at the centre of Swedish social administration.⁵⁷ As civil servants their formal position was different from that of the university professors – they were the experts within the state bureaucracy and in charge of the continuous monitoring of the labour market. As Heclo has shown, that position did not diminish their influence, and the specialists in the new department actually defined themselves as an association for social reform and promoters of social peace. They were highly active within the reform networks linked to the Central Association for Social Work.⁵⁸

Collecting, arranging and publishing of all kinds of labour statistics – on occupations, wages, yearly incomes, food and lodging, accidents, conflicts etc – were of course the main tasks of the new department. Investigations into unemployment were not a top priority, but the Department was instructed to collect data from the growing number of local labour exchanges, run by the municipalities, in order to create an objective picture of balance between supply and demand of work over time; the labour exchanges reported their monthly figures to the department in the capital who published them quarterly (bi-monthly from 1908).[59] As already noted, objective quantified knowledge about the society was in high demand and the principles guiding the reorganisation of Sweden's labour statistics were certainly not uniquely Swedish. Nor was the great interest in labour exchanges as the premium tool stopped by national borders.

In Sweden, this interest derived from many sources, among them the question of emigration, a topic which in the early 20th century was about to receive status as a national problem elevated above partisan politics and the well-known opposition to far-reaching social policies among important groups in the *Riksdag*. Emigration caused shortage of manpower; there were hardly any skilled workers to be found in engineering and agriculture lacked labourers, ran the complaints. The fear of continuing emigration, causing further shortages, made the situation even graver and called for economic modernisation. One may question the gravity of these complaints, but the emigration was nevertheless perceived as a national problem of great magnitude.[60]

Labour exchanges, clearly in line with economic doctrines stressing market efficiency, were seemingly uncontroversial; they were mainly a technical issue and the offices were established and financed by the municipalities. Apart from the low costs and low levels of controversy, the free impartial exchange was an imported social policy innovation – Made in Germany – that met the highest standards of the day, an innovation much needed to make hiring procedures modern, efficient and rational. [61] This would, it was argued, minimise unemployment and through the cooperation of local and regional exchanges improve the organisation of the national labour market. Consequently, the promotion of labour exchanges became an integral part of the leading labour statisticians' work and both Elmquist and Huss published articles about the new developments abroad and the principal issues involved.[62]

The priority given the labour exchanges became even more evident when Huss in August 1907 published his report on unemployment insurance, a survey of different programmes adopted abroad of the kind that Westergaard and the Danish Unemployment Commission had published in the preceding years. Huss discerned seven types of unemployment, each with its special causes and remedies, singling out labour exchanges as without a doubt the most important remedy, with an effective and encompassing system of exchanges needed to provide the base for all other measures, such as relief work programmes and maybe even an insurance reform. The exchange had another vital task: to control if those who called themselves unemployed really were to be regarded as such.[63] Controlling and testing the applicants, responsibilities that the Danish system transferred to the benefit funds, remained official tasks in the same way as within the poor relief system. Huss, who included the recent Norwegian and Danish insurance reforms in his survey, did not speak out in favour of the insurance at this time. The practical argument said that it was too early to make any judgements on the performance of the reforms and the principle arguments warned against the favours that a voluntary publicly subsidised insurance administered by union-linked funds would offer organised labour – and above all against the voluntary insurance's inability to protect the weakest groups in the labour market. For Huss, the conclusion, based on principle and practical considerations, was evident: a centralised organisation of public labour exchanges must precede any publicly organised or financed insurance. The free and neutral labour exchanges could be used to discriminate between deserving and undeserving job-seekers and they must be used to collect reliable data about the labour market.[64]

As the economic situation worsened in 1908, the interest in unemployment insurance began to increase somewhat. The *Riksdag* 1908–10 turned down the first private bills which requested a commission on unemployment insurance at the same time as the labour statisticians conducted yearly censuses of the unemployed and published special reports.[65] These inquiries, set up in accordance with standards developed in similar investigations abroad, established unemployment as a category at the national level by providing aggregated data and detailed investigations into the different characteristics of the unemployed (branches, duration, age groups, marital status etc). The statisticians proceeded in the established way in order to first measure the extent and gravity of the problem before they made any concrete policy recommendations. Consequently, their reports focused on the performance of the labour market in general and had little to say about positive counter-measures. This silence was probably motivated by the increasing public interest, which made unemployment insurance politically controversial and not a proper topic for administrators, and by statistician's daily preoccupation with the technical side of the censuses.[66] Relief work programmes introduced by the municipalities and the state made up the important measures in the years 1908–1910.

In 1911, the Swedish Liberals (*Liberala Samlingspartiet*), including unemployment insurance in their election platform, won the first election with general male suffrage and entered government. Immediately, the young labour statistician and Social Democrat Otto Järte (1881–1961) at the Board of Trade was appointed to draft the new policy, using the new knowledge produced by the recent statistical investigations and drawing on foreign experiences, and in January 1914, the minister in charge signalled that a bill proposing a voluntary insurance with limited public contributions would soon be presented. Nothing happened. Instead, the lengthy and heated conflicts over defence spending and parliamentary power forced the Liberals out of office that same spring. A conservative, non-partisan bureaucratic government replaced them, and then the war came and all reform plans were shelved. 'For the moment ... the impetus behind Sweden's first efforts at unemployment insurance had been lost', Heclo sums up.[67] In 1914, Sweden had no unemployment insurance but about one hundred public labour exchanges, run by municipalities, county councils and agricultural societies, supervised by the labour statisticians.

The importance of experts and the making of social policies

The limited contrastive Danish-Swedish comparison highlights numerous dissimilarities and produces an even longer list of possible explanations. The national contexts were different so it is futile to search for a single factor which can explain the diverging national labour market policies. In opposition to one-sided labourite interpretations, my argument holds that neither the smooth introduction of the Danish unemployment insurance nor the primacy of labour exchanges in Sweden can be satisfactorily explained by the position and actions of the Social Democrats. On the contrary, they were largely due to the work done by the social economists, the knowledge-bearing experts who prepared the ground and imported the blueprint for reforms. This is especially true of Denmark, where the work of Professor Westergaard from the mid-1890s onwards was a decisive factor in domesticating the insurance and making it the natural and acceptable alternative. Admittedly, the labour movement's campaigns for state-organised provision of the unemployed surely increased public support, but the Social Democrats were still on the outside, whereas academics and bureaucrats were on the inside. They possessed the highly valued expertise in social policy and they belonged to the established society, and this gave them a privileged position and meant that their views, reports and recommendations had political significance of the highest order. By giving the voluntary insurance their blessing and laying out the principles for a ideologically and financially sound reform, Professor Westergaard and the other leading social policy experts helped make the insurance more attractive or at least more acceptable to those who found labour's demands dangerous.

The voluntary unemployment insurance introduced 1907 did not correspond to the demands made by the Social Democrats during the preceding years. It was a compromise based on the principles of self-help, limited public subsidies and state supervision. The workers themselves were to bear the main burden; their own contributions were to fund the insurance, so it would be in their own best interests to closely scrutinise all applicants. All daily administration was to be handled by the benefit funds and these had to be kept, at least formally, completely separated from the unions. These key features, included in the experts' plans, made the unemployment act easier to swallow for the non-socialist majority. The subsequent positive effects on the strength of the Social Democrats through the established custom of double membership in union and union-linked unemployment fund were consequences, foreseen by some contemporaries and surprising to others, and they cannot explain the introduction of the insurance.

In Denmark, the problem of unemployment was framed as a question of insurance, a problem to be solved by modern social policies. In Sweden, labour exchanges made up the standard answer and shortage of work was best handled by making the labour market modern and efficient. Unemployment insurance was an available alternative, but Swedish labour market specialists opted for labour registries and public placement. Many different explanations can be found for these diverging first conceptualisations of the problem. Sweden's pre-democratic character narrowed the possibilities for broader political compromises and its lack of major social insurance reforms made the prospects of the unemployment insurance pretty bleak. Conversely, the relatively developed landscape of Danish social reform had two important effects: the knowledge-bearing social policy experts had demonstrated their expertise through their work with older reforms and the idea of encompassing social reforms was not alien to the established elites. For want of anything better, this can be labelled a discursive path-dependence.[68]

The Swedish experts at the Department of Labour focused on the promotion of public labour exchanges, the neutral service that both employers and workers held in the highest regard. Labour exchanges gained support in all camps and Sweden was far ahead of most countries in this area, Gunnar Huss claimed in 1908.[69] A state-subsidised insurance could be financially risky and unfair since it serviced the better-off workers and was consequently ill-equipped to do what the labour exchanges already did, i.e. balance the changes in supply and demand of labour. Publicly organised insurance might even be unnecessary, as Gustav Cassel argued, providing a theoretical foundation for the efficiency-oriented perspective. The statisticians, who never absolutely rejected an insurance reform per se, added that exchanges were needed in order to monitor the labour market, provide accurate data about its current state and discriminate between the real unemployed and the undeserving. By stressing the importance of labour statistics and labour exchanges as the foundation for further reforms Sweden provides almost a textbook example of early unemployment policies. Norway's and Denmark's early start in 1906 and 1907 rather have the nature of exceptions.

The argument forwarded here challenges hardcore social democratic interpretations of the origins of modern social policies where 'the welfare state is a product of labour organization and political rule by labour parties', but it is compatible with later studies in that tradition, such as Walter Korpi´s underlining of the significance of the state elites' strategic action introducing reforms in order to foster social peace.[70] The new experts belonged to the elite and it would be possible to see the insurance reform of 1907 as a result of a coalition between the elite, which then has to include social scientists, state bureaucrats, non-socialist politicians and social reformers, and non-elite political forces such as the labour movement. In the Scandinavian countries in 1890–1914, the latter was of course the junior partner and the key non-elite force consisted of the farmers, it must be added.[71] Comparative studies yield little support for the argument that the size of organised labour or the actual level of unemployment had the final word when *Folketinget* opted for the insurance and *Riksdagen* turned down similar proposals. Clearly, the Danish bad winters in the first years of the new century influenced the public debate and the pressure from organised labour made an impact. Whether sympathy or rejection dominated the reactions of non-socialist decision makers to the demonstrations and petitions is harder to find out, and it also possible to blur the picture further through a comparison of Sweden and Finland, two countries where the economy performed well, with the Finnish social policy elite opting for both labour exchanges and unemployment insurance. The Finnish reforms, introduced by a modernising elite and hardly brought about by the pressure from a weak labour movement, were of a preventive kind, and none of the Nordic cases shows a simple connection between high unemployment levels and insurance reforms although they support the conclusion that bad times heightened an interest in reforms.[72]

In my view, studies focusing on class coalitions and pressure from non-elite groups have a hard time accommodating this active and modernising nature of the early social policies promoted by experts and bureaucrats.[73] Instead, they tend to stress the reactive character and pacifying motives of social reform and leave ample room to social forces at the expense of actors and discourses. Reform proposals and decisions were not only answers brought about by social changes but products of the continuous processes of puzzling and political learning conducted by different policy makers, as Hugh Heclo made clear in his seminal work. Political learning within the country and from abroad, the transfer of concepts, problems and policies, played an equally important part in Denmark and Sweden. The major policies were imported and modified to suit the domestic settings and demands and the knowledge-bearing groups were instrumental in this process. These processes were of course highly complex, but it is evident that the knowledge-bearing groups, interconnected in different national and transnational networks, played a central role.[74] The swift introduction of Belgian unemployment insurance and German *Arbeitsnachweis* in Denmark and Sweden demonstrates the importance of transfer and the transnational character of social reform.

Statistics, public placement and insurance defined unemployment. Unemployment is an institutionally constructed category, a social fact created through a process of conventionalisation where certain forms of joblessness are included, others excluded. Like other statistical entities it is simultaneously real and constructed, discovered and invented.[75] When the Danish union measured a shortage of work among their members, they used a simple questionnaire without any definition of what being unemployed might mean. The official census in 1901 tried to provide more details and the report took different causes into account when trying to separate between different forms of joblessness due to sickness, conflicts and bad times, and the insurance act of 1907 included further regulations which delimited unemployment proper. A year later, Swedish statistician Huss found seven different types of unemployment ranging from shortage of work unemployment caused by inadequate knowledge about available jobs via recurring seasonal unemployment and those unemployed due to disability and illness to the substratum of those 'unemployable' due to degeneration, drinking and indolence. Similar classifications are easily found – Westergaard and Cassel were both preoccupied with the demarcation of involuntary unemployment from other forms of joblessness and statisticians and reformers all over the world shared this preoccupation.[76] The classifications and categorisations, developed by the experts and established through the insurance and labour exchanges, constitute a vital contribution as they gave the concept of unemployment a clearer definition. They were neither arbitrary nor directly given by economic conditions. Changing economic and social conditions in the industrialising societies were certainly important, but they only provide parts of the story and the making of unemployment, a protracted and contentious process, depended just as much on new categorisations and new forms of regulation designed by the knowledge-bearing elite.

Notes

1 Like German, the Scandinavian languages nowadays have one term, arbetslöshet (Swedish)/arbejdsløshed (Danish)/arbeidsledighet (Norwegian), to cover loss of work and employment.
2 Denmark had a population of 2.45 million in 1901. The questionnaire on unemployment in the census excluded agriculture.
3 *Folketællingen i Kongeriget Danmark den 1. Februar 1901*, 1904, pt. 2, pp. 77–83, Co-

penhagen. For the different ways in which the German and French censuses of 1895 and 1896 defined shortage of work, Bénédicte Zimmermann, 2000B; Christian Topalov, 1994, ch. 12.
4   Alexander Keyssar, 1986; William Walters, 2000, ch. 1–3; Bénédicte Zimmermann, 2000, introduction, ch. 1–3.
5   See e.g. Christian Topalov, 1994, ch. 3–4; Madeleine Herren, 1993; Nils Edling, 2008, pp. 23–40.
6   Although the Norwegian insurance had a difficult start, these reforms make the claim that 'the United Kingdom was the first nation to adopt a national unemployment policy' highly disputable, Michael Hanagan, 1997, p. 450.
7   A voluntary insurance based on the Ghent system was introduced in Iceland in 1955. For different reasons, the Finnish unemployment insurance programme of 1917 had a difficult start and saw limited growth.
8   The timing of reforms is discussed in Nils Edling, 2006, pp. 101–108.
9   See e.g. Hugh Heclo, 1974; Dietrich Rueschemeyer & Theda Skocpol, 1996; Sven E. (Olsson) Hort, 1992, ch. 1; Rune Ervik & Stein Kuhnle, 1993.
10 See, for example, the works of Iver Hornemann Møller, 1981 and Søren Kolstrup, 1996; where different socio-economic and class-based analyses prevail. Of the two, Kolstrup has definitely produced the more interesting, theoretically nuanced and empirically substantial studies.
11 E.g. Björn Wittrock & Peter Wagner, 1996, pp. 93–104.
12 Björn Wittrock, Peter Wagner & Hellmut Wollmann, 1991, pp. 28–38.
13 Data from Christiansen & et al. 2006, appendix.
14 For Denmark, Georg Nørregaard, 1977, pp. 342–351; for Sweden, Nils Edling, 2002, pp. 308–312.
15 Fred Nilsson, 1970, pp. 170–184.
16 Knut Kjeldstadli, 1990, pp. 32–33, and p. 207 Anne-Lise Seip, 1994, pp.131–137. The capital's name was officially changed from Christiania to Kristiania in 1898, and in 1925 it was renamed Oslo.
17 In Danish: 'At det er arbejderbevægelsens krav og kampe, der har initieret en forsikringsdannelse', Per H. Jensen, 2007, p. 34.
18 Søren Kolstrup, 1995, pp. 14–21; p. 52; p. 135.
19 *Beretning om Arbeidernes faglige landsorganisations virksomhed fra 1ste juli 1905 til 1ste januar 1906*, 1906, pp. 14–15. See Nils Edling, 2005, pp. 117–139.
20 Nils Edling, 2005, pp. 124–126; Bent Jensen, 2006, pp 221–225.
21 Bent Jensen, 2006, pp. 182–192; Jens Toftgaard, 2008, pp. 59–96.
    In 1900, roughly 85% of all male Danes over 30 held the right to vote and Norway had universal male suffrage since 1898 (for those over 25 years of age). Several restrictions excluded poor relief recipients, servants and all those with outstanding taxes, and in practice they reduced the number of voters. Nevertheless, Swedish figures were still considerably lower: three out of four men over the age of 21 lacked voting rights in 1900.
22 Quote Berndt Schiller, 1975, p. 199; Nils Edling, 2006, p. 102.
23 Søren Kolstrup, 1995, pp. 16–18.
24 Characteristic is his dating of the other parties' interest in the insurance. He acknowledges the early initiatives made by individual politicians, but Kolstrup, 'A-kasselovgivningen', p. 21, note 21, dates the Conservatives' first 'pronounced social policy statement' to November 1907, six months after *Folketinget* passed the unemployment insurance. It is however clear from their manifesto, *Højres*

manifest, and the party programme *Højres program*, both dated and printed April 1905, and from the secret election handbook from 1906, *Valgbog. Udgivet af Højres Forretningsudvalg*, pp. 47–52, that the Conservatives developed such a programme, which included unemployment insurance as a major item, well before the autumn of 1907. For these printed leaflets, 'Politik: Højre', Småtrykssamlingen, Det Kongelige Bibliotek, (Uncatalogued Printed Material Section, Royal Library), Copenhagen.

25 Harald Westergaard, 1894, pp. 1–11.
26 On Westergaard, Anne Løkke, 2002, pp. 393–422; Niels Kærgård & Thorkild Davidsen, 2005, pp. 349–366; Lars Schädler Andersen, 2009, pp. 49–59.
27 Harald Westergaard, 1898, pp. 372–378; 1902, pp. 602–607; 1903. For other early Danish contributions, Aleksis Studnitz Petersen, 1888, pp. 225–229; Marcus Rubin, 1894, pp. 540–544; Birger Hansted, 1897, (detailed examination of the Swiss and German programmes); idem, 1896. Hansted published several texts on Swiss and British labour legislation in the 1890s. On Westergaard's work on unemployment, Lars Schädler Andersen, 2005, pp. 239–259. My perspective and argument have many affinities with Andersen's study.
28 Harald Westergaard, 1899, p. 28.
29 Harald Westergaard, 1903, p. 141.
30 Aleksis Studnitz-Petersen, 1899, pp. 381–390.
31 Birger Hansted, 1897, pp. 418–431; Harald Westergaard, 1903, pp. 147–148. On professor G. Schanz' proposals, Karl-Christian Führer, 1990, pp. 47–48.
32 Nils Edling, 2008; Westergaard, 1903, p. 149.
33 Harald Westergaard, 1903, pp. 151–154.
34 On parliamentary process and party politics, Asbjørn Sonne Nørgaard, 1997, ch. 5.
35 Unfortunately, no minutes from the commission's meeting are available.
36 'Et Lovforslag om Arbejdsløshed', *Berlingske Tidende*, 1 April 1903. Of course, Westergaard insisted that the MP Poul Rasmussen, not widely known for his interest in social policy, had thoroughly studied the topic himself. Special thanks to Lars Andersen who generously provided me with this reference.
37 Actually, the Danish insurancesystem, where the level of public subsidies was calculated on the basis of the funds' revenues instead of on the sums paid by the funds to their unemployed members, resembled another Belgian insurance model, that of Liège. However, the Danes themselves claimed to pattern the example set by Ghent and no other Belgian insurance model was mentioned.
38 Hugh Heclo, 1974, p. 74.
39 Aleksis Studnitz-Petersen, 1888, pp. 259–260.
40 Laurids Bruun, 1895, p. I [translation by the author], Copenhagen.
41 *Det Statistiske Departement (Statens Statistiske Bureau) 1896–1920*, 1920, pp. 9–10 and p. 95.
42 'Compte-rendu de la troisième session de l'Institut International de Statistique', *Bulletin de l'Institut International de Statistique*, 1892, pt. 4, sec. 1, vol. 1, pp. 176–177; Marcus Rubin, 1900, pp. 34–41.
43 Theda Skocpol & Dietrich Rueschemeyer, 1996, p. 11.
44 Michael Koefoed & Harald Westergaard, 1898; Jens Warming, 1909–1913, pp. 537–545.
45 Frantz Pio, 1903; Jens Warming, 1903; Laurits V. Birck, 1903; Einar Einarsen, 1904. Cf. Theda Skocpol & Dietrich Rueschemeyer, 1996, pp. 303–304.

46 Hugh Heclo, 1974, pp. 70–78 and pp. 301–304, quote p. 301. Heclo refers to state administrators, not experts in general.
47 Nils Edling, 2002, pp. 310–312.
48 Nils Edling, 2006, pp. 101–108; idem, 2005, pp. 129–130.
49 Rune Ervik, 1993, pp. 192–198.
50 For a detailed analysis, Mauro Boianovsky & Hans-Michael Trautwein, 2003, pp. 385–436. A summary of Wicksell's lecture 'Arbetslösheten. Dess orsaker och botemedel' was printed in the social democratic daily *Arbetet*, March 22–23 1901, and has been published in Knut Wicksell, 1998, pp. 114–123.
51 Benny Carlson, 1994, p. 118 [quote from Cassel, 'Det sociala värdets problem', *Ekonomisk Tidskrift*, 1903, vol. 5, p. 280].
52 Gustav Cassel, 1902, p. 103. Quoted from Boianovsky & Trautwein, 2003, p. 408 [with a few minor changes of their translation and Cassel's original italics added].
53 Benny Carlson, 1994, p. 217.
54 Hugh Heclo, 1974, p. 67 and p. 76 (quote); Gustav Cassel, 1904, pp. 21–35 and pp. 51–81. Karl J. Höjer, 1952, p. 55, cautiously states that Cassel's book probably had some effects on – the non-socialist – public opinion on social policy. Benny Carlson, 1990, p. 155, claims that *Socialpolitik* was highly influential in shaping the new non-socialist interest in social policy.
55 E.g. Johan Leffler & al., 1894–1902; Gustav Sundbärg, 1902. On the important Lorén foundation, Per Wisselgren, 2000.
56 There is a substantial literature on the nature of Swedish labour market policies before the 1930s and above all on the genesis of the new economic policies of the 30s, for references Nils Edling, 2006, pp. 115–117 and pp. 120–123.
57 Elmquist was in charge of labour statistics from 1898 to 1912, headed the Board of Social Affairs (Socialstyrelsen, established in 1912) from 1912 to 1919 and became minister of social affairs 1920–21, and for many years he acted as arbitrator in industrial conflicts. He co-chaired the labour exchange in Stockholm and became the city's royal governor in 1928. Huss became national inspector of the labour exchanges in 1910, headed the Board of Social Affairs 1921–37 and was from 1914 subsequently secretary, co-chairman and from 1931 finally chairman of the National Unemployment Commission (Statens Arbetslöshetskommission).
58 Hugh Heclo, 1974, p. 76 and pp. 301–304; David Östlund, 2003, pp. 282–292 and pp. 321–335, esp. p. 287 note 523 and p. 289 note 530; Nils Edling, 2008, pp. 33–34.
59 Close monitoring of the labour market of this kind was of course nothing typically Swedish but a primary task of every national bureau, office or department in charge of labour statistics. For the instructions, 'Den officiella arbetsstatistiken i Sverige. Särskilda kommitterades utlåtande angående det arbetsstatistiska arbetets anordnande under år 1903', *Meddelanden från K. Kommerskollegii afdelning för Arbetsstatistik*, 1903:1, vol. 1, pp. 15–17.
60 On the crucial ideological and discursive importance of the emigration, Bo Stråth, 1996, pp. 72–78.
61 Nils Edling, 2008, pp. 31–32.
62 E.g. Henning Elmquist, 1903, vol. 3, pp. 327–329; idem, 1904; Gunnar Huss, 1906, pp. 77–82; idem, 1906, pp. 317–320; idem, 1907, pp. 25–28; idem, 1908, pp. 36–44 and pp. 52–59.
63 [Gunnar Huss], *P.M. angående arbetslöshetsförsäkring*, 1907, p. 3; cf. Nils Edling,

2008, p. 32; Cf. Desmond King, 1995, ch. 2.
64 [Huss], 1907, p. 35.
65 [Gunnar Huss], *Promemoria angående arbetslösheten i Sverige hösten 1908 samt kommunala åtgärder i anledning af arbetslöshet*, 1908; *Arbetslösheten i Sverige under vintern 1908–1909*, 1910; *Arbetslösheten i Sverige den 31 januari 1910*, 1911.
66 Cf. Hugh Heclo, 1974, p. 301.
67 Quote Hugh Heclo, 1974, p. 78; for details, Per-Gunnar Edebalk, 1975, pp. 71–90.
68 In his Swedish-Norwegian comparison Norwegian historian Svein Ivar Angell, 2002, in a similar way contrasts the primacy of economic modernisation in Sweden with the political modernisation in Norway.
69 Gunnar Huss, 1908, p. 43.
70 Quote John D. Stephens, 1979, p. 72; Walter Korpi, 2001, pp. 251–254.
71 For a complex and convincing coalition analysis, Ann Shola Orloff, 1993. On the crucial importance of agrarian interests, Peter Baldwin, 1990, esp. ch. 1.
72 Nils Edling, 2006, pp. 101–108; Hugh Heclo, 1974, pp. 286–287; Jens Alber, 1981, pp. 173–175.
73 Cf. Pauli Kettunen, 2006, pp. 33–42.
74 Cf. Hugh Heclo, 1974, pp. 304–312 and note 142 above.
75 Christian Topalov, 1994, ch. 13; Alain Desroisières, 1998, pp. 1-12.
76 Cf. Christian Topalov, 1994.

References

Alber, Jens 1981: 'Government Responses to the Challenge of Unemployment. The Development of Unemployment Insurance in Western Europe', Peter Flora & Arnold J. Heidenheimer (eds.), *The Development of Welfare States in Europe and America*, New Brunswick & London.

Andersen, Lars Schädler 2005: 'Et socialt onde eller selvforskyldt elendighed? Om begrebet arbejdsløshed omkring år 1900', Lars Schädler Andersen, Poul Duedahl & Louise N. Kallestrup (eds.), *De måske udstødte. Historiens marginale eksistenser*, Aalborg.

Andersen, Lars Schädler 2009: 'The Discovery of Professional Risk. Social Science and the Industrial Accident in Denmark 1880–1900', *Ideas in History*, vol. 4.

Andersen, Lars Schädler, Poul Duedahl & Louise N. Kallestrup (eds.) 2005: *De måske udstødte. Historiens marginale eksistenser*, Aalborg.

Angell, Svein Ivar 2002: *Den svenske modellen og det norske systemet. Tilhøvet mellom moderniseirng og identitetsdanning i Sverige og Noreg ved overgangen til det 20. hundreåret*, Oslo.

Baldwin, Peter 1990: *The Politics of Social Solidarity. Class Bases of the European Welfare State 1875–1975*, Cambridge.

1906: *Beretning om Arbeidernes faglige landsorganisations virksomhed fra 1ste juli 1905 til 1ste januar 1906*, Oslo (Kristiania).

Birck, Laurits V. 1903: *Bidrag til en Teori om de økonomiske Perioder*, Copenhagen.

Boianovsky, Mauro & Hans-Michael Trautwein 2003: 'Wicksell, Cassel and the Idea of Involuntary Unemployment', *History of Political Economy*, no. 3, pp. 385-436, vol. 35.

Bruun, Laurids 1892: 'Compte-rendu de la troisième session de l'Institut International de Statistique', *Bulletin de l'Institut International de Statistique*, pt. 4, sec. 1, vol. 1.

Bruun, Laurids 1895: *Officiel statistik. Undersøgelser af Statsbureauernes Organisation og Virksomhed fra et Studieophold i Tyskland, Schweiz, Østrig, England, Frankrig og Italien* [translation by the author], Copenhagen.

Carlson, Benny 1990: 'Gustav Cassel', Christina Jonung & Ann-Charlotte Ståhlberg (eds.), *Ekonomporträtt. Svenska ekonomer under 300 år*, Stockholm,

Carlson, Benny 1994: *The State as a Monster. Gustav Cassel and Eli Heckscher on the Role and Growth of the State*.

Cassel, Gustav 1902: *Socialpolitik*, Stockholm.

Cassel, Gustav 1903: 'Det sociala värdets problem', *Ekonomisk Tidskrift*, vol. 5, pp. 258-280.

Cassel, Gustav 1904: 'Om kriser och dåliga tider 1–2', *Ekonomisk Tidskrift*, vol. 6.

Christensen, Lars K., Søren Kolstrup & Anette Eklund Hansen 2007: *Arbejdernes historie i Danmark 1800–2000*, Copenhagen.

Christiansen, Niels Finn et. (eds.) 2006: *The Nordic Model of Welfare – A Historical Reappraisal*, Copenhagen.

Desrosières, Alain 1998: *The Politics of Large Numbers. A History of Statistical Reasoning*, Cambridge Mass. & London.

1920: *Det Statistiske Departement (Statens Statistiske Bureau) 1896–1920*, Copenhagen.

Edelbalk, Per-Gunnar 1975: *Arbetslöshetsförsäkringsdebatten. En studie i svensk socialpolitik 1892–1934*, Lund.

Edling, Nils 2002: 'Den svenska arbetslösheten tar form', Pauli Kettunen (ed.), *Lokalt och internationellt. Dimensioner i den nordiska arbetarrörelsen och arbetarkulturen*, Tampere.

Edling, Nils 2005: 'Statistik och arbetslöshetspolitik i skandinavisk arbetarrörelse omkring år 1900', *Arbeiderhistorie. Årbog for Arbeiderbevegelsens historie*, Oslo.

Edling, Nils 2006: 'Limited universalism. Unemployment Insurance in Northern Europe 1900–2000', Niels Finn Christiansen et al. (eds.), *The Nordic Model of Welfare – A Historical Reappraisal*, Copenhagen.

Edling, Nils 2008: 'Regulating Unemployment the Continental Way. The Transfer of Municipal Labour Exchanges to Scandinavia 1890–1914', *European Review of History*, vol. 15, no. 1, pp. 23-40.

Einarsen, Einar 1904: *Gode og daarlige tider. En undersøgelse med særligt hensyn til den økonomiske udvikling i Norge og Danmark i den sidste menneskealder*, Copenhagen.

Elmquist, Henning 1903: 'Staten och arbetsförmedlingen', *Social Tidskrift*, vol. 3.

Elmquist, Henning 1904: *Offentlig arbetsförmedling*, Stockholm.

Ervik, Rune 1993: 'Kunnskap og sosialpolitikk: Arbeidsløyse som sosial risiko i Noreg og Sverige', Ervik, Rune & Stein Kuhnle (eds.): *Kunnskap, risiko og sosialpolitikk. Institusjonelle perspektiver på skandinavisk utvikling*, Bergen.

Ervik, Rune & Stein Kuhnle (eds.) 1993: *Kunnskap, risiko og sosialpolitikk. Institusjonelle perspektiver på skandinavisk utvikling*, Bergen.

1904: *Folketællingen i Kongeriget Danmark den 1. Februar 1901*, Copenhagen.

Flora, Peter & Arnold J. Heidenheimer (eds.) 1981: *The Development of Welfare States in Europe and America*, New Brunswick & London.

Führer, Karl-Christian 1990: *Arbeitslosigkeit und die Entstehung der Arbeitslosenversicherung in Deutschland 1902–1927*, Berlin.

Hanagan, Michael 1997: 'Citizenship, Claim-making and the Right to Work. Britain 1884–1911', *Theory and Society*, vol. 26, pp. 449-474.

Hansted, Birger 1896: 'Det schweiziske Arbejdersekretariat samt Forsikring imod Arbejdsløshed', *For Industri og Haandværk*, vol. 5.

Hansted, Birger 1897: 'Om Forsikring imod Arbejdsløshed', *Nationaløkonomisk Tidsskrift*, vol. 35.

Heclo, Hugh 1974: *Modern Social Politics in Britain and Sweden. From Relief to Income Maintenance*, New Haven.

Herren, Madeleine 1993: *Internationale Sozialpolitik vor dem Ersten Weltkrieg. Die Anfänge europäischer Kooperation aus der Sicht Frankreichs*, Berlin.

Höjer, Karl J. 1952: *Svensk socialpolitisk historia*, Stockholm.

Hort, Sven E. (Olsson) 1992: *Social Policy and Welfare State in Sweden*, Lund.

Huss, Gunnar 1903: 'Den officiella arbetsstatistiken i Sverige. Särskilda kommitterades utlåtande angående det arbetsstatistiska arbetets anordnande under år 1903', *Meddelanden från K. Kommerskollegii afdelning för Arbetsstatistik*, vol. 1.

Huss, Gunnar 1906: 'Offentlig arbetsförmedling i Sverige', *Social Tidskrift*, vol. 6.

Huss, Gunnar 1906: 'Arbetsförmedling för barn vid utträdet ur folkskolan', *Social Tidskrift*, vol. 6.

Huss, Gunnar 1907: 'Arbetsförmedlingskonferensen i Stockholm. Dess förutsättningar och resultat', *Social Tidskrift*, vol. 7.

Huss, Gunnar 1907: *P.M. angående arbetslöshetsförsäkring*, Stockholm.

Huss, Gunnar 1908: 'Arbetsförmedling' and 'Arbetslöshet', G. H. von Koch (ed.), *Social Handbok. På uppdrag av Centralförbundet för Socialt Arbete under medverkan av flera författare utgiven av G. H. von Koch*, Stockholm.

Huss, Gunnar 1908: *Promemoria angående arbetslösheten i Sverige hösten 1908 samt kommunala åtgärder i anledning af arbetslöshet*, Stockholm.

Huss, Gunnar 1910: *Arbetslösheten i Sverige under vintern 1908–1909*, Stockholm.

Huss, Gunnar 1911: *Arbetslösheten i Sverige den 31 januari 1910*, Stockholm.

Jensen, Bent 2006: *Træk af avisdebatten om de arbejdsløse fra 1840'erne til 1940'erne. pt 1: Debatten indtil 1907*, Copenhagen.

Jensen, Per H. 2007: 'Grundlæggelse af det danske arbejdsløshedsforsikringssystem i komparativ belysning', Jesper Hartvig Pedersen & Aage Huulgaard (eds.), *Arbejdsløshedsforsikringsloven 1907–2007. Udvikling og perspektiver*, Copenhagen.

Kettunen, Pauli 2006: 'The Power of International Comparison. A Perspective on the Making and Challenging of the Nordic Welfare State', Christiansen et al. (eds.): *The Nordic Model of Welfare – A Historical Reappraisal*, Copenhagen.

Keyssar, Alexander 1986: *Out of Work. The First Century of Unemployment in Massachusetts*, Cambridge etc.

King, Desmond 1995: *Actively Seeking Work? The Politics of Unemployment and Welfare Policy in the United States and Great Britain*, Chicago.

Kjeldstadli, Knut 1990: *Oslo bys historie*, vol. 5: Den delte byen. Fra 1900 til 1948, Oslo.

Koefoed, Michael & Harald Westergaard 1898: *Grundrids af Danmarks Statistik*, Copenhagen.

Kolstrup, Søren 1995: 'A-kasselovgivningen. Loven om statsanerkendte a-kasser, et klassekompromis med arbejderbevægelsen som dynamo', *Arbejderhistorie*, no. 1, pp. 14-21.

Kolstrup, Søren 1996: *Velfærdsstatens rødder. Fra kommunesocialisme til folkepension*, Copenhagen

Kolstrup, Søren: 'Fra 1900 til 1945'.

Korpi, Walter 2001: 'Contentious Institutions. An Augmented Rational-action Analysis of the Origins and Path Dependency of Welfare State Institutions in Western Countries', *Rationality and Society*, no. 2, vol. 13, pp. 235-283.

Kærgård, Niels & Thorkild Davidsen 2005: 'Harald Westergaard. From Young Pioneer to Established Authority', Warren J. Samuels (ed.), *European Economist of the Early 20th Century, vol. 1: Studies of Neglected Thinkers of Belgium, France, The Netherlands and Scandinavia*, Cheltenham.

Leffler, Johan & al. 1894-1902: *Det ekonomiska samhällslifvet. Handbok i nationalekonomi*, 2 vols. Stockholm.

Løkke, Anne 2002: 'Creating the Social Question. Imagining Society in Statistics and Political Economy in the Late Nineteenth-Century Denmark', *Historie Sociale – Social History*, vol. 35, pp. 393-422.

Møller, Hornemann 1981: *Klassekamp og sociallovgivning 1850–1970*, Copenhagen.

Nilsson, Fred 1970: *Emigrationen från Stockholm till Nordamerika 1880–1893. En studie i urban utvandring*, Stockholm.

Nørgaard, Asbjørn Sonne 1997: *The Politics of Institutional Control. Corporatism in Danish Occupational Safety and Health Regulation & Unemployment Insurance, 1870–1995*, Aarhus.

Nørregaard, Georg 1977 (1st ed. 1943): *Arbejdsforhold indenfor dansk haandværk og industri 1857–1899*, Copenhagen.

Orloff, Ann Shola 1993: *The Politics of Pensions. A Comparative Analysis of Britain, Canada, and the United States, 1880–1940*, Madison.

Pedersen, Jesper Hartvig & Aage Huulgaard (eds.) 2007: *Arbejdsløshedsforsikringsloven 1907-2007. Udvikling og perspektiver*, Copenhagen.

Pio, Frantz 1903: *Økonomiske Depressioner*, Copenhagen.

'Politik: Højre', Småtrykssamlingen, Det Kongelige Bibliotek, (Uncatalogued Printed Material Section, Royal Library), Copenhagen.

Rubin, Marcus 1894: 'Arbejdsløshedspørgsmaalet', *Nationaløkonomisk Tidsskrift*, vol. 32.

Rubin, Marcus 1900: 'Om befolkningens sociale Gruppering', *Forhandlinger ved det 6. fællesnordiske statistiske Møde i København 27–30 August 1900*, Copenhagen.

Rubin, Marcus 1903: 'Et Lovforslag om Arbejdsløshed', *Berlingske Tidende*, 1 April 1903.

Rueschemeyer, Dietrich & Theda Skocpol 1996: *States, Social Knowledge, and the Origins of Modern Social Policies*, 1996, Princeton.

Rueschemeyer, Dietrich & Theda Skocpol: 'Conclusion', Rueschemeyer & Skocpol (eds.).

Samuels, Warren J. (ed.) 2005: *European Economist of the Early 20th Century, vol. 1: Studies of Neglected Thinkers of Belgium, France, The Netherlands and Scandinavia*, Cheltenham.

Schiller, Berndt 1975: 'Years of Crisis 1906–1914', Steven Koblik (ed.), *Sweden's Development from Poverty to Affluence 1750–1970*, Minneapolis.

Seip, Anne-Lise: 'At det er arbejderbevægelsens krav og kampe, der har initieret en forsikringsdannelse'.

Seip, Anne-Lise 1994 (1st ed. 1984): *Sosialhjelpsstaten blir til. Norsk sosialpolitikk*, Oslo.

Skocpol, Theda & Dietrich Rueschemeyer, 'Introduction', Rueschemeyer & Skocpol (eds.).

Stephens, John D. 1979: *The Transition from Capitalism to Socialism*, Urbana & Chicago.

Stråth, Bo 1996: *The Organisation of Labour Markets. Modernity, Culture and Governance in Germany, Sweden, Britain and Japan*, London & New York.

Studnitz-Petersen, Aleksis 1887: Review: Arbejdsløsheds-Statistik. Eighteenth Annual Report of the Bureau of Statistics of Labor. December 1887. Boston.
Studnitz-Petersen, Aleksis 1888: 'Om Arbejdsstatistik', *Forhandlingarne paa det nordiske Nationaløkonomiske møde i Kjøbenhavn 1888*, Copenhagen.
Studnitz-Petersen, Aleksis 1888: *Nationaløkonomisk Tidsskrift*, vol. 28.
Studnitz-Petersen, Aleksis 1899: "'Det sociale Spørgsmaal'. Litteratur-Anmeldelser II, *Nationaløkonomisk Tidsskrift*, vol. 37, pp. 381-90.
Sundbärg, Gustav (ed.) 1902: *Sveriges land och folk. Historisk-statistisk handbok*, Stockholm.
Toftgaard, Jens 2008: *Kampen om København. Magt og demokrati i byens rum 1870–1901*, Copenhagen.
Topalov, Christian 1994: *Naissance du chômeur, 1880–1910*, Paris.
von Koch, G.H. (ed.) 1908: *Social Handbok. På uppdrag av Centralförbundet för Socialt Arbete under medverkan av flera författare utgiven av G.H. von Koch*, Stockholm.
Wagner, Peter et al. (eds.) 1991: *Social Sciences and Modern States. National Experiences and Theoretical Crossroads*, Cambridge.
Wagner, Peter, Claude Didry and Bénédicte Zimmermann (eds.) 2000: *Arbeit und Nationalstaat. Frankreich und Deutschland in europäischer Perspektive*, Frankfurt am Main.
Walters, William 2000: *Unemployment and Government. Genealogies of the Social*, Cambridge.
Warming, Jens 1903: *Gode og daarlige tider. Besvarelse af en konkurrence-opgave*, Copenhagen.
Warming, Jens 1909-1913: *Haandbog i Danmarks Statistik*, Copenhagen.
Westergaard, Harald 1894: 'Om Forholdsregler mod Arbejdsløshed', *Nationaløkonomisk Tidsskrift*, vol. 32.
Westergaard, Harald 1898: Review. G. Cornil: L'assurance municipale contre le chômage involontaire. Bruxelles 1898, *Nationaløkonomisk Tidsskrift*, vol. 36.
Westergaard, Harald 1899: *Socialismen og Samfundsudviklingen*. Copenhagen.
Westergaard, Harald 1902: 'Forsikring mod Arbejdsløshed i Gent', *Nationaløkonomisk Tidsskrift*, vol. 40.
Westergaard, Harald 1903: 'Forsikring mod Arbejdsløshed', *Nationaløkonomisk Tidsskrift*, vol. 41.
Wicksell, Knut 1998: *Stridsskrifter och samhällsekonomiska analyser*, Stockholm.
Wisselgren, Per 2000: *Samhällets kartläggare. Lorénska stiftelsen, den sociala frågan och samhällsvetenskapens formering 1830–1920*, Stockholm.
Wittrock, Björn & Peter Wagner 1996, 'Social Science and the Building of the Early Welfare State. Toward a Comparison of Statist and Non-Statist Western Societies', Rueschemeyer & Skocpol (eds.), *States, Social Knowledge, and the Origins of Modern Social Policies*, Princeton.
Wittrock, Björn, Peter Wagner & Hellmut Wollmann 1991: 'Social Sciences and the Modern State. Policy Knowledge and Political Institutions in Western Europe and the United States', Peter Wagner et al. (eds.), *Social Sciences and Modern States. National Experiences and Theoretical Crossroads*, Cambridge.
Zimmermann, Bénédicte 2000: *La constitution du chômage en Allemagne. Entre professions et territoires*, Paris.
Zimmermann, Bénédicte 2000B: 'Arbeitslosigkeit um die Jahrhundertwende: Zwei Formen der statistischen Konstruktion einer nationalen Kategorie', Peter Wagner, Claude Didry and Bénédicte Zimmermann (eds.), *Arbeit und Nationalstaat. Frankreich und Deutschland in europäischer Perspektive*, Frankfurt am Main.

The 'psy – experts' and the minds of children: Transfer of knowledge in inter-war Norway and Sweden

Kari Ludvigsen

The crucial role of experts in defining the norms of a good and healthy childhood during the twentieth century has inspired several analyses during the last decades, also in Scandinavia.[1] Scholars have also showed an increasing interest in the processes whereby the mental health of children gradually became a point of interest for governmental agencies and what Rose has named 'the psy- experts'.[2] Ideas and knowledge related to mental hygiene, child guidance and psychoanalysis have been regarded as important for this increasing focus on child mental health during the inter-war period. It has been pointed out, however, that the ideas of the international movements received different interpretations and merged in various ways in different national contexts.[3] Recent studies indicate variations in the definition of policies and the organisation of services taking care of aspects of child mental health.[4] Therefore, to study the child mental health care, one has to take into consideration the various historical, professional and intellectual interests projected into this area. This article represents an attempt towards an understanding of the processes that shaped the Norwegian mental health care for children in the period from 1920 until the 1950s, through an analysis of the transformation of international impulses into the national contexts of constraints and traditions, and the role of particular agents in the process. In particular the role of the psychological and psychiatric expertise transferring ideas of mental hygiene, child guidance and psychoanalysis into a Norwegian context will be studied.

In Norway, as in the rest of Scandinavia and other European countries, experts nurtured their views and understandings by close relations to these international movements. The transfer of the ideas of mental hygiene, child guidance and psychoanalysis is seen as merging processes, in line with the analytical framework suggested by historians Andresen and Grønli.[5] They argue that in processes of transferring knowledge, impulses may go in different directions, from various sources. The analytical framework of this article underlines how the object of study itself may become transformed through the process of transfer. This assumption corresponds well with the analytical perspective used by Thom and Stewart in their studies of the implementing of the American-inspired child guidance ideas and activities in England and Scotland.[6] In her analysis of the English child guidance clinics and their incorporation of different schools of thought, Thom shows that the history of these clinics was not uniform, and their theoretical foundations and organisation differed. These variations are seen as emerging from variations in political, economic and administrative contingencies. Further, Stewart's study of Scottish child guidance clinics has pointed out that the homogeneity of the American child guidance ideas as well as the distribution of a unitary clinic model can be questioned. Thus, the actual role played by the American models that were imported through funds and study trips has to be empirically analysed, taking into account the influence of various other models of thought and practice in specific national and local settings. The analytic framework of this article may add further to our understanding of the ways international ideas of mental hygiene, child guidance and medical and psychological measures were implemented and transformed in various institutional settings in different countries.

It is important, however, to recognise the various natures of these streams of thought and models for policy and practical mental health work. It is crucial also to consider the variations in the way these thoughts and models became spread internationally and by whom. Ideas of mental hygiene were promoted through American associations, and spread through extensive information work, international congresses, the establishing of local, national and international associations and economic funding for travels and study trips from around 1920. The child guidance model also spread from the United States, partly related to the networks of mental hygiene. The methods and ways of thinking about the mental health of children were spread through scholarly networks, study trips and academic reports, partly supported by foundations like the Commonwealth Fund[7]. Child Guidance has been seen as a conceptual framework forming the thinking of child mental health, a particular method for practical work with children, and a model for organising this work in out-patient clinics and experts teams. The ideas of child guidance were related to the thoughts of mental hygiene, but were also inspired by various psychotherapeutic ideas. In particular, aspects of psychoanalysis were important as a powerful but also controversial therapeutic method and way of thinking about the child, individual mental development and society. Psychoanalysis developed on the European continent, and experts in psychology, psychiatry and other academics travelled to study these thoughts in Berlin and Vienna. During the 1930s, continental scholars moved to Britain and to the United States, and the academic travellers followed them to study at their clinics and university institutes.

This article will try to grasp some of the particular merging of these thoughts and models of understanding and working with the child mental health in Norway. The framework suggested by Andresen and Grønli will serve as a tool for this analysis. First, the specific exchange situations and production of knowledge on the mental health of children is looked at. The particular focal point here is the international meeting points formed by conferences and associations, as well as 'model clinics' and academic settings where visitors from abroad met with the new understandings and methods of work related to children's minds. At such arenas, experts from many countries met an explicit ambition to spread ideas on the prevention of mental illness. Who were the spokesmen travelling to exchange ideas in such arenas, and how did they present their ideas to a domestic audience? Secondly, the receiving and reinterpretation of the ideas in the national context is scrutinised by regarding some of the contextual factors labelled 'filters' by Andresen and Grønli: The compatibility of the ideas with hegemonic understandings and solutions, and with the norms and ethics of science and politics, the positions of the spokesmen, and the economic and political situation and the correspondence of the ideas with priorities. To grasp how new knowledge is received, evaluated, negotiated and reinterpreted, such factors may ease transformation or hinder it, according to Andresen and Grønli. The third question raised by this analytic framework is the implementation of the ideas of mental hygiene, child guidance and psychoanalysis into practical work and governmental policies. How did the activities become organised, and in which institutional setting? Building on an earlier analysis of the establishing of Norwegian child psychiatry, the end of the chapter will briefly also address these questions, with respect to the organisation of the clinics and teams and the professional relationships and authority as well as the relationship to other activities and forms of financial support.

The transfer of mental hygiene ideas: the international arenas and the Norwegian spokesmen

In 1930, several European experts on psychiatry travelled to Washington to attend the first international mental hygiene congress. Two Norwegian psychiatrists travelled as official attendants. Both held central positions in Norwegian hospital psychiatry. Dr. Hans Evensen (1868–1953) was head of the largest and oldest state mental asylum near Oslo, Gaustad, from 1915. Dr. Sigurd Dahlstrøm (1882–1933) was from 1916 head of the first psychiatric clinic in Norway, the 6th department at Ullevål hospital. Together with Ragnar Vogt (1870–1943), the first professor of psychiatry from 1915, formerly head of Gaustad and from 1926 the first head of the new university psychiatric clinic in Oslo, these men represented the Norwegian psychiatric elite. Also, prominent representatives of Swedish and Danish psychiatry went to the US for this event. As Quarsell has pointed out, it was not very common for these Scandinavian experts to gather knowledge across the Atlantic.[8] Scandinavian psychiatrists were traditionally strongly oriented towards the international trends of the field. But until the inter-war period, their main contacts had been with the psychiatric ideas and practices of continental Europe. Through their Atlantic crossing, the Norwegian psychiatrists got in contact with an international movement that presented a programme for the psychiatric ward and the mental well-being of the population.

From 1909, the American National Committee for Mental Hygiene had worked for the establishing of out-patient advisory clinics and child and adolescent mental health clinics. The core idea was to prevent mental illness and social programmes and promote mental health through information and clinical advice to the population. A mentally healthy population was to be achieved through social work and psychiatric counselling, as well as regulations of immigration, reproduction and marriage. The idea of a mental health care for children and the importance of the right upbringing of children became a central aspect of this programme. These ideas influenced expert attention towards child mental health for many decades, although the American movement changed concepts and perspectives over the years.[9]

The 1930 congress was a gathering of experts from many countries, and a broad range of questions was discussed. Aspects of child mental health were a core topic at several sessions and a range of speeches addressed questions related to this theme. Quarsell has argued that the contact with the international mental hygiene movement had a direct impact on the establishing of child psychiatric activity in Sweden in the thirties.[10] In addition, it stimulated the strong interest in popular educational activities on psychological questions in general, and child psychology in particular. Mental hygiene ideas on the increasing interest in minds and behaviour of children had an impact on health and social services aimed at children. It also, however, had a strong influence on how children were perceived, emphasising the child's mind and mental health as a area of expert and public policy interest, not only its physical condition.[11]

The mental hygiene ideas presented to Norwegian psychiatrists in the early 1930s were immediately received as important, and led to the establishing of out-patient clinics and associations. Leading psychiatrists became spokesmen for the ideas of mental hygiene, and for the importance of childhood in the prevention of social problems and mental illness. But these thoughts were not entirely new to the Norwegian psychiatric experts.[12] During the early 1920s, an international congress was arranged and several associations working with mental hygiene were established in Europe. The Norwegian psychiatrists showed an interest in these matters, and Hans Evensen was a central force in the early initiatives to make these ideas known to the psychiatric community. Dr. Dahlstrøm had also worked for the promotion of mental hygiene ideas for some years. Early in his career, he took a strong interest in crime and youth delinquency, and he stressed the social environment as a central force behind crime and mental illness. His doctoral dissertation from 1922 presented a translation of the tests made by Binet and Simon for the purpose of testing young prisoners. Dahlstrøm wrote a large number of articles and speeches on mental hygienic issues. Dahlstrøm's active involvement in the questions of mental hygiene increased as a result of his several stays in the USA. His trip in 1930 was not his first one. He visited USA in 1926, and was welcomed by the National Committee for mental hygiene. As was their custom, the representatives of American Mental hygiene made him a travel route and introduced him to many useful contact persons.[13] In 1927, Dahlstrøm introduced the concept of mental hygiene to a meeting of the Norwegian hygienist association.[14] In his lecture at that meeting, Dahlstrøm pointed out the growing influence of the mental hygiene movement. Dahlstrøm was concerned about the level of public information about the societal consequences of mental illness. The population had to be informed that most of the major social problems, like pauperism, crime, prostitution and alcoholism, were grounded in the weak mental equipment of the individuals. Even social disorder and strikes could be seen from a mental hygiene perspective, he told the hygienists. Dahlstrøm saw mental hygiene as an expansion of medicine from health care into the social sphere, and argued that the role of the psychiatrist had changed, from a public administrator taking care of the state properties, to a hospital doctor. He considered the knowledge of these doctors as an important government resource that could be used in local community social work.

Several leading psychiatrists took an interest in the perspectives and plans presented to them during the 1920s and early 1930s. But the idea of preventing mental illness and the thought of psychiatrists contributing to the solving of social problems were articulated among the leading Norwegian psychiatrists several years before Evensen presented the ideas of mental hygiene to his colleagues in 1923. [15] As in other countries, Scandinavian psychiatrists took an interest in questions of childhood, delinquency and education from the turn of the century onwards. The importance of childhood and the emphasis on preventive acts to avoid social problems and mental illness had been focused on by a wide range of experts. The mental hygiene way of thinking seems to have been in line with a central understanding of the challenges in mental health care and the handling of social problems since the turn of the century.[16] Norwegian care of the mentally ill was predominately in public lunatic asylums and private care in families and so-called colonies. The state government and the local governments shared the expenses of the care for persons declared mentally ill. There were few privately owned asylums in Norway, and few nursing homes and clinics. Compared to Sweden, the capacities of the asylums of Norwegian mental health care were far more limited. The public asylums experienced a rising level of over-booking from 1920 onwards. Only people declared insane were admitted to the asylums, and until 1935 no one was admitted at their own request, whilst in England 60% of the patients of mental hospitals were admitted on their own wish.[17] The Norwegian mental asylums were thus largely filled with chronically and severely ill patients, and the ambitions of the psychiatrists to hospitalise them along the lines of somatic hospitals largely remained programmatic until World War II. The professional status of psychiatry and the legitimisation of psychiatric knowledge as expertise for the state were based on an involvement in a broadening range of social problems from the turn of the century.[18] This orientation out of the asylum also included a growing interest in the problems of childhood and crime. Psychiatrists also became deeply involved in questions of mental hygiene and the mental health, mind and behaviour of children, whether they advocated a biologically oriented perspective or a social perspective. The psychiatrists argued for more differentiated care for children with different problems. They saw themselves as advisors for the local and central government, the public and other experts related to the education system, special education and the child care system.

The programme and thoughts introduced from 1905 by the first Norwegian professor of psychiatry, Ragnar Vogt (appointed 1916) emphasised psychiatry as a kind of social science, with its main task to prevent and cure different social problems. Vogt has been considered an eclectic, inspired by a broad range of ideas, from psychoanalysis to psycho-techniques and eugenics. However, emphasis has also been placed on his medical-psychological views.[19] The central point of the programme was to reduce mental illness through prophylactic interventions regarding both social factors and eugenics. Important elements of Vogt's programme were followed up by Norwegian psychiatrists during the 1920s and 1930s. A similar tendency was seen in Sweden, where there was also an increasing interest among Swedish psychiatrists in open care, prophylactic measures and psychotherapy aimed at nervous problems. Together, medical actors, public health care and voluntary organisations took initiatives to establish counselling activities and out-patient clinics during the 1920s.

Also in Norway, ideas of mental hygiene became closely linked to the role of childhood early on. The psychiatrist could contribute to the prevention of mental illnesses through advisory work aimed at schools, the child care system, poor system and the courts. Early intervention, the right care and education were seen as important measures to improve the mental health of the population, and to start with children was a crucial device. Out-patient activities related to the mental hospitals had to be a central part of the proposed system. To Dahlstrøm, a most important part of mental hygienic work was the child-guidance clinics. Dr. Dahlstrøm saw a healthy environment as an important part of a healthy childhood. In the Norwegian context, he saw the work of the local child care committees as a central force in mental hygiene. He also argued that most parents had too little knowledge about mental hygiene and the upbringing of children, and he viewed popular information on such matters as a crucial task for experts in psychiatry. During the following decades, Norwegian psychiatrists and psychologists worked to increase the knowledge of the citizens regarding mental health and child mental development, through new associations and information in books, journals and meetings.

Receiving the of mental hygiene ideas: local associations, popular information and clinical activities

After returning from the international conference, the Norwegian psychiatrists published scientific and popular works inspired by the mental hygienic ideas, and initiated the establishment of associations and clinics promoting the ideas and techniques associated with mental hygiene. The central elements of mental hygiene work argued for by these experts were still the establishing of out-patient clinics, the crucial role of child mental health work, and the emphasis on popular information.

Evensen and Dahlstrøm started to work for the establishing of a Norwegian association. Dr. Dahlstrøm played a central part in establishing the Oslo Mental Hygiene Association in 1930, and he became the first leader of the association.[20] Dahlstrøm was a leading force in mental hygienic work in Norway for a few years, until his early death in 1933. Ideas of mental hygiene received support from the psychiatric and medical elite in Norway in the early 1930s. Several other leading psychiatrists and psychologists took part in the work of this association, which saw it as a main task to do social work among the part of the population that was unable to get help and advice on its own. Professor Ragnar Vogt had a central role in the Norwegian mental hygienic work, including being a member of the board of the first mental hygiene association in Norway from 1930. During the thirties, new mental hygiene associations were set up in the largest Norwegian towns. A national association was established, and became affiliated with the new World Federation for Mental Health from 1948.

One of the spokesmen of mental hygiene work was the psychiatrist Gunnar Rohde Moe (1901–1988), who stated that mental hygiene of the child was the core activity of mental hygienic work, something in which the individual, the school, physicians and society shared an interest.[21] Out-patient activities had been tried out since 1928 by one of the county asylums, the Lier asylum, on the basis of an initiative taken by the head of the asylum, Dr. Grimsgaard. In 1930, Dr. Evensen suggested that such initiatives by mental hospitals should be reinforced. It became essential to devise a service aimed at both children and grown-ups, and Evensen placed considerable emphasis on the importance of cooperation between mental health care, the social services and the education system. He suggested a system of out-patient clinics, in cooperation with the schools, the nursing associations and the child care system.[22] From the early 1930s, pioneer out-patient clinics were established by several of the mental hygiene associations in the largest Norwegian cities, receiving both adults and children as their patients.

Public information on mental health and child upbringing became core activities of the Norwegian mental hygiene spokesmen and -women from the early 1930s.[23] The Association participated in the publishing of a journal on public health issues, called 'Folkehelseforeningens Tidsskrift', with its members eagerly publishing articles in this journal. Members of the Association also held various public speeches, some of which were published with great success in the booklet 'Mentalhygiene' in 1931 and 1937. Mental hygiene offices were established in several towns and cities, the main purpose of which was to give people advice on questions of mental hygienic relevance.

Ideas of mental hygiene seem to have been welcomed by the Norwegian experts in psychiatry in the early 1930s. The spokesmen held central positions in academic medicine, like Vogt, and in psychiatric care, like Evensen and Dahlstrøm. These experts were also involved in broader social and educational matters, in relation to children with learning disabilities, the child care system and the question of juvenile delinquency. The ideas of mental hygiene were first presented in the late 1920s to an expert audience of physicians, hygienists and psychiatrists. Through the establishing of local and subsequently national associations, the ideas of mental hygiene were disseminated to the population through extensive efforts of popular information on mental illness and health, mental development, child rearing and related topics.[24] After 1930, the associations took up this task, informing the public through journals, books and meetings.

Also in Sweden, psychiatrists initiated an association for mental health. The association worked for the prevention of mental illness and asocial behaviour, for the improvement of mental health care and the promotion of mental hygiene in the population.[25] It was proposed that counseling clinics should be established in Sweden. A program for the Swedish association was launched in 1932.[26] The importance of the environment for the upbringing of children was underlined as the first task for mental hygiene. According to Jönsson, the Swedish association was mostly concentrated to the Stockholm area. It did not have a numerous member list, but worked closely with the governmental representatives. Quarsell has pointed to the close ties between the Swedish mental hygiene association, established in 1931, and the new orientation of Swedish social policy in this period.[27] Questions of children and motherhood, upbringing and reproduction were a central part of the social policy. This, he argues, made the Swedish mental hygiene association influential, despite a relatively small number of members. With its social orientation, the mental hygienic movement worked as a bridge between the biologically oriented hygienism at the turn of the century, and the socio-political reforms of the inter-war period. Like their Swedish counterparts, the Norwegian associations did not recruit large numbers of members. The ideas seem to have gained influence, however, among both the experts and the public. The thoughts promoted at the international conference in 1930 can be seen as a further underlining of what was already viewed as important by the experts on mental health. It seems, however, to have further stimulated both activities related to expert advice on mental hygiene towards the population and practical work among the population. During the 1930s, several initiatives were taken to establish clinics and other measures to improve the mental health of the population. First and foremost, it seems like these initiatives were both aimed at and used for the improvement of the mental health and psychological development of children.

Implementation of mental hygiene ideas: The establishing of out-patient clinics

As pointed out, the ideas of early intervention to prevent severe mental illness were a central aspect of the mental hygiene movement, and corresponded to the striving of Norwegian psychiatrists to gain a base for themselves outside the narrow limits of the mental hospital and the mental health act. In 1926, the fifty-year-long battle for an independent psychiatric university clinic was over, and Professor Ragnar Vogt became the first director of the clinic at Vinderen in Oslo. During the following years, psychiatrists argued for the establishing of dispensaries related to the mental hospitals, to broaden the scope of their services to also embrace patients suffering from less serious mental problems. As mentioned, one of the first initiatives came from the head of the mental hospital in Lier, Dr. Grimsgaard. His views on this issue were strongly inspired by mental hygienic ideas, seeing prevention as a central task of modern medicine generally, and particularly as an important part of psychiatry.[28] Dispensaries were regarded as an important tool in the care for the mentally ill, and a crucial part of the mental asylums.

Dr. Grimsgaard also argued that medical expertise on the mind and soul could assist in all phases of human life, from early childhood onwards. Earlier mental hospital patients should be given advice, assistance and care at the out-patient clinic. The testing of school children, however, was a central task, demanding cooperation between psychiatrists, teachers and school physicians. Grimsgaard also wanted the dispensary staff to supply expert knowledge on mentally retarded children and problem children. The role of the dispensary would be to create a cooperation link between the home, the school and child care system. Grimsgaard's plans received support from professor Vogt. Among problems that could be prevented through this kind of out-patient care, Vogt also mentioned abnormal and psychopathic children. Inspired by the American and French systems, the Norwegian psychiatrists embraced the idea that every asylum should have its own dispensary.[29]

Dr. Grimsgaard opened his dispensary at the asylum in 1928. It was open one day a week, the doctors doing the work for free. In addition, a nurse was employed. The dispensary moved to the city of Drammen in 1930, and later to the hospital of the city. This was an attempt to increase interest among the public by establishing a setting more autonomous from the asylum. A few years later, the activity was expanded by the establishing of a new service in the southeastern town of Tønsberg. The work of the dispensary focused on advising physicians, hospitals, schools and parents on the diagnosing and prescribing of treatment of mental illness.[30] In terms of numbers, issues regarding children seem to have remained a small part of the consultations, under 10% until 1933. But the dispensary psychiatrists regarded children as an important group, in line with Grimsgaard's ideas.

In 1931, a mental hygienic out-patient clinic for adults opened in Oslo, in close cooperation between the Mental Hygiene Association, the Norwegian Nurses' Organisation and the Public health association (Folkehelseforeningen).[31] So-called advisory stations were also established in Bergen, Trondheim and Stavanger through the work of the local Mental Hygiene associations. Journals on the activities of these stations have been difficult to trace. However, some understanding of the nature of the work at the Oslo office can be gained through the accounts given by leaders and staff members in popular publications. The following is based on those sources.

In Oslo, the work was from the start led by Dr. H.H. Dedichen, who also became leader of the Mental Hygiene Association in 1937. Three physicians, representing the medical disciplines of psychiatry and neurology, each worked one afternoon a week. The physicians worked for free, while the Nurses Association provided for the office and paid a nurse. Public support was given to the activity in the late thirties. The clinic moved to the Oslo health board building in 1937, and in 1938, the town council raised money for a social worker and assistance at the clinic.[32] The following year this financial support was doubled, after a warm recommendation from the Oslo health board.[33] At the same time, the members started to work for an increased cooperation with public policlinics for mothers and children.[34]

In a speech, Dr. Hans Dedichen described the first five years of work at the clinic. The purpose of this office, as well as the ones in Drammen and Trondheim and other towns, was to provide the public with a place to seek advice and help. It was not supposed to serve people with fully developed illness; those cases were to be provided for by special doctors. In five years, around 2,000 patients visited the office. According to Dedichen, the public understood the purpose of the clinic extremely well. It was meant for people with troubles of different kinds, problems that 'got on their nerves'. The obviously ill did not seek advice at the office, and Dedichen preferred to call his clients 'the public' instead of 'patients'. Children and young persons made up the majority of clients, and thus most of the speech dealt with the youngest clients at the clinic. This was also in accordance with the central ideas of mental hygiene. To start with the children and to regulate as early as possible was crucial.

Mostly parents, but also schools and children's homes sought advice at the clinic, and the cooperation went smoothly, according to Dr. Dedichen. Parents and teachers sought advice about particular groups of children: not the severely ill, but those demonstrating different kinds of odd or deviant behaviour. They were often considered troublesome by teachers or parents, with visible nervous dispositions, like nail-biting, bed-wetting, and stuttering or raging.

The ideas of mental hygiene, focusing on prevention of social and mental health problems, reinforced the attention paid by psychiatrists and other medical experts towards childhood. The out-patient clinics established in Norway around 1930 were initiated by psychiatrists who were central spokesmen of the mental hygiene movement. Children became an important part of the clientele of the early out-patient mental health clinics in Norway. It was considered important to start with the children in work to prevent severe societal problems. Informing the public about mental health and mental hygiene work was a central part of the mental hygiene movement, also in the Norwegian context. And the public saw the new out-patient clinics as a way of handling children causing trouble and worries in schools, child care and families. With inspiration from American and British Child guidance clinics, the measures and methods for the work with troublesome and deviant children in families, schools and other settings were further developed. New expert groups became crucial agents of these ideas in Norway, first and foremost the psychologists.

The psy - experts and the transfer of child guidance ideas

The mental hygiene movement raised the issue of child mental health as an important part of the prevention of mental illness and social problems. The ideas and practice labelled child guidance were closely related to the mental hygiene work, but they can also be viewed as a movement in itself. As indicated in the introduction to this article, the term child guidance refers to a multifaceted movement, and child guidance was a term used in different ways, according to Jones.[35] It described the system of specialised mental hygiene clinics for the treatment of problem children, but also referred to a particular interpretation of the behaviour of children, mainly based on a psychodynamic view. In addition, child guidance could mean a particular therapeutic approach aimed at solving the problematic behaviour of children. It also described a specific way of organising the work through teams of experts trained to work together to treat problem children. Child guidance was also the term used for the expert attempts to educate the public on matters of child rearing.

The ideas of child guidance and the establishing of clinics spread throughout the United States from around 1920, and clinics became established in several other countries as well, a crucial role being played by The Commonwealth Fund. The fund was supposed to address the problem of juvenile delinquency, by conducting clinic-based assessments of young offenders. During the 1920s, the fund contributed to the establishing of clinics and education of staff in several countries, as has been analysed by Thom and Stewart in a British context.[36] The first American child guidance clinics were closely linked to the juvenile courts. After some years, the fund was reoriented towards more general preventive social functions. The central idea was early intervention to prevent criminal deviance. Over 200 clinics were funded in the United States over the following years.[37]

As pointed out, the American movement of child guidance was multifaceted, based on diverse historical contingencies and various intellectual interests. The organisation of the American clinics varied.[38] The English child guidance clinics were organised differently from their American counterparts. The representatives of the funding organisations promoted particular ways of organising the clinics they supported, but, as both Thom and Stewart show, the contingencies varied and the English and Scottish child guidance clinics were based on a diversity of organisational and financial models, displaying a diversity of approaches. According to Thom, the work in the English clinics established between 1920 and 1939 was informed both by the British child study tradition, psychoanalysis, and American psychological medicine. The American and British teams most often came to consist of psychiatric, psychological and social work experts, but research into the work of child guidance clinics has showed that the professional authority of relationships was often negotiated, and the division of labour and authority between the experts of the teams differed.

The ideas and models of these clinics inspired experts from many countries – Scandinavian psychologists and psychiatrists also visited them and brought home the models. The pioneering activities in this field were initiated during the 1930s in the Scandinavian countries, a decade or so later than their British and American counterparts.[39] These initiatives were not followed by economic support from large funds; they were established by experts travelling abroad to visit clinics and learning from the work there. These early child mental health clinics in Scandinavia were unsystematic and mostly on a small scale, being based upon free and idealistic work by a few pioneers.

Psychological expertise was a crucial part of the child guidance teams in England, Scotland and the United States. During the early 1930s, child guidance ideas were transferred to a Norwegian context by one of the country's psychology pioneers, Åse Gruda Skard. There were few psychologists in Norway in the early thirties. Psychology was still a very young and mainly academic discipline. Skard was one of the first educated psychologists, and she remained a leading force in Norwegian child psychology for many decades.

Also in Norway, psychological expertise was needed by the outpatient clinics established in the late 1920s. To classify the clients and their needs, testing skills was considered important. The above-mentioned clinic in Drammen, established on the initiative of Dr. Grimsgaard, focused on child and school hygiene. The medical staff of the clinic asked for psychological expertise to carry out the testing, and Åse Gruda Skard was engaged to carry out this work in the early 1930s. Besides working directly with the children, she did consultant work for the schools in the counties of Vestfold and Buskerud.[40]

Skard made it her programme to establish methods for the prevention of mental illness and other problems among children.[41] She became an important spokesperson for the ideas of child guidance and introduced new knowledge on child psychology. The clinical work, research and popular information carried out by Skard became a strong force in Norwegian child psychology and mental health care. Skard was strongly inspired by Dr. Sigurd Dahlstrøm and was deeply committed to the work of the Mental Hygiene Association in the early 1930s. On Dahlstrøm's advice, she went to the States for further studies after her degree in psychology. She visited the Judge Baker Centre in Boston, and studied and worked with the pioneers Healy and Bronner. The models she learned there became important, but it became a central feature of her work to transform the ideas from abroad into a Norwegian context. It was important for her to base her work on clinical experience with Norwegian children, and she worked to achieve such experience from a variety of jobs, some of which were even unpaid. A central aspect of the child guidance work was to view the child and its problems in relation to the environment in which it was brought up. This made it important to take the particular characteristics of a Norwegian upbringing and childhood into account when using these models.

Skard placed great emphasis on cooperation with parents. The psychologist saw an important role for the clinic in establishing a link between the school and the home. Inspired by her work at the American Judge Baker Clinic, Skard visited the homes of the children and tried to establish relationships with the parents.[42] The out-patient work with children was also based on cooperation with the school system. She further worked to achieve close ties with the teaching profession. Her ideas of handling problem children seem to have fitted well into the pedagogical ideas of representatives of the school system. Through close contacts with some of the radical reform-pedagogical oriented female teachers of the capital in the early thirties, she gained access to school children material for her research. This was important for her ambition to transfer child guidance ideas into a Norwegian context.

Skard's clinical work was based on what have been called a psychological counselling model. The mental hygienic school clinics should have as their main tasks to work with the difficult children at school, and pick out those who needed a special education. The psychologist's testing skills played an important role in the out-patient clinic team work. As described by Dedichen, the physicians first spoke with the adults, to get information on the child and its conditions. Then they spoke thoroughly and inspecting with the child to discover possible illness that could cause the problems.

Skard's close relations with the school system implied that psychologists were entering an arena where psychiatry had a certain foothold since the early 1920s in Norway. The role of psychologists in the testing of school children implied a replacing of the psychiatrists in this setting. Such tasks had been performed by the school psychiatrists that were employed by the municipalities of the two largest cities since the early 1920s.[43] Based on IQ-testing, Dr. Lofthus in Oslo and Dr. Looft in Bergen helped the teachers to differentiate between children with different learning disabilities. Earlier analysis has pointed out that the teachers welcomed the psychiatric and psychological experts into the schools, to handle the segregation of pupils with learning disabilities.[44] According to one of the Oslo school psychiatrists, the purpose of school psychiatry was to meet the needs of teachers to take care of troublesome and less gifted children in an efficient and legitimate way. Via the psychiatric examination schools secured expert decisions on classifications of children, and thus reduced criticisms from parents. In his report on his work as a psychiatrist at the 'særskole', the special classes for the slow learners in Oslo, the school psychiatrist underlined how he was welcomed by the teachers when he started his work there, and how easy and light his work felt because of this very positive cooperation with the teachers. It seems as if the new initiatives represented by mental hygiene clinics were also positively considered among school staff. This cooperation contrasts starkly with the sceptical views towards psychiatrists that the teachers of the schools for the mentally retarded showed in Norway during the twenties and thirties, but it corresponds with analyses made by other Scandinavian researchers on troublesome children. Swedish social scientists Börjeson and Palmblad, for instance, have seen testing, classification and segregation of troublesome children as a cooperative project between experts.[45]

The material from the mental hygiene out-patient clinics indicates that school staff also consulted these clinics when they needed advice on the handling of troublesome children. According to Dr. Dedichen, the Oslo out-patient clinic experienced smooth cooperation with parents, teachers and staff from children's homes that sought advice at the clinic for the handling of troublesome children. A suitable classification of the child in the school system seems to have been a central solution to many problems. Children with low learning abilities were strongly advised to be removed from the homes and to attend special schools. Many of the children attending the clinic, however, were considered to have good abilities, but behaved badly. These children needed to spend their energy on the right things, and placing them at the right educational level would often solve their problems. Thus, a properly differentiated education was a central solution for both psychiatrists and psychologists. This situation differs from the Dutch experience described by Bakker.[46] She points out that in the Netherlands the child guidance experts nurtured a sceptical attitude towards the school system, placing emphasis on the exhaustion of the children and the lack of knowledge in mental health among teaching staff. Also the Norwegian experts, however, could consider the social situation of the school or the home as the cause of the child's problems. In such cases, the child had to be placed in new environments.[47]

The school system was not a strong and enduring field of work for psychiatry. When counseling activities grew in relation to the school system, psychology acquired an increasing role. In 1938, when a small clinic was established in Oslo on the initiative of a psychologist, the clients were mainly school children.⁴⁸ In 1940, a team consisting of a school psychiatrist and a psychologist started to examine school children that had shown problems with their schoolwork. The psychologist took care of the testing, while the psychiatrist did a neurological-psychiatric examination. This work continued after the Second World War, connecting a social worker to the team.⁴⁹

The reinforced testing skills and knowledge of psychologists were important for their work with the school system. During the 1930s, Skard also worked in connection with the University of Oslo, where psychology was now emerging as an academic discipline. During her first years there, she did testing, diagnostic work and partly treatment of children for free, in cooperation with the clinic nurse at the Department of Psychology. The testing experience became important for the development of Norwegian psychology after WW II, when educational psychology became a central field of work for the fast-growing psychology profession. During the inter-war period, the psychiatrists resisted the autonomy of psychologists to carry out testing without the supervision of psychiatrists, but during the 1950s, they had to leave this task to the psychologists.⁵⁰

When child psychiatry was established as a professional field in the early 1960s, the ideas of child guidance remained influential in the organising of team work and the understanding of child mental problems closely linked to the social environment of the child. ⁵¹ The ideas of child guidance merged, however, with therapeutic models related to psychoanalysis during the 1950s. After WW II, travels to the US led to transformed ideas of child guidance being brought back to Scandinavia, with their stronger emphasis on psychoanalytic and psychodynamic aspects of treatment and understanding of the child's mind. This became an important source of inspiration for the first Norwegian child psychiatric wards, established during the 1950s, as well as the comprehensive system of child psychiatry that was institutionalised during the 1960s.⁵²

Transferring and merging ideas of psychoanalysis

During the late 1930s, American mental hygiene went through a redefinition, marked by a stronger emphasis on psychoanalysis and a conceptual shift from hygiene to mental health. The Norwegian branch of mental hygiene work, however, became strongly based on the traditional program of the American mental hygiene movement, according to Haave. He relates this to the weak position of psychoanalysis among Norwegian psychiatrists, and the strong position of hospital care in Norwegian mental health care.[53] When it comes to the establishing of expertise on child mental health, however, psychoanalytic thought seem important from the 1930s onwards. Other studies have pointed out a certain impact of psychoanalytic ideas on early Norwegian psychiatry, but underline that different versions of psychoanalytic ideas received different receptions among the Norwegian experts.[54] Here, the main point will be to trace the particular merging of psychoanalytically inspired thoughts and practice with other streams of thought and the process that made these ideas crucial in early Norwegian child psychiatric work. The role of particular actors will again be addressed in order to grasp this process.

Among the first to pick up the ideas of psychoanalysis in Norway were members of the politically radical group 'Mot Dag', several of whom influenced Norwegian psychiatry, social medicine and health services in important ways during the 1940s and 50s. One of the medical members of this group was the female student Nic Waal, who has been considered a main force behind Norwegian child psychiatry. Her strong influence on the predominantly psychodynamic and social psychiatric perspective of the services is often underlined. Already as a medical student in the twenties, Waal had a strong interest in social medicine. From the late twenties, Waal underwent psychoanalytical therapy by the Norwegian professor of philosophy Harald Schjelderup. This interest became reinforced through her travels abroad, where Waal also came into contact with child mental health work and child psychotherapy. In Berlin in 1932–33 she studied both psychoanalysis and child psychiatry under Professor Kramer. During a stay in Britain in 1935, she visited several London child guidance clinics and schools for nervous children, amongst them Summerhill school and the Tavistock clinic.[55]

One of the first initiatives to introduce a psychotherapeutic practice to Norway was taken by Waal when she established her own private clinic in Oslo. The patients were both adults and children. She also engaged in other kinds of work involving children. During the 1930s, Waal worked as an advisor for the Child Care Council of Oslo. The ideas of child guidance also inspired advisory work towards mothers on child rearing. During the late 1930s, however, Waal mainly worked with adult psychiatric patients. In 1938, she became employed at the state mental hospital at Gaustad in Oslo. In accordance with the common practice there, she used different methods of therapy, also pharmaceutical. After the war, she continued this work at Gaustad.

During the first after-war years, new study trips inspired her work in crucial ways. Her journey to the United States, where she visited the Menninger clinic, was important. This journey has been said to have changed her intellectual views and her professional interests. At the Menninger clinic, child psychiatric therapy was dominated by a psychodynamic orientation. Waal was inspired both by this perspective and methods and the clinic model, combining therapeutic activities, research and education. After this journey Waal decided to devote herself to child psychiatry. She became a specialist in psychiatry in 1951 and in child psychiatry in 1953.

In 1953 Waal also started her own clinic, the Nic Waal's Institute, which she developed into a major child psychiatric clinic in Norway. By 1955, the Institute counted 30 full-time therapists, and 10 working part-time. Following the program of the Menninger clinic, the institute combined the examination and treatment of children and juveniles with adaptation problems with the training of team workers in child psychiatry and research in this field.[56] The institute was a private foundation from the beginning. Representatives of the Directorate of Health sat on the board, and several big Norwegian companies gave financial support. The day-to-day running costs were met partly by health insurance refunds, and partly by support from local government, and the Directorate for Health. The Department of Education financed the training of team workers, which became a significant part of the institution. The training program for the teamwork was very thorough. The Institute trained physicians, psychologists and social workers. And, as in the Mental Hygiene Clinic, a lot of the work was unpaid, or done for low salaries, even if Waal used her close relationship with the powerful Director General of Health, Karl Evang, who also had been part of the 'Mot Dag' group, to apply to the World Health Organization for financial support for the institute.

Studies in other countries have pointed out that the role of different intellectual ideas related to child psychiatry and child guidance was disputed among different expert groups. In Britain, it was the medical doctors who introduced psychoanalytical thinking into the clinics in the 1930s, according to Thom.[57] In other countries, the role of psychoanalytic ideas and therapy seem to have been contested among medical experts. The question of the role of psychoanalysis has also been viewed as important for the forming of Norwegian child psychiatry. Several writers have underlined the controversial position that Nic Waal occupied among the medical elite, and the role that her radical position played in the forming of Norwegian child psychiatry.[58] During the inter-war period, there were tensions among the Norwegian psychiatrists about the role of psychoanalytic ideas. But as Skålevåg has pointed out, there was not a general rejection of psychoanalytic thought among Norwegian psychiatrists.[59] His analysis shows that the medical elite were in favour of a Freudian version, whereas other more marginal representatives of the medical profession tried to import versions that were rejected. This case has also been discussed by Andresen and Grønli, pointing to the filters hindering the implementation of psychoanalysis with a Jung/Bleuler inspiration: The low status of Dr. Strømme, who took the initiative to import the ideas, as well as the contesting of these ideas with the norms and interests of psychiatry, were obstacles to the acceptance of this version of psychoanalytic ideas in Norway. According to Skålevåg, this opened up space for a new group of experts taking over psychoanalysis from psychiatry. A leading figure was Nic Waal's analyst, Harald K. Schjelderup, who received psychoanalytical training in Vienna and Zurich, and was appointed to a chair in philosophy in Oslo in 1928. This chair was later transformed into the first chair of psychology in Norway. Politically radical young doctors like Waal became inspired by Schjelderup to train as analysts, but still Skålevåg argues that psychoanalysis broke away from Norwegian psychiatry during the 1930s. The arrival of Wilhelm Reich in Norway in the 1930s also influenced the Norwegian psychiatrists' view of psychoanalysis. Reich had been dismissed from the International Psychoanalytical Association, and the dispute about his ideas and role also involved Nic Waal. According to her son and biographer, Helge Waal she did not completely defend the theories of Reich, but wanted his case to be properly treated by psychiatrists.[60] Even so, her standpoints in this matter were not embraced by the psychiatric elite of the country.

During the forties, a new conflict arose between Nic Waal and members of the academic medical elite, a dispute that has also been linked to the medical elite's problems with accepting Waal's radical standpoints. Norway did not have any psychiatric ward for children before 1950. In 1949, it was decided to establish a child psychiatric ward and a position for a psychiatrist connected to the children's ward at Rikshospitalet, the state general hospital in Oslo. According to Helge Waal, the medical professors became worried when Nic Waal applied for this position, and no one was employed. When the position was again announced, Nic Waal did not apply, deciding instead to establish her own clinic.

The small ward in the basement of the hospital employed the psychiatrist Hjalmar Wergeland as its first head. This ward at the National hospital was the only ward of its kind in Norway until 1962. It was important because specialist training in child psychiatry required practice here. When Norwegian child psychiatry was defined as a medical speciality and part of the mental health care system during the early 1960s, it was based on institutions separate from the adult mental health hospitals. The important first clinics were the ward at Rikshospitalet, the Nic Waal Institute and the State established 1962 centre for child psychiatry in Oslo. The system established during the 1960s was based on out-patient clinics spread around the country. As in Sweden, a psychodynamics-oriented therapy had a dominating role. [61] Like Waal, Hjalmar Wergeland had been studying in the United States, and his long-lasting work in Norwegian child psychiatry was strongly inspired by the American model of child guidance. This made the psychodynamics-oriented child guidance model important in Norwegian child psychiatry.

Åsmund Seip has pointed out that there were important differences between the approaches used at the Nic Waal Institute and the other central child psychiatric clinics in Norway in the early 1960s.[62] The structure at NWI was less hierarchical than at the state centre for child and adolescent psychiatry (SSBU). The so-called ego-psychology, a form of psychodynamic thought shaped by Anna Freud and Heintz Hartman, was important for all the Norwegian child psychiatric clinics. At the NWI, the therapy was based on a broad approach with long-lasting individual therapy of children and parents, and seeing the child and its environment as a whole.

The controversial role of Nic Waal's standpoints regarding both politics and therapy has been interpreted as a crucial factor for the particular organisation of Norwegian child psychiatry.[63] But also close relationships between experts and central health government actors and the merging of psychodynamic thoughts with other ideas central to Norwegian psychiatry and child mental health care must be considered important for the form and content of the services developed during the 1950s. Nic Waal seems to have been a woman of great initiative, with a wide network of contacts, both at home and abroad. Waal was very well educated in psychoanalysis, and brought with her modern ideas from leading international institutions. During the 1950s, the model she and others brought home from the American clinics became important, combining the methods of psychodynamic therapies with a child guidance teamwork model. Waal took part in conflicts on the role of psychoanalysis in psychiatry and stood up against the medical elite in questions related to this, although she also continued some of the traditions central to Norwegian psychiatry: the eclectics in therapy, the holism, the combination of a psychological and a social perspective. Merged with psychodynamic thoughts and methods and child guidance-inspired team work this also became an important platform for the central practices and measures related to Norwegian child psychiatry. The child mental health services, however, were established on the borders between education policies, social policies and health care, and the policies, the organising of services and the education of experts varied from the adult mental health services. In the last section of this chapter, I will discuss some of the central features of the definition of child psychiatry as a field of expertise and public policy in Norway, compared to some other European countries, based on the previous analysis of the transferring processes.

Travelling knowledge and the establishing of child psychiatry as a public policy field

Ideas of mental hygiene, child guidance and psychoanalysis inspired experts in psychology and psychiatry to reinforce their interest in the minds of children. Measures aimed at preventing mental illness and social problems through advice and counselling and the right classification of childhood problems were important. Such initiatives were supported by prominent members of the medical professions and became established in close relationship between the experts, the voluntary organisations and government representatives. There were, however, variations in the implementation of the new knowledge on children's minds.[64] Through mental hygiene, psychiatrists in particular reinforced their concerns about the prevention of mental and social problems, and the need to start with classifying and care for childhood problems to cope with these challenges. They became spokesmen for these ideas through popular information, associations and the establishing of clinical work. Psychiatric experts saw themselves as an important contributor of understanding and handling of problems related to the school system, the care for the mentally ill as well as juvenile delinquency and other areas. The role of these experts in these areas varied between countries, as did that of mental hygiene ideas. Also child guidance became linked to different areas of policy and care in different countries. What will be discussed here are some features of the policy definitions and the organisation of the services aimed at child mental health in Norway, and an attempt to link these features to the way ideas of mental hygiene, child guidance and psychoanalysis merged in particular ways in the Norwegian case.

As mentioned, the early American child guidance clinics were linked to the system of juvenile courts. However, the link weakened over time, and it also seems that the relationships between the child guidance activities and the legal system varied between countries. A study of Swedish child psychiatry places emphasis on the influence on the mental health professions and care from the system taking care of juvenile delinquency.[65] It also seems as if some of the Swedish child guidance-inspired clinics became established with close ties to the Child Care system. In a paper on the construction of the Swedish juvenile delinquent, Nilsson has pointed out that the psychiatrist Olof Kinberg contributed strongly to the Swedish leap in the categorisation of the juvenile delinquent in the 1930s. In Sweden, a nation-wide system of reformatory prisons developed, characterised by an increasing medicalisation. Nilsson argues that from the 1950s, the medical and social approach melted together, forming a powerful treatment-oriented discourse that dominated the discussions of youth criminality for a long time.[66]

In both Norway and Sweden, central psychiatrists engaged in questions related to criminology. The links between the Norwegian child guidance clinics and the system taking care of juvenile delinquency are not as visible, but like in Sweden, some of the central members of psychiatry shared broad interests in questions of children, youth and social problems. Norwegian psychiatrists saw the categorisation of delinquents and possible delinquents as a task where they could supply the local boards and the special schools with techniques of classification. Also, the special schools made up laboratories where groups of children could be examined. Professor Vogt was involved in discussions on this question around the turn of the century, and he assisted several public reform committees.[67] In the 1920s and 1930s, Norwegian spokesmen of mental hygiene assisted local child care boards in their work, among them were the psychiatrists Dr. Dahlstrøm and Dr. Lofthus. As pointed out earlier in this article, Dr. Dahlstrøm was involved in these questions from the early phase of his career, and he published several works on these matters. Dahlstrøm saw the child welfare or 'vergerådssystem' as one of the most important factors in the promotion of mental hygiene. But when the idea of child guidance clinics was put into practice, these clinics did not establish close links to the field of juvenile delinquency. As in England, they came to take care of other problems regarding childhood. The loose links to the system of child welfare may have made it easier to achieve trust in the guidance work from the parents, but maybe also among the teachers, who welcomed the IQ-testing of children to help them in their assignment of pupils to the proper level and institution of education.[68]

The analysis has pointed to the close relationship established between teachers and psy-experts in Norway during the 1930s. Unlike both the US and the Norwegian case, Bakker has pointed out that in the Netherlands, the school was considered of little importance in the crusade for the prevention of mental illness. What Bakker has labelled the Dutch child guidance lobby monopolised the care, treatment and knowledge of problem children, in relation to child guidance clinics, discrediting the expertise of both teachers and parents.[69] In Norway as in other Western countries, both psychiatrists and psychologists were involved in the educational system during the inter-war period, in particular through the testing of the learning abilities and mental development of the pupils. The Norwegian psychologists' contribution to mental health work with children was welcomed by the psychiatrists. Among the teaching profession, too, the ideas of child guidance were met with a cooperative spirit. Norwegian psychiatrists did not see a central role for themselves in the practical work with these children. Their role was to supply the teachers, social workers, nurses and parents with tools for defining and classifying pupils, to give advice to other experts and the public, and to treat the small group of troublesome children defined as having real mental illnesses and problems. The psychiatrists argued for a professional cooperation in this field through a medical-pedagogical system where the psychiatrists supplied the knowledge and the differentiation, and the teachers did the practical work with the children. The solution most often defined as a way of handling the troublesome and deviant was to secure the right education of the children. Through testing, children in need of a special education were categorised and separated from the others. The Norwegian psychiatrists and psychologists saw themselves as experts on such matters, but defined their expertise in a way that was considered useful for the teachers of the larger city schools. It became an arena for the new psychology profession. But after the Second World War, the psychiatrists gave up their ambition to control and regulate the testing of school children, and left this field of work to the young and rapidly growing Norwegian psychology profession that became crucial when the school counselling activities were developed during the 1950s.[70]

The split between child mental health work, child care and school psychology widened around 1960. During the 1950s and 60s, child psychiatry gained acceptance as a medical discipline and child mental health services became a public policy responsibility in many countries, also in Scandinavia. At the same time, the content of the services was redefined, and child mental health was to a larger extent seen as a health policy matter. Norwegian initiatives seem to have come somewhat later, and the number of out-patient clinics grew slower than in other Scandinavian countries during the 1930s. In Sweden this redefinition took place during the late 1940s. A handful of socialist medical doctors contributed to the redefinition of child psychiatric and psychological work, according to Zetterquist Nelson. The activities of these agents supported the establishment of a nation-wide system where Child and Youth psychological care became part of the health care system rather than the child welfare boards.[71] She dates the beginning of state-subsidised care in Sweden to February 1945, when a proposal was made where psychological care for children was to be linked to the pediatric units at the county hospitals. Nelson argues that a group of physicians with explicit socialist visions and ideals became central experts in the process where child psychiatry in Sweden became defined as a health issue. Nelson further argues that the political contexts of the reforms had certain implications for the aims and methods of the child psychological care system. The system established was one of the medical experts advising other expert groups with the aim of preventing mental health problems, through parental advice and education. Children with graver problems were referred to treatment based on various kinds of psychotherapy. A connection between the psychological care system for children and youth, socialistic political visions of central medical actors and psychoanalytic therapeutic methods was established, Zetterquist Nelson argues.

The close Swedish relationship between the health system and psychiatric activities were not self-evident at this point in time, according to Nelson. Until the 1950s, public policy in the field of child psychiatry in Norway was very modest. A few out-patient clinics got some financial support from the government, but not on a regular basis. This changed during the 1950s. Several initiatives were then made to strengthen the work with troublesome children. Clinics with public support were established. Through a complex process, Norwegian child psychiatry became more clearly defined as a part of the public health policy, but with features differing from the Swedish system, where there was established close links between child psychiatry and the somatic child health care in hospital paediatric units.

As in several other western countries during the 1920s and 30s, mental hygiene ideas strengthened the focus on childhood as an important interest for the Norwegian experts of mental health and illness. Expert advice and popular information on mental hygiene and child guidance made the population aware of a new way of seeing childhood problems as an issue for experts on the mind. Child guidance also represented a way of organising expert teams that was adapted to the Norwegian scene in specific ways, where the structure of teams and expert groups involved seems to have differed slightly from other countries. And the 1950s wave of American child guidance thoughts that combined a psychodynamic therapeutic approach with the focus on the child's environment as a crucial factor for mental health and illness inspired the Norwegian experts already familiar with the thoughts of psychoanalysis.

Concluding remarks

In early 1960s Norway, child mental health was not any longer seen as a task to be handled through social policy or educational policy, but became part of a new and broader health policy, carried out by the strong Norwegian social democratic state. The 1961 Mental Health Act cut ties between child guidance activities and the community child care service. Child psychiatry was defined as part of the mental health system. A state planned regional system of child psychiatry with close connections to central health authorities was established, based mainly on out-patient clinics. But the Norwegian child psychiatry system became organised through a specific set of clinics and institutions, separate from the adult psychiatric hospitals, and the multidisciplinary expertise on children's minds was taught in the two Oslo clinics that combined perspectives and therapeutic methods by psychodynamic thought and in teams based on the principles of child guidance in different ways.[72] And the traditional ideas of mental hygiene, placing emphasis on the prevention of mental illness, became an important part of the governmental plans for the improvement of public health in Norway after World War II. For the first decades after the war, however, the main task was to get enough hospital beds. In the early 1970s, ideas of preventing mental problems among children became important again, as part of the local public health work.

As in several other Western countries during the 1920s and 30s, mental hygiene ideas strengthened the focus on childhood as an important interest for the Norwegian experts of mental health and illness. Expert advice and popular information on mental hygiene and child guidance made the population aware of a new way of seeing childhood problems as an issue for experts on the mind. Child guidance also represented a way of organising expert teams that was adapted to the Norwegian scene in specific ways, where the structure of teams and expert groups involved seems to have differed slightly from other countries. And the 1950s wave of American child guidance thoughts that combined a psychodynamic therapeutic approach with the focus on the child's environment as a crucial factor for mental health and illness inspired the Norwegian experts already familiar with the thoughts of psychoanalysis.

Notes

1   Roger Cooter, 1992; Kari Ludvigsen, 2004; Åsmund Arup Seip, 2004; Kari Ludvigsen, Kari & Åsmund A. Seip, 2009, p. 20, 5; Karin Zetterquist Nelson, 2007.
2   Nikolas Rose, 1998; Deborah Thom, 1992, Kathleen W. Jones, 1999; John Stewart, 2001, p. 50; Nelleke Bakker, 2006.
3   Deborah Thom, 1992; John Stewart, 2001 & 2004.
4   Karin Z. Nelson, 2008; Kari Ludvigsen & Åsmund Seip, 2009.
5   Astri Andresen & Tore Grønli, 2007.
6   Deborah Thom, 1992; John Stewart 2001; 2004.
7   John Stewart, 2001; 2004.

8   Roger Quarsell, 1997.
9   Andrew Abbott, 1988.
10 Roger Quarsell, 1997.
11 John Stewart, 2001 p. 50.
12 Harry Hendrick, 1994; Harry Hendrick, 1997; Roger Quarsell, 1997.
13 Sigurd Dahlstrøm, 1931.
14 Sigurd Dahlstrøm, 1928, pp. 1070-1085.
15 Bård Brekke, 1952, pp. 279-28; Helge Waal, 1991, p. 219.
16 Kari Ludvigsen, 1998; Svein Atle Skålevåg, 2003; Per Haave, 2009.
17 Christofer Lohne Knudsen, 1952, pp. 271-277.
18 Kari Ludvigsen, 1998.
19 Svein Atle Skålevåg, 2003, pp. 333-354.
20 Norsk Mentalhygienisk Forening changed its name to Oslo Mentalhygienisk Forening.
21 Geir Evjen, 1983.
22 The child care act from 1896 established a system of local boards, called vergeråd, with lay people and experts given the task of deciding on the use of various measures to prevent delinquency and of taking care of children in danger.
23 Kari Ludvigsen, 2008.
24 Kari Ludvigsen, 2008.
25 Ulf Jönsson, 1997.
26 Viktor Wigert, Emilia Fogelklou & Kerstin Hesselgren, 1932.
27 Roger Quarsell, 1997.
28 Wilhelm Grimsgaard, 1928, pp. 857-866.
29 Per Haave, 2009.
30 Rohde Moe, 1935, pp. 3-6.
31 Bård Brekke, 1952, p. 283.
32 *Folkehelseforeningens Tidsskrift*, 1937, årg. 18, no. 2, no. 3, 1938, no. 6, p. 31.
33 *Folkehelseforeningens Tidsskrift*, 1938, årg. 19, no. 2, pp. 26-28, no. 6, p. 18.
34 *Folkehelseforeningens Tidsskrift*, 1939, årg. 19, p. 26.
35 Kathleen Jones, 1999, pp. 6-16.
36 Deborah Thom, 1992; Stewart, 2001; 2004.
37 Deborah Thom, 1992, p. 206.
38 John Stewart, 2001.
39 Roger Quarsell, 1997.
40 Siri Gullestad & Anna Louise von der Lippe, 1984, p. 187.
41 Siri Gullestad & Anna Louise von der Lippe, 1984, p. 185; Åse Gruda Skard, 1959.
42 Synnøve Hernes, 1991.
43 Kari Ludvigsen, 2004.
44 Jan Froestad & Bodil Ravneberg, 2006.
45 Mats Børjeson & Eva Palmblad, 2003.
46 Nelleke Bakker, 2006.
47 H.H. Dedichen, 1936, pp. 3-13.
48 Geir Evjen, 1983, pp. 15-16.
49 D. Oftedal, 1952, pp. 7-10.
50 Bodil Ravneberg, 1999; Eva Simonsen, 1998.
51 Synnøve Hernes, 1991; Kari Ludvigsen and Åsmund Seip, 2009.
52 Kari Ludvigsen and Åsmund Seip, 2009.

53 Per Haave, 2009.
54 Svein Atle Skålevåg, 2006.
55 This journey was made possible by a scholarship from the municipality of Oslo.
56 Nic Waals Institutt, *Virksomheten gjennom de første 2 år. 1953–1955*, 1957, Oslo.
57 Deborah Thom, 1992.
58 Helge Waal, 1991; E. Moe, 2003.
59 Svein Atle Skålevåg, 2006, pp. 125-138.
60 Helge Waal, 1991.
61 Kari Ludvigsen and Åsmund Seip, 2009.
62 Kari Ludvigsen and Åsmund Seip, 2009.
63 E. Moe, 2003.
64 Kari Ludvigsen, 2004.
65 Ulf Jönsson, 1997.
66 Nelson, 2007.
67 Kari Ludvigsen, 1998.
68 Jan Froestad & Bodil Ravneberg, 2006.
69 Bakker, 2006, p. 782.
70 Synnøve Hernes, 1992.
71 Karin Zetterquist Nelson, 2007, p. 11.
72 Kari Ludvigsen and Åsmund Seip, 2009.

References

Abbott, Andrew 1988: *The system of professions: an essay on the division of expert labour*, The University of Chicago Press, Chicago & London.

Andresen, Astri et al. 2004: 'US Influences on the development of Child Guidance and psychiatric Social Work in Scotland and Great Britain during the Inter-war period'.

Andresen, Astri (ed.), *Public Health and preventive medicin 1800-2000*, Bergen.

Andresen, Astri and Tore Grønli 2007: 'Travellers and travels of health: from inspiration to adaptation', Andresen and Grønli (eds.), *Transferring Public health, medical Knowledge and Science in the 19th and 20th Century*, Conference Proceedings, Stein Rokkan Centre for Social Studies, Report, Bergen.

Bakker, Nelleke 2006: 'Child Guidance and mental health in the Netherlands', *Paedagogica Historica*, no. 6, vol. 42.

Brekke, Bård 1952: 'Mentalhygiene', Storsteen, Einar (ed.), *Sosial håndbok for Norge*, bind I, Norsk forening for sosialt arbeide.

Børjeson, Mats og Eva Palmblad 2003: *I problembarnens tid*, Förnuftets moraliska ordning, Stockholm.

Cooter, Roger (ed.) 1992: *In the name of the child: health and welfare 1880–1940*, London.

Dahlstrøm, Sigurd 1928: 'Litt om 'mental-hygienebevægelsen'', foredrag holdt ved Norsk hygienisk foreningsmøte i Oslo 1927, *Tidsskrift for Den norske lægeforening 1928*, årg. 48.

Dahlstrøm, Sigurd 1931: 'Mentalhygiene', foredrag ved åpningsmøtet for Mentalhygienisk forening, *Mentalhygienisk forenings småskrifter*, no. 1, Oslo.

Dedichen, H.H. 1936: 'Fra den Mentalhygieniske arbeidsmark', foredrag holdt for

Mentalhygienisk Forening 3. desember 1936, *Folkehelseforeningens Tidsskrift*, årg. 16, no. 8.
Evjen, Geir 1983: *Pedagogisk-psykologisk rådgivning - et historisk perspektiv*, Brandbu.
Froestad, Jan and Bodil Ravneberg 2006: 'Education Policy, the Norwegian Unitary School and the Social Construction of disability', *Scand. Journal of History*, no. 2, vol. 31.
Grimsgaard, Wilhelm 1928: 'Om sindets hygiene og i forbindelse dermed paatænkt dispensærvirksomhet ved Lierasylet', *Tidsskrift for Den norske lægeforening 1928*, årg. 48.
Gullestad, Siri and Anna Louise von der Lippe (eds.) 1984: *Kvinner i psykologien. Portrett av ni pionerer*, Oslo.
Haave, Per 2009: *Ambisjon og handling. Sanderud sykehus og norsk psykiatri i et historisk perspektiv*, Sanderud asyl 1908–2008, Oslo.
Hendrick, Harry 1994: *Child Welfare: England 1872-1989*, London.
Hendrick, Harry 1997: *Children, Childhood and English Society 1880-1990*, Cambridge.
Hernes, Synnøve 1991: *Velferdsstat, barnevernsreformer og profesjonalisering av psykologien*, LOS-senteret, Notat 92/21, Bergen.
Jones, Kathleen W. 1999: *Taming the Troublesome Child: American Families, Child Guidance, and the Limits of Psychiatric Authority*, Cambridge, Mass.
Jönsson, Ulf 1997: *Bråkiga, løsaktiga och nagelbitande barn. Om barn och barnproblem vid en rådgivningsbyrå i Stockholm 1933-1950*, Linköping Studies in Arts and Science 159, Linköping.
Knudsen, Christofer Lohne 1952: 'Omsorgen for de sinnslidende og nervøse', Storsteen, Einar (ed.), *Sosial håndbok for Norge*, bind I, Norsk forening for sosialt arbeide.
Ludvigsen, Kari 1998: *Kunnskap og politikk i norsk sinnsyke resen, 1820-1920*. Rapport no. 63, Institutt for Administrasjon og organisasjonsvitenskab, Bergen.
Ludvigsen, Kari 2004: 'Child Guidance and Mental Hygiene in Inter-War Norway', Andresen, A., Kari Tove Elvbakken and William Hubbard (eds.), *Public health and Preventive Medicine 1800-2000*, Rokkansenteret, Report 1, Bergen.
Ludvigsen, Kari 2008: 'Hensiktsmessige vaner i et hensiktsmessig miljø', Elvbakken and Stenvoll (eds.), *Reisen til helseland. Propaganda i folkehelsens tjeneste*, Bergen.
Ludvigsen, Kari and Åsmund A. Seip 2009: 'The establishing of Norwegian Child Psychiatry: ideas, pioneers and institutions', *History of Psychiatry*.
Moe, E. 2003: *Nic Waals Institutt. Pioner og aktør i norsk barne- og ungdomspsykiatri gjennom 50 år*, Oslo.
Nelson, Karin Zetterquist 2007: 'The development of Swedish Child and Youth Psychological Care System - the role of socialist medical doctors', Paper, In the Name of the Child, SHCY-conference, Norrköping, Sweden.
Nic Waals Institutt 1957: *Virksomheten gjennom de første 2 år. 1953–1955*, Oslo.
Oftedal, D. 1952: 'Utviklingen av arbeidet ved Skolepsykologisk kontor i Oslo'. *Impuls*, no. 6.
Quarsell, Roger 1997: 'Mentalhygien och psykisk hälsovård', Eriksson, B.E. og R. Quarsell (eds.), *Hur skall själen läkas. Forändringar innom den psykiatriska vården*, Borås.
Ravneberg, Bodil 1999: *Normalitetsdiskurser og profesjonaliseringsprosesser. En studie av den spesialpedagogiske yrkesutviklingen 1880-1990*, report no. 69, Bergen.
Rohde, Moe 1935: Et kort foredrag om Lierasylets polikliniske virksomhet, *Folkehelseforeningens Tidsskrift*, årg. 15, no. 4.
Rose, Nikolas 1998: *Inventing our selves: Psychology, Power and Personhood*, Cambridge.

Seip, Åsmund Arup 2004: 'Private Initiative for Public health: The Emergence of Child Psychiatry in Post-War Norway', Andresen, A. (ed.), *Public health and Preventive Medicine 1800-2000* Rokkansenteret, Report 1, Bergen.

Simonsen, Eva 1998: *Vitenskap og profesjonskamp. Opplæring av døve og åndssvake i Norge 1881-1963*, Oslo.

Skard, Åse Gruda (ed.) 1959: *Psykologi og psykologar i Norge*, Oslo.

Skålevåg, Svein Atle 2003: *Fra normalitetens historie. Sinnssykdom 1870-1920*, Rokkansenteret, report no. 10.

Skålevåg, Svein Atle 2006: 'Psychoanalysis and /as science. Norway, 1900-1930', Andresen and Grønli (eds.).

Stewart, John 2001: 'The most precious possession of a nation is its children: The Clyde Committee on Homeless Children in Scotland', *Scottish Economic and Social History*, vol. 21.

Thom, Deborah 1992: 'Wishes, anxieties, plays and gestures: Child guidance in Inter-War England', Cooter, Roger (ed.): *In the Name of the Child: Health and Welfare 1880-1990*, London.

Waal, Helge 1991: *Nic Waal. Det urolige hjerte*, Oslo.

Wigert, Viktor, Emilia Fogelklou and Kerstin Hesselgren 1932: *Om psykisk hälsovård: Et försummat samhällsproblem*. Svenska föreningen för psykisk hälsovård småskrifter, no. 1.

Power, knowledge and acknowledgement of expertise: Signe and Axel Höjer's strategies to launch public health ideas, 1919–1970

Annika Berg

People acknowledged as experts played crucial roles in the construction of modern welfare states. This was also very much the case in Sweden during the long rule of Social Democracy. But who were those people who established themselves as experts? And how did they manage to claim expertise in various fields? This text primarily aims to explore the second question, but will also help to illuminate the first.

In recent historiography, and even more so in popular media discourse, Alva Myrdal and Gunnar Myrdal have often stood out as *the* experts who shaped the Swedish welfare system. But they were hardly alone in this, not even as an expert-couple. I will examine the careers of two other, married and more or less co-working, partners – Signe Höjer and Axel Höjer – who came to play significant parts in public health and social policy making, in Sweden but also internationally. By studying Signe Höjer and Axel Höjer as a couple, I will try to shed light on the acknowledgement of expertise, or, more precisely, how certain people came to be recognised as experts in some different contexts and processes of policy making. I will explore how the Höjers' attempts to establish themselves as experts – and their varying success in doing so – were influenced by factors such as gender, class and education, and I will apply a transnational perspective to the use of knowledge in the construction and government of welfare states.

A twentieth century couple

Axel Höjer was born in Visby in 1890 and grew up in Stockholm. His father was a high-school teacher with a doctoral degree in political science, his mother was a housewife, although trained as a singer, and Axel was the oldest child among eight siblings, the majority of whom, both sisters and brothers, made brilliant careers within politics, public management and union work.[1] Axel himself was educated as a medical doctor and reached fame and notoriety when, between 1935 and 1952, he acted as an unusually radical, and often controversial, Director-General of the Swedish Medical Board.

Signe Höjer was born in Malmö in 1896. Her maiden name was Signe Dahl. She was the youngest daughter in a relatively affluent family that adhered to the Swedish Evangelical Mission. Her family would not allow her to pursue a university education, allegedly for health reasons – her elder sister had protracted tuberculosis while studying. Instead, Signe Dahl trained as a nurse and a social worker. In time, she became active as a Social Democratic politician and a member of various public commissions. She also became well known as a peace activist and an author.

Axel Höjer and Signe Dahl met in Paris in the summer of 1919 and got married in the following spring. After three decades in increasingly central positions within the Swedish political system, the couple devoted themselves full-time to international development work, mainly in the newly independent states of India (Kerala and Assam) and Ghana. Their international commitment continued after their return to Sweden in the 1960s, when they engaged in campaigns against leprosy and nuclear armament, and worked more generally to promote Swedish development aid to the third world.

Axel Höjer died in 1974 after a period of illness. Signe Höjer survived him by fourteen years, being active to the end. She died in March 1988, at the age of nearly 92. Her last book was published posthumously.[2]

Definitions of expertise

To understand the place and function of people like Axel Höjer and Signe Höjer, respectively, in the welfare state context, I will claim that we need an inclusive definition of the concept expertise. The British sociologist Nikolas Rose uses the term expertise to refer to 'a particular kind of social authority, characteristically deployed around problems, exercising a certain diagnostic gaze, grounded in a claim to truth, asserting technical efficacy, and avowing humane ethical virtues.'[3] His fellow sociologist Zygmunt Bauman traces a similar line in his definition of expertise as a specifically modern form of authority:

'The essence of expertise is the assumption that doing things properly requires certain knowledge, that such knowledge is distributed unevenly, that some persons possess more of it than others, that those who possess it ought to be in charge of doing things, and that being in charge places upon them the responsibility for how things are being done. In fact, the responsibility is seen as vested not in the experts, but in the skills they represent. [...] For those who do not possess the know-how responsible action means following the advice of the experts. In the process, personal responsibility dissolves in the abstract authority of technical know-how.'[4]

In a similar way, when I speak of experts, I refer to people who are supposed to possess a more or less exclusive knowledge about how to solve different social problems. Expertise, thus, simultanously refers to *knowledge* about how things should be done and to the *people* who represent this knowledge.

The centrality of expertise in modern welfare states can be explained in terms of a rationality inherent in modern governance, i.e. what Michel Foucault and some of his followers have referred to as governmentality. This concept implies that the exercise of power in modern democracies is based on a kind of paradox. At the same time as modern governance strives to control people's behaviour, and reaches ever further into people's private and everyday lives, it is fundamentally dependent on their freedom of action. This dependence on freedom is not only a matter of ideology. It is also a practical necessity. The more complex a society gets, the more impossible for its government to manage the amount of knowledge needed to control it. Thus, a great part of actual governance needs to be delegated and exercised outside of the politically elected centres of power. Governments need to employ a growing amount of self-regulating technologies, with the aid of which people can be formed as subjects and enabled to govern themselves in directions perceived as desirable by the rulers as well as by themselves.[5]

But, for power to diffuse ever further out into the capillary networks of society, experts in possession of specific knowledge are crucial as mediators.[6] And, as I will claim in this text, the power of knowledge very much depends on it being acknowledged as such. And, perhaps needless to say: knowledge can be used in different ways, and what counts as knowledge varies depending on context.

The emergence of expertise

In order to understand the role of expertise in the construction of the modern welfare system, it is necessary to look outside the narrow group of persons officially appointed as experts. Signe Höjer and Axel Höjer did not always act as experts in an official sense, and they certainly did not start out as such. Primarily, they had to claim expertise for themselves, and try to gain acknowledgement of those claims. In other words, they had to appoint themselves as experts.[7] In order to reach influence as self-appointed experts, it was essential for them to invoke unique knowledge.

An example of this can be drawn from the Höjers' very first years as a cooperating couple. When they first met in Paris in the summer of 1919, they were united by a common interest in healthcare and children's welfare, as well as a shared sense of commitment to a social task of almost boundless proportions. For practical and ideological reasons, however, they decided to start by reforming Swedish child healthcare.

Young and unestablished as they were, they had to use a variety of strategies to implement their ideas. Central to these strategies was the claim of unique international experience. As soon as Axel Höjer returned to Sweden in 1920, he wrote a report on French and English child healthcare to the Medical Board of Sweden, which had financed part of his stay abroad. The travel report was remarkably long, almost taking on the appearance of a commission report with suggestions for reform. Axel Höjer also wrote several journal articles, directed towards different professions in the fields of health and social work.[8] Signe Höjer gave lectures on social childcare and child healthcare and apparently helped Axel with the report and some articles.[9]

In the report, as well as in other texts, Sweden was consistently presented as a backward country. In order to compete with the dominant countries in Europe, Sweden was exhorted to strengthen its public health system. Children's health would act as a key to public health and foreign reforms should serve as models for reforming child healthcare.[10] Axel Höjer emphasised that many of the best ideas for reform of child healthcare originated in France.[11] However, it was primarily England that he and Signe Höjer highlighted as an example worth following. The English were described as less innovative than the French, but more able to implement reforms – many of them more or less imported from other countries – such as the system of so-called health visitors and the state-sponsored Infant Welfare Centres, where new mothers were encouraged to breastfeed their children and taught various aspects of 'good mothercraft'.[12] England was presented as a formerly very backward and still quite conservative country that nevertheless was now moving quickly forward. By doing this, Axel Höjer implied that Sweden, being even more backward but in possession of more innovative, reasonable and progressive citizens, would be able to implement similar (although not identical) reforms even faster than England.[13]

The strategy used in writing these texts can be defined as lesson-drawing, that is, to use the words of the political scientist Richard Rose, 'an action-oriented conclusion about a programme or programmes in operation elsewhere; the setting can be another city, another state, another nation or an organization's own past'. A 'lesson', so defined, is more than an evaluation of a programme in its original context. It also implies an estimation of the value of doing the same – or something similar – somewhere else.[14] Lesson-drawing in this case could be used for at least a couple of different, although closely related, purposes. First, the Höjers could use references to well-acknowledged experts, well-known institutions and more developed nations in order to strengthen their own arguments and anchor their ideas. Second, by indicating international experience and contacts with world-renowned academics and medical authorities such as Frederic Truby King, Adolphe Pinard and Antoine Bernard-Jean Marfan, they could enhance their own professional status.[15]

However, lesson-drawing does not necessarily result in change. For example, actors may draw *negative* lessons from different experiences, and warn against programmes and innovations that should *not* be imitated.[16] This kind of strategy too is evident in the Höjer case. While both used England as a source of positive lessons, Axel Höjer largely used his French experience as a warning example. Although he stressed that the French were worthy of respect for their brilliant ideas and innovations, he argued that they suffered from lack of morality and practical inability to cope with social problems. The most important lesson to draw from the French, thus, was *not* to follow their lead.[17]

But, I would like to add, lesson-drawing not resulting in change may also be due to a lack of the kind of power relevant to an expert – i.e. the acknowledgement of a person as being in possession of special knowledge. Aspiring policy-makers in non-governmental positions may well influence policy-making, but they have to do it by indirect means. When the young Höjer couple had drawn their lessons, their next step could not possibly be the immediate implementation of policies. Instead, their process of learning had to be complemented by different kinds of influencing strategies to make the transfer of ideas or policies possible.[18] Such strategies, I propose, may include both rhetoric and practice. Obviously, writing reports and articles are rhetorical strategies, and so is lecturing. A practical strategy may be to launch a project to serve as a 'pilot' or model for future institutionalisation.

Lacking professional status and with limited access to channels to speak through, the Höjers had to add strategies of a more practical nature to advance their ideas. In the summer of 1920, the newly-wed couple moved to the impoverished suburb of Hagalund in Solna, just outside Stockholm, where Axel started a private practice and Signe Höjer took assignments as a social childcare inspector.[19] Additionally, and of much greater consequence in a longer-term historical perspective, they reformed the existing Solna Milk Drop into a network of infant healthcare centres. The milk drop – derived from a French model – had focused on providing cow's milk for poor mothers and their babies. At the new infant clinics, as the healthcare centres were called initially, the Höjers' main emphasis was on encouraging mothers to breast-feed and to teach them how to behave as rational, observant and hygienic mothers. The infants were regularly weighed and monitored at the clinics, where Axel – and sometimes Signe – Höjer also gave lectures on a range of topics. They focused on the benefits of breast-feeding, but also treated more controversial subjects, like birth control. The Höjers imagined their project as a model for a future system of similar clinics which was eventually to cover the entire country.[20] Via information, education and training, the reforms ultimately aimed at creating women who could look after their children in the way medical science considered most appropriate. Their objective was to 'make' families in a new, more efficient way, but not necessarily to create a new type of family. Rather, the aim was to make working-class women adapt their behaviour to an established bourgeois – although in the eyes of Axel Höjer truly socialistic – norm, with families dependent on a male breadwinner.

The Solna milk drop was not the first in Sweden to change its emphasis from the distribution of cow's milk to the encouragement of breastfeeding. Similar experiments had been carried out at other Swedish milk drops.[21] But the reforms initiated by Axel Höjer and Signe Höjer were among the most ambitious and systematic. The

Höjers, and particularly Signe, were also unusually careful to point out that their system was not meant to serve as a charitable institution. Its ultimate goal was to reach all mothers, not only the poorest, and to get the healthcare centres financed by public funds.[22]

Both Signe Höjer and Axel Höjer were happy to admit that their Solna project had drawn inspiration from other countries, and especially from the so-called Infant Welfare Centres and Schools for Mothers they had visited in England. These references helped to legitimise their own practical endeavours, at the same time as their pilot project could be used to demonstrate that their foreign ideas, adapted to a Swedish context, actually worked. This could be helpful when launching their ideas in more influential circles, which they, and particularly Axel, continued to do.

Ultimately, these attempts did have effects at a national level. Axel Höjer initiated a discussion and, in 1923, joined together a group of pediatricians to make a common statement on the need of child healthcare reforms. Later, he was attached to a couple of governmental commissions as an expert on maternal and child healthcare. His recommendations on the subjects were included in the reports of several state commissions and had an impact on the bills they put forward. From 1937 onwards, when new legislation granted state support to a nationwide network of child healthcare centres, Axel Höjer would monitor their institutionalisation as Director-General of the Medical Board of Sweden.[23]

These developments show how Axel Höjer could refer to a certain kind of medical expertise to reinforce his attempts at reform, but they also indicate how this reinforcement, in return, helped to enhance Höjer's status as an expert. His partner in the process of lesson-drawing, Signe Höjer, was not as clearly recognised as an expert. Consequently, she has all but disappeared from the historiography of Swedish mother and child healthcare reform. This difference in recognition, I will argue, had to do with such factors as gender and professional status, which in combination helped to either strengthen or diminish their respective claims to expertise.

Different regimes of expertise

Through socially-minded physicians like Axel Höjer, actively engaged in what has been characterised as the Swedish public health project, medical expertise came to play an important part in the construction of the Swedish welfare state. This kind of commitment, surely, had historical precedents. The medical corps nurtured a long tradition of making statements in relation to different issues concerning government and society. In more general terms, the strong position of medical experts, and especially medical doctors, can be explained by the great importance given to the optimisation of the population in the governance of modern societies. The experts and reformers of the nineteenth century formulated a series of social problems, mostly connected to life in the growing cities, and, remarkably often, they did so with the aid of a medical vocabulary. These, often self-appointed, medical experts focused on getting to know human beings but they also strived to reform and transform them. Medical experts helped to categorise the population into problem groups. Crime, drunkenness and poverty were defined as diseases of the social body, exacerbated by poor housing and other precarious living conditions. Epidemic outbreaks led to further medical problematisation of city life, and on to surveys and numerous reform proposals. In this process, the medical doctor could emerge as a leading expert and adviser on the art of monitoring and improving the social – as well as the individual – body and of maintaining its health and productivity.[24]

However, the welfare state meant something more, and partially other than earlier attempts at social policy reform. The growing scope of the welfare state was connected to an ever-expanding network of expertise, increasingly diverse in its claims to knowledge and use of power technologies.[25] What, then, did these developments mean in terms of *medical* power and expertise?

For Axel Höjer, the growth of the welfare state gave opportunities to advance professionally, but not as a medical scientist and academic, as he himself for a while had hoped. Instead, he became what the American sociologist Ron Eyerman would define as a professional expert. Eyerman uses Gunnar and Alva Myrdal to exemplify how Swedish intellectuals from the inter-war period and onwards could combine the two intellectual roles formerly predominant within Swedish Social Democracy – the agitator and the expert – to enter into the service of the emerging welfare state. According to Eyerman, this new set of professional experts (Eyerman also calls them, alternately, expert intellectuals and rationalising intellectuals) set as their goal to rationalise all sectors of society: agriculture, industry, home, community, research and education, etc. They presented themselves as representatives of an objective, value-neutral science, with the competence, on the one hand, to examine and diagnose society's ills, and on the other hand, in their roles as agitators, to mobilize the public and, if necessary, change its attitudes to governmental intervention.[26] Axel Höjer was named Director-General of the Royal Medical Board in 1935, at the beginning of the long era of Social Democratic rule in Sweden. During his 17 years as Director-General, Axel Höjer was arguably the most powerful professional expert in Sweden where questions of public health were concerned. In this powerful position, his ambitions grew. As the goal for his work he would now state nothing less than the complete physical, mental and social health of all citizens.[27]

As a medical doctor *and* public official, Axel Höjer could operate from a unique position and claim a dual professional expertise. When represented by a person like Axel Höjer, the state itself could claim medical expertise, just as well as the medical profession could. As a representative of medical expertise, Axel Höjer could act on behalf of the medical profession, for example by trying to limit the work opportunities for people who made therapeutic claims without belonging to the medical profession, and who could be written off as quacks.[28] At the same time, as a representative of the State, and relieved from previous academic ambitions, Axel Höjer could when he so wished act contrary to the interests of the organised medical corps. The prime example of this was when Höjer in the spring of 1948 presented the report of a commission, led by him, on the future organisation of out-patient medical care in Sweden. Höjer looked upon this report as his 'will'. His stated objective was that healthcare would be equally accessible to all citizens, and in particular that preventive healthcare would be expanded to the point that, in a long-term perspective, the treatment of diseases would be increasingly superfluous. This process, he claimed, could only be made possible through a publicly funded and publicly organised health system, with regular health examinations and publicly employed doctors on a fixed salary.[29] Axel Höjers proposals met with strong opposition, mainly from the Swedish Medical Association, whose leading figures claimed that the Höjer report formed a serious threat against medicine as a free profession and, not least, as a free trade.[30] Eventually, Höjer's line of argument would prevail and, although he himself was then long gone as Director General of the Medical Board, the healthcare system was reformed in a manner quite similar to the one Höjer and his commissioners had suggested.[31] Another example of action on behalf of the interest of the state, rather than the medical profession, was the infected debate on the 'import' of doctors in 1939–1940, where Axel Höjer, in opposition to many members of the Swedish medical establishment, argued for the need of an expansion for the medical work force and – referring to this as well as to humanitarian reasons – advocated that a suitable selection of German-Jewish specialist doctors would be given work permits in Sweden.[32]

Axel Höjer's double role must be seen in relation to his special position as a medical doctor connected to the very core of the welfare state. But it should also be seen in connection to the emergence of a new, professionalised set of social sciences, within governance as well as within academia.

In December 1935, some months after his entry as Director-General, Höjer and the Medical Board suggested the establishment of a National Institute for Social Hygiene, divided into five departments that would engage in social hygiene, medical and health statistics, infection control, industrial and technical hygiene, and food hygiene. As science gained more evidence of the connection between poor health and 'social phenomena', and practical medicine progressively focused more on preventive medicine, the tasks of social hygiene were increasing, they argued. Therefore, the new institute would have to survey social problems such as poor housing conditions, unfit food, unhealthy work, harmful habits, prejudices and errors in child rearing and education, poverty, crime, and so forth. Also, it should demonstrate how the harmful effects of such environmental factors could be prevented, and support society in the fight against major endemic diseases. Social hygiene should also include more generally preventive care, such as maternity care, childcare, social dental care, home care, public nutrition, eugenics and sexual hygiene. Research, the Medical Board suggested, should be an important part of the Institute's activities. So should health information or 'hygienic propaganda' and the training of social health officials: social hygiene was still largely perceived as a problem of public education.[33]

The experts from the Ministry of Social Affairs, when responding to the proposed programme, suggested that the institute's responsibilities should be concentrated on 'scientific-practical' research, education and information within three main areas, namely general hygiene, occupational hygiene and nutritional hygiene/food control.

They also wanted to change the name to the State Institute for Public Health (*Statens institut för folkhälsan*).³⁴ Further, they suggested that the institute should be supervised by a board of representatives from different government agencies, including the Medical Board, but not giving it an exclusive position.³⁵

The Medical Board, in turn, criticised the Ministry of Social Affairs' proposal for being too narrow, while the head of the Ministry, Gustav Möller, instead pointed to the new institution as too diverse to fit into the medical administration, although parts of its activities should be planned in collaboration with the Medical Board. The parliament went for the Möller line, and in 1938 the State Institute for Public Health was started, belonging under the Ministry of Social Affairs.³⁶

The historian of ideas Karin Johannisson has characterised this competition as a battle between 'the strict, scientific-oriented medical society and a social policy institution with the ambition to 'socialise' areas that medicine had considered as its own'. This antagonism, she claims, can also be illustrated by the terminology: social hygiene versus public health.³⁷ I do not quite agree with this interpretation. Rather, a principal dividing line went between the 1935 Medical Board proposal and earlier suggestions to establish an institute for state medicine that had principally focused on integrating bacteriology, forensic chemistry and pharmaceutical laboratory research.³⁸ Also, the medical doctors that Johannisson refers to, i.e. mainly Axel Höjer, were themselves in the process of changing terminology during this period in time. As Johannisson herself remarks, Höjer frequently used the concept 'folkhälsa' (public health, or, more precisely, people's health or population health) in order to mark an epochal transition.³⁹

Moreover, Höjer's wish to put what he defined as social hygiene under the jurisdiction of the Medical Board does not necessarily imply that he, in comparison to Gustav Möller, was less interested in recognising the problems in question as 'social'. The Medical Board definition of the tasks of social hygiene show that they too wanted to focus on environmental and social factors behind illness, rather than point at biological factors behind 'social' problems. Höjer and Möller often worked closely together and also shared a common agenda more generally: they wanted to substitute a universal welfare system for an outdated system relying on charity and poor relief.⁴⁰

The conflict around the public health institute was, I would argue, rather based in disagreements on where to place the responsibility for things mutually defined as social policy and problems with social roots. Since Axel Höjer, as Director-General of the Medical Board, could act both as a medical doctor and a socially oriented expert, and therefore could present himself as qualified to assume a dual responsibility, I think the 'battle', above all, shows how Höjer strived to redefine the meaning of medical expertise, so that this expertise could also include the methods of social science and the social distribution policy that he personally supported.

In the 1940s, to motivate his suggestions to reform the healthcare system, Höjer very directly referred to the emergence of social medicine as a new discipline, and to the need of a new sort of medical doctor, with a double competence. This doctor must be able to combine scientific excellence with knowledge of basic health-promoting factors and the outlook of a social worker, without losing his medical authority. In order to broaden the new doctors' skills, studies in social sciences – sociology, social medicine and psychology – would have to be integrated into the medical curriculum. Höjer would, he said, like to see doctors as the natural leaders of the new 'social' medicine, but on condition that they favoured a social perspective and did not bury themselves in medical technicalities.[41]

This assertion of a specific public health expertise that incorporated the methods of modern social science and a social, or even Social Democratic, approach into the medical field of expertise, can be seen as a statement of expertise directed towards the more conservative parts of the medical profession, but also towards the emerging elite of social scientists who established themselves as professional experts within, or closely connected to, the state apparatus.

The Swedish so-called public health project that was connected to the construction of a welfare state and had Axel Höjer as a major actor, has sometimes been characterised as an attempt to 'place a biological and medical perspective on society'.[42] The public health project, thus defined, is regarded as part of a classical medicalisation process, where more and more problems, formerly defined as non-medical, are looked upon, defined and treated as medical problems, diseases or disturbances.[43] However, I would argue that to study the Swedish public health project from such a medicalisation perspective is somewhat problematic. Firstly because it does not really consider other actors than medical doctors within the 'project'. But public health problems were also highlighted by other actors, in a broader context of social policy: Signe Höjer provides but one example of such an expert. Karin Johannisson does acknowledge this when talking about the 'sociologisation' of public health in the 1930s.[44] Another problem with this perspective, which persists even if one chooses to focus on the doctors involved, lies in its simplification of the concept medicine. As the historian Ludmilla Jordanova points out: taking medicalisation for granted, without due regard to tensions, conflicts and negotiations between different groupings and actors, augments the risk of becoming trapped in a teleological model of explanation. Importantly, it cannot really explain conflicts *between* medical professionals.[45] To understand why Höjer's sociomedical proposals led to such controversy one must, I would claim, rather focus on differences *within* the field of medicine and health policy.

True enough, an important part of the public health project – very much in line with liberal rationalities of governance – focused on health education. By focusing on strategies to avoid disease, health education was definitely a way of suggesting medical solutions to different problems. Axel Höjer very much promoted and also involved himself in public health education. However, this was hardly controversial. Rather, it was exactly what was expected of him as a medical doctor, let alone as a public health officer.

What made Axel Höjer's project of public health and social medicine novel and provocative was, I would claim, rather those aspects of it that were the very opposite of medicalization, if medicalization is primarily seen as what I would rather call biomedicalization. Besides providing medical solutions to problems that might be perceived as social, it aimed to highlight the social basis of a range of medical problems.[46] Further, Höjer's project very much relied on large-scale systematic solutions that were connected to the claims and hopes of the new social sciences.

Axel Höjer's strategies of public health must be seen in the light of the establishment of modern social science in Sweden, of his connections to international authorities on social medicine, of his and Signe Höjer's connections to the Swedish social science elite of the day and their earlier connections to the London School of Economics and the Fabian Society, and of the high hopes that Swedish Social Democracy in general had of social scientific surveys and investigations. The growth of disciplines like social hygiene and social medicine were deliberate attempts by medical science – broadly defined – to claim a place among the social sciences. Or, in other words, to prove that medical doctors did possess a somewhat unique, scientifically grounded social expertise. Other defendants of social medicine made this just as clear as Axel Höjer did.[47]

Höjer supposed that social reforms, health surveillance and proactive health promotion, and, not least, a more fair and democratic access to healthcare by way of putting the system under state or regional control, would lead to higher costs in the short run. His plans relied on the hope that a general, mandatory health insurance would soon be introduced in Sweden. In a longer perspective, however, he supposed that the biopolitical solutions he suggested would eventually make healthcare more and more superfluous. For him, thus, public health work and social medicine were not primarily about invading society with biological explanations to all sorts of problems – a sort of activity just as well associated with doctors and health educators of an older generation – but rather about the integration of social, social scientific or even socialist perspectives into the medical field. Höjer and his adversaries cordially agreed on this.

However, that does not necessarily mean that Axel Höjer and other proponents of social medicine were promoting what Peter Conrad has identified as demedicalisation.[48] Social medicine was just as concerned about asserting its medical expertise as the more conservative disciplines were. And it certainly was not prepared to let go of its jurisdiction over 'demedicalised' areas. Instead, it wanted to integrate the methods of social science within medicine, and thus expand medical jurisdiction over problems defined as social or psychosocial. So, by referring to a sociomedical expertise, combining the expertise of medicine and social science, Höjer contributed to a kind of medicalisation, but one quite different from biomedicalisation.

As a nurse with some further education within the social sciences, Signe Höjer might appear to be even more justified in claiming expertise in both social and medical science. But although her background made it possible to claim a double competence, her lack of a Swedish university education made it quite likely that such claims would be doubted, questioned, or simply neglected. People who consider themselves as experts are not necessarily acknowledged as such. And, presumably, being a woman complicated things further, as expertise, let alone scientific expertise, was a highly gendered concept. In other words, an expert was generally supposed to be male. Some aspects of Signe Höjer's career will now be used to illuminate the gendered aspects of expertise.

The gender of expertise

Right from the start of their relationship, Signe Dahl and Axel Höjer identified themselves as co-working partners in a mutual life project.[49] But it was hardly a cooperation on equal terms. Their cooperation, although it changed considerably along the way, was continously shaped by the gendered dimensions of expertise. In other words, the Höjer case indicates how gender has functioned as a decisive factor when people have tried to claim expertise in public contexts, and not least where the expert role was integrated into the growing welfare state apparatus. In line with Joan Scott, I can see two main aspects of gender involved in this process, analytically distinct although closely intertwined in practice: gender as a fundamental element in social relations, based on perceived difference between the sexes; and gender as one of those primary fields where relations of power found – and still find – expression. Within this field, referrals to differences between male and female were used to legitimate superior power or justify submission. They also contributed to shaping different fields of action for men and women.[50]

The Höjers' mutual public health project included gender division and hierarchisation at various levels. First, it included strong views on men's and women's complementary roles in the creation of a better and more healthy society, especially in so far as it focused on mothers and child-rearing, while presuming men to act as breadwinners and heads of their families. Second, the Höjers were allocated, and assigned each other, different roles in the implementation of the project. From the outset, Signe clearly positioned and identified herself as a professional woman, but her professional identity was soon renegotiated so that she increasingly worked as a wife and mother, while Axel made a professional, and at least initally more public career.

At the same time, however, both Signe Höjer and Axel Höjer can be defined as intellectuals in a relatively political and action-oriented sense. Both were strongly influenced by the intellectual traditions defined by Ron Eyerman as dissenting and progressive: their reforms of the Solna Milk Drop were really only part of a larger social project, where the couple drew inspiration from the settlement movement and the Fabian Society.[51] In the longer run, however, Signe – by Eyerman's definition – was mainly active as a movement intellectual, in contrast to Axel, who had the opportunity to advance as a professional expert or expert intellectual, forming part of the growing welfare state elite on a professional basis.[52] This development points to a weakness in Eyerman's distinction between different intellectual roles: due to the lack of a gender perspective in his analysis, Eyerman remains blind to the fact that his distinction contains important gender aspects. Those who were recognised as experts and were given the opportunity to advance in the growing welfare state administration were primarily male academics and intellectuals. Most female intellectuals had to stay on within the organisational structures of an older generation and continue their work as movement intellectuals. This position usually offered them more limited opportunities to make themselves heard in their own, individual voices. It also contributed to the fact that they rarely became recognised as experts in the same sense as many professional men did.[53]

Signe Höjer had limited opportunities to make a professional career – a fact made even clearer by a comparison with Axel Höjer. Her comparative disadvantage can be traced back to agreements within their marriage as well as to external conditions, but was clearly linked to the prevailing gender order. Somewhat paradoxically though, thanks to the same gender segregation that hindered her professional career, she had the opportunity to make a kind of alternative career within female-dominated social movements such as the women's peace movement (as chairman of the Swedish section of Women's International League for Peace and Freedom Signe Höjer came to play a prominent role in the Swedish peace movement and also internationally, not least during World War II) and the Swedish Federation of Social Democratic Women. Her commitments as a movement intellectual then enabled her to make a kind of career in politics and public committee work as well. Between 1936 and 1952 she was a member of the executive committee of the Federation of Social Democratic Women.[54] When moving to Ålsten in Stockholm in 1935 she had also joined the local Social Democratic women's club, which nominated her for the Stockholm City Council, where she was elected a member in 1938.[55] Her political credentials then helped her to be appointed chairman of the special women's delegation that was linked to the 1941 population committee, and a member of several other investigations and commissions.[56]

Within the public committee system, a person like Signe Höjer could make her voice heard both as an individual expert and as a representative of a social movement. Sometimes she could refer to her knowledge as representative of the lay person's view, in other cases to knowledge more unique to her. But she was not considered a professional expert in the same sense as Axel Höjer. Her expertise was rarely linked to training and profession. Rather, it was predominantly gendered, in a double sense.

To the extent that she was seen as an expert, it was mainly on issues related to women, children and family. Signe Höjer proves that the emerging welfare state could offer opportunities for some of the female movement intellectuals to increase their influence. When they were allowed into politics, administration and investigation committees, however, it was usually in subordinate positions, and often only after they managed to claim that a 'female' perspective was needed on different issues. They were, therefore, primarily able to claim what I would define as a specific women's expertise. It was not necessarily a successful strategy for gaining influence in areas other than those considered female, or to reach higher political offices.[57]

Women's difficulties in gaining recognition as experts has been explained by referring to the welfare state as a fundamentally patriarchal structure, which incorporated the notion of a hierarchical family with men as breadwinners and women as carers.[58] This in turn has been linked to an old contractual philosophy that did not count women as citizens.[59] Another, not necessarily conflicting, explanation may be that women themselves chose to organise themselves in movements and to speak as representatives of groups rather than individuals because it gave them more impact in a male-dominated society, and that they chose to focus on 'female' issues because they saw them as poorly represented in the public debate.[60] In a Swedish context, the historian Josefin Rönnbäck has described how the strategies of the women's suffrage movement helped to construct a 'gender trap' for future generations of women politicians.[61]

As historian Nina Almgren notes, nearly all the women who had the chance to advance in the welfare state – Almgren chooses to call them state feminists – belonged to an elite of relatively wealthy and well-educated upper- and middle-class women, active in the upper echelons of the women's associations, with close links to the political top layer but without too burdensome family obligations.[62] Signe Höjer was no exception: no doubt her class – reflected in cultural capital as well as in access to domestic assistance and influential social networks – was crucial for her possibilities to advance as far as she did. Considering the elite status of Signe Höjer and those other women who were able to make a kind of alternative public career, it is even more remarkable how they chose to, or had to, refer to their expertise as women rather than to expertise based on education or professional experience. The tactic of referring to female expertise did indeed gain them certain positions in decision-making bodies, and some influence in those areas recognised as female, but it failed to gain them much influence, let alone acknowledgement, in other areas.[63]

The influence of female experts on 'women's' issues was no certainty either. For example, the special women's delegation, chaired by Signe Höjer, that was part of the 1941 population committee was not always allowed to participate in the committee's discussions on 'women's' questions – even if most of those questions had initially been raised by those women's political organisations that were represented by Höjer and the other members of the delegation. Also, in contrast to nearly all of the committee's other reports, the final report of the women's delegation was neglected, and not even acknowledged as a product by the committee. This, among other things, meant that the delegation's attempts to define family policy as a distinct policy area did not bear fruit until nearly a decade later.[64] Also, as Signe Höjer herself pointed out, the history of the Social Democratic women's movement may illuminate how many issues that were first raised by women 'experts' or politicians were not seriously acknowledged as matters of social policy until they caught the attention of male politicians.[65] However, the expertise of those men was seldom referred to as gendered. Instead, and a bit ironically, by leaning on their professional or political qualifications, these men could even speak about 'female' issues with greater authority than those women who raised them initially.

The difficulties of women experts might also be traced back to something paradoxical in the whole notion of a special women's expertise. Certainly the strategy to refer to specific knowledge on the grounds of one being a woman must have been easy to question, when the whole argument about a need of expertise in the first place was based on a presumption that women had no natural skills in these matters, or at least that their natural skills had been lost in the modern, urbanised and industrialised society within which the women experts claimed to represent a particularly modern cadre.

Towards the ends of their working lives, when the Höjers expanded their public health project to reach abroad, they found themselves in new positions. However, in those new positions the Höjers were still separated by a professional/semi-professional divide. Axel Höjer continued to work as a professional expert, but now on duty for the World Health Organization rather than the Swedish State. Signe Höjer's role was less clearly defined. Without an official assignment, she had fewer restrictions, but also no obvious framework to operate within. In order to complete the tasks she assigned herself, she must once again become a kind of social policy entrepreneur, or, in other words, construct her own reform projects.

Those reform projects, in turn, were facilitated by her advantages in terms of class and, perhaps, race. With a range of servants, Signe Höjer suddenly had a lot of free time on her hands. This made it possible for her to engage in a variety of contexts, and to begin a new career as a writer.[66] She engaged in childcare and healthcare matters, started up organisations and began to engage in some amateur historical and anthropological studies. She also held a number of lectures at various venues, about the UN, the World Health Organization and Swedish social services.[67] And, as once upon a time in Solna, she strived to materialise lessons drawn into various pilot projects.

The transnational expertise

The meeting of Signe Dahl and Axel Höjer in Paris 1919 marked the beginning of many years of travelling, together or separately. Through the years, the Höjers continued to actively use and point at international experience in their reform efforts. In doing this, they aimed at what British political scientists David Dolowitz and David Marsh define as policy transfer, that is, processes in which 'knowledge about policies, administrative arrangements, institutions and ideas in one political setting (past or present) is used in the development of policies, administrative arrangements, institutions and ideas in another political setting.'[68]

Throughout the 1920s, in discourse and practice, the Höjers continued to use England as a model for Sweden. This was never done on the grounds of Britain being an imperial superpower. On the contrary, it was the country's demonstrated ability to rapidly raise itself, or at least its children, from depths of poverty that was rhetorically put forward as a model for Sweden. Sweden, in this context, was presented as a country still seriously marked by poverty, and further hampered by geographical marginalisation and backwardness in the development of social institutions.[69]

In his committee report on outpatient healthcare, 20 years later, Axel Höjer continued to use strategic comparisons with other countries, although somewhat differently. Now, he argued that many other countries were well on their way to build modern systems for the promotion of population health, and that there was a striking consensus on the requirements of modern healthcare in countries as ideologically diverse as the Soviet Union, USA, France and England. Sweden was no longer presented as backward, but as a country that was ahead of the others in several respects. The current situation was presented as a race between nations, where Sweden must take care not to lose its leading position. Still, Axel Höjer stressed, it would be 'a mistake to suppose that we can learn only from countries that are more advanced than us in terms of results'.[70]

Although Axel Höjer was now placed in a central leadership position, his arguments show that he still needed to make use of rhetorical strategies to enable the transmission of ideas and health programmes. An important motive behind his references to other countries was undoubtedly the strong opposition he met from part of the Swedish medical profession.

When moving their operations to newly decolonised countries in the 1950s and 60s, the Höjers continued their attempts to transfer policies and technologies, but now the direction of transfer went largely from their country of origin to other countries. Now, *Sweden's* successful attempts to raise itself quickly from poverty could be used as a model for others. In the developing countries, the Höjers could act as experts on Western welfare technologies and strived to be acknowledged as such. Their experience of social policy making and public health work in a Swedish context was thus used in attempts to reform healthcare and medical education or introduce family planning measures in countries generally perceived as underdeveloped. Presumably, these reform efforts also included attempts to transfer 'Swedish' ideals in a wider sense. This may be seen in Signe Höjer's attempts to start kindergartens and educational institutions for kindergarten teachers, as well as institutions for family planning, and in Axel Höjer's attempts to initiate the start of a network of child healthcare clinics. All these – apparently successful – attempts drew inspiration from similar reforms that the Höjers had helped to initiate in Sweden. In India, they also hoped that their old dream of integrating such institutions would be realised, as this fitted well with Indian central planning.

In newly independent Ghana, a few years later, Axel Höjer got the opportunity to plan the future healthcare system of the country, as he had once tried to do in Sweden. In Ghana, he particularly stressed the importance of fostering domestic experts not stuck in the thought patterns of the old colonial administration. He was also careful to begin with a long inventory trip through the country together with Signe. Still, the reforms were clearly inspired by earlier reform suggestions, both Höjer's own, Swedish, ones, and late colonial reform proposals in India and Ghana. Höjer obviously believed in some kind of universally applicable healthcare structure, although it necessarily had to be adapted to local conditions and circumstances.[71]

In Swedish or other Western contexts, on the other hand, the Höjers rather aimed at acknowledgement as experts on the developing countries and on the roles of experts in those countries. As a member of the so-called *U-beredningen*, an influential preparatory committee for Swedish development aid, Signe Höjer was also officially recognised as a development expert. Axel Höjer spoke more specifically on healthcare related assistance, often to an international audience.

As development experts, the Höjers attempted to increase Swedish and Western understanding of the sort of help needed in the newly decolonised parts of the world, as well as the roots of these needs. They pointed out the rich countries' possibilities, and even obligations, to extend their sense of solidarity outside their own group or nation by including people in the rest of the world as well.[72] In line with the WHO constitution, Axel Höjer now also claimed that everyone, not just the citizens of Sweden, had the right to complete health.[73]

However, the people in the emerging 'third' world were not always presented as needy and victimised. Sometimes, the direction of lesson drawing or policy transfer was reversed. In texts addressed to the World Health Organization or Swedish audiences, the Höjers particularly emphasised India as a country that, despite many serious problems, could provide positive lessons for countries such as Sweden.[74] Axel Höjer, after a couple of years as Principal at the Medical College of Travancore-Cochin, no longer wanted to include the state among the underdeveloped areas of the world. Today, he wrote in his final report to the WHO, the state rather belonged in an intermediate position between the rich Western countries and the least developed countries in the world.[75] In some areas the state was even more developed than Sweden, he claimed, and stressed that Travancore-Cochin had hired the world's first female state medical officer of health.[76] He also pointed out that there were things that Swedish physicians could learn from India, for example in the field of tropical medicine.[77] After two additional years as professor of social and preventive medicine in Dibrugarh, Assam, he also implied that the development of preventive healthcare as a university subject went both faster and smoother in India than in Sweden. The same, he claimed, was true of the development of an infrastructure for health controls of people of different ages.[78] In Axel Höjer's opinion, Swedish healthcare professionals were too firmly rooted in old habits and seldom understood the importance of education in social and preventive medicine as well as their Indian colleagues did. Perhaps, he concluded, lobbying for a Nordic college of public health, in the next few years Swedish public health administrators would need to go to Delhi for further training.[79]

The Höjer example belies any idea of a simple transfer process in international or transnational aid and development activities, with a transmitter and a receiver, even though inherent power relations are asymmetrical. Although the 'beneficiaries' of the Höjers' reforms and reform suggestions are hard to reach, I would suggest that traces of resistance are indicated by the way the Höjers' perceptions, both of their own work and of the relationship between Sweden and other countries, changed through their experiences in the third world. The couple's transnational activities thus raise questions about what happens when a rationality that deals with appropriate ways to control the population within the boundaries of a nation state is confronted with ideas of internationalism and international healthcare, and, not least, with practical field experience.[80]

Axel and Signe Höjer wanted to stress that poverty in the formerly colonised world depended on geopolitical power relationships rather than on any innate inferiority on the part of the poor countries. They emphasised that the duty of the West, after centuries of oppression, was to bring the people in the underdeveloped parts of the world into a position where they would be able to help themselves build their own welfare states, without reproducing old relationships of dependency. Foreign, and in a longer run domestic, expertise was seen as a key factor in this process.[81]

But how to bring the people in the former colonies into this position? And how westernised did this position need to be? The Höjers' opinions on these things changed considerably during their stay in the former colonies. Before going to India, Axel Höjer claimed that what the non-industrialised part of the world needed to do now was simply to catch up with countries like Sweden. This process would not take 200 years, as everything needed to transform the poor countries was already known; the knowledge just needed to be transmitted by Western experts. In a 1950 article, Axel Höjer wrote that the consultants and demonstration groups of the WHO would work as 'enzymes, spreading their blessing powers into the big, inert mass'. Through these enzymes, the brightness of enlightenment would dispel the darkness of superstition.[82]

After more than a decade in international health work, much of it on location in developing countries, he expressed himself differently. An expert, he wrote in an advisory text to a UN audience in the early 1960s, can never arrive with a ready-made plan. The specific conditions of every individual country must be studied in detail, on the spot. The more general the plan under construction, the more important that the expert acquired profound knowledge of the country's natural and cultural history, its relationship to surrounding countries and its integration into greater ethnographic and geographical units, as well as local knowledge of social, economic and psychological conditions. Newly-arrived experts were strongly recommended to make tours lasting several months, like those he and Signe Höjer had made. Crucially, the expert must show humility and realise that even the present state of knowledge was very incomplete. An expert should never under any circumstances approach the people as a 'prophet' knowing exactly how things should be done, presenting model solutions from more developed countries.[83] Instead, the expert must act as a good teacher:

> 'Exported experts have always to be teachers. Merits in teaching are good, a teaching spirit, not to say a Missionary spirit is even more useful. The disposition of an exported expert must be optimistic, his patience as well as his energy without limits. He ought to listen to objections and advice and not impose himself when not necessary. He should closely study the conditions of his new country, where his teaching is to be applied, before introducing schemes from the advanced countries. He should contact a very big number and be intimate with few. He must know that though the truth is often one, its practical application might be one of several.'[84]

So, even the outlook of a missionary of health was commendable, as long as the expert did not act in an almighty fashion. Local health experts, in turn, must, because of their scarcity, primarily serve as teachers for local school teachers.[85]

To delegate responsibility to local employees and give them the opportunity to take credit for the effort was also seen as crucial for other reasons: 'It strengthens self-esteem, which is one of the tasks of the expert, and if people long for recognition and appreciation ... and who does not? ... they will afterwards participate much more willingly'.[86] Using local teachers was considered necessary also because those secondary experts could speak both figuratively and literally in a language that the people understood.[87] For to implement a project in practice, no matter how well-planned, it was necessary to ensure public participation – and this must be done with the help of enlightened teachers and 'community development' centres. Comprehension was a key concept. There was, Axel Höjer emphasised, no point in giving slogans to people unless there was someone to introduce them and explain the context and purpose of various health projects in the local language, someone who also had knowledge of local conditions and ways of thinking.[88] To ensure that self-help projects were appropriate and constructive, both staff and physical facilities must, as far as possible, be collected locally. Otherwise, Höjer warned, there was a great risk that gifts remained unused, were used wrongly or would hamper domestic production and trade.[89]

However, people's participation did not necessarily imply active participation. Axel Höjer basically talked about learning and education as a one-way process, with teachers as the extended arms of health experts. That the knowledge conveyed by local experts or sub-experts must be fully compatible with Western science was taken for granted. Höjer was even prepared to fine people who violated basic health rules.[90]

Signe Höjer's plans to introduce family planning in the state of Travancore-Cochin – strongly supported by Axel Höjer – were more clearly guided by liberal ideals of governance, or, in other words, guided by a stronger sense of governmentality. Her plans built on a conviction that Indian women would be able to regulate their own reproductive behaviour, by using methods that required a high degree of self-control, such as so-called safe periods, contraceptive herbs, if such were found, or pessars, if such could be provided more cheaply, and thereby ensure both population control and personal health. Later on in the Indian family planning programmes, when such self-regulatory technologies came to be regarded as ineffective, they were replaced by more enforcive methods, such as sterilisations or IUD application, by incentive or even force. The Höjers did not reflect on such drastic methods during the time when they had some power to influence family planning programmes in India, although the kind of integrated mother and child healthcare/childcare/birth control clinics that they supported eventually came to form an infrastructure for more drastic family planning measures, such as those large-scale sterilisation campaigns carried out in Kerala, as in other parts of India, in the 1960s and 70s.[91] Signe Höjer was also careful to stress the importance of cooperation with the local population and, not least, that women must be involved in the development of plans – both in order to make planning better adapted to local needs, and to increase women's status in local societies.[92]

The possibility of speaking of governmentality in a colonial context has been eagerly discussed in recent years. Some historians are highly sceptical about applying the concept of governmentality to the European colonies, as colonised peoples were never free in the sense that one can speak of modern governance.[93] Other researchers stress that the concept of colonialism must be historicised. Although no colonies were administered in the same way as their European 'mother' countries, colonial governments acted differently in different periods, had differing objectives and used different methods. Therefore, those researchers claim, it may be plausible to think about governmentality in *some* colonial contexts.[94] Historian Gyan Prakash argues that in the context of colonial India, it may be reasonable to talk of a certain colonial governmentality, one that incorporated some parts of the liberal modes of governance simultaneously developed in the West, but left out others.[95]

Although the Höjers operated in a post-colonial context, such questions are highly relevant in connection to their work as well. Decolonisation should not be seen as an abrupt break. Rather, it must be seen as a lengthy process that differed in different countries and also incorporated new forms of colonialism, side by side with remains of the old colonial structures. My study shows that the Höjers' couple's work in India and Africa should not simply be seen as part of a new kind of Western imperialism, cultural and economic rather than administrative in nature. Nevertheless, they too were unavoidably trapped in colonial and neocolonial thought patterns and administrative structures. As peace and development scholar Maria Eriksson Baaz points out, varieties of the kind of 'partnership' discourse that Axel and particularly Signe Höjer began to engage in, got increasingly dominant in aid and development circles in the latter half of the twentieth century. This new way of speaking may, she warns, help to hide the assymmetrical power relations inherent in development work. It may also create an oversimplified picture of 'good' and 'bad' aid donors, and thus reinforce the donors' images of neocolonialism as something that only 'the Others' are involved in.[96] Those are important remarks. My point, however, is that the Höjers at least nurtured a hope or desire that the donor-recipient relationship could be based on equality and mechanisms of self-help and self-formation, even though this desire for liberal governance was not always realised in practice. Possibly, this desire could be supplemented by an openness for tougher measures in case liberal governance failed: however, such measures were hardly believed necessary at this early stage.

The ideal, thus, was to create self-governing people, or, in other words, to teach people to steer themselves in the right direction. However, Signe Höjer admitted, this direction was not necessarily the same that Sweden had chosen. The greatest adventure, she claimed after leaving Ghana, had been to reeducate herself:

> 'To learn, as we did in Asia, not to apply Western values on phenomena encountered, such as worship of ancestors and spirits, magic drums, autocracy, polygamy, women's oppression, nudity and other customs and traditions. To learn humility in what we white people can offer our dark brother, trying to help him choose wisely among our inventions, our merchandise and – our patterns of moral behaviour.'[97]

Signe Höjer warned that Western attempts to foster and educate would wipe out rich and vital cultural traditions.[98] The more she learnt about African conditions, the more convinced she had become that the heart of African darkness consisted in the Europeans' ignorance of the continent. A fundamental problem, she said, was that most Europeans in Africa isolated themselves from the local population, constructing their own small enclaves in resemblance of their home countries. Instead, experts must make efforts to understand the foreign cultures and, if possible, learn the local languages. Also, the Europeans should not take for granted that their own preconceptions about gender roles or sexuality were more natural, normal or morally sane.[99] For example, Burmese, Tibetan and Ghanaian people could testify that polygamy was often a good solution, she argued.[100] Thus, at the same time as Signe Höjer favoured a Western-style small nuclear family model as a solution to international population problems, she could strongly challenge Western family norms on other grounds. Also, she did not want to presuppose that traditional societies were either less democratic or less equal in their gender relations.[101] In conclusion, she warned that assistance from the West would wipe out the poorer countries' own cultural values. 'There is a need', she said, 'of self-questioning on the part of us Europeans, if we are to begin a new kind of *cooperation on equal footing* with the new states'.[102] However, when it came to health-related matters, neither Signe Höjer nor Axel Höjer would accept any relativism. The Höjers estimated that, due to colonialism, third world people were left with a large degree of ignorance on these matters. This fact made foreign expertise crucial in a transitional stage.

The activities of foreign expertise were also justified by a dichotomisation between 'good' and 'bad' expertise. A medical expert, Axel Höjer claimed, must know foreign languages, be committed, well-informed on local conditions and willing to get to know people from different ethnic and social groups. A doctor on a developmental mission must also be humble, but not too humble, and have a strong psyche:

> 'He must not be obtrusive, but has to be very stubborn to realise his project in a certain amount of time: just never throw the axe into the lake. If the door is closed in front of you, you enter through the window. These are always open in the tropics.'[103]

The expert was also presupposed to be a heterosexual male, preferably in similar family circumstances as Axel Höjer: Höjer advised that the medical expert were to be accompanied by a democratically-minded and socially interested wife.[104]

Axel Höjer and Signe Höjer advertised themselves as humble advisers who had taken the time required to get acquainted with local conditions and thus build confidence in the domestic staff.[105] To further exemplify good expertise, both Signe Höjer and Axel Höjer highlighted the Norwegian fishery project in Quilon, Kerala, where, according to Signe, cooperation with the Indians was given pride of place. The Norwegians, she stressed, had also been exemplary in executing a sociological study of the fishing community before starting the actual project.[106] As an example of a 'bad' expert Axel Höjer, in his memoir, took his successor in Ghana, Daniel Brachott. As Axel Höjer described the matter Brachott was forced to leave Ghana earlier than originally planned, when his military style and over-rapid implementation of reform plans turned the entire Ghanaian health administration against him.[107] Bad experts could also be those that were primarily driven by a wish to convert people to Christianity, or by an interest in personal benefits. Good experts, in contrast, were perceived as neutral, always prepared to help and open to the other party's needs.

The reciprocity that was always presumed in the Swedish welfare project, based on notions of social solidarity, had no real equivalent in this vision of global solidarity. The silence on poor people's reciprocal duties may be explained by the audiences that the Höjers addressed and the frameworks that they worked within. Their primary mission as experts on developing countries was to stir up empathy and generosity in the Swedes or in people within the WHO or other UN organisations. This made it appropriate, as far as possible, to present people in the developing countries as needy, deserving and able to use aid in a proper way – and by extension able to help themselves in a way that would benefit themselves as well as the donors. Axel Höjer spoke of a 'silent cry from the wild forest', and of a debt that needed to be repaid, from the 'white' world to the 'black'.[108] Occasionally, he also spoke of this as a necessity for the world's survival – hinting too at the survival of the Western world. [109]

Small countries like Norway, Sweden, Denmark or Israel, Signe Höjer argued, enjoyed a certain good-will in the former colonies, due to their fairly non-imperialistic history and, in the case of Israel, their own experience of racial harassment.[110] Swedish experts also had the advantage of belonging to a non-aligned country, in the middle of the cold war era, of taking a secular stance in questions of sexual politics, and, not least, of having gone through a quick process of modernisation. Now that Sweden had evolved into a welfare state, it would be natural for the Swedes to widen their perspective and help the poor people of the world. However, Signe Höjer stressed, it was less obvious how to assist wisely. Decisions on such matters demanded special knowledge of a kind that she, as a self-appointed expert on development aid, would gladly contribute with.[111]

According to the Höjers, principal programmes and budgets should preferably be administrated by the UN and its special organisations. The UN was seen as a future world government in which WHO might function as the health department.[112] Well into the 1960s, Axel Höjer wrote about a natural 'transition from national to world Government'.[113] Countries in Africa and Asia, Axel Höjer said, were happy to receive capital and technical expertise from the international aid agencies but afraid of 'bilateral agreements coupled with political and commercial demands'.[114] In addition to their criticism of the former colonial powers, the Höjers were highly sceptical of the emerging superpowers – the United States, the USSR and to some extent China – in their attempts to make formally decolonised countries dependent on them in a neo-colonial way.[115]

Both being convinced of the necessity of a multi-angled approach to aid – hunger, disease, analfabetism, overpopulation and general poverty must be combatted simultaneously – however, they, like Gunnar Myrdal and other contemporaries, claimed that bilateral aid would be needed for certain areas too controversial for the international health community to handle. Family planning was the most obvious of those areas.[116]

Concluding remarks

For more than half a century Axel Höjer and Signe Höjer worked, more or less together, in what could be defined as a mutual life project, largely centred on public health problems in a wide sense. By following them through the years, I have shown how they continually tried to launch reform proposals and concrete projects by referring to special expertise. However, the knowledge referred to changed through the years, and so did their positions as experts and their ways of claiming expertise. Variations over time and differences between the two of them can be linked to a range of factors, such as educational background, professional status, gender, audience, private circumstances, and the perceived state of development of the settings between which policies might be transferred. The Höjers' views about Sweden as recipient or provider of lessons changed with their perception of the Swedish state of development. At the same time, their ways of communicating new lessons were modified according to their own changing positions. Their international health work may, in many respects, be seen as an extension of a Swedish, or more generally Western, public health project. Even so, the Höjers would rather see themselves as helpers in other national health projects which were supposed to eventually drive themselves forward by the same mechanisms that were thought to be pivotal in the Swedish development process. These included large-scale biopolitical solutions such as health insurance and generally accessible healthcare, but were nevertheless thought to be ultimately dependent on self-regulating citizens. In a longer perspective, the Höjers imagined some kind of world government where WHO functioned as a health ministry, but where actual governance was largely delegated to the lowest level possible. And so basically, in the Sweden of the 1920s as well as in the Africa of the 1960s, the Höjers were largely driven by a liberal rationality of governance, where experts such as themselves were perceived as crucial components in the process of making people able to govern themselves in the 'right' direction.

However, as I have shown, acting as an expert was never enough in itself. For knowledge to turn into political power, mediators such as Signe Höjer and Axel Höjer had to achieve acknowledgement of their expertise in each relevant context. In the Höjer case, this meant that they had to be acknowledged as experts on the construction of specific welfare solutions, on the governance of modern welfare states, and even world improvement.

Notes

1   His sister Gerda became chairman of both the Swedish Nurses' Association and the International Council of Nurses, and was also a member of Riksdagen, the Swedish parliament. Sigrid, also a nurse, became director of a vocational school for physically disabled young people. Furthermore, no less than three of the brothers became Director-General of different government agencies.
2   Annika Berg, 2009.
3   Nikolas Rose, 1998, p. 86.
4   Zygmunt Bauman, 1989, p. 196.
5   Michel Foucault, 2000, vol. 3, pp. 340-342; Nikolas Rose & Peter Miller, 1992, pp. 175–176; Thomas Osborne, 1997, p. 175; Graham Burchell, 1991, p. 191. However, delegating power does not necessarily mean that more outright disciplinary technologies have vanished. In 'Technologies of the Self', Foucault describes governmentality as the meeting point between technologies of power (that is, technologies to govern other people) and technologies of self (that is, technologies to form one's own body, thoughts and behaviour in order to reach goals such as happiness, wisdom or perfection). Michel Foucault, 1988, pp. 18-19.
6   Nikolas Rose & Peter Miller, 1992, p. 175.
7   Compare e.g. with Thomas Osborne's thoughts on the increasingly important

roles of 'mediators', or John Kingdon's on 'policy entrepreneurs', in the complicated processes of launching ideas and policy proposals to politicians and/or the general public. Thomas Osborne, 2004; John W. Kingdon, 1984, p. 129 and pp. 134-137.

8   Axel Höjer, 'Reseberättelse, inkommen till Medicinalstyrelsen 5/10 1920, d:nr 1703/1920 M', Medicinalstyrelsen, Medicinalbyrån, EIII, at the National Archives of Sweden, Stockholm; Axel Höjer, 1920; Axel Höjer, 1920B; Axel Höjer, 1920C.

9   'Mjölkdroppar' [manuskript by Signe Höjer, early 1920s], in the archives of Signe and Axel Höjer at the National Archives of Sweden, Stockholm (*Signe och Axel Höjers arkiv*, hereafter referred to as SAHA), 2b vol. 1. Axel Höjer asked Signe for special advice on English childcare and child healthcare. Axel Höjer to Signe Dahl, Jan. 24 1920 in SAHA, 3b vol. 5.

10 Axel Höjer, 1920; Axel Höjer, 1920B; Axel Höjer, 1923; Axel Höjer, 'Reseberättelse', appendix IV.

11 Axel Höjer, 'Reseberättelse', A1–A15; Axel Höjer, 'Något om fransk barna- och modersvård'.

12 Axel Höjer, 'Reseberättelse', Ba–Bd; Axel Höjer, 1920A; Axel Höjer, 1920C; Signe Höjer; Signe Höjer, 1922, pp. 65-67.

13 Axel Höjer, 1920C, pp. 30-33; Axel Höjer, 'Reseberättelse', IV. Both clearly stated that some adaptations would be necessary in the Swedish context. Signe Höjer, 'Mjölkdroppar' (including additional comments by Axel Höjer); Signe Höjer, 1922.

14 Richard Rose, 1991, quot. 7.

15 Axel Höjer, 'Reseberättelse', especially appendices A1, A7–10, IV.

16 Richard Rose, 1991. See also David P. Dolowitz & David Marsh, 1996, p. 351.

17 Axel Höjer, 'Reseberättelse', A1–A15; Axel Höjer, 1920B.

18 Diane Stone have explored such processes when investigating think tanks and other 'policy entrepreneurs' as agents of policy transfer, and their strategies for spreading ideas. See e.g. Diane Stone, 2000; Diane Stone & Andrew Denham, 2004.

19 Axel Höjer, 1975, pp. 72-97; Signe Höjer, 1979, pp. 133-140.

20 Axel Höjer, 1921, pp. 1-2; Signe Höjer, 'Mjölkdroppar'; Axel Höjer, 1923. Compare with Axel Höjer, 'Reseberättelse'; Axel Höjer, 1975, pp. 62-63; Signe Höjer, 1979, p. 11.

21 Birger Broman, 1938, pp. 149–150; Gena Weiner, 1995, pp. 81-86.

22 Signe Höjer, p. 16; Gena H. Weiner, 1995, pp. 86–92, pp. 152–153; Allan Gunther, 1966, p. 21.

23 Birger Broman, 1938, pp. 152–156; Allan Gunther, 1966, p. 21; Axel Höjer, 1975, pp. 160–161; Axel Höjer, Hjalmar Fries, Carl Gustaf Hulting, Adolf Lichtenstein & Gotthilf Stéenhoff, 1923, pp. 570–82; SOU, 1929, vol. 28, pp. 44–55 and pp.186–206; SOU, 1935, pp. 92–100.

24 Nikolas Rose, 1994, pp. 49-56. See also Nikolas Rose and Peter Miller, 1992, p. 180; Nikolas Rose, 1993, p. 284 and p. 291. On the early formation of a 'social' sphere in Sweden, see Frans Lundgren, 2003.

25 Nikolas Rose, 1994, pp. 51–52.

26 As corresponding to the Swedish professional experts in an American context, Eyerman identifies a group of *public intellectuals* who entered the public sector in the USA around World War I. Ron Eyerman, 1994, p. 92, pp. 150–186 and pp.

126–127. See also Ron Eyerman, 1995. Compare with Per Wisselgren, 2009 who instead uses the term *public intellectual* when discussing Swedish 'professional experts' such as Alva and Gunnar Myrdal and Kerstin Hesselgren.

27 Axel Höjer's goal of full health and the ambition to act preventively in a long-term perspective meant that although he would entitle everyone to the best healthcare possible, not everyone would be allowed to breed. Axel Höjer was dedicated to a kind of reform eugenics, enforcing sterilization of certain groups with supposedly genetic flaws, and especially those groups categorised as *sinnslöa* (feeble-minded).

28 'Kvacksalveriets vackra skylt av vetenskaplighet och människokärlek rena bluffen', *Östergötlands Folkblad*, 1937, (Apr. 16), p. 12; 'Samhället måste snart ingripa mot kvacksalveriet', *Norrköpings Tidningar*, 1937, (Apr. 16), pp. 6–7; Axel Höjer, 1943, pp. 190-192.

29 SOU, *Den öppna läkarvården i riket: Utredning och förslag*. See also J. Axel Höjer, 1948.

30 See particularly the extensive debate in *Svenska Läkartidningen*, 1948.

31 Urban Janlert, 1978, pp. 5–8; Arthur Engel, 1975, p. 1786.

32 Compare Axel Höjers own account of the events in Axel Höjer, 'Ur J Axel Höjers minnen', Johan Axel Höjers arkiv, The National Archives of Sweden, pp. 515–517 and pp. 545–546 (a shortered version of this account is published in Axel Höjer, 1975, p. 140 and pp. 148-149) with my account in Annika Berg, 2009, chapter 2 p. 2.

33 The official letter from the Medical Board is reproduced in SOU, *Betänkande med förslag angående inrättande av ett statens institut för folkhälsan avgivet av tillkallade sakkunniga*, 1937, vol. 31, pp. 16–19.

34 SOU, 1937, vol. 31, pp. 22–40.

35 SOU, 1937, vol. 31, pp. 60–62.

36 Erik Björkquist & Ivar Flygare, 1963, pp. 80-82; Karin Johannisson, 1991, pp. 179–180.

37 Karin Johannisson, 1991, p. 180.

38 SOU, 1937, vol. 31, pp. 7–16.

39 Compare Karin Johannisson, 1991, p. 180 and p. 189. The picture of a marked conflict is also complicated by the fact that two out of five members of the investigating committee were medical doctors, as were the majority of those experts (including Axel Höjer) that the committee asked for advice. Höjer gave advice on 'the general foundations for the institute's organisation and tasks'. SOU, 1937, vol. 31, pp. 5–6.

40 Möller was also, generally speaking, very positive towards the original 1935 Medical Board suggestion. SOU, 1937, vol. 31, p. 22. Möller and Höjer worked closely together. Axel Höjer, 'Ur J. Axel Höjers minnen', p. 525.

41 SOU, 1948, vol. 14, pp. 107–109, p. 216, p. 293 and p. 390; Axel Höjer, 1948, p. 123; Axel Höjer, 1941, p. 154.

42 Quotation from Mattias Tydén, 2002, p. 35.

43 Compare Peter Conrad, 1992, particularly p. 209 and p. 211.

44 Karin Johannisson, 1991, p. 172.

45 Ludmilla Jordanova, 2004, pp. 345-346.

46 Surely, social medicine and social hygiene may be squashed into a rather conventional medicalization perspective, with that peculiarity that social problems are regarded as diseases of the social body. However, the social body was an old

metaphor, by no means monopolised by the medical corps. Mary Poovey, 1995. Notably too, Axel Höjer himself very seldom talked about society in corporal terms. For an exception, see Axel Höjer, 'Present day interdependence', culturally, politically, economically, [manuscript for a speech at the WILPF International Seminar, Leangkollen, Norge, 1 aug (Norway, 1 Aug. 1961]', SAHA, 2b, vol. 3, 2b vol. 7.

47 Dorothy Porter & Roy Porter, 1988, pp. 90–106; Annika Berg, 2009, pp. 268–272.
48 Peter Conrad, 1992, pp. 224–226.
49 See e.g. Axel Höjer to Signe Dahl, July 23, 1919, SAHA, 3b, vol. 4; Signe Dahl to Axel Höjer, July 14, 1919, reproduced in Signe Höjer, 1979, p. 17.
50 Joan Wallach Scott, 1999, pp. 28-50. In a similar way, from a Swedish horizon, Yvonne Hirdman has discussed dichotomy and hierarchy as fundamental components of what she defines as the 'gender system'. Yvonne Hirdman, 1988, vol. 9, pp. 49–63. Compare Yvonne Hirdman, 2003.
51 In London in 1919, they both lived in so-called settlements, where they actively participated in various activities designed to bring together well-educated middle-class youngsters with working-class people. The house the Höjers built in Solna a couple of years later was supposed to perform a similar function, and also did so to quite some extent. In the house, the growing Höjer family shared their living quarters with Axel Höjer's laboratory, but also with a more or less public library and meeting facilities for the local branch of the Social Democratic educational society (ABF). Signe Höjer, 1979, p. 105, pp. 166–169 and p. 180. See also several letters from Signe and Axel Höjer to Signe's mother Louise Dahl 1920–1921, SAHA, 3b, vol. 17.
52 Ron Eyerman, 1994, pp. 100-101, 107-109, describes the *movement intellectuals* as people based in different social movements who have primarily worked with formulating collective identities and who have therefore more seldom been able to assert themselves as separate intellectual voices. Traditionally, the movement intellectuals were more rarely formally educated and mainly expressed themselves through the channels of their own social movements. This may help to explain their tendency to disappear in historiography. (Eyerman has also written about social movements in cooperation with Andrew Jamison. See e.g. Ron Eyerman and Andrew Jamison, 1991.
53 The flora of social movements that was active before and during the welfare state's constructional phase offered a new arena for many female intellectuals, even though they were often contested within male-dominated movements such as the workers' movement. Gunnel Karlsson, 1996; Christina Carlsson, 1986, pp. 276-277; Yvonne Hirdman, 1979, pp. 65–67 and pp. 359–361.
54 Helge Moberg, 1967, pp. 75-76.
55 Signe Höjer, 1982, pp. 54-59 and p. 72.
56 Signe Höjer, 1982, p. 83, p. 115 and pp. 141–144.
57 Josefin Rönnbäck, 2002, pp. 113-114; Kjell Östberg, 1997, pp. 200-205; Gunnel Karlsson, 1996, p. 114.
58 Elizabeth Wilson, 1977; Jane Lewis, 1980.
59 Carole Pateman, 1988; Carole Pateman, 1989, particularly ch. 8.
60 These kinds of strategies have been analysed in terms of 'welfare feminism' or 'maternalism'. Olive Banks, 1986, pp. 153-179; Seth Koven and Sonya Michel, 1990, pp. 1076–1108; Theda Skocpol and Gretchen Ritter, 1991, pp. 36–93. The results of these strategies are, however, debated, as is the definition of 'mater-

nalism'. Ann Taylor Allen, 2005, p. 8; Jane Lewis, 1994, pp. 37-55.
61 Rönnbäck, 2002, pp. 113-114.
62 Almgren, 2006, pp. 5-6.
63 Influence, as the political scientist Anna G. Jónasdóttir, 1986, p. 163, points out, is not necessarily the same as authority (by which she means legitimate, openly acknowledged power).
64 Annika Berg, 2009, ch 2 p. 5. Compare with Ann-Sofie Ohlander, who in an often-referred text dates the formulation of a distinct family policy to the 1950s, not mentioning the attempts of the women's delegation or even earlier attempts by the Social Democratic women's movement. See also Ann-Sofie Ohlander, 1991.
65 Signe Höjer, 1951, pp. 20-29. Compare with Gunnel Karlsson, 1996.
66 Signe Höjer, 1982, p. 167.
67 Axel Höjer, 'Report to World Health Organization, Regional Office for South East Asia by Dr. J. Axel Höjer, India 22, T. A. India 26: Final Report', SAHA, 2a, vol. 2, p. 13; Signe Höjer, 1955, p. 156; Signe Höjer, 1982, p. 189; Signe Höjer, 1953.
68 David P. Dolowitz and David Marsh, 2000, pp. 5–23, quot. 5. See also Dolowitz and Marsh, 1996. Policy transfer, in their definition of the concept, can involve different categories of actors, transfer of different objects, including negative lessons (Dolowitz and Marsh count with lesson drawing as a subcategory of policy transfer) and different degrees of transfer.
69 Signe Höjer, [1920s manuscript], SAHA, 2b, vol. 2; Signe Höjer, 1922; Axel Höjer, 1923; Axel Höjer, Hjalmar Fries, Carl Gustaf Hulting, Adolf Lichtenstein and Gotthilf Stéenhoff, 1923.
70 SOU, 1948, pp. 193–198, quot. 194; Axel Höjer, 1948, pp. 298–305.
71 Annika Berg, 2009, ch 3, 4.
72 Signe Höjer, 1959, p. 12, p. 210; Axel Höjer, 1961; Axel Höjer, 1963; Annika Berg, 2009, ch 3, p. 5.
73 Axel Höjer, 1958B. p. 11.
74 See e.g. Signe Höjer, 1955, pp. 99–118; Signe Höjer, 1960A; Signe Höjer, 1960B; Signe Höjer, 1970.
75 Axel Höjer, 1954 B, p. 22..
76 Axel Höjer, 1954, p. 75.
77 Axel Höjer, 1995, p. 11, (First published in *Världshorisont*, 1954, vol. 8, issue 12, pp. 15–19, continuing in vol. 9 (1955), issue 1, pp. 9–13.), Svenska FN-föreningen Mellanfolkligt Samarbete, Stockholm.
78 Axel Höjer, 1957, pp. 16–18; see also Axel Höjer, 1958, pp. 381–385.
79 Axel Höjer, 1958, p. 385.
80 The use of expertise in forming various programs and institutions is rarely limited to a strictly national context, but this dimension is often lost in governmentality analyses – rather paradoxically, as these theories very much aim to problematise the concept of the nation state. Nikolas Rose and Peter Miller claim that their analysis of governmentality could just as well be applied to geo-political phenomenona like diplomacy, international agreements, national borders, customs, war and colonialism. Nikolas Rose and Peter Miller, 1992, p. 178.
81 See e.g. Axel Höjer, 1995, pp. 12–13; Signe Höjer, 1955; A. Höjer, 1961.
82 'Det är endast genom administrativa och organisatoriska anvisningar, genom

att lära folken att hjälpa sig själva, som VHO kan utföra sitt verk. Dess utsända konsulter och demonstrationsgrupper verkar som enzym, som sprider välsignelsebringande krafter i den stora tröga massan. Så skingrar den distinkta upplysningens klara ljus vidskepelsens mörker.' Axel Höjer, 1950, pp. 557–60, quot. 560.
83 Axel Höjer, 1962.
84 Axel Höjer, 1962, 7.
85 Axel Höjer, 1962, 3.
86 Axel Höjer, 1963B, p. 164.
87 Axel Höjer, 1962, 3.
88 Axel Höjer, 1963; compare Axel Höjer, 1962, 3.
89 Axel Höjer, 1962, 7.
90 Such crimes could consist in refusal to use extant latrines. Axel Höjer, 1962, 3.
91 Sterilisation was introduced as a birth control measure in India from the late 1950s, then escalated until the 1970s, when, as historian Sunniva Engh has shown, the Swedish development aid agency, Sida, helped to sponsor campaigns for several years. During the so-called emergency period of 1975–77 the number of sterilisations reached alarming levels. Annika Berg, 2009, ch. 3, p. 2; Sunniva Engh, 2005; Sunniva Engh, 2007.
92 Signe Höjer, 1955, 2.
93 See e.g. Megan Vaughan, 1991, pp. 10-12.
94 David Scott, 1995, pp. 191-220.
95 Gyan Prakash, 1999, particularly ch. 5.
96 Maria Eriksson Baaz, 2001; Louis Faye and Michael McEachrane 2001, pp. 159-186.
97 Signe Höjer, 1961, pp. 9-11, quot. 10-11.
98 Signe Höjer, 1960, pp. 16–17; Signe Höjer, 1961, pp. 238–244.
99 Signe Höjer, 1960, pp. 17–20.
100 Signe Höjer, 1960B; see also Signe Höjer, 1957; Signe Höjer, 1960A, pp. 19–20.
101 Signe Höjer, 1960B; see also Signe Höjer, 1969; Signe Höjer, 1961, pp. 19–20; Signe Höjer, 1961.
102 Signe Höjer, 1960, p. 14. Self-questioning (*självprövning*) was a term that Axel Höjer had used similarly, in a radio speech at New Year's eve 1954. Axel Höjer, 1955, pp. 1–4.
103 Axel Höjer, 1963B, quot. 164.
104 Axel Höjer, 1963B, quot. 164.
105 Axel Höjer, 'Report on Ghana 13: Draft', SAHA, 4b, vol. 4, p. 9; Kari Molin, 1976. How they were perceived by the local people is, of course, another matter and, unfortunately, hard to find out.
106 Signe Höjer, 1960, pp. 17-20; Axel Höjer, 1995, p. 14.
107 Axel Höjer, 'Ur J Axel Höjers minnen', pp. 718-719. Compare S. Kojo Addae, 1997, p. 76, where no mention is made of Brachott's militant style; also, Addae claims that Brachott stayed for two years in Ghana.
108 See e.g. Axel Höjer, 1958, pp. 733–752.
109 Axel Höjer, 1959, p. 23; Axel Höjer, 1967, pp. 350–351. Compare speech manuscript marked 'Som hälsoexpert i främmande miljöer, Västerås 1962', SAHA, 4b, vol. 5.
110 Signe Höjer, 1961, quotation from caption at p. 80f.
111 Signe Höjer, 1958, p. 6.

112 Signe Höjer, 1955A, p. 3; Axel Höjer, 1963, p. 14; Axel Höjer, 'Ur J Axel Höjers minnen', p. 730; Axel Höjer, 1961, XIII.
113 Axel Höjer, 'Report on Ghana 13: Draft', p. 12. See also Axel Höjer, 1963, p. 14; Axel Höjer, 1961.
114 Axel Höjer, 1959, quot. 22.
115 Axel Höjer, 1995, pp. 12–13; S. Höjer, 1960A, p. 23.
116 Axel Höjer, 'Som hälsoexpert i främmande miljöer', SAHA, 4b, vol. 5; Axel Höjer, 'Anförande vid United Nations conference on the application of science and technology', p. 1; Annika Berg, 2009, ch. 3, p. 2.

References

Addae, S. Kojo 1997: *History of Western Medicine in Ghana 1880-1960*, Edinburgh & Cambridge & Durham.
Allen, Ann Taylor 2005: *Feminism and Motherhood in Western Europe 1890-1970: The Maternal Dilemma*, New York & Basingstoke.
Almgren 2006: *Kvinnorörelsen och efterkrigsplaneringen: Statsfeminism i svensk arbetsmarknadspolitik under och kort efter andra världskriget*, Umeå.
Banks, Olive 1986: *Faces of feminism: A study of feminism as a social movement*, Oxford.
Bauman, Zygmunt 1989: *Modernity and the Holocaust*, Cambridge.
Baaz, Maria Eriksson 2001: 'Biståndet och partnerskapets problematik', Louis Faye and Michael McEachrane (eds.), *Sverige och de Andra: postkoloniala perspektiv*, Stockholm.
Berg, Annika 2009: *Den gränslösa hälsan: Signe och Axel Höjer, folkhälsan och expertisen*, Uppsala.
Björkquist, Erik and Ivar Flygare 1963: 'Den centrala medicinalförvaltningen', Wolfram Kock (ed.), *Medicinalväsendet i Sverige 1813-1962: Utgiven med anledning av Kungl. Medicinalstyrelsens 300-årsjubileum*, Stockholm.
Broman, Birger 1938: 'Barnavårdscentralernas uppkomst och utveckling i Sverige', *Nordisk hygienisk tidskrift*, vol. 19.
Burchell, Graham 1991: 'Peculiar Interests: Civil Society and Governing 'The System of Natural Liberty'', Graham Burchell, Colin Gordon and Peter Miller (eds.), *The Foucault Effect – Studies in Governmentality: With Two Lectures by and An Interview with Michel Foucault*, Chicago.
Carlsson, Christina 1986: *Kvinnosyn och kvinnopolitik: En studie av svensk socialdemokrati 1880-1910*, Lund.
Conrad, Peter 1992: 'Medicalization and Social Control', *Annual Review of Sociology*, vol. 18.
Dolowitz, David P. and David Marsh 1996: 'Who Learns What from Whom: A Review of the Policy Transfer Literature', *Political Studies*, vol. 44.
Dolowitz, David P. and David Marsh 2000: 'Learning from Abroad: The Role of Policy Transfer in Contemporary Policy-Making', *Governance*, vol. 13.
Engel, Arthur 1975: 'En hälsans, fredens och den sociala rättvisans missionär', *Läkartidningen*, vol. 72.
Engh, Sunniva 2005: 'Population Control in the twentieth Century: Scandinavian Aid to the Indian Family Planning Programme', (unpublished Ph.D. dissertation) Oxford University.

Engh, Sunniva 2007: 'Det internasjonale folkhemmet? Styringsmentalitet i velferdsstat og bistand', Christina Florin, Elisabeth Elgán and Gro Hagemann (eds.), *Den självstyrande medborgaren? Ny historia om rättvisa, demokrati och välfärd*, Stockholm.

Eyerman, Ron 1994: *Between Culture and Politics: Intellectuals in Modern Society*, Oxford.

Eyerman, Ron 1995: 'Rationalizing Intellectuals: Sweden in the 1930s and 1940s', *Theory and Society*, vol. 14.

Eyerman, Ron and Andrew Jamison 1991: *Social Movements: A Cognitive Approach*, Cambridge.

Faye, Louis and Michael McEachrane (eds.) 2001: *Sverige och de Andra: Postkoloniala perspektiv*. Stockholm.

Foucault, Michel 1988: 'Technologies of the Self', Luther H. Martin, Patrick H. Hutton and Huck Gutman (eds.), *Technologies of the Self: A Seminar with Michel Foucault*, Amherst.

Foucault, Michel 2000: 'The Subject and Power', James D. Faubion, (ed.), *Essential works of Foucault, 1954–1984*, vol. 3, New York.

Gunther, Allan 1966: *'Mjölkdroppen' – ett socialmedicinskt pionjärarbete*, Stockholm.

Hirdman, Yvonne 1979: *Vi bygger landet: Den svenska arbetarrörelsens historia från Per Götrek till Olof Palme*, Solna.

Hirdman, Yvonne 1988: 'Genussystemet – reflexioner kring kvinnors underordning', *Kvinnovetenskaplig tidskrift*, vol. 9.

Hirdman, Yvonne 2003: *Genus: Om det stabilas föränderliga former*, Liber, Stockholm

Höjer, Axel: 'Ur J Axel Höjers minnen', Johan Axel Höjers Arkiv, The National Archives of Sweden.

Höjer, Axel: 'Som hälsoexpert i främmande miljöer, Västerås 1962', SAHA, 4b vol. 5.

Höjer, Axel: 'Anförande vid United Nations conference on the application of science and technology'.

Höjer, Axel: 'Report on Ghana 13: Draft', SAHA, 4b vol. 4.

Höjer, Axel: 'Report to World Health Organization, Regional Office for South East Asia by Dr. J. Axel Höjer, India 22, T. A. India 26: Final Report', SAHA, 2a vol. 2.

Höjer, Axel 'Reseberättelse, inkommen till Medicinalstyrelsen 5/10 1920, d:nr 1703/1920 M', Medicinalstyrelsen, Medicinalbyrån, EIII, at the National Archives of Sweden, Stockholm.

Höjer, Axel 1920: 'Något om barnmorskeväsendet i England: Intryck från en studieresa där sept-dec 1919', *Jordemodern*, vol. 33.

Höjer, Axel 1920B: 'Något om fransk barna- och modersvård', *Vårdarebladet*, vol. 10.

Höjer, Axel 1920C: 'Något om engelsk barna- och modersvård', *Vårdarebladet*, vol. 10.

Höjer, Axel 1921: 'Mjölkdroppen i Solna och dess verksamhet', *Stockholms förstadsblad* (Nov. 5).

Höjer, Axel 1923: 'Om 'Mjölkdroppar' som övervakningsställen för späda barn', *Hygienisk revy*, vol. 12.

Höjer, Axel 1941: 'Aktuella socialmedicinska uppgifter', *Socialmedicinsk tidskrift*, vol. 18.

Höjer, Axel 1943: 'Hälsoarbetare', *En bok till Karl Hovberg på 50-årsdagen 24 marts 1943*, Framtiden, Malmö.

Höjer, Axel 1948: *Hälsovård och läkarvård: i går – i dag – i morgon*, 14, KF, Stockholm.

Höjer, Axel 1948B: 'Engelsk hälsovårdsreform och svensk', *Tiden*, vol. 41.

Höjer, Axel 1950: 'Världshälsoorganisationen och sjuksköterskorna: Anförande vid Nordiska sjuksköterskekongressen i Göteborg den 3 juli 1950', *Tidskrift för Sveriges sjuksköterskor*, vol. 17.

Höjer, Axel 1954: 'Hälsningar från Travancore och J Axel Höjer', *Tidskrift för Sveriges sjuksköterskor*, vol. 21.
Höjer, Axel 1954B, 'Note on Health and Medicine in Travancore – Coshin with an Introduction on Generel Conditions and Culture [Appendix to find Report to WHO], dated June 22, 1954, in SAHA, 4b, vol. 5.
Höjer, Axel 1955: 'Självprövning', *Studiekamraten: Tidning för det fria och frivilliga bildningsarbetet*, vol. 37.
Höjer, Axel 1957: 'Undervisningen i förebyggande och social medicin i Indien', *Världshorisont*, vol. 11.
Höjer, Axel 1958: 'Assam och hälsovårdsarbetet', *Tidskrift för Sveriges sjuksköterskor*, vol. 25.
Höjer, Axel 1958B: 'En dröm som kan bli verklighet', *Vårt Röda Kors*, vol. 13.
Höjer, Axel 1958C: 'Det tysta ropet från urskogen', *Sociala meddelanden*.
Höjer, Axel 1959: 'En världsdel vaknar' [manuscript marked 'Speech at the Stockholm Consert Hall Meeting Jan. 27, 1959'], SAHA, 2a vol. 1.
Höjer, Axel 1961: 'Present day interdependence', culturally, politically, economically, [manuscript for a speech at the WILPF International Seminar, Leangkollen, Aug. 1, Norway], SAHA, 2b vol. 3 and 2b vol. 7.
Höjer, Axel 1962: 'Experience of Health Service Planning' [Agenda Item F.1.2. at United Nations Conference on the Application of Science and Technology for the Benefit of the Less Developed Areas, marked E/CONF.39/F/52, 10 Oct], SAHA, 2a vol. 4 and 4b vol. 5.
Höjer, Axel 1963: 'En friskare värld', *Världshorisont*, vol. 17.
Höjer, Axel 1963B: 'Vidga Flaskhalsen', 1963, Vol. 22.
Höjer, Axel 1967: 'En procent av den taxerade inkomsten till u-land?', *Farmaceutisk revy*, vol. 66.
Höjer, Axel 1975: *En läkares väg: Från Visby till Vietnam*, Bonniers, Stockholm.
Höjer, Axel 1995: *Liv och död i det nya Indien*, Svenska FN-föreningen Mellanfolkligt samarbete, Stockholm.
Höjer, Axel, Hjalmar Fries, Carl Gustaf Hulting, Adolf Lichtenstein and Gotthilf Stéenhoff 1923: 'Betänkande rörande övervakning av späda barn: Till pediatriska sektionen av Svenska Läkaresällskapet', *Hygiea*, vol. 85.
Höjer, Signe: 'Mjölkdroppar' [manuskript, early 1920s], in the archives of Signe and Axel Höjer (SAHA) at the National Archives of Sweden, 2b vol. 1 and 3b vol. 5, Stockholm.
Höjer, Signe: 'Synpunkter på kvinnliga studiecirklar' [1920s manuscript], SAHA, 2b vol. 2.
Höjer, Signe 1922: 'Om 'hemhjälp'', *Vårdarebladet*, vol. 12.
Höjer, Signe 1951: 'Befolkningsproblemen', *Socialdemokratisk kvinnogärning: Festskrift i anledning av Disa Västbergs 60-årsdag den 17 maj 1951*, Sveriges Socialdemokratiska Kvinnoförbund & Tiden, Stockholm.
Höjer, Signe 1953: 'Social welfare and the family' [manuscript for lecture at the Indian Institute of Culture, Bangalore], SAHA, 2b vol. 7.
Höjer, Signe 1955: *Travancore – välsignat land*, Tiden, Stockholm
Höjer, Signe 1955B: 'Women in the Underdeveloped Countries: Statement Submitted as Basis for Discussion to the International Socialist Women's Conference', 1955, (9-10 July) [marked International Socialist Women's Secretariat, Circular No. W.10/55, 27 May, 1955], SAHA, 2b vol. 8, London.
Höjer, Signe 1957: 'På struma-jakt i Himalaya' [manuscript marked Assam, Jan.],

SAHA, 2b vol. 7.
Höjer, Signe 1958: *Angår Indien oss?*, Stockholm.
Höjer, Signe 1959: *Levande begraven: En bok om spetälska*, Stockholm.
Höjer, Signe 1960: 'Civilisering av färgade – eller av vita?' [manuscript for speech at Oslo City Hall, UN Day], SAHA, 2b vol. 9.
Höjer, Signe ca. 1960B: 'Är det vi som är efterblivna?' [manuscript, marked 'Artikel i Hertha'], SAHA, 2b vol. 3.
Höjer, Signe 1961: *Slav stig upp...*, Stockholm.
Höjer, Signe 1969: 'Mammies och andra kvinnor i Västafrika' [manuscript for lecture at the Stockholm section of Fogelstadsförbundet, Nov. 30], SAHA, 2b vol. 4.
Höjer, Signe 1970: *Kvinnomakt – könsroller i tropikerna*, Stockholm.
Höjer, Signe 1979: *Vägen till Hagalund*, Stockholm.
Höjer, Signe 1982: *Mitt i livet*, Stockholm.
Janlert, Urban 1978: 'Sjukvård efter kriget', *Motpol*, vol. 56, issue 3–4.
Johannisson, Karin 1991: 'Folkhälsa'. Det svenska projektet från 1900 till 2:a världskriget, Stockholm.
Jónasdóttir, Anna G. 1986: 'Kön, makt, politik: Sammanfattning av en pågående teoriutveckling om grundvalarna i det formellt jämlika samhällets mansvälde', Hillevi Ganetz, Evy Gunnarsson and Anita Göransson (eds.), *Feminism och marxism: En förälskelse med förhinder*, Stockholm.
Jordanova, Ludmilla 2004: 'Social Construction of Medical Knowledge', Frank Huisman and John Harley Warner (eds.), *Locating Medical History: The Stories and their Meanings*, Baltimore.
Karlsson, Gunnel 1996: *Från broderskap till systerskap: Det socialdemokratiska kvinnoförbundets kamp för inflytande och makt i SAP*, Lund.
Kingdon, John W. 1984: *Agendas, Alternatives, and Public Policies*, Boston.
Koven, Seth and Sonya Michel 1990: 'Womanly Duties: Maternalist Politics and the Origins of Welfare States in France, Germany, Great Britain and the United States, 1880-1920', *The American Historical Review*, vol. 95.
1937: 'Kvacksalveriets vackra skylt av vetenskaplighet och människokärlek rena bluffen', *Östergötlands Folkblad*, (Apr. 16).
Lewis, Jane 1980: *The Politics of Motherhood: Child and Maternal Welfare in England, 1900–1939*, London & Montreal.
Lewis, Jane 1994: 'Gender, the Family and Women's Agency in the Building of 'Welfare States': The British case', *Social History*, vol. 19.
Lundgren, Frans 2003: *Den isolerade medborgaren: Liberalt styre och uppkomsten av det sociala vid 1800-talets mitt*, Hedemora.
Moberg, Helge 1967: *Stockholms stadsfullmäktige 1938–1963: Biografiska data och porträtt*, Stockholm.
Molin, Kari 1976: 'Signe Höjer 80 år: Frågan om fred viktigast i dag', *Dagens Nyheter*, (Aug. 8).
Ohlander, Ann-Sofie 1989: 'Det osynliga barnet? Kampen om den socialdemokratiska familjepolitiken', Klaus Misgeld, Karl Molin and Klas Åmark (eds.), *Socialdemokratins samhälle: SAP och Sverige under 100 år*, Stockholm.
Ohlander, Ann-Sofie 1991: 'The Invisible Child? The Struggle for a Social Democratic Family Policy in Sweden, 1900–1960s', Gisela Bock and Pat Thane (eds.), *Maternity and Gender Policies: Women and the Rise of the European Welfare States, 1880s-1950's*, London/New York.
Ohlander, Ann-Sofie 1992: 'The Invisible Child? The Struggle over Social Democratic

Family Policy', Klaus Misgeld, Karl Molin and Klas Åmark (eds.), *Creating Social Democracy: A Century of the Social Democratic Labor Party in Sweden*.

Osborne, Thomas 1997: 'Of Health and Statecraft', Alan R. Petersen and Robin Bunton (eds.), *Foucault, Health and Medicine*, London & New York.

Osborne, Thomas 2004: 'On Mediators: Intellectuals and the Ideas Trade in the Knowledge Society', *Economy and Society*, vol. 33.

Östberg, Kjell 1997: *Efter rösträtten: Kvinnors utrymme efter det demokratiska genombrottet*, Stockholm & Stehag.

Pateman, Carole 1988: *The Sexual Contract*, Cambridge.

Pateman, Carole 1989: *The Disorder of Women: Democracy, Feminism and Political Theory*, Cambridge.

Poovey, Mary 1995: *Making a Social Body: British Cultural Formation, 1830–1864*, Chicago & London.

Porter, Dorothy and Roy Porter 1988: 'What Was Social Medicine? An Historiographical Essay', *Journal of Historical Sociology*, vol. 1.

Prakash, Gyan 1999: *Another Reason: Science and the Imagination of Modern India*, Princeton, N.J.

Rose, Nikolas 1993: 'Government, Authority and Expertise in Advanced Liberalism', *Economy and Society*, vol. 22.

Rose, Nikolas 1994: 'Medicine, History and the Present', Roy Porter and Colin Jones (eds.), *Reassessing Foucault: Power, Medicine and the Body*, London.

Rose, Nikolas 1998: *Inventing Our Selves: Psychology, Power, and Personhood*, Cambridge & New York & Melbourne.

Rose, Nikolas and Peter Miller 1992: 'Political Power beyond the State: Problematics of Government', *The British Journal of Sociology*, vol. 43.

Rose, Richard 1991: *What is Lesson-Drawing?*, Glasgow.

Rönnbäck, Josefin 2002: 'Den fängslade modern: Om samhällsmoderlighet som ideologi, taktik och praktik i kampen för kvinnors rösträtt', Helena Bergman and Peter Johansson (eds.), *Familjeangelägenheter*, Stockholm & Stehag.

1937: 'Samhället måste snart ingripa mot kvacksalveriet', *Norrköpings Tidningar*, (Apr. 16).

Scott, David 1995: 'Colonial Governmentality', *Social Text*, vol. 43.

Scott, Joan Wallach 1999: *Gender and the politics of history*, New York & Chichester.

Skocpol, Theda and Gretchen Ritter 1991: 'Gender and the Origins of Modern Social Policies in Britain and the United States', *Studies in American Political Development*, vol. 5.

SOU 1948: *Den öppna läkarvården i riket: Utredning och förslag*.

SOU 1929: *Betänkande angående moderskapsskydd*, vol. 28.

SOU 1935: *Kungl. Medicinalstyrelsens utlåtande och förslag angående förebyggande mödra- och barnavård*, vol. 19.

SOU 1937: *Betänkande med förslag angående inrättande av ett statens institut för folkhälsan avgivet av tillkallade sakkunniga*, vol. 31.

SOU 1948: vol. 14.

Stone, Diane 2000: 'Non-Governmental Policy Transfer: The Strategies of Independent Policy Institutes', *Governance*, vol. 13.

Stone, Diane and Andrew Denham 2004: *Think Tank Traditions: Policy Research and the Politics of Ideas*, Manchester.

Tydén, Mattias 2002: *Från politik till praktik: De svenska steriliseringslagarna 1935-1975*, Stockholm.

Vaughan, Megan 1991: *Curing their Ills: Colonial Power and African Illness*, Cambridge.

Weiner, Gena 1995: *De räddade barnen: Om fattiga barn, mödrar och fäder och deras möte med filantropin i Hagalund 1900–1940*, Uppsala.
Wilson, Elizabeth 1977: *Women & the Welfare State*, London.
Wisselgren, Per 2009: 'Women as Public Intellectuals: Kerstin Hesselgren and Alva Myrdal', Christian Fleck, Andreas Hess and E. Stina Lyon (eds.), *Intellectuals and their Publics: Perspectives from the Social Sciences*, Farnham.

Experts at work.
A micro-study of architects and school buildings in Denmark, 1940–1970

Ning de Coninck-Smith

Introduction

When in 1957 the parish council of Nørre Lyndelse on the island of Funen made the decision to build a new school, they were not aware they were making history. But they were, and the new comprehensive school with its seven classrooms, its area for the 'Mellemskole' [middle school] and its graduating 'Realklasse' or lower secondary pupils had many visitors from other parts of the country. Before then children had had to travel into the nearby city of Odense if they – or their parents on their behalf – felt that they should continue after the seven first compulsory classes. This was all to be changed, and in the new school a class was even created for children with speech, hearing and sight disabilities. These were the years in which reserves of intelligence were to be mobilised, and with its new school the small parish of Nørre Lyndelse leapt forward into the era of educational expansion. The number of pupils taking the final school-leaving exam had already started to grow substantially, and a most important impetus for this development – alongside a mechanisation of agriculture that allowed young people greater freedom of choice in the labour market – was the creation of the many new central schools. They were not only central to this development; they were also centrally located in the community. Such a symbolic location indicated the importance of education even in the countryside, where children as late as in the 1950s frequently went to schools with two or four classes without age divisions and with school days that were considerably shorter than in the towns.

This increase in the number of people with a 'mellem' [middle] or 'real' school exam had started several generations back. Since the turn of the century, the number had doubled every 25 years.[1] For children coming from the countryside taking these exams was only possible if they attended a private school. The state schools – the so-called folk schools [folkeskoler] did not offer this option. With the rise of the many new central schools like the one at Nørre Lyndelse, giving children equal educational opportunities became a task for the welfare state.

The central school in Nørre Lyndelse was not any ordinary school. It was located in the parish where the composer Carl Nielsen (1865–1931) had been born and was equipped with a concert hall capable of seating 300 people with acoustics that would make a small orchestra feel at home. The creation of this hall was in itself a challenge, one taken up by the architectural firm of Johannes Folke Olsen (1908-2002). However – though it is hard to believe – a separate challenge was presented in getting the Ministry of Education to approve its new lavatories. The architects had located them inside the building and not in a separate outbuilding with direct access from the school playground, which was the prescribed norm. For every two classes they had even provided two lavatories, one for girls and one for boys, together with a wardrobe and a sink. According to their own words, they had been inspired by a pamphlet published by the Ministry of Education about classroom function and design.[2]

In contrast to the traditional desks placed in rows next to each other with the teacher's desk at the front, the pamphlet had recommended a more flexible classroom design, with light tables and chairs that would enable new group-based teaching methods. According to the text and the illustrations, schools of the future were to have a more homely look than the existing schools with their long bare corridors with rows of classrooms leading off. Experience from England and Sweden, where the architects and planners had looked at kindergartens, showed that the youngest pupils in particular had a need to feel at home. Schools were to be divided into smaller sections, and children were to have the right to use the lavatory when they needed to and not, as tradition had it, only during breaks.[3]

Adherents of the new system argued that once new flexible teaching methods had been introduced, it would not disturb the teaching if a child left the class during lessons. The more sceptical feared that the new 'individual approach to discipline', as the advisory architect of the ministry of education, Henning Hansen, put it, could make it difficult to control what the children did during their visits to the lavatories, when the teacher was busy teaching the other children.

But the fact of the matter was that the system had already been approved by the ministry at a different school, also designed by Folke Olsen's firm. This, however, was a smaller school with only four classrooms. The authority's approval could not be ignored, and as a compromise the ministry suggested that Nørre Lyndelse School was to be accorded the status of being a trial school for the new system. But only on the condition that complementary lavatories were located in a separate outbuilding with direct access from the school playground.[4]

History does not tell us anything about the result of the experiment, but a preserved copy of the school rules and regulations contains a number of sections relating to the use of the indoor toilets, which is evidence of the importance for the teachers of regulating this new school space. Playing in the toilets was not allowed, and only one pupil at a time was permitted to use the facility.[5] At more and less the same time, the indoor facilities at a school at the parish of Ryslinge were approved by the ministry. According to Folke Olsen (1908–2002), it had taken about 15 years for the ministry to accept the new system, but clearly this did not imply that indoor toilets had become a standard for the new schools. Quite the opposite, and the following year the authority's advisory architect, Henning Hansen, turned down a proposal to build indoor toilets at the school in Skrøbelev, arguing that there was no rush to acquire the newest of the new. It goes without saying that it was not within the power of the Svendborg-based firm to make its own rules, regardless of the fact that they could refer to a report published by the ministry.[6]

The story is illustrative of the role (some) architects played in relation to the modernisation of children's environment during the early days of the welfare state. Behind the disagreements about the indoor lavatories lay differing attitudes not only towards school pupils but also towards more general phenomena such as recognition and respect of individual physical and mental needs. This was a basic dilemma within the architecture of the welfare state, which was constructed to cater for the many but was to an increasing extent perceived as caring for the individual.[7]

A micro-study approach to the history of architecture

The story also contains another point with regard to who were the architects of the welfare state. Such a statement is frequently thought to refer to 'the social engineers', those highly educated bureaucrats and politicians who designed the welfare state[8] and only more rarely to the literal engineers, the architects and engineers. The purpose of this chapter is to investigate how architects participated in constructing the welfare state and how they handled the dilemma between the collective and the individual. The focus is on institutional architecture, more specifically on those school buildings that provided the setting for the educational explosion of the 1960s and 1970s, an explosion that raised the percentage of a youth cohort completing higher secondary education [gymnasium] from 5–6 percent to about 20 percent.[9]

I am interested in the dialogue between architects and educators from the 1940s and to the end of the 1960s, and also by the collaboration between architects and other experts. These were formative and experimental years for institutional architecture, rooted in a wish to cater more for the needs of the individual child. This development was first visible within the kindergarten movement, where children's right to be self-reliant made an impact on kindergarten architecture and playground design.[10] The inspiration came from Sweden, where the educator and social democratic politician Alva Myrdal collaborated closely with a social housing agency (HSB) in Stockholm on the design of collective housing and kindergartens. In Denmark, the social housing sector was also a pioneer when it came to the development of new urban spaces for children. In 1929, the Copenhagen social housing agency (KAB) asked the landscape architect C.Th. Sørensen (1893–1979) to design the playground in conjunction with a housing complex in the north-western part of the city. Sørensen chose to design with children and not roses in mind. The playground was moved from the shade to the sun; the children were provided with a circular paddling pool and a circular sandbox but very little in the way of playground equipment, since Sørensen believed that too much equipment would limit children's creative play.[11]

My contribution to the discussion about the experts of the welfare state deals with one single case, the architectural firm of Johannes Folke Olsen, located at the city of Svendborg at the island of Funen and practising between 1944 and 1974. During this period the firm designed about 20 elementary schools. Sometimes the schools were central schools like the one in Nørre Lyndelse, mentioned above, while at other times the firm dealt with refurbishments or extensions. During the 30 years of the firm's existence, educational architecture changed. During the 1950s, schools were built as parish centres [sognegårde] for the benefit of all the local inhabitants. Their construction was crafted with care and details were drawn 1:1 to make sure that architects could follow the construction process to the minutest detail.

During the late 1960s and early 1970s, school was just one of the many institutions of the welfare state – but it was an important one. These later schools were built using industrialised construction methods, arriving like pieces of scenery on a truck and put up overnight. The role of the architect changed radically once the modules had been designed.

Olsen's firm belonged in many respects to the vanguard of educational design. During the 1950s it travelled to England to get ideas for group collaboration and for methods for rationalising the construction process, but also to study school architecture in a country where more attention was paid to the needs of the individual child than was the case in Denmark. During the 1960s, Olsen went on a study tour to the US to glean further ideas about industrialised architecture. Whenever the ministry of education issued invitations to seminars and meetings about school architecture, Olsen and his employees would be sitting in the front row, and the firm was also present in 1963 when twelve architectural drawing offices decided to collaborate on a new modular school building system, entitled The Funen Plan [Fynsplanen]. Over the next ten years, about 50 new schools were designed according to this new modular system.

It is very likely that other architectural firms had the same professional profile, and Folke Olsen's firm has not been selected for this article because it is representative but because it was persistent – some might even say stubborn – in its efforts to clothe the newest educational ideas in architectural form. It was not always a success, and as Olsen stated it himself at the 25th anniversary of his firm, '…. Over all these years we have had our failures, but it's my impression that we have mostly been successful with our buildings…'[12] The buildings still stand today, though in several cases with new functions, and testify to the fact that these schools were far from ordinary or run-of-the mill. Furthermore, the study of the firm is of relevance, since the architecture of the welfare state has recently been the subject of new interest. This interest has mostly focused on well-known architects like Kay Fisker, C.F. Møller, Svenn Eske Kristensen, Palle Suenson, Ib Martin Jensen and Erling Langkilde.[13] In this context, Folke Olsen's firm, which in its heyday during the 1960s had twelve employees, is an unknown name on a par with hundreds of other small firms outside Copenhagen circles with relatively easy access to the pages of the professional journal Arkitekten [The Architect]. A study of this small firm's drawings and working practices gives a unique and micro-historical perspective on how the policies and expectations of the welfare state as regards equal educational opportunities were translated and dealt with in local contexts.

This approach to architectural history differs from classical architectural history[14] in having a focus on the construction processes and on the network of relations between the architectural firm and other experts, local politicians and various public authorities, and on their handling of rules and regulations. The classical approach prioritises the finished building in all its detailed materiality and the creative architect, while the processes and conditions that made the building possible are frequently left out of the picture. In contrast to this I want to inscribe the architecture in a broader social and cultural historical narrative and, more specifically for educational architecture, in a historical narrative of childhood and education. The approach could be called the historical sociology of architecture, since the focus is on the social context as well as the social role of these constructions.

When the firm closed down in 1974, its records, drawings, reports and correspondence were taken to the refuse dump. An era was over, Folke Olsen retired and two of his trusted employees started a new firm on their own. The idea behind not preserving the archives of the firm could have been that the buildings were thought to speak for themselves. It is an honest impulse but, to a historian, an impossible thought, if our aim is to illustrate how architects performed as one body of experts who helped design the welfare state. But nobody can run completely away from their history, and the welfare state did not arrive out of the blue. As a state structure it built upon the heritage of an administrative tradition dating back to the absolutist state of the 17th century. Since then, the number of intermediate bureaucratic stages in the planning process had not diminished. In the 1950s, a new school building had to be negotiated with the local parish council, the school commission, the teachers' council, the county education authority, the county school adviser, the county doctor and the national teaching inspectors before it was sent to the ministry of education and from there to the advisory architect Hans Henning Hansen. The drawings were then returned with his comments to the architectural firm, which might have to start the process all over again.[15] This long – and tiresome – process left a long paper trail, and this article is based on tracking that trail in the archives of the ministry of education, in the archive of the advisory architect and in the archives of the local parishes in which the new schools were being planned. Apart from visits to the schools, I have interviewed Kaare Lund Rasmussen, who's father was employed by Folke Olsen for 25 years, the architect Hans Lund Rasmussen. I have also been assisted by Folke Olsen's grandchild, Nanna Folke Olsen, who is the former director of Svendborg town archives and by the janitor at Tre Ege School in Ryslinge, Leif Kristensen, who went to the school as a child. The School was also designed by Folke Olsen's office.

School architecture during the inter-war years

In 1937, the Danish parliament voted on a new Education Act. Its purpose was to bring into line the schooling offered in the countryside with that in urban areas. In rural schools age-differentiated teaching had not been introduced in all areas, and most children left school after their seven compulsory years. The curriculum expanded and the number of school hours increased, which meant that the traditional every-other-day school system for the oldest pupils had to be abandoned. It was not a popular decision among many parents – and smallholders – who depended on children as a labour force. [16]

Parishes could apply for state grants to build new schools, but the demands made of the new school buildings prompted a centralisation process. The new schools had to be equipped with gyms and special facilities for Home Economics and Woodwork. Through centralisation, costs could be limited, and gathering all the children under one roof made the introduction of age-differentiated teaching seem (more) sensible. Centralisation was not always popular in areas with sparse populations, even though older children who had more than 3.5 km and younger ones with more than 2.5 km to school could receive free transportation by bus.[17] In many instances this transportation problem was solved by turning existing local schools into preschools and letting the oldest – from about the age of 10 – walk or bike to school. So in practice, centralisation of the educational system was a gradual process which was not completed until around 1970.

Resistance towards the new system was not only rooted in the long distances being travelled. It was also fed by concerns about children's time and about money needed for overcoats and bikes, as the parents of the Gryderup school district in the centre of the island of Zealand wrote in a protest note in the early 1930s.[18] Their anger was triggered by the parish's plan to build a new school located centrally in the community. The new Boeslunde school was the first central school and a model for those that followed. With its three classrooms it was in reality not much bigger than other rural schools. The major difference consisted in the impressive gym with a balcony, from where spectators could watch plays or gymnastic performances, and in the two special classes, one for Woodwork, one for Home Economics. This was a school built with the future in mind. Until the late 1940s, only two of the classrooms were in use, the third was used as a public library, and the two special classes in the basement were only used by young people who took classes in the evening. The 1930s were a time of depression, and to save money the furniture from the old school was repaired, painted and reused. The 'school palaces' of the 1950s and 1960s were unimaginable, with ambitions nurtured by the school still limited and having to be adjusted to the need for child labour.

Local politicians as well as members of the Danish parliament [Folketing] had high expectations of the new central schools. Inspired by the history of the folk high school movement, the ruling Social Liberal party imagined that the schools could develop into local cultural centres, with a public library and free access to the local community after school hours for study groups and sport clubs.

The Danish government and its advisory architects were not alone in this. In 1933 the fourth international CIAM conference – a forum for modern architecture – had advocated this idea. School should be merged with other public institutions, like the town hall, but with the school as the most important construction, because it was fundamental to the preservation of national culture. A model school, designed by the ministry's advisory architect, Thomas Havning (1891–1976), was erected in conjunction with the agricultural exhibition at Bellahøj in 1938, and in 1941 an exhibition sponsored by the ministry of education travelled around the country demonstrating how schools could be built as cultural centres [sognegårde]. The examples showed schools that were not only built to be kept open after the school day was over, but that also had offices for the parish council, public baths, a library and large assembly rooms where it was possible to show films and hold concerts and political meetings. In the introduction, the Social Radical minister of education, Jørgen Jørgensen (1888–1974), viewed the new cultural centres as related to the folk high school movement of the second half of the nineteenth century, in which teachers had frequently played an important part. This heritage should not be forgotten when new schools with 'light and spacious rooms' were built. The exhibition was followed by the publication of a pamphlet.

According to the foreword, this new initiative should be used particularly to make sure that local young people had the opportunity to practise sport and take evening classes. Concern for the young may have been rooted in the high unemployment rates of the 1930s, but the German occupation and the risk that young people might be attracted to Nazi rhetoric and take the 'wrong door', as it was put at the time, spurred an effort to create youth clubs in the towns and in the country. For this purpose, many new schools would be equipped with youth club room.[19]

But local politicians were not prepared to spend more than the minimum necessary on the new schools. As a symbol of this attitude – and, of course, for practical reasons – the 1938 model school was to be built of wood. The ministry of education also tried to calm the local authorities by stating that there was no need for houses that could last an eternity. Nothing was more certain than that within two generations, new educational ideas would appear and 'stones had to give away to ideas', wrote the ministry advisor in educational matters, F. C. Kaalund-Jørgensen (1890–1962). Therefore there was no need for educational palaces, like those constructed in many urban areas, with aulas and big windows and a plethora of technical facilities. What was needed '…was plain and simple, practical and light school rooms, which could create a space around the refurbished rural school, an appealing and healthy work place for children and teachers…'[20] But before the ink was dry on the paper, the German occupation and the subsequent lack of construction materials put a temporary halt to the wish to build new schools equipped in line with the 1937 educational act.

Value for money. Architects and parish councils during the 1950s

The wish to create cultural centres in rural areas survived the war, stimulated, too, by the many reports from the so-called 'Youth Commission' published between 1945 and 1952. Young people were seen as essential to the consolidation of democracy, not only as future political voters, but also – and mainly – as democrats in daily life.

Democracy, argued the chairman of the committee, Hal Koch (1904–1963), was to be understood as a way of life, and the earlier people started to practise – e.g. in self-governed youth clubs or by having access to evening classes and public libraries – the better for democracy.[21] Such visions had a considerable impact, even in Folke Olsen's small architectural firm, and the ideas materialised in the schools designed by the firm from the end of the 1940s until the middle of the 1960s. These schools were equipped with public libraries, a separate entrance to the gym, which also had a stage and provided a space for meetings, talks and film projection, and one room reserved for local youth. A few schools also incorporated public baths complete with a sauna. 'The Alpha and Omega …', explained Folke Olsen at his 50 years anniversary, '…has been that the school, as well as being a space where school children learn their lessons, also became a natural cultural centre for the people of the parish. Therefore there should be a certain affinity between the new schools and the old village hall [forsamlingshus].'[22] This was hardly surprising. It was in line with the thinking of the ministry of education and in line with Folke Olsen's personal background in the folk high school movement. His father had been a teacher, while he was a trained carpenter and he had taken a course in woodwork at one of the most famous Danish folk high schools at Askov. After three years at the building construction school [konstruktørskole] in Odense, he started out as an architect in the firm of Einar Mindedal at village of Ollerup, not far from Svendborg. Mindedal was also closely related to the folk high school movement. Another of the leading employees at Folke Olsen's firm, the architect Hans Lund Rasmussen, had a similar background.

Employees in the firm made good use of the standard drawings published by the ministry of education in connection with the new educational act in 1937 and designed by Thomas Havning and the architect Knud V. Barfoed (1888–1965). As royal inspector of buildings, Havning's office had to approve every set of drawings before either the government grant or the much coveted grant for construction materials could be obtained. The standard patterns were an expression of modular housing of the most simple kind. The individual blocks could be combined in various ways and could also used as extensions to already existing school buildings. The classroom measured 48 m^2 and could house 36 pupils, had plenty of natural light, light colours on the walls and linoleum on the floor. The new buildings were to contribute to the improvement of the pupils' health.

The location of schools was therefore of importance, and they were not to be in the vicinity of sewage plants or landfill sites. There had to be water inside the building, and all children had to be able to wash their hands before eating and after visits to the outdoor toilets, which themselves were easily accessible for inspection. If possible, the school should have a separate dining room, so that it was possible to ventilate the classroom during the lunch break.[23]

These demands were not easily met – and the targets were not realised from one day to the next. When the building research committee from the ministry of education visited Ryslinge School on the island of Funen as late as 1954, they witnessed a depressing sight. The light on the blackboard was 'terrible', there was a provisional classroom for woodwork at the attic, the children had their lunch in the classroom or outside, weather permitting, the floor was not cleaned in the gym and the privvies were ' horrible, with no mitigating circumstances...', according to the report written after the visit. The local doctor was completely aware of the poor conditions, but everybody knew that 'it had to work', so nothing had so far been done. What was also shocking to the visitors from Copenhagen were the standards of teaching. The young teacher who showed them around defended the traditional every-other-day school system, and they clearly got the impression that there was not much room for 'experiments with new teaching methods'. All this stood in stark contrast to the new central school, which was inaugurated in 1960 and designed by Folke Olsen and his team of architects. The new school in Ryslinge was equipped with a public bath and sauna in the basement, special classes for children with various handicaps, a gym with a balcony, classrooms with outdoor access, which made open-air teaching possible, and indoor toilets.[24]

If the old Ryslinge School did not comply with the demands of the 1937 Act, this was not only because hygiene standards were higher in the city than in the country. A continuous lack of building materials during the 1950s resulted in tough competition between residential construction and school construction for the attractive grants for building materials. Furthermore, the growing number of children born right after the war, the baby boom, also put pressure on the construction of school buildings, especially in the suburbs, as rural populations gradually gravitated towards larger conurbations. All this contributed to placing rural parishes like Ryslinge at the end of the queue – and the ministry of education's final deadline for when the school's buildings were to comply with the act had to be extended several times. The final deadline was 1970, and according to the educational historian Erik Nørr, who has investigated the effect – and lack of effect – of the 1937 Act, '…in rural areas there were still in the 1960s schools of the old 'thatched' type, which could date their history back to the school act of 1814 without any modern facilities'… but their number was fast dwindling.[25] As late as in 1957 only 37 percent of rural parishes had schools with seven grades. Most had three or four grades, with the same teacher teaching nearly all the subjects.[26]

Folke Olsen stopped designing buildings in 1954–55, when his partner, Werner Madsen (1904-1984), left the firm. After that he spent all his time working for formers, for which he was apparently very well-qualified. He managed to get large contracts for his firm, and he was especially proud of the collaboration with Ryslinge parish. The firm had had a project here every year since its start.[27] In 1958, it was the new school, and Folke Olsen was invited to a meeting with the local decision-makers in the community hall. The group decided to make a study tour to the island of Zealand for the purpose of studying a 'very modern' prefabricated school, a traditionally built school and a high school that was under renovation. The participants were very satisfied with what Folke Olsen and his contractor had shown them, and especially happy that the price per square metre seemed reasonable. A month later, the local building committee visited two newly built schools designed by Olsen's firm.

According to the minutes of the meeting with the parish council, members of the parish council were very pleased, and next step consisted in setting up a contract with the architects. The only condition was that the school should be built by local craftsmen. On several occasions over the ensuing months the parish council had to deal with budget outruns. The central heating system became more expensive, and the architects suggested facing the buildings overlooking the school yard with mosaic tiles instead of concrete tiles. The argument – to which the council agreed after some grumbling – was that they were more attractive, more durable and maintenance-free.

More serious problems arose when it came to discussing furniture. Once again it was important to the parish council that the furniture was made by local labour. The teachers also had their views about the design. They wanted to retain the old pencil groove and the podium in front of the blackboard kept in its full length. This was a reaction to the suggestion from the firm that the teacher's desk should be placed at the same level as the pupils' light and movable desks.

The reactions from the teachers might seem of minor importance, but they reflect how difficult it was to abandon old teaching practices – and they also illustrate the cultural distance between teachers and architects. Asked about whether his teachers actually made use of the new teaching methods and moved the tables around so that the children could work individually or in groups, the janitor, Leif Kristensen – a former pupil at Ryslinge school (now Tre Ege school), where he started in 1962 – answers 'We sat where we had been seated the first day – and there we remained'. According to his memoirs, the teachers marched up and down the long corridor during lunch breaks and knocked on the windows, if the children became too violent. Soccer was absolutely banned from the school playground. The new school had to be protected, although the children were allowed to throw a ball to each other.[28] The rules the children had to abide by at Nørre Lyndelse school – mentioned earlier – also suggest a wish to keep strict discipline. The pupils had to demonstrate obedience, politeness and good behaviour. When the teacher or any visitor entered the class, they had to stand up. At Nørre Lyndelse pupils were not to enter the school of their own free will but had to line up in the school playground and wait to be called. Only in bad weather could they remain indoors during breaks.[29]

Even the architects, who were members of the ministry's building research committee, recall the teachers as being conservative as regards making use of the opportunities offered by the new school. One of them was Tyge Arnfred (1919 -), who during the 1950s participated in many study tours with the committee.

'I recall one teacher at a pavilion school that had been 'architect designed' in a provincial town, to whom the new school was more like a catastrophe. Why? Because the greater distance between the staff room across the playground to his class had forced him to shorten the well-planned lessons he had been teaching for the past 15 years. 'I've had to rearrange my teaching completely', he told me. But he was completely indifferent to what it could have meant to the children that they didn't have to line up in the school playground before class anymore. It was of no interest.'[30]

Tyge Arnfred's comments echo a feeling at the time – and later – that the many new school buildings constructed in accordance with the reports from the building research committee of the ministry of education were ahead of their time. Ahead of their time in making space for a variety of teaching methods, making it possible for children to enter the school on their own, making it possible for them to leave class to go to the lavatory – and trying to adapt the school to the scale of the child. The 1957 report on classroom design, which had inspired Olsen's employees with its focus on young children and their needs, in many ways anticipated the so-called blue report [Den blå betænkning] from 1960, which is commonly considered as an important step in the modernization of the Danish elementary school system. The report stated that pupils should 'grow up as harmonious, happy and good people', and it recommended the teaching methods to be adapted to the needs and abilities of the pupils.[31]

The school at Ryslinge, like other schools in the area of South Funen designed by Folke Olsen and his team of architects, testifies to the firm's awareness of the latest educational ideas and of its ability to give them an independent architectural form. The key word was flexibility – as few stairs as possible and as much light as possible. The ideal shape was the single storey school, but the undulating Funen landscape made it possible to create high-ceilinged basements and build in split levels. The basements were frequently used for special classes like Woodwork and Home Economics. The public baths could also be located here and have a separate entrance.

From the early days the firm had its battles with the advisory architect for the ministry of education, Hans Henning Hansen. These related not only to the usefulness of indoor toilets but also to the amount of space required by schools. The firm had to accept Hansen's verdict on several occasions, when he found that the planned halls or the corridors were too big. A creative solution to this problem that was frequently used was a combination of the entrance area with the hall. It made good sense if the school building was L-shaped and the entrance located where the two wings met.[32]

Despite the firm's preference for the single-storey school, the local parish councils were not always easily persuaded. The problem was not the price of land, as was the case in urban areas. It was their sense of getting value for money that was the challenge. Through experience the firm learned that the best way to persuade the local decision-makers was to arrange a study tour. In January 1954, the parish council from Stenstrup went on a trip to Zealand to visit two of the most advanced and high-profiled schools of the time, the Skovgaard school in Gentofte from 1951, designed by the architects Hans

Erling Langkilde and Ib Martin Jensen, and Rungsted school from 1952, designed by Professor Steen Eiler Rasmussen. The two schools, built of that classical Danish building material, red brick, had borrowed their lightness from British school architecture. Both were single-storey schools, and the firm was to borrow much of the detail for their own future schools. The more traditional of the two, the Skovgaard school, shaped like a farm with three blocks surrounding a school playground, made the stronger impression on the members of the parish council, while the school at Rungsted with its simple architecture, with detached single-storey buildings was judged to be a rather minimalist construction. That the school expressed and allowed a new educational programme based on individualised and group teaching methods[33] did not seem to have impressed members of the parish council from Stenstrup.

Once back in Svendborg, the architects returned to the drawing board and made new calculations of the costs. At the subsequent meeting with the parish council, Folke Olsen informed them that a single-storey school would be about DKK 150,000 cheaper than a school with two storeys. Furthermore, a state grant could be applied for if the basement could be designed to house an emergency hospital for use in the event of a nuclear attack on Denmark. This last piece of information tipped the balance in the council, or, as stated in the minutes of the meeting, 'after several rounds of questioning, criticism and reflection – the council agreed upon the single-storey building.'[34] Reasons for voting for the single-storey building were clearly financial and not educational. When the architects came back with the first set of drawings, in which all classrooms had doors opening onto the surrounding play area, the members of the parish council could not really see the point – the fact that the firm could refer to the recommendation of the report from the ministry of education, mentioned earlier, about the need to build schools in such a way that children could move around more freely did not make any impression. The doors were therefore replaced by (cheaper) windows.

From craftsmanship to 'engineership'. Two generations of modular schools.

Schools of the 1950s were a matter of prestige, and it mattered to the local members of the parish council that their school would be attractive to all members of the community. Or as Folke Olsen put it in 1958: 'The inhabitants have to be able to visit their school with pleasure, they have to feel at home. If we can get this far, and create a physical space around local cultural life, then it is up to the teachers and the community to flesh it out. With a 100 percent contact between homes and school, school buildings have their complete justification. This is what matters to us when we design schools.'[35]

Halls were equipped with a stage, and schools had several entrances, so the public use of facilities like the library, the baths, the gym or the hall did not interfere with the building's other functions. The schools were built of the best materials available, red or yellow brick walls, roofing tiles, and with many details demonstrating the diligence of the local craftsmen. Most visible are the detailing in the brickwork and the iron balustrades surrounding stairs and entrances. But a light and harmonious colour scheme was also used – in line with experiences from Rungsted school – and the schools were decorated with various works of art. The firm chose local artists, who created indoor murals, stage curtains and outdoor wall sculptures. On the walls of the school in Espe, a Mother Funen could be seen caring for a boy and a girl, and the school at the village of Stenstrup was decorated with a large clock, a gift from the architectural firm. Twelve o'clock had the shape of the cross of faith, 3 o'clock was the heart of love, 6 o'clock an hourglass and 9 o'clock an anchor. At the inauguration of the school building in 1959, Folke Olsen explained the symbolism as follows: 'I hope the children will come to school in the morning with hope and faith, leave it with love, and once school is over, continue to make good use of their time.' [36]

Regardless of the many regulations, circulars and standard designs, schools were to have their individual character, and to satisfy parish councils members and a budget that just undercut what other firms could offer. The firm also borrowed design elements from schools that had been mentioned in the professional journal The Architect [Arkitekten]. There are many examples, such as the chimneys with their sharp profile, a detail on several contemporary schools designed by the architect Kay Fisker; or the map in the linoleum floor at Stenstrup school, which was an idea inspired by a similar map at the School on the Sound in Copenhagen, designed by Kaj Gottlob, from the 1930s. The wind shelters around the doors could be found at Skovgårdsskolen, which had been a stop on one of the study tours to the island of Zealand (see above). The broad corridors where children could eat their lunch was first introduced in Danish school architecture by the architect Steen Eiler Rasmussen in the design of Rungsted school.

It was no coincidence that the architects frequently referred to these two last-mentioned schools and took their potential clients on study tours to visit these two schools. Both schools were inspired by British school architecture and whenever possible the firm's employees went on study tours to England. The single-storey British school buildings with plenty of light were very attractive to Danes, as was the attempt to work on an intimate and human scale that would enable young children not to feel lost. Experiments with rationalisation and industrialisation of the school buildings were also of considerable interest to Danish architects and school planners. The British school architects had looked to the nursery school in their efforts to design schools 'from the inside out' with children's needs in mind. Children's independence should be encouraged and their creativity stimulated. Classes should be equipped with lightweight furniture children could move around without asking an adult, and special areas should be reserved for creative activities like drawing or theatre performances.

The county of Hertfordshire was especially active in this regard, and in the summer of 1954 two of its central architects, the couple Mary and David Medd (1907–2005 and 1917–2009), were invited by the building research committee under the Danish ministry of education on a study tour with the purpose of evaluating the most recent Danish schools and teaching Danish architects more about how to work with the users, both young and old, from the very beginning of the building process. Together with their Danish hosts, they visited some of the most highly profiled schools at the time. And, even though the British inspiration was very visible, their assessment was rather negative: 'Our real fear is that in recent trends in school buildings we have seen in Denmark there is an increased tendency towards standardization and regimentation of the plan...'. In their opinion 'buildings for children should not be regimented and military in character but should have the same kind of charm, liveliness and spark that the children do themselves...'.[37]

The regimentation that the British couple had noted was a result not only of educational disagreements but also of the bureaucratic system that all school buildings had to go through to obtain state grants and the attractive grants for materials. Based on what is left of the correspondence between Folke Olsen's firm and the many public bodies involved, the impression is that it was very difficult to bend rules and regulations in order to tone down the 'square' and standardised image.

But local parishes got value for money, once they had hired Olsen and his team. In contrast to other local building firms, they had gradually learned their lesson and knew the kinds of drawings that needed to be sent to the advisory architect for him to spend time on them – and hopefully give his approval. The shelters in the basement were especially important to remember. After 1950, they were obligatory in all public buildings. It was also important to enclose a description of the distance to neighbouring properties and to include elevations, sections and facades in the drawings.

But there was a price to pay, which the local decision-makers were not always aware of when they engaged Olsen's team. As mentioned several times, the firm's employees were avid readers of the reports published by the research council of the ministry of education. The report on the classroom written in 1957 was a particularly frequently used point of reference. The main author was the psychologist Svend Skyum Nielsen, who advocated school spaces that acknowledged the fact that there could be substantial differences in children's intellectual abilities.[38] It was not enough to cater for the inhabitants of the local parish and ensure that they felt 'at home' in the new school. It was just as important that the scale of the child was given physical form in the design and furnishings.

New features appeared such as 'smart interior', which meant lightweight tables for two people with individual chairs, or the mosaic tiles used on walls facing the school playground, protecting the facade against children's play and ball games; another novelty was to have special sections of the school designed for young children with lowered ceilings and smaller proportions, as well as doors opening onto the outside – not to mention the indoor toilets. Olsen defended the expensive tables and the tiles on the walls by arguing that in the long run it would pay off to buy quality. Pragmatism ruled when dealing with the local decision-makers, but the finer details were left to discussions internally in the firm. According to the memoirs, his employees completely changed his sketches once he was back from a visit to the parish officials.[39]

During these years of hectic activity at Olsen's firm the school landscape underwent dramatic changes. The preponderance of small schools disappeared – according to calculations made by the ministry of education, the number of primary and secondary schools was reduced from 4,500 to 2,800 between 1936 and 1966.[40] The many new central schools lay like islands in the landscape, frequently located on an elevation with glorious views across the landscape. They were solid buildings and flexible at the same time, a new block could be added without changing the overall idea of the complex. This flexibility came to be increasingly used during the 1960s when schools had to be enlarged to make room for the growing number of students who continued after grade 7. Olsen's firm participated actively in the development of flexible and pre-fabricated solutions. In 1963, the firm joined – as mentioned – 11 other architectural firms in the so-called 'Funen Plan' [Fynsplan] with the aim of developing modular school buildings that could be constructed without much craftsmanship. The plan was very successful and much praised by the ministry of education. Members of parliament as well as other architects were sceptical and felt that the buildings lost their individuality – while the professional organisations of craftsmen complained about losing out to entrepreneurs and unskilled labour. The partners in the Funen Plan – among them Folke Olsen's firm – could not see the problem; if raw concrete was not an option, then the buildings could be faced in brick. In their mind there was plenty of room for the individual architect, even though he chose to make use of prefabricated building elements. The controversy was as old as the welfare state and could be found within the housing sector as well. Some argued that standardisation was a precondition for individuality, since it lowered costs and thereby made it possible for people in general to improve their living conditions. Others feared that the variations within the architectural landscape would disappear and that people would end op living a boring and monotonous life.[41]

By joining the Funen Plan, Olsen's firm took a step into the age of the second generation of standard schools, since in many ways the schools of the 1950s were also standard buildings. Variation was limited, and the firm had a preference for the farm design with three blocks surrounding a school playground. Traditionally, this type of farm was especially widespread on the island at Funen, and in this way they connected their schools with the architectural heritage of the area. Another much used plan was the L-shape, where the class rooms were located in one bloc, the offices and special classes in another. A third option was the T-shape, where the administrative and class building was crossed by a gym.

But there were recognisable differences between the standard schools of the 1950s and those of the 1960s. The schools from the

1950s were built of red or yellow brick, and built with craftsmanship and a care for detail. In the 1960s the schools came in sections on a truck, the elements were ready-made in concrete and could be put up without much professional skills.

Another difference between the two generations of schools was the teacher accommodation. The shortage of teachers during the 1950s especially in rural areas made teacher accommodation a way of attracting applicants. When teachers were asked about the plans for a new school, they very rarely had comments about the school building. Instead they commented on their own accommodation. Frequently they would move into the old school that the children had abandoned for the new one. Or they would get an apartment in the school building, or in a separate building. Noise and the wish to protect their private life were important issues, as well as access to modern facilities like a fridge, indoor bathrooms, central heating or shower.[42] During the 1960s, teacher accommodation disappeared; there was no longer a shortage of teachers, and the new generation of teachers did not see their job as a round-the-clock vocation. They preferred to live at a distance from the school. The former teachers' residences were gradually converted into special classes of various kinds.

During the 1960s and 1970s, school buildings became more a matter of routine. Olsen's firm was busy with the construction of extensions to the schools the firm had designed in the 1950s. More and more pupils took classes 8, 9 and 10, and more and more pupils were going to special classes for children with various learning difficulties. The majority of these buildings were constructed with the use of standard systems like the ones produced by the Funen Plan. This development was common across the country and encouraged by the ministry of education. When selecting which parishes should be allocated building and material permits, the ministry prioritised those who had decided to make use of standard solutions. Olsen's firm had been a frontrunner in this development, and in 1967 he was included in a tour to the US organised by the ministry to study rationalised educational architecture, primarily the open-plan school, which in subsequent years became part of the standard design incorporated into the Funen Plan.[43]

Conclusion

Through a micro-study of Folke Olsen's small Svendborg-based firm of architects and the part of their work relating to school buildings, it has been possible to track (a group of) experts of the welfare state at work. We have seen them dealing with local decision-makers, participating in debates in building design and in ministerial circles and seen them reading and studying the many reports and articles about educational architecture produced at the time in Denmark and internationally. Pragmatism and financial responsibility are two of the words which could characterise the group of about twenty schools designed by the firm during its 30 years of existence between 1944 and 1974. But employees of the firm also featured a certain creativity, curiosity and willingness to adopt more progressive ideas about designing schools with children's individual needs in mind. Knowledge about these new developments was gained both through reading and study tours in Denmark and abroad.

The case also shows that experimentation had its limits. The local decision-makers were more interested in pleasing their voters by keeping expenses down than making space for new progressive educational ideas, and teachers seem to have cared more about their own accommodation than about the school's buildings. But the lack of construction materials was also a constant challenge. It took time to get the buildings from the drawing table out onto the open fields, but the straitened financial situation generated creative solutions – primarily collaboration between firms, standardised plans and continuing rationalisation and industrialisation of the building processes. In this the Danes looked to England, especially to experience gained in the county of Hertfordshire.

There existed, of course, experts before the welfare state, but its expansion developed new ones. Rules and bureaucracy demanded that there were educated people to understand and follow them; to be a local master builder was no longer enough. Engineers and architects from smaller firms like Folke Olsen's were given many commissions and managed to position themselves so as to be the inevitable choice of designer when the many new institutions were decided on and constructed during the era of the consolidation of the welfare state in the 1950s and 1960s. The industrialisation of the building sector added a new link to the chain, the entrepreneurs pushing the craftsmen further down the ladder. Only those architects who managed to adjust to the new industrialised and rationalised building sector stood a chance of survival. Among them was Folke Olsen's firm, which in addition was very active as regards rationalisation and prefabrication in the building sector.

The many central schools and their extensions, speak of a time when the school fought hard to become more central to children's lives in rural communities. This took place within just one generation, and the school became so natural that the school building itself went from being a local status symbol to being an amenity to be constructed as quickly and cheaply as possible. The architecture testifies to this story – the classic red bricks, the iron balustrades, the fine detailing and saddle roofs were replaced by simple facades in concrete and glass and built-up roofs. Some mourn this development. There may be cause for that, but the purpose of this chapter has been to discuss why it happened and to show that the educational explosion of the second half of the twentieth century could not have taken place without these radical changes to the physical shaping of the school. In this development the architects were indispensable.

Notes

1. Agústin Escolano Benito, 2003, p. 59; U-90, vol. 1, pp. 22-23.
2. *Klasserummet, dets function og udformning*, written by the building research committee within the Ministry of Education. (Hans Henning Hansen's archive, correspondence regarding Nørre Lyndelse school, no. 41-974, 401-1346, 401-1835 and 401-3388; minutes, Nr. Lyndelse school commission 1943 – Landsarkivet for Fyn) The Funen Regional Archive.
3. *Klasserummet*, 1957, pp. 68–69.
4. Newspaper article 6.4.1958, Svendborg town archives and Hans Henning Hansen's archive, correspondence concerning Nørre Lyndelse skole, records no. 41-974, 401-1346, 401-1835 and 401-3388.
5. Rules and regulations for pupils at Carl Nielsen School, minutes of Nørre Lyndelse Parish teachers' committee. [Ordensregler for eleverne på Carl Nielsen skolen, i kuvert i Nr. Lyndelse sogns lærerråds forhandlingsprotokol, 1953 – Landsarkivet for Fyn].
6. Skrøbelev school, 1960, Hans Henning Hansen's archive journal no. 41-2267, 401-497 and 2496.
7. The argument is made in the article by Ning de Coninck-Smith and Mogens Rudiger, 2007.
8. Cecilie Felicia Stokholm Banke, 1999.
9. U90, vol. 1, pp. 22-23.
10. Ning de Coninck-Smith, 2008 b.
11. Ning de Coninck-Smith, 2008 a.
12. Newspaper cuttings, Svendborg town archives, 1.3.1969.
13. Poul Sverrild, 2008.
14. As an example of this see Kim Dirckinck-Holmfeld, Martin Keiding and Marianne Amundsen, 2004.
15. Ministry of Education, circular, 16.6.1938.
16. Erik Nørr, 2008.

17   Sognegården, 1938, p. 7.
18   Cited in a letter from the parish council at Boeslunde parish to the Ministry of Education, 28.2.1938. UM 1. dept. 1 kt., Journal no. [record no.] 3725/43.
19   Ning de Coninck-Smith, 2010.
20   Quotation, Ning de Coninck-Smith, 1989, p. 40.
21   Ning de Coninck-Smith, 2010.
22   Newspaper cutting, Svendborg town archives, 7.4.1958.
23   Ministry of Education, circular, 16.6.1938.
24   Report, Hans Henning Hansen's archive, Ryslinge School, 41-2188 and newspaper cutting, 18.11.1959, Svendborg town archives.
25   Erik Nørr, 2008, p. 218.
26   Erik Nørr, 2008, p. 196.
27   Newspaper cuttings, Svendborg town archives.
28   Interview with Leif Kristensen, 15.1.2009.
29   Rules, Nørre Lyndelse School, minutes of the teachers' council 1953 - , Landsarkivet for Fyn.
30   Tyge Arnfred, 1990, p. 101.
31   Ida Juul, 2006, p. 78.
32   Hans Henning Hansen's archive, case no. 41-1757, case no. 41-255, 21-2318, 401-165, 2135 and 2952. The idea may have been borrowed from Rungsted school, built in 1953 and designed by Steen Eiler Rasmussen, see Rasmussen, 1953.
33   Steen Eiler Rasmussen, 1953.
34   Minutes [Forhandlingsprotokol] Stenstrup parish council 1954-57, meeting 15.1.1954, Landsarkivet for Fyn m.m.
35   Newspaper cutting, 7.4.1958, Svendborg town archives.
36   Stenstrup Centralskole, 1957–2007, p. 12.
37   Report 2.9.1954, inbox 5, The building research committee, The ministry of Education [Byggeforskningsudvalget, Undervisningsministeriet], Rigsarkivet.
38   *Klasserummet*, p. 15.
39   Interview with Kaare Lund Rasmussen, 6.5 2008.
40   U-90, vol. 1, p. 20.
41   *Dpa-bladet*, 1967, no. 10, p. 28; *Dpa-bladet*, 1965, no. 3, pp. 13 and p. 31; *Rationelt skolebyggeri på Fyn*, 1963, p. 25. The argument is developed further in Ning de Coninck-Smith and Mogens Rüdiger, 2007.
42   See for example Thurø school, Hans Henning Hansen's archive, 41-822, the comments of the teachers union [Fælleslærerrådets udtalelse].
43   A report on the trip can be found in *Uddannelse*, 1969, no. 9, vol. 69 – *Uddannelse* [Education] is the official journal of the Ministry of Education.

References

Andersen, Jens (ed.) 2008: *København i en jazztid*, København.
Arnfred, Tyge 1990: 'Set fra en tegnestue', Ellen Nørgaard and Ning de Coninck-Smith (eds.), *At lære og være – I hvilke rammer?*, pp. 99-107, København.
Banke, Cecilie Felicia Stokholm 1999: *Den sociale ingeniørkunst i Danmark, familie, stat og politik fra 1900 til 1945*, Roskilde.
Benito, Agústin Escolano 2003: 'The School in the City: School Architecture as Discourse and as Text', *Pedagogica Historica*, no. 1 and 2, vol. 39, pp. 53-64.

Christiansen, Niels Finn, Kurt Jacobsen and Mogens Rüdiger (eds.) 2007: *Ole Lange – fra fætter til koryfæ*, København.
Coninck-Smith, Ning de 1989: *Vor lærdoms bygning. Folkeskolens bygninger 1814-1940*, 1989, report no. 2, Planstyrelsen.
Coninck-Smith, Ning de and Mogens Rudiger 2007: 'Typehuset, velvære og modernitet. Danmark 1950-1973', N. F. Christiansen, K. Jacobsen & M. Rüdiger (eds.), *Ole Lange - fra kætter til koryfæ*, pp. 196-216, København.
Coninck-Smith, Ning de 2008a: 'Buksetroldenes boliger. Børn på Bispebjerg og Nordvest i mellemkrigsårene', Jens Andersen (ed.), *København i en jazztid*, pp. 136-153, Golden days og Politikens Forlag.
Coninck-Smith, Ning de 2008b: 'PH og børnenes rum: Børneinstitutionen ved Dehns Vaskeri' (1948) and 'Københavns Rundskuedags børnerekreationshjem Mindet' (1952), Jørn Guldberg and Niels Peter Skou (eds.), *Kritik og formidling. Studier i PH's kulturkritik*, pp. 35-62, Odense.
Coninck-Smith, Ning de 2010: *Arkitektur og barndom. Rum til børn gennem 250 år*, (Manuskript under udarbejdelse med henblik på publicering i 2010).
Dirckinck-Holmfeld, Kim, Martin Keiding and Marianne Amundsen (eds.) 2004: *Dansk arkitektur 250 år / 250 years of Danish Architecture*, Arkitektens Forlag.
Juul, Ida 2006: 'Den danske velfærdsstat og uddannelsespolitikken', *Udannelseshistorie*, pp. 72-99.
Guldberg, Jørn and Niels Peter Skov (eds.) 2008: *Kritik og formidling. Studier i PH's kultur og kritik*, Odense.
Hansen, Else and Leon Jespersen (eds.) 1990: *Samfundsplanlægning i 1950'erne. Tradition eller tilløb?* København.
Hansen, Hans Henning 1977: 'Skolebyggeri gennem skiftende tider', *Årbog for dansk skolehistorie*, pp.106-115.
Nørgaard, Ellen and Ning de Coninck-Smith (eds.) 1990: *At lære og være – hvilke rammer?* København.
Nørr, Erik 2008: 'Hvorfor blev skoleloven af 1937 først gennemført i 1950'erne og 1960'erne?', Else Hansen and Leon Jespersen (eds.), *Samfundsplanlægning i 1950'erne. Tradition eller tilløb*, pp. 153-226, København.
Rasmussen, Steen Eiler 1953: 'Rungsted Skole', *Arkitekten M.*, pp. 125-141.
Rationelt skolebyggeri på Fyn. Et oplæg til det fynske skolebyggeris rationalisering udarbejdet af 12 fynske arkitektfirmaer i kontakt med amtsskolekonsulenterne og produktivitetsudvalget, marts 1963.
Rationelt skolebyggeri. Fynsplanen fortsætter, (u.å.) Odense.
Rationelt skolebyggeri. Redegørelse for system 1 og system 2, 1968.
Steffensen, Inga 2007: *Fra 5 små skoler til Stenstrup Centralskole 1957-2007. Glimt af historien*, Svendborg.
Sognegaarden. Centralskole. Forsamlingshus. Aftenskole. Bibliotek, Sogneraad. Alderdomshjem, Copenhagen.
Sverrild, Poul 2008: *Velfærdssamfundets Bygninger. Bygningskulturens Dag 2008*, Kulturarvsstyrelsen.
Undervisningsministeriets byggeforskningsudvalg og statens byggeforskningsinstitut *Klasserummet. Funktion og udformning. Nyt skolebyggeri 5*, 1957, Copenhagen.
U 90 samlet uddannelsesplanlægning frem til 90'erne, 1978, bd. 1.
'USA rapport. Skolebyggeri', *Uddannelse*, no. 9, vol. 69 (temanr.), Undervisningsministeriet.

Part III
Experts, Research and the Nordic Welfare State

Gendered understandings of agrarian population in early Finnish social studies

Ann-Catrin Östman

In 1898, an influential study on the situation of the crofters in Finland was published by the young scholar Aksel Warén. Warén described his subject as novel and unstudied. According to the preface, Warén had gathered material in the midst of the people (kansan keskuudesta). When depicting the collecting of material, he used the word 'exploration expedition' (tutkimusmatka).[1] The use of the expression may well be descriptive: to underline the scientific character of the enterprise; or, to illustrate his conception of agrarian people. For the expression implies that the studied group was unknown, distant and/or unfamiliar.

The article examines how the agrarian population was described in social studies presented in Finland in the late nineteenth century. It describes how the problems of the rural population was depicted, understood and conceptualised in the studies and texts written by a middle-class group interested in social reforms. Initially, ideas of social reform engaged the urban educated group, including university teachers as well as rural estate-owners. By focusing on how the problems associated with agrarian society were interpreted, the article illustrates how understandings of cultural differences between different groups – uneducated and educated, urban and rural – shaped the depictions of agrarian problems. In the Nordic countries, the countryside and agricultural sector developed quickly during the late nineteenth century. Despite this, few scholars have studied how this development was interpreted by scholars and other activists propagating social reforms.[2]

In Finland, the social question was considered rural;[3] it was mainly presented and defined as a 'land question'.[4] Several of the early texts about – or studies of – social problems dealt with the rural population. These studies had been made in relation to discussions about land reform, which was a central political issue in Finland for many years – and it was more important here than in the other Scandinavian countries. One other aspect makes the Finnish case somewhat special: in Finland many of the early social studies were carried out by historians.[5] In 1884, a group of politicians and scholars – including Professor Yrjö Koskinen and other leading historians – initiated studies of the actual economic conditions in rural districts. Subsequently, the group which had been influenced by *Verein für Sozialpolitik* formed a society called Kansantaloudellinen Yhdistys. Persons related to this organisation initiated a number of other studies related to rural issues.[6] Historical writing was practised in different ways. There was, however, an emphasis on mass phenomena, which provided a framework for studies of the peasantry and other rural groups.[7] In a country which lacked a history of an independent state, social, economic and cultural history was emphasised at an early stage.

The focus here is on historical studies of agrarian society and of early social studies of agrarian and/or rural society. The study by Aksel Warén as well as the reports initiated in 1884 have been taken into consideration. The article analyses the discursive frameworks which characterised the studies of the peasantry. Furthermore, I point to the connections between gender ideals and understandings of the social position of the country group. Viewing the studies of rural society from the perspective of gender, the article focuses on understandings of femininity and masculinity – as well as the family. This will illustrate how understandings of societal development and social problems were presented in gendered frameworks.

Gendered understandings of evolutionism and civilisation

Literature on agriculture and the peasantry was shaped by various historiographical traditions. Late nineteenth-century Finnish historians linked scientific ideas about the writing of history with theories of social evolutionism and the tradition of German historicism.[8] Strong traditions of nineteenth-century statistics characterised many of the historical studies published during this period. Furthermore, leading historians were influenced by the German historical school of economic thought.

This mixture of ideas, including social evolutionism and nationalism, formed the depictions of the rural groups. In addition, the studies were based on an understanding of a social and cultural gap between the 'educated' and the rest. According to Yrjö Koskinen, it was important to help the landless and the rural poor materially and economically, but also morally.[9] Likewise, Hannes Gebhard underlined the importance of enlightening and edifying the people. Gebhard, a historian who was engaged in studying contemporary social problems in the Finnish countryside, frequently emphasised the concept of morality (in Finnish siveellinen, cf. Sittlichkeit). Furthermore, ideas of evolutionism and morality were elaborated within a group of scholars influenced by the German Historical school.[10] Ideas like these shaped the studies and depictions of the peasantry.

The social position and the characteristics of the peasantry were frequently presented and interpreted in a gendered way. In this article I show how groups placed at different stages of evolutionary progress are related to understandings of gender differences and gendered characteristics. Gender, according to Joan Scott (1988), is an inseparable part of the reproduction of the social order. Scott calls for an examination of the ways in which meanings of sexual differences are constructed and used to signify power and hierarchy.[11] Drawing on this theory, I discuss how gender operated in these texts and discuss how conceptions of gender structured the articulation of development, civilisation and problems.[12] According to evolutionary ideas, developed cultures were characterised by clear gender differences. Furthermore, the position of women functioned as a catalyst for understandings of progress.[13] I study how the positions of women and of men are depicted. The structure of the family is also taken into consideration. Lastly, the article focuses on how men in different social groups were ascribed gendered characteristics.

History and social studies, social reform and elements of philanthropy

There were strong links between history and politics. The process of nation building engaged historians and other scholars, many of whom were connected to the Fennomen movement, i.e. the Finnish language movement.[14] Early on, leading historians considered it important to deal with questions of 'societal' relevance. In 1874, the historian Georg Zacharias Yrjö-Koskinen, who often used the signature Yrjö Koskinen[15], published an article, later famous, about the 'working class question' in Finland. He was also the leader of the Finnish party. Combining the role of scholar and politician, Yrjö Koskinen wrote about the position of crofters and landless groups.[16] Several historians placed a strong emphasis on social and economic history. E.G. Palmén, who held the chair in Finnish and Scandinavian history for decades, gave lectures about topics which would provide historical guidance related to 'the greatest social and economic currents of the present day'.[17] As a professor, he supervised many studies and dissertations dealing with social or economic aspects. One of his students wrote about the ownership of cattle in early modern Finland. This topic was chosen because 'economic questions were central in our societal life.'[18] Furthermore, scholars of history laid the foundation for new academic disciplines dealing with contemporary social and economic aspects – in for instance the fields of agricultural economics, statistics and sociology.[19] Consequently, historical thinking and historical notions of development had formed the thinking of these scholars.

The connections between the association of economics (Kansantaloudellinen Yhdistys) and the Historical Association, which was founded in 1890, were strong. Several persons were engaged in both societies, and many of the members were politically active in different groupings.[20] By publishing the early reports, the Finnish Literature Society (Suomen kirjallisuuden seura, SKS) was also engaged in the social question. In 1894, Aksel Lilius, a journalist and accountant who had written one of the above-mentioned reports, donated inherited money to the Finnish Literature Society for a major investigation into the situation of crofters. Aksel Warén, who had written a long report about the situation in Kuortane, was assigned this task.

Several studies of the social and economic situation of the countryside were carried out in relation to political discussions about land reforms and land tenure. The legislation of land tenure was changed several times – in 1892, 1902 and 1909. The studies were used and referred to when reforms were discussed and presented. The studies initiated in 1884 were related to parliamentary discussions about reforms of land taxation and to a public discussion about tenure contracts. The first studies dealt with the situation of the whole rural population. The study carried out by Aksel Warén dealt with the situation of the crofters. In the preface, Warén stated that studies which could be used when preparing reforms were needed. Warén's study was due to be published as early as 1896. But as the issue of land tenure was not dealt with in parliament, the book was not published until later. In 1901, a comprehensive study of the position of the landless was carried out by Hannes Gebhard. Gebhard was a historian and social scientist who had studied in Germany in the mid-1890s; he was appointed to be an associate professor of history in 1890, and gained a similar position in statistics and agricultural economy in 1899. At the turn of the century, Gebhard, who is also known for his work on co-operative organising, greatly influenced the definition of the land issue.[21]

In a lecture on the land question, Gebhard's notion of the relationship between science and social reform was made explicit. He presented the system of landholding in ancient Greece and Rome. Furthermore, he presented examples from English and Finnish history. Finally, he criticised land legislation in Finland. He asked his students whether this was tendentious. He himself answered: 'Tendentious it is! And I also wanted it to be tendentious'. This lecture was probably given in 1899 or in 1900. He wanted science to be purposeful; the aim was not only to objectively gather facts. That was only a science of the second rank.[22] In an earlier lecture, he discussed liberalism and socialism. According to Gebhard, both of these groups had forgotten their duties. Nevertheless, now the time of duty had come; the duty to enlighten oneself, the duty to work for equity, the duty to require the state to work for those who were poor. He stressed love of mankind, Christian values and virtues.[23] In these lectures Gehbard mixed philanthropic, religious ideals with understandings of science and social reform. In a review he emphasised the moral position of Aksel Warén; although Warén was badly paid, and given less money than crofters, he had spent three years studying the situation of crofters.

Women's work and the position of women

Entitled *Tutkimuksia ialoudellisista oloista Suomen maaseudulla* and in twelve short booklets, the studies initiated in 1884 were published between 1885 and 1893. These short booklets were written by various persons, including landlords and priests. One booklet, the one regarded as the best, was written by the above-mentioned Warén. Many questions about land owning, the size of the units and the division of land were posed in the original programme. One section dealt with the standpoint of agriculture, and among other things the methods used and the work done by women was mentioned.[24]

The question about women's work in the fields was dealt with in most of the answers. Several authors mentioned that women performed many tasks, also in agriculture. Especially in the descriptions of areas regarded as backward, women's field work was stressed. In addition, these descriptions seem to have been the most negative and distanced.[25]

The aim of the study was to understand the variation between different regions in Finland. There were differences regarding women's work. Several of the writers had Swedish names, and were members of upper-class families. One report was provided by Matti Kivelä from Kemi. Besides depicting problems, he also reviewed an area with relatively big farms. According to Kivelä, women only performed easier tasks in the fields.[26] According to an answer from Laukkaa, the mistress of the house mainly performed household tasks, whereas other women worked outdoors.[27] When describing the situation in Ostrobothnian parish in Western Finland, Warén depicted the heavy work done by women in a positive way. Moreover, he also underlined that women's wages were quite good.[28]

Interestingly enough, the position of the writer also influenced the depictions. Since they had middle-class values, it is clear that some writers tended to underline the domestic chores of women.[29] From a similar perspective, some of the writers mentioned women's outdoor work in an almost victimising way. Victimising elements are most obvious in depictions from Eastern Carelia. The people in this region are regarded as 'uncivilised' and ascribed an almost pagan faith. The men are depicted as tall and strong, whereas the women were said to be short and malformed due to work and early marriage. The wife is depicted as the hardest worker of the house.[30] In line with evolutionary thinking, hard-working women were related to countries or areas seen as underdeveloped.[31]

In ordinary historical work, as for instance in dissertations published in the late nineteenth century, the position of women was seldom discussed. Several historical studies about economic or social 'conditions', which were supervised by E.G.Palmén, were presented during the late nineteenth century. However, in some of the studies of the conditions in peripheral regions topics like these were briefly touched on. For instance, in Petrus Nordmann's book about Finns in Swedish backwoods, women's work was discussed. Furthermore, in a study about Ingria during the eighteenth century marriage customs were also considered.[32]

Interestingly enough, the position of women was most explicitly and thoroughly discussed in a study which was strongly characterised by evolutionary theories and notions of causality. In 1890, Yrjö Koskinen Yrjö-Koskinen, the son of Professor Yrjö Koskinen,[33] defended a thesis about the development of agriculture in Finland. His aim was to demonstrate that permanent field cultivation had been established in a pagan period. In line with traditions of evolutionary thinking, he was convinced that each society had developed in a similar way. Embracing unilinear understandings of evolutionism, he depicted ascending stages of economy: hunting, cattle-raising and field cultivation. Mobile hunting communities had been replaced by cattle-keeping households. From an evolutionary perspective, strongly emphasised in late-nineteenth century historiography, field cultivation was regarded as more developed and civilised. According to this theory, only permanent field cultivation enabled more organised societal systems. Mobile communities were contrasted to more permanent settlements, and the latter were regarded as less backward. Permanent agricultural practices were, according to several scholars, brought to Finland during the period of Swedish colonisation and settlement. At the same time, it was also emphasised that primitive communities of swidden cultivation, a main form of agriculture in Eastern Finland, could not build states – thus they 'lacked history'.[34]

Using evolutionary theory and pointing to the early introduction of field cultivation, he argued that societal structures were established before the period of 'Swedish rule'. But also the position of women functioned as a catalyst for understandings of civilisation and development in this text. In the first chapter of the book, which discussed general development, the poor conditions of women in societies at a low stage of civilisation are touched on. In earlier periods, women were said to have been slaves, and they were also said to be responsible for agriculture in primitive cultures.[35] Furthermore, the heavy work done by Russian women was depicted, and Yrjö-Koskinen also mentioned the custom of bridal looting.[36]

In addition, he discussed the structure of the family. Extended families were mainly related to mobile and cattle-raising societies, and these large households in particular were characterised by almost unlimited patriarchal power. Women were more or less owned by men. However, the rights of Finnish women had improved; this was a process which according to the younger Yrjö-Koskinen still was to come to an end.[37]

Victimisation of the male peasants
– and notions of prehistoric individualism

In the late 1880's, professor Palmén supervised several studies on social relations. In 1887, a thesis about the enfeoffment, i.e. the growing power ascribed to landlords, during the 17th century was defended. The comment made by the opponent illustrates how the widespread interest in social questions also influenced historical studies: the study was considered too limited, as it didn't deal with the 'socio-political' aspect of the topic. The opponent required further discussions about the conditions of the peasants and asked whether injustice had been done. In historical studies on economic and social conditions, the peasant was mainly depicted as a victim suffering from miserable conditions, although the simplicity and the common sense of the people was sometimes described in a positive way. These studies also covered other groups than the peasantry, but questions about agrarian history were paid attention to and frequently emphasised.[38] When criticising one of the early studies in this tradition, Professor Palmén pointed to the need for a more thorough disposition of the material; this would have illustrated 'how the Ingrian peasantry had endured the hardest of destinies'. Apparently, the social ambition and the idea of social history resulted in a victimising picture of the peasantry.

The peasantry of Finland and Sweden had been relatively free, whereas peasants in many other countries had endured serfdom. The freedom of the peasantry was seldom mentioned in the historical studies about the 'conditions' in different parts of Finland.[39] A study entitled 'Depiction of the conditions in Finland 1617–1632', where the situation of different social groups was described, stressed the oppression of peasants and showed how the peasants approached the King himself for help. In addition, tormentors of peasants (*bonde_plågare*) were described.[40] Another study dealt with the early eighteenth century, a period when Finland was occupied by Russia. It illustrated the sacrifices on the peasants' part, but also how the country people demonstrated fighting spirit.[41] A very victimising picture was given in a study about the province of Viipuri, the region which came under Russian rule during the eighteenth century; according to the author the peasants in this region experienced virtual serfdom.

From the 1850s onwards, there were strong attempts to show that Finland had a long and continuous history, despite its lack of a state. This attempt was based on the ideals connected to the Finnish-speaking part of the population – the Finnish people. Nevertheless, the peasantry was seldom depicted in an idealised way in these studies. Masculinity can be conceived as a trope structuring historical writing, and understandings of masculinity were formulated and used by the historians. In historiography, individualism, men's individualism, has often represented and symbolised the position of the nation.[42] However, in these studies the peasants were depicted in a victimising way; the notion of free, equal and individual peasants was seldom alluded to.

Interestingly enough, in the evolutionary influenced study carried out by the younger Yrjö-Koskinen individualism is ascribed to the peasants of the past. His aim was to study the introduction of field cultivation. In explorations of this development, aspects which were both implicitly and explicitly connected to men and masculinity were frequently paid attention to. In late-nineteenth century historiography, there was an interest in the history of the family,[43] and the development of the marital relation was regarded as a central element of a social evolution.[44] In Yrjö-Koskinen's discussion of the diminishing importance of patriarchy, the position of men was pivotal. The extended family, which characterised a certain evolutionary stage (i.e. societies relying on cattle-breeding), could consist of more than two nuclear families – and of more than two grown-up men. To be in a dependent position, not being the master of the house was considered in negative terms, and in the extended family it was not possible for every man to gain the status of a male householder.

At a more developed stage, families – according to this idea of progress and cultural evolution – had become smaller. A family now resembled the nuclear family, which created space for male individuality. In his text, Yrjö-Koskinen deals with the introduction of field cultivation, the development of the family and the position of men in an intertwined way. The family was central also for men – especially for men. Frequently Yrjö-Koskinen used words with references to individuality. In this framework also words like 'self-respect' and 'independence' were employed.[45] Besides the position of women, individualism was a sign of development; it placed the studied nation at a higher level of civilisation. While the primitive was characterised by collectivism, individuality was related to more developed stages.

Moral characteristics and the position of the family

Questions about land taxation as well as indebtedness were formulated in the programme of the launched investigation in 1884. Not least questions about the size of land holdings were seen as central. Also the position of crofters and cottagers were mentioned as central themes when the studies were initiated.[46] Maybe because of their interest, several of the authors wrote in detail about agriculture and about agricultural conditions. It was frequently stated that agriculture was undeveloped.

When discussing agriculture and questions of indebtedness, the authors often paid attention to moral characteristics. In several reports it was underlined that debts were due to an inability to handle money; the peasant lived beyond his means and, due to commercialisation, country people had become used to a higher standard of living. The consumption of coffee was mentioned as a problem. In a report from Savonia, Nils Grotenfelt and others who supplied information stated that the landless would be able to be self-sufficient if they only were hard-working, industrious and economic. This was, however, seldom the case.[47] In the report from Kuopio, Aksel Lilius who later donated money for Warén's major study, stressed that practical attainments and skills in handicraft had declined.[48] In another report, a taunting description of a landless man who behaved like his master was made. In addition, it was stated that people were just living for the day and that they were getting married too young.[49]

In some of the reports the simplicity of the country is depicted in a positive way. Moreover, the vulnerability of smallholders was underlined in several of the studies. Even so, there was a degrading view of the peasantry in the early studies. Not being able to understand the need for development, the agrarian groups, and especially the landless, were considered backward. In a review of the studies, the inability to save money was compared with economic 'virtues' of other undeveloped groups. The Finnish rural population was said to be hospitable; however, hospitality was exaggerated and the people were considered dishonest.[50] Partly, the educated authors seem to have been unable to understand the situation of the rural group, which was considered undeveloped, childish, and uncivilised.

Questions about the role of the family or the structure of the household were not posed in the initial programme. Nevertheless, the family was referred to in comments about the studies. Aksel Lilius chose to write an appendix to his report.[51] Here, he listed measures to be taken in order to solve the problems. Instead of poor relief, one should require the poor to work. Houseless lodgers should be helped so they could get a place to live. Subsequently, the male worker (työmies) would become 'the master of the house' (asutuksen isäntä); he would – in other words – be given a more independent position, the cottager, often called 'vuokramies' (i.e. legoman, 'lease man'), would be helped to get land. At length, Lilius discussed how the position of the working man could be improved. Among other things, the tasks of the wife were mentioned. She was to take care of cows. It was presupposed that the man was married, and Lilies explicitly discussed family relations in a section entitled 'moral standpoint' (siveellinen kanta).

During this period, marriage was considered to improve the position and vitality of men.[52] The family was considered central for men; this was also made clear in the presentation of the studies published in the journal Valvoja in 1890. When evaluating the studies which had been published, the author underlined that land holding enabled men to support families. Crofts were regarded as the only way of offering the landless an opportunity to work; this would in addition make them good citizens and enable them to support a family. The text was written by Onni Hannikainen, a historian who had written a study about provinces annexed by Russia in the eighteenth century. The tradition of living in with others families was, according to him, harmful and immoral. But due to ignorance and laziness, the poor people lived in a borrowed part of a room. Here, the author underlined that the country people had left the stage characterised by extended families. Nevertheless, new and harmful forms of cohabitation had evolved. Lastly, Hannikainen regarded the reports to be reliable, and he encouraged the educated to help civilise the landless.[53] This was how the nation could be bound together.

Rights and citizens: Warén's interviews

Was there a 'crofter-question', Akseli Warén asked explicitly in the first chapter of his book about the crofters. Or was it a consequence of exaggerated complaints and agitating? According to Warén, the discussion was an outcome of 'the awakening of the lower classes'. Even if there had been problems and arbitrariness earlier, nobody had believed that things could change.[54] To begin with, Warén had stressed economic questions. However, when publishing the book he also underlined the legal aspects of leasehold.[55]

Later regarded as modern and epoch-making, the study was based on both oral and written sources. The author called the study descriptive. When discussing his methods, Warén noted that he had interviewed both landholders and leaseholders. If the information given by the former was deemed unreliable, it was not taken into consideration. On the other hand, all the information provided by the land leasers had been dealt with.[56] Crofters on peasant land and crofters on estates were seen as separate groups. As the group of leaseholders was very heterogeneous, the writer pointed to insufficient statistics.[57]

In addition, the author underlined that he had not considered the locality of where a certain thing had happened. Therefore, the depictions were not related to particular places. His main aim was to demonstrate that certain things had occurred. He wanted to treat a delicate subject in an objective way. Furthermore, he wanted to protect the interviewees; he didn't want them to be victims of science.[58] In earlier studies, the differences between regions were paid attention to in, to some extent, a hierarchical way. The peripheral position as such explained the state of conditions. Here, the spatial aspects were not emphasised.

Partly due to rumours about land division, the land question was paid more attention during the final years of the century. Even so, the main goal was not self-ownership. Although being critical of the liberal economic system, Yrjö-Koskinen had defended the right to ownership in the 1880s; according to him, the system of land tenure was to be reformed but not abolished. In the late 1890s, this was also the position held by Gebhard.[59] According to Warén, the system was not suitable for developed agriculture, but he regarded it as important for the country.[60]

A committee formed by land holders and liberal economic thinkers presented the idea of independent landowning as early as the mid-1890s. During the 1890s, the crofters demanded longer periods of tenure, fixed workings hours, and the right to compensation for improvements made on the land.[61] The early legal reform limited the length of the tenure period, the maximum being 50 years. According to the regulation made in 1902, the maximal number of days' work demanded by the land holder was to be settled. The amount of the day-work was not regulated, neither the shortest period of tenure.[62]

Whereas Warén's notion of country people had become more positive, Yrjö-Koskinen's view had changed in the other direction. While

Yrjö-Koskinen in earlier years had stressed the abilities of the landless, he later regarded them as passive.[63] In the study published in 1893, Warén depicted country people as morally undeveloped. In this book, the image had changed.[64] Even if this 'class of citizens' stood for a lower level of civilization,[65] there were few depictions of their moral state in this book. He defined the issue as 'societal'. At the same time, Warén stated that the group was not yet sufficiently aware to organise itself. To begin with, many lacked the capability to define their problems.[66] In order to make them a 'more economically independent and morally conscious class of people' legislation was needed.[67] This would secure the rights of the crofters. Warén underlined the need for regulations of the tenure period, compensations, and claims laid to day-work. According to Aksel Warén, the responsibility of the state was no longer to regulate economic and private life, but to create opportunities for development.[68]

Notions of independence and unmanliness in Gebhard's lectures

Explicitly masculine terms and understandings of masculinity are not used in Warén's book. He invoked the concepts of 'rights', and he used the term 'citizen'. These concepts refer to understandings of equality, and Warén also explicitly stated that leaseholders were not always treated as equal citizens. Notably, Hannes Gebhard took recourse to explicit masculine rhetoric and to metaphoric use of the word 'man' when presenting the 'agrarian question'. In a lecture probably given in 1899, he presented examples of misery in a gendered way. He presented the rural labourers in England; their wives had to work. He pointed to bad standards of living, making family life difficult. As the system of poor relief increased, so did the number of illegitimate children, which he considered to be immoral. This was also the case with the Finnish system, which treated grown-up men in a patriarchal and patronising way.[69] These men were not given the right to think and act themselves, he claimed. Invoking a causal notion of history, he underlined that a growing group of dependent working men would lead to demands for land reforms.

In 1895, Gebhard published a book about agrarian statistics. This scholar was mainly influenced by German ideas. When it came to co-operative land reform, Ireland was often referred to. Presenting statistics, he discussed examples from several countries, mainly nations regarded as civilised. In this book he emphasised that the size of the holding was more important than the formal ownership and forms of taxation. Rhetorically, he asked about 'independence': who is more 'independent' – a crofter relying on a good contract or a self-owning smallholder with three cows?[70] Independence and responsibility can be seen as key elements attached to middle-class manhood during this period.

According to Gebhard, the position of the landless, not the situation of the crofters, was the most burning issue. Whereas the latter group was tied to the land, the former, a mobile group, would also have influence on the urban situation.[71] In 1901, information about every rural household in Finland was gathered. Questions about land owning, about housing and the number of rooms as well as number of cows and pastures were asked. These questions concerned the position of the male householder (called huvudmannen), the living standard of the family and the possibilities of keeping cattle. Thus, formal as well as social aspects were touched on. But there were no questions about the tenancy – central from a strictly economic perspective.[72] However, the scope of the investigation, which covered every rural household in Finland, exemplifies the belief in statistics and science.

Even if Gebhard frequently invoked such terms as rights and equality in the lectures he gave, he also stated in 1902 that it was not possible to give these ignorant men land and then leave them without guidance. Here, Gebhard propagated co-operative organising.[73] A mixture of ideas about social reform, evolutionism, and on the other hand, an understanding of a social and cultural gap between the educated group and the agrarian poor produced an ambiguous picture. Men in this group were ascribed other characteristics than middle-class men. Here, the approach outlined by the American historian Gail Bederman can be pointed to. Studying late nineteenth century America, Bederman illustrates how the term manliness was used to depict characteristics like self-control, self-mastery and honesty – special civic values – whereas the term masculinity was associated with aggression, strength and virility. Furthermore, Bederman shows how 'whiteness' was linked to 'manliness' through a use of a discourse on civilisation. What is central in her approach in relation to this article is her way of studying how men placed at different stages of cultural and evolutionary progress are endowed with diverse gendered characteristics and moral qualities.[74] While Warén mainly presented citizenship in terms of rights, Gebhard seemed to a higher degree to have related this concept to such characteristics as activity, morality and civilised forms of behaviour.[75] The landless were to become independent landholders, but they were also to be enlightened and edified in order to become responsible and active.

Gendered understandings of social reform

In this article I discuss how the stage of development as well as the moral status of the peasantry, especially the rural poor, was understood in gendered terms. The themes which were discussed in these studies – the situation of women, the position of the family in society, men's capability to be breadwinners and act as citizens – have been important in many social studies. In the early studies made by historians, in particular, these themes were discussed in discursive contexts which were strongly influenced by ideals of social evolutionism. According to evolutionary ideas, the position of women was pivotal when seeking to understand the stage of progress. According to middle-class values, or according to an evolutionary conception of society, women's field work and women's subordinated position was related to a low level of development. However, also the position of men and individuality ascribed to men functioned as a catalyst for understanding of development. Likewise, perceptions of the family were at issue when the position of different social groupings was discussed.

The studies were made in a discursive context influenced, on the one hand, by positivism and evolutionism, and on the other hand, by understandings of civilisation and morality. Especially in the historical studies, development was compared to the situation in other countries and areas. However, the depictions were based on understandings of internal differences, i.e. cultural differences between the 'educated' and the rest. Nationalistic arguments were evoked when the studies were initiated. The peasantry was a part of the depicted nation, but had an ambiguous position; the educated group could identify itself with the agrarian groups, but the latter also functioned as a category against which the upper classes could position themselves. Here, the rural poor were seen as incapable of measuring up to the moral standards of other groups of the population. Considered backward and morally undeveloped, the rural population itself constituted a problem.

Notes

1. Aksel Warén 1898, p. I.
2. For a discussion about earlier studies, see Per Wisselgren, 2000, pp. 14-15 and Pertti Haapala, 2007. Several scholars have discussed gender and social reform. However, these studies have often focused the twentieth century. See for instance Yvonne Hirdman, 1997; Åsa Lundqvist, 2007; Ann-Katrin Hatje, 2009.
3. Matti Peltonen, 1998; Sakari Heikkinen et al. 2000, pp. 108-109.
4. The Finnish term 'maakysymys' was often used, especially during the last years of the century.
5. Pertti Haapala, 2007, p. 56.
6. Viljo Rasila, 1961, pp. 111-116.
7. Pekka Ahtiainen and Jukka Tervonen, 2000, pp. 52–50; Mylly, 2002, pp. 226–229; Päiviö Tommila, 1989, pp. 138–154.
8. Pekka Ahtiainen and Jukka Tervonen, 1996, pp. 48–62; Pertti Haapala, 2007.
9. Rasila, 1961, p. 163.
10. Heimer Björkqvist, 1986, pp. 471-473; cf. Risto Eräsaari, 1976. For a discussion about the meaning and the importance of the term 'siveellinen' in Finland at the turn of the century, see Heidi Grönstrand et al. 2007.
11. Her leading statement on gender as an analytical tool, her analytical definition, has two parts: 'gender is a constitutive element of social relationships based on perceived differences between the sexes, and gender is a way of signifying relations of power' (Joan Scott, 1988, p. 42).
12. For a discussion about masculinity and the writing of history, see Stefan Dudink, 2004. See also Ann-Catrin Östman, 2006.
13. Cf. Ann-Catrin Östman, 2008.
14. The upper classes and the nobility had historically been Swedish-speaking. At the turn of the century, the Swedish-speaking minority in Finland amounted to 12.9 percent (approximately 350,000 people). The Swedish-speaking population was heterogeneous and consisted of different groups, including an agrarian rural group as well as urban and rural working classes.
15. E.g. Georg Zacharias Forsman; his name Forsman was changed to the Finnish Koskinen.
16. Viljo Rasila, 1961, pp.111-120; Matti Peltonen, 2004, p. 222-223.
17. The Archive of Helsinki University, Historisk filosofiska sektionens protokoll 20.9.1900 (minutes, historical and philosophical section). 'En historisk ledning till förståendet av nutidens förnämsta sociala och ekonomiska strömningar'.
18. Joho Heikki Vennola 1900, preface. Vennola later held a chair in economics and he was also an active politician, for instance as prime minister.
19. Päiviö Tommila, 1989, pp. 145-147; Pertti Haapala, 2007, pp. 56-57.
20. Päiviö Tommila, 1989, pp. 145-147; Pertti Haapala, 2007.
21. Viljo Rasila, 1961, pp. 111-120 and pp. 159-163; Matti Peltonen, 1998, 95.
22. National Archives, the archives of Hannes Gebhard, Manuscript ('Yliopistoll. Luentoja') File 28.
23. A lecture given at the university in 1896. National Archives, the archives of Hannes Gebhard, Manuscript ('Yliopistoll. Luentoja') File 28.
24. Tutkimuksia, I, 1885, pp. 1-4.
25. Tutkimuksia I: No. 11, p. 6, No. 22, p. 3, No. 23, p. 5.
26. Tutkimuksia I: No. 24, p. 6.

27 Tutkimuksia IV: No. 18, pp. 6-7.
28 Tutkimuksia V: Aksel Warén, 1890, p. 32.
29 Cf. Pirjo Markkola, 1989, pp. 52-53.
30 Tutkimuksia V. Brander, p. 32.
31 Cf. Ann-Catrin Östman, 2008.
32 Cf. Petrus Nordmann, 1888, p. 70 and p. 106; Ann-Catrin Forsström, 1890.
33 I.e. Georg Zacharias Forsman.
34 Jussi Raumolin, 1987, p. 191.
35 Y.K. Yrjö-Koskinen, 1890, p. 5 and p. 36.
36 Y.K. Yrjö-Koskinen, 1890, pp. 29-30 and p. 49.
37 Y.K. Yrjö-Koskinen, 1890, pp. 11-12 and p. 63.
38 By comparison it can be said there were fewer, historical studies on agrarian history in Sweden, cf. Janken Myrdal, 2004.
39 In Danish historiography, a victimised picture was formed in late-nineteenth century studies of agrarian history. Here, aspects of feudalism were stressed. Cf. Thorkild Kjærgaard, 1979; Peter Henningsen, 2006, pp. 57-85.
40 K.R. Melander, 1887.
41 K.O. Lindeqvist, 1886.
42 Cf. Joan Scott, 1988, pp. 68-90. Joan Scott has discussed the gendered aspects of the book 'The Making of the English Working Class'. Cf. Dudink, 2003. Dudink discusses the relationship between masculinity and the history of Dutch historiography.
43 Cf. Bente Rosenbeck, 1985, p. 17.
44 Judith Surkis, 2006, pp. 125-127; Jonas Liliequist, 2006, p. 201.
45 Y.K. Yrjö-Koskinen, 1890, pp. 51-53.
46 See Tutkimuksia I, p. 3.
47 See for instance the different studies of *Tutkimuksia:* No. 11, p. 11; No. 22, p. 6; No. 23, p. 10).
48 Tutkimuksia III: p. 5.
49 Tutkimuksia IV: No. 16, p. 16-22.
50 Olli Hannikainen, 1890, p. 341.
51 *Tutkimuksia taloudellisista oloista Suomen maaseudulla*, 1888, Kolmas vihko III, Helsinki. Tilattoman väen oloista Kuopion läänissä.
52 Cf. Jonas Liliequist, 2006, p. 201; Judith Surkis, 2006, p. 12 and pp. 125-127.
53 Olli Hannikainen, 1890, pp. 340-342.
54 Aksel Warén, 1898, p. 9.
55 Aksel Warén, 1898, p. 11 and 20.
56 Aksel Warén, 1898, pp. 3-4.
57 Aksel Warén, 1898, pp. 32-33.
58 Aksel Warén, 1898, p. 6.
59 Viljo Rasila, 1961, pp. 137-138, p. 163 and p.170.
60 Aksel Warén, 1898, pp. 26-27.
61 Viljo Rasila, 1961, p. 136 and 158.
62 Viljo Rasila, 1961, pp. 203-204.
63 Viljo Rasila, 1961, pp. 116-117.
64 Cf. Matti Peltonen, 2004, pp. 222-223.
65 Aksel Warén, 1898, p. 27.
66 Aksel Warén, 1898, pp. 11-12.
67 Aksel Warén, 1898, p. 402.

68 Aksel Warén, 1898, p. 27.
69 National Archives, Hannes Gebhard's archives, Kansio 22, Käsikirjoitukset: 'yliopistolliset luennot'.
70 Aksel Warén, 1898, p. 59.
71 Villjo Rasila, 1961, pp. 215-218.
72 Cf. Matti Peltonen, 1998, p. 91.
73 National Archives, Hannes Gebhard's archives, Kansio 22, Käsikirjoitukset: 'yliopistolliset luennot'.
74 Gail Bederman, 1995, pp. 20-23; Sigridur Matthíasdottír and Ann-Catrin Östman, 2003.
75 Cf. Henrik Stenius, 2003, pp. 312-313.

Studies

Forsström, O.A. 1890: *Kuvaus Inkerimaan oloista Ruotsinvallan aikana*, Sortavala.
Gebhard, Hannes 1895: *Maanviljelystilasto meillä ja muualla*, Helsinki/Otava.
Hannikainen, Olli 1890: 'Tutkimuksia taloudellisista oloista Suomen maaseuduilla', *Valvoja*, 11:4, pp. 333–348.
Lindeqvist, K.O. 1886: *Suomen oloista ison vihan aikana*. Akatemiallinen väitöskirja, J.C. Frenckell ja poika, Helsinki.
Melander, K.R. 1887: *Kuvaus Suomen oloista vuosina 1617-1634*, I. Akatemiallinen väitöskirja, Helsinki.
Nordmann, Petrus 1888: *Finnarne i mellersta Sverige*, Helsingfors.
Tutkimuksia taloudellisista oloista Suomen maaseudulla, Ensimäinen vihko I, 1885, Helsinki.
Tutkimuksia taloudellisista oloista Suomen maaseudulla, Toinen vihko II, 1887, Helsinki.
Tutkimuksia taloudellisista oloista Suomen maaseudulla, Kolmas vihko III, 1888, Helsinki.
Tutkimuksia taloudellisista oloista Suomen maaseudulla, Neljäs vihko IV, 1889, Helsinki.
Tutkimuksia taloudellisista oloista Suomen maaseudulla, Viides vihko V, 1893, Helsinki.
Warén, Aksel 1898: *Torpparioloista Suomessa*, SKS, Helsinki.
Vennola, Juho Heikki 1900: *Pohjois-Suomen maalaisvarallisuus 16: llä ha 17:llä vuosisadalla*, Helsinki.
Yrjö-Koskinen, Y.K. 1890: *Suomalaisten heimojen yhteiskunta-järjestyksestä pakanuuden loppu-aikoina*, Jyväskylä.

References

Ahtiainen, Pekka and Jukka Tervonen, 1996: *Menneisyyden tutkijat ja metodien vartijat*, Helsinki.
Ahtiainen, Pekka and Jukka Tervonen, 2000: 'A journey into Finnish historiography from the end of the nineteenth century to the present day', Meyer, Frank and Jan Eivin Myhre (eds.), *Nordic Historiography in the 20th century*, Oslo.
Bederman, Gail 1995: *Manliness & Civilization*, Chicago.
Björkqvist, Heimer 1986: *Den nationalekonomiska vetenskapens utveckling i Finland intill*

år 1918, Åbo.
Bock, Gisela and Thane Pat (eds.) 1991: *Maternity and Gender Policies. Women and the Rise of the European Welfare states 1880s-1950s*, Routledge.
Christiansen, Niels Finn, Klaus Petersen, Niels Edling and Per Haave (eds.) 2006: *The Nordic Model of Welfare. A historical Reappraisal*, Copenhagen.
Dudink, Stefan 2004: 'Masculinity, effeminacy, time: Conceptual change in the Dutch age of democratic revolutions', Stefan Dudink, Karen Hagemann and John Tosh (eds.), *Masculinities in Politics and War. Gendering Modern History*, Manchester.
Dudink, Stefan, Karen Hagemann and John Tosh (eds.) 2004: *Masculinities in Politics and War. Gendering Modern History*, Manchester.
Engman, Max 1999: 'The Finland-Swedes: a case of a failed national history?', Michael Branch (ed.), *National History and Identity*, Helsinki.
Eräsaari, Risto 1976: *Historiallinen taloustiede – katederisosialismi – Verein für Sozialpolitik. Sosiaalipolitiikan synnyn ongelma Saksassa*, Helsinki.
Eskola, Hanna (ed.) 1997: *Models, Modernity and the Myrdals*, Helsinki.
Frederiksson, Göran et al. (eds.) 2003: *Könsmaktens förvandlingar*, Göteborg.
Grönstrand, Heidi et al. 2007: 'Suomalaisen omakuvan muutos', *Historiallinen Aikakauskirja*, vol. 3, pp. 389-392.
Gustafsson Harald et al. (eds.) 2007: *Den dubbla blicken. Historia i de nordiska samhallena*, Lund.
Haapala, Pertti 2007: '*Kulturgeschichte* i den finländska historieskrivningen', Harald Gustafsson et al (eds.), *Den dubbla blicken. Historia i de nordiska samhällena*, Lund.
Hatje, Ann-Katrin 2009: *Svensk välfärd, genus och social rationalism under 1900-talet*, Umeå.
Heikkinen, Sakari et al. 2000: *The history of Finnish economic thought*, Helsinki.
Henningsen, Peter 2006: *I sansernas vold. Bondekultur og kultursammenstød i enevældens Danmark*, Copenhagen.
Hirdman, Yvonne 1997: 'Social planning under Rational Control', Pauli Kettunen and Hanna Eskola (ed.), *Models, Modernity and the Myrdals*, Helsinki.
Kjærgaard, Thorkild 1979: 'Gårdsmanslinien i dansk historieskrivning', *Fortid og Nutid*, no. 27, pp. 178-191.
Kostonis, Yanni 1999: *Making Peasants backward. Agricultural Cooperatives and the Agrarian Questions in Russia, 1861-1914*, New York.
Liliequist, Jonas 2006: 'Sexualiteten', Jørgen Lorentzen and Claes Ekenstam (eds.), *Män i Norden. Manlighet och modernitet 1840-1940*, Hedemora.
Lundqvist, Åsa 2007: *Familjen i den svenska modellen*, Umeå.
Markkola, Pirjo 1989: 'Maaseudun työläisvaimot', Leena Laine and Pirjo Markkola (eds.), *Tuntematon työläisnainen*, Vastapaino.
Matthíasdottír, Sigriður and Ann-Catrin Östman 2003: 'Möte mellan manligheter. Nationalism, bondeideal och (åter)skapandet av de övre skiktens manlighetsideal', Göran Fredriksson et al. (eds.), *Könsmaktens förvandlingar*, Göteborg.
Mylly, Juhani 2002: *Kansallinen projekti: historiankirjoitus ja politiikka autonomisessa Suomessa*, Turku.
Myrdal, Janken 2004: 'Agrarhistoriens etablering som universitetsdisciplin', *Bebyggelsehistorisk tidskrift*, no. 47, pp. 7-18.
Peltonen, Matti 1998: 'Från osäkerhet till hat. Torparfrågans moraliska ekonomi i sekelskiftets Finland', *Bebyggelsehistorisk tidskrift*, no. 35, pp. 91-98.
Peltonen, Matti 2004: 'Torpparikysymys', Matti Peltonen (ed.), *Suomen maatalouden historia II*, Helsinki.

Peltonen, Matti (ed.) 2004: *Suomen maatalouden historia II*, Helsinki.
Rasila, Viljo 1961: *Suomen torpparikysymys vuoteen 1909. Yhteiskuntahistoriallinen tutkimus*, Helsinki.
Raumolin, Jussi 1987: 'Introduction to the study of swidden cultivation', *Suomen antropologi*, 12:4, pp. 185-212.
Rosenbeck, Bente 1985: 'På sporet af kvindernes historie. Historisk kvindeforskning', Anna-Birte Ravn and Marianne Rostgård, *Kvindefælleskaber*, Aalborg.
Sinha, Mrinalini 1999: 'Giving Masculinity a history', *Gender & History*, no. 11, pp. 445-460.
Scott, Joan 1988: *Gender and the politics of history*, New York.
Stenius, Henrik 2003: 'Kansalainen', Matti Hyvärinen et al (eds.), *Käsitteet liikeessä. Suomen poliittisen kulttuurin käsitehistoria*, Vastapaino.
Surkis, Judith 2006: *Sexing the citizen. Morality and masculinity in France, 1870–1920*, Ithaca.
Tommila, Päiviö 1989: *Suomen historiankirjoituksen. Tutkimuksen historia*, Helsinki.
Wisselgren, Per 2000: *Samhällets kartläggare*, Stockholm.
Östman, Ann-Catrin 2006: 'Från eländighet till manligt medborgarskap. Bonden i det tidiga 1900-talets finländska historieskrivning', *Historisk tidskrift*, 126:4, pp. 749–766.
Östman, Ann-Catrin 2008: 'Den civiliserade skillnaden – om kvinnors arbete och könsarbetsdelning i tidig historisk och etnologisk forskning', *Nätverket*, no. 15, pp. 8-25, (nättidskrift ISSN:1651–0593), Uppsala.

From the common good to the efficiency of policy means – Research on alcohol and drugs in Nordic social science

Svanaug Fjær

This article investigates the special case of social science research on alcohol and drugs in the Nordic countries. This is a research area which in many countries has been dominated by medical expertise, but where sociological and multi-disciplinary research has played a strong and independent role in the Nordic countries. It is also an area where research has coexisted with policy-making structures to the extent that it sometimes seems to have become integrated in the policy sector for the regulation of alcohol and drugs. Researchers have committed themselves to the policy aim of dealing with the drug and alcohol problems in their society, and in this sense participated in the the policy community together with policy makers at all levels of governance.

Thus, the tradition of social science research on alcohol and drugs developed from the early 1960s as an integrated part of the community's response to what was conceptualised as the alcohol and drug problem in public discourse and politics. The research theme was defined by the social and political construction of the 'alcohol and drug problem'. This quite integrated position in the policy field has naturally influenced research issues during the whole period, but with only few conflicts – with the important exception of research on drug policy.[1] During the 1990s, the research groups in the different countries underwent a series of reorganisations linked to major political and administrative changes, and management reforms. While the tradition back to the Nordic sociology of the post-WWII period is quite explicitly articulated in the research community in the early period, it is not so easy to tell what the motive of the researchers within this tradition is in this later period, and how the reforms have influenced on the tradition. This article will discuss if these changes can be understood in terms of a change of focus *from one on the impli-*

cations of politics into one on the *efficiency of policy*. It will also discuss the impact of these changes on the independence of the research and the potential to do basic social science research in the present state.

The term *politics* describes the process of the formation of interests, and how they are represented and balanced against each other. Politics covers the whole of the decision-making process, including public discourses. *Policy* as a term is restricted to the practical outcome of politics, such as means and strategies in a policy field.[2] The change from politics to policy has a potential impact at two levels. Firstly, it affects the research issues and themes for research; secondly, it affects the role of the research community in the policy-making process. In the latter case, the research community gets a more external role as an advisor, whereas it had earlier been fully participating in the politics of the drug and alcohol field. This article will elaborate further on the content of this change and discuss possible explanations. How is this research field moving from being a participant in politics to becoming a tool in administration of politics in the Nordic countries?

A considerable change in public opinion and public policy has taken place over the last 15 years when it comes to regulating alcohol in the Nordic societies.[3] The Nordic countries have turned from 'dry' into 'wet' societies, both in terms of alcohol policy and in terms of consumption. When Finland and Sweden became members of the EU in 1995, the shift towards more liberal regulation became even stronger. Drug policy is a different kind of issue, because of the marginal position of the users in the society, but this is also an area where the moral- and value-based questions have recently been asked in a different way from only a few years ago. Thus, a quite deep-rooted change seems to have taken place in the motives of the policy which influences the role of alcohol and drug research in many dimensions, the balance between research traditions, the priorities of research themes and the way research is used in the policy process.

The organisational change of the traditional corporative structures of the Nordic welfare states is part of the political process, but it should also be addressed on its own terms. Applied science has been an important part of this research field from the start, with researchers participating in politics along with interest groups, civil servants and politicians. Among the most important sources of change to the traditional model of politics was the gradual introduction of ideas from New Public Management (NPM) in the 1990s.[4] It influenced the organisation of politics as well as the role and status of research in policy making. NPM gave research an independent role as a regulating tool because of its preference for evaluations, reviews, meta-analysis and benchmarking strategies[5] The depth of this change is emphasised even more by Pekka Sulkunen (2009) in his book 'The Saturated Society', where he describes the present form of governance of lifestyles based on ideas of NPM as a 'new contract society'.[6]

How does the new task for research of providing politics with transparency and rationality from a neutral position differ from the traditional role of this research community? How has it altered the balance between social science research and other sources of scientific knowledge? How has it impacted on social science itself? Even if the Nordic countries are seemingly similar, differences in history and organisation of the research area make a comparison interesting and relevant in order to gain insight into how different national contexts influence the research-policy relation.

The study

The discussion about recent changes is based on empirical material from a study commissioned by the Nordic Centre for the Study of Alcohol and Drugs.[7] The aim was to create an overview of present development and priorities in social science studies on alcohol and drugs in the Nordic countries. The data material consists of interviews in focus groups and individual interviews with experienced researchers in all the Nordic countries. Some written documentation was also collected from all countries, such as annual reports from research institutions, recent research programmes of national research councils, strategy documents from the institutions and presentations of national research.

For the discussion in this article, this material is supplemented by earlier debates and presentations from the Nordic research community. I also use data from a more in-depth study of the science-policy relation in Norwegian drug policy as a background for this analysis.[8]

Sweden, Finland, Denmark and Norway have central research organisations with a special responsibility for social science research in the field of alcohol and drugs. They are, however, different in terms of history, size and organisational position. The Centre for Social Research on Alcohol and Drugs (Sorad), in Sweden, is a research unit within the Faculty of Social Science at Stockholm University. In

Finland, the Research Group on Alcohol and Drugs is included as a unit in STAKES (The National Research and Development Centre for Welfare and Health). In January 2009, STAKES merged with the National Public Health Institute to form one large single organisation for public health and welfare. In Denmark, the model resembles the Swedish model, with the Centre for Alcohol and Drug Research (CRF) organised at the Faculty of Social Sciences, Aarhus University. The Norwegian Institute for Alcohol and Drug Research (Sirus) has the most independent organisational position as a separate entity under the Ministry of Health. The size of the budgets of the institutions in 2006 shows that the Norwegian Sirus has double that of the other institutions.[9] Sorad and CRF have the largest proportion of external funding (about 50% of total), something that fits well with their position within universities rather than the civil service.

A twofold task and a sociological heritage

Drug and alcohol research in the Nordic countries is a genuinely multi-disciplinary tradition which includes methods, perspectives and theories of sociology, psychology, social medicine, education, law, history, anthropology and political science.

The longest history of social science research on the alcohol problem is to be found in Finland, with roots back to the inter-war period and the 1950s. The Norwegian tradition also has roots back in the early post-WWII period. The Norwegian National Institute on Alcohol Research was set up in 1960. In Finland research was funded by the strong national alcohol monopoly (Alko) while in Norway there was state funding and the Institute was organised within the central civil service. These models of organisation have for a long while represented a guarantee for continuity and an independence of the research communities, compared to the situation in other countries, where private funding of alcohol research by for instance the alcohol industry has dominated. To respond to social problems and social needs has been a natural part of the motivation for this research, as commented on by Babor in a study from the early 1990s:

> 'At times this mission-oriented model of research conflicts with the belief that science is best conducted in an atmosphere of complete intellectual freedom. Nevertheless, there is little in the literature on research centres that indicates that scientists are uncomfortable to make science relevant to social needs.'[10]

'Epidemiological research stands out as the fundament for the continuity in research as well as for the quite unique relation between research and politics in the Nordic drug and alcohol policy tradition. This harmonious relation meant that the institutions have neither established nor considered it important to make a distinction between research and administrative documentation.[11] This genuine cooperation between research, civil service, politics and voluntary organisations is based on the common agreement of the necessity and relevance of the numbers for research itself as a tool for policy-making. The sociological or academic contribution to epidemiological studies was to study consumption trends in a historical, social and cultural perspective.'[12]

'Nordic sociology seen internationally is considered to be a somewhat young tradition which combines continental and American influences via a combination of theoretical and conceptual interests and empirical research.[13] The academic breakthrough coincided with national efforts to develop research on alcohol consumption and politics. The strong interest in sociology among the public as well as among researchers from other disciplines is described by informants with experience from the 1960s.[14] The first director of the National Institute for Alcohol Research in Norway, Sverre Brun-Gulbrandsen, had an academic background in sociology. This is an example of the fact that the founders of the Nordic sociology were involved in the implementation and planning of institutions in the modern welfare state.'

In historical terms, two names should be mentioned as especially relevant as contributors to the perspectives of this research field. They are Kettil Bruun and Vilhelm Aubert – Bruun with a direct involvement in the field of alcohol and drugs research, and Aubert with a strong influence on how the sociological questions about social problems should be asked.

Tuka Tammi,[15] describes the goal of the Kettil Bruun tradition as protecting marginal or weak social groups against the suppression and demand of normalisation. On the basis of research, he recommended that alcohol policy should be directed towards general social control measures rather than to subgroups which often had other stigmatising characteristics as well. This perspective also gained a stronghold in international policy cooperation through the WHO-report *Alcohol Control Policies in Public Health Perspective*, written by Bruun and colleagues in 1975. It has been said that: 'Few books have had so much influence on the thinking and actual policy-making in this area. Its great impact was due to the authority of the group, to the very thorough way in which they did their work, and to the practical form in which they packaged their conclusions.'[16] Bruun's political programme was based on the insight that alcohol policy cannot alter the cultural dimensions of drinking – but has the capacity to affect the level of aggregate consumption, for example, by reducing availability.[17]

The challenge of living with diversity and opposing the pressure of conformity was even more clearly ezpressed in the opposition to the restrictive Nordic drug policy. Bruun was co-author with Nils Christie of the book *'The Ideal Enemy'*.[18] Nils Christie emphasised Bruun's importance in the analytical process leading up to the conceptualisation of the social role of the drug problem which is formulated in the title.[19] A critique of international drug policy had also been presented at an international level earlier, with the same practical recommendations for alcohol policy, in the book *The Gentlemen's Club*.[20] The political impact of this publication cannot be compared to the impact of the publication on alcohol policy of the same year. The idea of practical and political relevance of research was, however, the same.

Vilhelm Aubert formulated his programme in sociology as 'problem oriented empiricism', which is a formulation that explains how social epidemiology could become a part of studies that also included such themes as crime, disease, guilt and shame. The aim of the programme was of a both academic and political nature. Sociology should not only study 'deviants' but also enter into a relation with them in order to help them. In order to understand the causes of a problem it was necessary to study the whole of populations rather than individual cases and to focus on the level of consumption in the population rather than individual habits. The existence of deviance should be accepted as a natural part of society and marginalised people should be allowed ordinary civil rights. In Aubert's own words, it was a goal for social research: '...to defend rationality in public discourse...'[21] It was an obligation for research to resist the problem definitions of the media and the public.

The impact of these new perspectives and analyses of the social phenomenon of alcohol and drugs consumption was strengthened by the entry of new professionals in this area. Social work and social education contributed to new services in the welfare state, and used the insights of sociology quite actively as a basis for their work. Their ambition was not only to solve the problem but also to address the social and political causes of a problem. The combined efforts of new professionals, researchers and interest organisations were, for instance, significant in the process of the amendment of the Vagrancy Act in Norway in 1970.[22] Public drunkenness was decriminalised through this amendment and marginal people with drinking problems gained the same right as other poor people to social security benefits and medical treatment. The sociological interest in processes of integration and marginalisation in society and studies of civil society corresponded to the political effort of building the welfare state in this period. In this sense, the researchers were active participants in politics at both a national and international level.

This social science research tradition grew quite independently of medical research – and it is possible to argue that it was complementary with welfare politics during the 1960s and 1970s. There was strong criticism of closed institutions and a plea for self-determination for vulnerable people suffering from different kinds of social oppression. On the other hand, the 'problem' of alcohol and drugs as the main source of legitimation of the research also has a potentially negative influence on the possibility to ask important research questions. The change from the involvement in politics at an international as well as a national level took place as a gradual process when the research groups found themselves in a more restricted role in the 1980s. The integrated policy community of the 1960s, with participants from civil service, politics and research, did not exist any longer.

Stavseng[23] comments on the lack of development in this research during the 1980s and 90s, and claims that the attitude of both research and policy has been dominated by 'the logic of the spectator'.[24] This is a logic which presupposes that youth is at risk, in great danger, and that help must come from external sources (i.e. grownups, society or professionals). Stavseng points to a problem of paternalism that is recognised especially in connection with research on prevention and youth culture.

Organising transparency and changing the role of research[25]

The changes in organisation and research priorities of the 1990s took place against a background of major structural changes, such as changes in public opinion, ideas about management and the strengthening of the European dimension in Nordic policies.

The organisational changes for the research communities followed different paths in the individual countries, but all processes can be understood as part of a trend in the modernisation of public administration. Important goals of these reorganization processes were to provide transparency in policy making and to establish neutral and independent production of knowledge.

The Finnish Social Research Institute of Alcohol Studies was originally organised within the alcohol monopoly; Alko. Historically Alko was without comparison the strongest institution among the Nordic alcohol monopolies. It was not only a monopoly for the national manufacturing and sale of alcohol; it was also involved on a broad scale in treatment, prevention and research.[26] The dismantling of the monopoly was a quite direct result of the Finnish entry into the EU. In 1996, the Social Research Institute lost its quite protected and lucrative position in the monopoly institution, and became a part of the civil service, now called the Alcohol and Drug Research Group in STAKES (National Research and Development Centre for Welfare and Health).

Danish research on alcohol and drugs has by no means the long and strong tradition of that in Finland. Academic research in this area was conducted until the 1990s within the medical discipline. Social science research acquired its first small institutional basis at the Centre of Research on Alcohol and Drugs (CRF) in Århus in 1993. The basis of the centre was the work force of two professors at Aarhus University and external project funding. Research on drug policy and evaluations dominated from the start. Alcohol studies had gained a stronger position by the end of the 1990s, and from 2001 the centre received basic funding for alcohol research. The centre was also given the permanent task of running a monitoring system for the treatment sector (DANRIS). In 2002, a small new centre, the Center for Alcohol Research, was set up within the National Institute for Public Health in Copenhagen. This centre is more oriented towards medical and epidemiological research, but it has also a multidisciplinary activity in collaboration with CRF.

Swedish alcohol research has traditionally been dominated by medicine, but has also hosted one of the key figures in social science. Kettil Bruun was professor of sociology at the University of Stockholm. The structure of the research field differed, however, somewhat from the other countries. Not only because of the significant players both in sociology and medicine but also because the research area in the mid-1990s appeared to be rather fragmented. Paradoxically, the mixture of academic, voluntary and state actors in a traditional corporative structure produced this result in the field of research on alcohol and drugs. In order to cope with the fragmentation and to meet the national need for knowledge in the area, the Centre for Social Research on Alcohol and Drugs (Sorad) was set up at the University of Stockholm in 1999. During its first years, the centre was funded by external sources. After some uncertainty during 2006, since 2008 the centre has permanent funding as a Centre of Excellence and a fully integrated part of the Faculty of the Social Sciences.

The Norwegian National Institute for the Study of Alcohol (SIFA, from 2002 Sirus) was set up in 1960, and in formal terms is practically the same organisation today. It is organised as a part of the civil service under the Ministry of Health, but is independent as regards research,[27] as stated in the statutes. Some of the major institutions within public health and social service were reorganised in 2000. This process represented a strengthening of the Institute because of a more exclusive assignment to national monitoring activities and dissemination of research in the alcohol and drug area. The Institute has a responsibility as a focal point for the EMCDDA and hosts the national library on alcohol and drugs.

Research in Iceland has not taken place at one singular institution. Although traditionally a small group of researchers at Landsspitallin (psychiatric hospital) had continuous research activities in the area from the 1970s until the late 1990s. A new National Public Health Institute, set up in 2002, runs most of the national monitoring activities. Social science studies are handled by a small group of individual researchers without a common institutional basis. International cooperation in research both at Nordic and European level has been of great importance for the Islandic researchers in social science.

We see different models in the Nordic countries, where the location within civil service seems to be a traditional model and integration into a university structure is the model of the recent period. With the exception of Norway, all the groups have been included in larger organisational structures which include themes outside the alcohol and drug policy field. The research groups seem to be less protected in their new situation, where they have to compete on their academic merits as well as on their policy relevance. Epidemiological research and monitoring activities related to public health policies have been a permanent task, but with quite different organisational set up in the different countries.

To do social science in the field of public health has perhaps represented one of the most important challenges to the Nordic tradition in later years. The relation between social science research and public health is, as we have seen, organised differently in the various countries. The Finnish group became part of a public health institution and in Denmark, CRF in some ways got a competing centre within a public health institution. The Swedish centre is clearly organised outside the civil service for public health and the Norwegian Sirus has succeeded in maintaining an independent position outside the National Institute of Public Health through the reorganisations at the turn of the century. In Iceland public health happened to become a part of the civil service, while social science research on alcohol and drugs lost its small but still important institutional basis at Landspitallin.

Public Health and intoxicants: Impact on social science studies on alcohol and drugs

In the research communities of the Nordic countries there has been considerable scepticism regarding the impact of the public health perspective on politics and research, even though there clearly is potential common ground for medical and social science research on alcohol and drugs. It is also a policy field where both sociology and medicine have been considered important by politicians and public administration.

There are two main sources of scepticism from social science. These are factors that have also been pointed out in other studies of the science-policy relation in public health. Firsly, like what is found in studies from France and the UK, social science tends to become a more technical discipline within the framework of public health because of the dominance of surveys and evaluations.[28] Secondly, the emphasis on lifestyle and individual conduct, which Berridge (2007) sees as a policy result of the 'epidemiological transition' after WWII, is also considered by Nordic researchers as an obstacle to equality in health. As described earlier, the Nordic sociological tradition aimed at the integration of marginalised groups and looked for causes of social problems outside the focus on individual conduct.

By the turn of the century, the changes were being debated by several Nordic researchers, who commented both on the technicalisation and the orientation towards individual conduct:

> 'It is not accidental that alcohol research today to a large extent consists of the monitoring of statistical evidence for relations between consumption and different forms of health problems...'[29]

That this change also represents a normative shift is argued by Tigerstedt:

> 'In the name of individual freedom, social equity, and the abstract statistical (public health) solidarity – the traditional dominating moralistic and discriminator alcohol policy mentality – has been transformed into a more neutral, risk-based and consumption-oriented way of thinking...'[30]

The shift towards individual conduct and evaluations of policy means represented more than a thematic change for research. Combined with the organisational changes it seems to have shifted research from politics to policy, in terms of participation in political processes as well as in thematic interest. It is not least this emphasis on individual conduct that has been considered as a problem among Nordic researchers.

In the same time period, there was a discussion about research priorities in the Nordic research community. The Danes commented that it was easier to fund drug research and research directed towards practical social work than alcohol research.[31] The Norwegians commented on experiencing an intensification on demands from the 'users' (policy makers, administration and health and social services) – perhaps at the expense of '... independent, critical and long term development of knowledge ...'.[32] The Finnish group, which had experienced the reorganisation of the 1990s that caused them to fear for their tradition when they were included in welfare administration, commented on the positive side of being a part of a larger policy field. Jussi Simpura described closer contact between drug and alcohol research and the practical policy field at both national and municipal level and the research potential inherent in a closer contact with a broader spectrum of problems related to social marginalisation.[33]

How do the observations from the turn of the century match considerations about the situation some years later? Has a profound change taken place in institutional terms, one that influences the norms and values of the research community? Has the study of individual conduct, life style and evaluations of policy means now become dominant at the expense of the traditional studies of social, cultural and political dimensions in the field?

Politics and policy in present research

The national research groups' own presentations of their research could provide a basis for discussing these questions. How are the research themes presented in the plans of the groups by the year 2007?

The monitoring of consumption, patterns and trends are given quite a similar presentation in all groups. These themes are referred to as studies of *consequences* in Finland and Iceland, *explanations and consequences* in Norway, and the study of *problems* in Sweden. Studies of politics are presented as studies of *alcohol and drug politics* in Finland and Iceland, as *national and international alcohol policy* in Norway, and as study of *control policy* in Denmark. The Swedish institute Sorad does not use studies of politics as a category, but has 'Drug and alcohol problems in comparative perspective' as a theme. When it comes to studies of policy means, there is a similar description in Finland, Denmark and Iceland, where they are described as studies of 'prevention, treatment and control'. In Sweden this theme is described as studies of 'social responses to drug and alcohol problems, while it is termed simply 'research on policy means' in the Norwegian Sirus' programme.

Among the interesting small differences in the details of how the research is presented in the different countries are: the use of the term 'problems' in Sweden, the focus on control policy in Denmark, and the exclusion of drug policy as an object of study in Norway. The obligation to confront the alcohol and drug problems seems to be more explicitly expressed by Sorad. The Danish CRF focused from the start on control policy in the drug area, while in the Norwegian case it has been difficult to actually carry out independent research on drug policy because of the tense polarisation of the drug policy debate over a long period of time.[34]

Research priorities, independence and organisational change

The direct impact of politics on research was debated in the focus groups and among the informants. It is a common experience that large amounts of consumption data have been collected over the years which have not at all been fully exploited for analysis purposes. The same situation also holds good for many evaluations which often only have a purely legitimating role for the commissioning partner – whether it is public administration or private actors. All research groups experience some sort of challenge from stronger competition and the fragmentation of research. The Swedish focus group commented explicitly on how the scientific demands at the present stage mean focusing more on providing evidence for efficient means rather than on norm-breaking behaviour.

A stable funding from public sources is considered to be the best guarantee of independence in the Nordic research community. In this sense, the Finnish and Norwegian groups have had the greatest stability and the most generous funding compared to the others. Both Sorad and CRF have had more uncertainty about their funding situation. Independence has most of all been a topic in discussions about funding from the alcohol industry, and state funding has not been considered as problematic in the same sense, except when it is given on a too short-term basis. But the demand for applicable knowledge has, however, been commented on over the years. The portfolios of research in the different groups are a result of the balancing between the demand for applicable knowledge and more basic research generated on the basis of research interest.

In the interviews from the Nordic groups in 2007, the issue of independence was discussed differently in the different national contexts. No one described the influence from the political side as direct control, but the researchers both as individuals and as groups were participating in negotiations on the selection and relevance of research themes and methods. The researchers in the large welfare institution (STAKES in this case) – described how they balanced between the demands of the institute and the research interest of the group. As long as STAKES as an institution was part of the governance structure for the handling of social and health problems, they considered the problem orientation as a necessary part of their work. Sirus is an independent research institute, although organised as an extension of national central administration. Naturally, they will need to concentrate on the drug and alcohol problems as a topic for national policies. From the Norwegian side the comment is made that research sometimes seems to become more symbolic than anything else, especially when it comes to evaluations of policy interventions or means of regulation – i.e. research as a legitimation of policy.

Lack of political interest, and an emphasis on research being able to govern itself, as in Sweden after the election in 2006, was also mentioned as a quite surprising problem. This was seen especially as a problem for social science, which because of the strength of medical research, easily lost priority in a situation where there was a lack of any political demand for social science research. The head of Sorad argued that it was much harder to succeed in the competition with medicine and natural science when politicians did not indicate a problem.

Policy evaluations have always represented a significant part of the research at CRF in Århus. This situation is described in quite positive terms, especially as long as it is possible to combine data from several evaluations into larger research projects, and often in international collaboration. Traditionally, left-wing parties are considered to be more research-friendly than right-wing parties. The change of government in 2001 was therefore a source of concern. Recent experience, however, indicates that there is always a demand for evaluations – especially in a situation with large structural reforms such as in Denmark in recent years. The shift towards a stronger integration into the university has, according to the director of CRF, strengthened the independence of the research centre. To compete on the basis of academic merit is better than to depend on the Ministry of Social Affairs. The most problematic aspect of being so close to one single ministry is that the research groups can be included and used in controversies between different ministries. The university profile protects one from being identified with one party or the other in such controversies.

Modern public management and social science research on alcohol and drugs

Questions regarding how independence and academic quality should be safeguarded in this highly politicised research area are challenging. The research community has participated in welfare politics in this policy field for the last 30-40 years – with varying emphases in the different Nordic countries, though with high legitimacy and a reasonable influence on parts of the field. In all the Nordic countries, researchers from the social sciences are represented on advisory committees, public boards etc. – where they are hired exclusively because of their expertise and with an obligation to provide research-based advice on public policy. The recent changes, which might be associated with ideas of NPM, have on the one hand resulted in an even more prominent position of research-based knowledge. On the other hand, the demand for transparency in politics and the ideal of neutral, objective knowledge have impacted on the way research questions are being asked and the status of different methods. Attention seems to have turned towards efficiency of policy at the cost of more general social science studies in the field of intoxicants. There is an agreement among researchers about the necessity of a political interest for the continuity of this research. There is, however, some concern about what it takes for research to maintain this interest.

First, it seems to call for *compatibility* between research and policy. Compatibility between research and policy makes the relevance more obvious and easy to communicate. This seemed especially to be the case in alcohol research when the 'total consumption model' created a basic research-based foundation for regulation policy from the 1970s onwards. The principle of the model was that there is a correlation between aggregate consumption of alcohol in the population and various harmful effects.[35] The model thus supported the politics of regulating the supply side through restrictive means such as taxes and limiting the opening hours and number of outlets (monopoly systems). The 'prevention paradox' which was formulated in the late 1970s also supported stronger attention being paid to the everyday use of alcohol among moderate drinkers. As public health work such interventions were of greater effect than the treatment of people with severe alcohol problems.[36]

Second, the persistent social perspective that has characterised the research tradition has *participation* in politics as an integrated element. The demand for participation in politics was so strong that when Edman and Stenius (2007) analysed recent changes in the Nordic system of addiction treatment, they analysed the modernisation process as a process of de-politisation and professionalisation. They interpreted the demand for cost-efficiency and evidence-based practices as part of this kind of process. Edman and Stenius explain this process by the fact that the era of corporatism in the Nordic welfare states is over. This implies that the researchers have not only moved their research focus from politics to policy, the politics they have participated in – their arena of agency has – changed as well. There is much uncertainty among researchers about what the motive for participation in present politics should be.

The present politics, with its emphasis on transparency, efficiency and voluntarism, provides the Nordic social science research tradition with a new role, one which resembles but still differs from their earlier role. In all the Nordic countries, research is an integrated part of governance in the policy area of alcohol and drugs, in terms of providing applicable knowledge for policy making. The challenge against independence is twofold, coming from the dependence on political interest and from the lack of distance to the civil service and public opinion and media when formulating research questions on the problem of intoxicants in present society. At the organisational level, this study indicates integration in academic institutions as being important for independence in research. On the scientific side, the historical roots back to critical sociology are still an important source of reflection and independence.

Notes

1. Svanaug Fjær, 1998; 2005.
2. Tanja A. Börzel and Thomas Risse, 2000.
3. Pekka Sulkunen et al. 2000.
4. Tom Christensen and Per Lægreid, 2007.
5. Pons and van Zanten, 2007.
6. Pekka Sulkunen, 2009, pp. 182-83.
7. Svanaug Fjær, 2008.
8. Svanaug Fjær, 2004.
9. The numbers in mill. DKK: Sirus: 34.9, STAKES 12, Sorad 19.8, CRF 13. (Fjær, 2008, p. 16)
10. Thomas Babor, 1993, p. 59.
11. Svanaug Fjær, 2008, p. 37
12. Klaus Mäkelä, 1988.
13. Tore Lindbekk and Peter Sohlberg, 2000.
14. Svanaug Fjær, 2004; 2008.
15. Tuka Tammi, 2007.
16. Thomas Babor, et al 2003, VII.
17. Christoffer Tigerstedt 2001a, p. 120.
18. Nils Christie and Kettil Bruun, 1985.
19. Interview, January 2003.
20. Kettil Bruun et al. 1975.
21. Ragnvald Kalleberg, 2000.
22. Ragnar Hauge, 2007.
23. Stavseng, 2001.
24. The term 'tilskuerlogisk' in Norwegian.
25. The snapshots of the history of the research groups in the Nordic countries are based on documentation presented in Svanaug Fjær 2008.
26. Jarmo Ahonen, 2007.
27. The term in Norwegian: 'forskningsfaglig uavhengig'
28. Luc Berlivet, 2005.

29 Ragnar Hauge, 2001, p. 491.
30 Christoffer Tigerstedt, 2001b, p. 496.
31 Karen Ellen Spannow, 2001.
32 Sturla Nordlund, 2001, p. 97.
33 Jussi Simpura, 2001.
34 Svanaug Fjær, 2005.
35 Christoffer Tigerstedt, 2001a.
36 Olaf G. Aasland et al., 2008.

References

Ahonen, Jarmo 2007: 'Treatment as Adaptation. A-Clinics in Post-War Finland', Johan Edman and Kerstin Stenius (eds.), *On the Margins. Nordic Alcohol and Drug Treatment 1885-2007*, Helsinki.

Aasland, Olaf G., Peter Nygaard and Per Nilsen, 2008: 'The long and winding road to widespread implementation of screening and brief intervention for alcohol problems', *Nordic Studies on Alcohol and Drugs* vol. 25, pp. 469-476.

Babor, Thomas et al. 2003: *Alcohol: no ordinary commodity*, Oxford and New York.

Berlivet, Luc 2005: 'Uneasy prevention: the problematic modernisation of health education in France after 1975', V. Berridge and K. Laughlin (eds.), *Medicine, the Market and the Mass Media Producing Health in the Twentieth Century*, Routledge.

Berridge, Virginia 2007: 'Multidisciplinary public health: What sort of victory?', *Public Health* 121(6), pp. 404-408.

Börzel, Tanja A. and Thomas Risse, 2000: 'When Europe Hits Home: Europeanization and Domestic Change' *European Integration online Papers*, no. 15, vol. 4, http://eiop.or.at/eiop/texte/2000 - 015a.htm

Bruun, Kettil, Lynn Pan and Ingemar Rexed 1975: *The Gentlemen's Club. International Control of Drugs and Alcohol*, Chicago and London.

Christe, Nils and Kettil Bruun 1985: *Den gode fiende*, Oslo.

Christensen, Tom and Per Lægreid 2007: 'Introduction - Theoretical Approach and Research Questions', Tom Christensen and Per Lægreid, *Transcending New Public Management*, Ashgate.

Desrosières, Allain 1990: 'How to make things which hold together: Social science, statistics and the state', *Discourses on Society*, P. Wagner, B. Wittrock and R. Withley Kluwer Academic Publishers, XV, pp. 195-218.

Edman, Johan and Kerstin Stenius, 2007: 'From Sanatoriums to Public Injection Rooms. Actors, Ideas and Institutions in the Nordic Treatment System', Johan Edman and Kerstin Stenius, *On the Margins. Nordic Alcohol and Drug Treatment 1885-2007*, Helsingfors.

Edman, Johan and Kerstin Stenius (eds.) 2007: *On the Margins. Nordic Alcohol and Drug Treatment 1885-2007*, Helsinki.

Fjær, Svanaug 1998: 'Forskning med forbudet som premiss', *Tidsskrift for velferdsforskning*, no. 3, vol. 1, pp. 152-167.

Fjær, Svanaug 2004: 'From Social Radicalism to Repression: The Construction of the Norwegian Drug Policy in the 1970ties', Astri Andresen, Kari Tove Elvbakken and William Hubbard (eds.), *Public Health and Preventive Medicine 1800-2000. Knowledge, Co-operation and Conflict*, Stein Rokkan Centre for Social Studies, Report no. 1, Bergen.

Fjær, Svanaug 2005: 'Ubehaget i enigheten', *Arr – idéhistorisk tidsskrift*, no. 1-2, vol. 16, pp. 3-17.
Fjær, Svanaug 2006: ".. money talks..", *Nordisk alkohol- och narkotikatidsskrift*, no. 4, vol. 23, pp. 262-264.
Fjær, Svanaug 2008: *Nordisk samfunnsvitenskaplig forskning om alkohol og narkotika - utviklingstrekk og endringer i alliansen mellom kunnskapsproduksjon og politikk*, Notat 8, Rokkansenteret, Bergen.
http://www.rokkansenteret.uib.no/rPub/files/214_Notat_8-2008_Fjaer.pdf
Hauge, Ragnar 2001: 'Alkoholpolitikken - død eller levende?', *Nordisk alkohol- och narkotikatidsskrift*, no. 5-6, vol. 18, pp. 490-492.
Hauge, R. 2007: 'On the Demise of the Norwegian Vagrancy Act', J. Edman and K. Stenius, *On the Margins. Nordic Alcohol and Drug Treatment 1885-2007*, Nordic Centre for Alcohol and Drug Research, Publication no. 50, Helsingfors.
Kalleberg, Ragnvald 2000: 'the Most Important Task of Sociology is to Strengthen and defend. Rationality in Public discourse: On the Sociology of Vilhelm Aubert', *Acta Sociologica*, no. 4, vol. 43, pp. 399-411.
Lindbekk, Tore and Peter Sohlberg, 2000: 'Introduction: The Nordic Heritage', *Acta Sociologica*, no. 4, vol. 43, pp. 293-298.
Mäkelä, Klaus 1988: 'The Finnish Foundation for Alcohol Studies and the Social Research Institute of Alcohol Studies', *British Journal of Addiction*, no. 2, vol. 83, pp. 141-148.
Nordlund, Sturla 2001: 'Statens institutt for alkohol og narkotikaforskning/Statens institutt for rusmiddelforskning', *Nordisk alkohol- och narkotikatidsskrift*, no. 1, vol. 18, pp. 95-97.
Poikolainen, K., T. Paljarvi et al. 2007: 'Alcohol and the preventive paradox: serious harms and drinking patterns', *Addiction*, no. 4, vol. 102, pp. 571-578.
Pons, Xavier & Agnés van Zarten 2007: 'Knowledge circulation, regulation and governance', *Know & Pol*, Literature Revview.
Simpura, Jussi 2001: 'Alkohol- och drogforskning, STAKES', *Nordisk alkohol- och narkotikatidsskrift*, no. 1, vol. 18, pp. 97-99.
Spannow, Karen Ellen 2001: 'Forskning på Center for Rusmiddelforskning.' *Nordisk alkohol- och narkotikatidsskrift*, no. 1, vol. 18, pp. 92-94.
Stavseng, O. 2001: 'Ungdommen, skammen og pedagogikken', T. Wyller (ed.), *Skam. Perspektiver på ære og skamløshet i det moderne*, Bergen.
Sulkunen, Pekka, Caroline Sutton, Christoffer Tigerstedt and Katariina Warpenius, 2000: 'Introduction', Pekka Sulkunen, Caroline Sutton, Christoffer Tigerstedt and Katariina Warpenius (eds.), *Broken Spirits. Power and Ideas in Nordic Alcohol Control*, Helsinki.
Sulkunen, Pekka, Caroline Sutton, Christoffer Tigerstedt and Katariina Warpenius (eds.) 2000: *Broken Spirits, Power and Ideas in Nordic Alcohol Control*, Helsinki.
Sulkunen, Pekka 2009: *The saturated Society. Governing Risk and Lifestyles in Consumer Culture*, Los Angeles and London.
Tammi, Tuka 2007: 'How I would describe 21st century drug policy to Kettil Bruun', *Nordisk alkohol- och narkotikatidsskrift*, no. 3, vol. 24, pp. 288-290.
Tigerstedt, Christoffer 2001a: 'Alcohol policy, public health and Kettil Bruun', Christoffer Tigerstedt, *The Dissolution of the Alcohol Policy Field. Studies on the Nordic Countries*. Helsinki.
Tigerstedt, Christoffer 2001b: 'En lans för upplösningen', *Nordisk alkohol- och narkotikatidsskrift*, no. 5-6, vol. 18, pp. 495-498.

Wyller, Trygve (ed.) 2001: *Skam. Perspektiver på ære og skamløshet i det moderne*, Bergen.

Notes on contributors

Lars Schädler Andersen is an associate professor at the Department of History, International Studies and Social Relations at the University of Aalborg. He defended his doctoral dissertation The Battle of Responsibility. Policy and Administration in Workers Accident Insurance in Denmark 1898-1933 in 2006. He is the author of several articles on the history of social policy and currently engaged in writing a biography on the Danish economist Harald Westergaard (1853-1936). Lars Schädler Andersen is also involved in a major research project on 'Danish Welfare History' aiming at the production of a five-volume piece on the development of Danish social policy from 1800 to present time.

Annika Berg is a researcher at the Department of History of Science and Ideas, at Uppsala University. Berg's doctoral thesis explores the married couple Signe Höjer and Axel Höjer in their different roles as experts on health and welfare, and problematizes their views on public health as key to a better society and a better world. More generally, Berg's research interests are directed towards the social and cultural history of medicine and healthcare, postcolonial issues and gender history. Recent publications include Den gränslösa hälsan: Signe och Axel Höjer, folkhälsan och expertisen (Uppsala: Acta universitatis upsaliensis, 2009); "From Copycats to Double Agents: Axel and Signe Höjer and the Transfer of Public Health Policies in 20th Century Sweden", in Transferring Public Health, Medical Knowledge and Science in the 19th and 20th Century, Astri Andresen, Tore Grønlie (eds.) Bergen: Rokkansenteret, 2007).

Ning de Coninck-Smith is Professor at The Danish University School of Education, Århus University. She is a historian of childhood and education. Lately her interest has been focused on the materialities of childhood. Together with Marta Gutman she has edited the collection Designing modern childhoods. History, space and the material culture of children (Rutgers UP, 2008). She is currently writing a book with the title Arkitektur og barndom. Rum til danske børn gennem 300 år [Architecture and childhood. Spaces for Danish children through 300 years].The book is expected to be published in the fall of 2010.

Nils Edling is a senior lecturer at the Department of History, Stockholm University, Sweden. He has, during the last years, been studying the making of unemployment in Denmark, Norway and Sweden between circa 1850 to 1914. His new project will be a conceptual history of the Swedish welfare state up to the 1970s. Recent publications include "Regulating Unemployment the Continental Way. The Transfer of Innovations to Scandinavia 1890–1914", European Review of History (no. 1, 2008), and "Limited Universalism: Unemployment Insurance in Northern Europe 1900–2000", in Niels Finn Christiansen et al (eds.), The Nordic Model of Welfare – A Historical Reappraisal (Museum Tusculanum Press, Copenhagen, 2006).

Sara Edenheim is a Research fellow at the Centre for Gender Studies and Department of History, Umeå university in Sweden. She is currently working on a study on historical writing, social movements and legal changes, as well as a critical study of the hegemony of hermeneutics within the research field of history and its relation to the archive. Recent publications include Begärets lagar - moderna utredningar och heteronormativitetens genealogi (The Laws of Desire - modern public reports and the genealogy of heternonormativity), (Symposion 2005) and Anakronistiskt manifest (An Anachronistic Manifest), (Ink förlag 2010).

Svanaug Fjær is Head of Research at the International Research Institute of Stavanger (IRIS) in Norway. Her research interests include studies of drug policy, science policy relations and health service research. Recent publications include: "Berg de avholdende! Informasjon som holdningsskapende virkemiddel i narkotikaforebyggingen" (Save the abstainers! Information as health promoting strategy in drug prevention) i Elvbakken K.T. og Stenvoll, D. (eds.): Reisen til helseland - Propaganda for folkehelsen (Fagbokforlaget , 2008) and "From Social Radicalism to Repression: The Construction of the Norwegian Drug Policy in the 1970ties" in Andresen, A., Elvbakken, K.T. and Hubbard, W. (eds.) Public Health and Preventive Medicine1800-2000. Knowledge, Co-operation and Conflict (Stein Rokkan Centre for Social Studies, 2004).

Kari Ludvigsen is Research leader at Uni Rokkan Centre, Bergen, Norway. She is a political scientist with broad experience from research on professions, expertise and politics. Her empirical focus is on studies of psychiatry and mental health, child health and welfare, and public health policy and health promotion. Recent publications include "The establishing of Norwegian child psychiatry: Ideas, actors and institutions", History of psychiatry (no.1, 2009) (with Åsmund Arup Seip); "The public, the mother and the child: Public health initiatives promoting the strong and happy child" (with Kari Tove Elvbakken), in Abreau, Lucinda (ed.) The price of Life: Welfare Systems, Social Nets and Economic Growth. (Cidadania. Lisboa: Edicoes Colibri/CIDEHUS, 2008).

Åsa Lundqvist is associate professor in sociology at the School of Social Work, Lund University, Sweden. Lundqvist's research interests include analysis of the history of the welfare state and the development of welfare policies, especially social- and family policy. Recent publications include: "Construction(s) of Swedish Family Policy, 1930-2000", Journal of Family History (no. 2, 2009) (with Christine Roman); Changing Relations of Welfare. Family, Gender and Migration in Britian and Scandinavia, co-edited with Janet Fink (Ashgate 2010), and Family Policy Paradoxes. Gender Equality and Labour Market Regulation in Sweden, 1930-2010 (Policy Press, forthcoming in November 2010).

Carl Marklund is a post-doctoral researcher at the Center for Nordic Studies and the Network for European Studies at University of Helsinki, Finland. Marklund's research interests include the political theory and social history of science and politics, especially the problems of social planning and social rationalization. In particular, he has studied the concepts and discourses of social engineering and technocracy in American and European social science. His recent works include Bridging Science and Politics: The Concept of Social Engineering in Sweden and the USA, Circa 1890-1950 (PhD, 2008) and "The Social Laboratory, the Middle Way, and the Swedish Model: Three Frames for the Image of Sweden" in Scandinavian Journal of History (2009).

Klaus Petersen is Professor at the Centre for Welfare State Research, University of Southern Denmark. He has published a number of books and articles on Danish and Nordic welfare state history. Is currently co-editor of and co-author to "Dansk Velfærdshistorie 1800-2000" [Danish Welfare History 1800-2000] - a 6-volume history of Danish social policy (vol. 1 to be published in November 2010). He works with his colleague Jørn Henrik Petersen on a comparative study of the history of the term "welfare state" in Britain, US, Germany and Denmark 1840-1960. Most recent publication in English: The Politics of Age. Basic Pensions in a Historical and Comparative Perspective, co-edited with Jørn Henrik Petersen (Peter Lang 2009).

Ann-Catrin Östman is a senior lecturer in history at Åbo Academy University in Finland. Her doctoral thesis Mjöl och jord (Milk and oil), published in 2001, discussed peasant work and understandings of femininity and masculinity in a small Finnish community between 1870 and 1940. She has published articles on the history of agricultural history and co-operative organizing. Currently, she is part of the project "Male Citizenship and Societal Reforms in Finland, 1918-1960"